Copyright Perspectives

Brian Fitzgerald • John Gilchrist
Editors

Copyright Perspectives

Past, Present and Prospect

 Springer

Editors
Brian Fitzgerald
Thomas More Academy of Law
Australian Catholic University
East Melbourne, VIC
Australia

John Gilchrist
Thomas More Academy of Law
Australian Catholic University
East Melbourne, VIC
Australia

ISBN 978-3-319-15912-6   ISBN 978-3-319-15913-3   (eBook)
DOI 10.1007/978-3-319-15913-3

Library of Congress Control Number: 2015941314

Springer Cham Heidelberg New York Dordrecht London

Printed on acid-free paper

Springer International Publishing AG Switzerland is part of Springer Science+Business Media (www.springer.com)

Foreword: The Future of Copyright[1]

I am delighted to have the opportunity to participate in this Conference. I commend the Faculty of Law of the Queensland University of Technology (QUT) and the principal organizers of the Conference, Professor Brian Fitzgerald and Ben Atkinson, for taking up the gauntlet thrown down by the digital society.

Few issues in intellectual property or, if I may suggest, cultural policy are as important as the consequences of the revolutionary structural change introduced by digital technology and the Internet. Recently, as the number of people in the world with access to the Internet passes two billion,[2] support for addressing the consequences of this fundamental change has come from the highest levels. Both President Sarkozy of France and President Medvedev of the Russian Federation have called for the G20 to consider the issue. In his speech at Davos earlier this year, President Medvedev stated that "the old principles of intellectual property regulation are not working anymore, particularly when it comes to the Internet". That, he stated, "is fraught with the collapse of the entire intellectual property rights system".

Digital technology and the Internet have created the most powerful instrument for the democratization of knowledge since the invention of moveable type for printing. They have introduced perfect fidelity and near zero-marginal costs in the reproduction of cultural works and an unprecedented capacity to distribute those works around the globe at instantaneous speeds and, again, near zero-marginal costs.

The enticing promise of universal access to cultural works has come with a process of creative destruction that has shaken the foundations of the business models of our pre-digital creative industries. Underlying this process of change is a fundamental question for society. It is the central question of copyright policy. How can society make cultural works available to the widest possible public at

---

[1] Address to Future Directions in Copyright Law Conference, February 25, 2011, Sydney.

[2] International Telecommunication Union, *The World in 2010: ICT facts and figures.*

affordable prices while, at the same time, assuring a dignified economic existence to creators and performers and the business associates that help them to navigate the economic system? It is a question that implies a series of balances: between availability, on the one hand, and control of the distribution of works as a means of extracting value, on the other hand; between consumers and producers; between the interests of society and those of the individual creator; and between the short-term gratification of immediate consumption and the long-term process of providing economic incentives that reward creativity and foster a dynamic culture.

Digital technology and the Internet have had, and will continue to have, a radical impact on those balances. They have given a technological advantage to one side of the balance, the side of free availability, the consumer, social enjoyment and short-term gratification. History shows that it is an impossible task to reverse technological advantage and the change that it produces. Rather than resist it, we need to accept the inevitability of technological change and to seek an intelligent engagement with it. There is, in any case, no other choice—either the copyright system adapts to the natural advantage that has evolved or it will perish.

Adaptation in this instance requires, in my view, activism. I am firmly of the view that a passive and reactive approach to copyright and the digital revolution entails the major risk that policy outcomes will be determined by a Darwinian process of the survival of the fittest business model. The fittest business model may turn out to be the one that achieves or respects the right social balances in cultural policy. It may also, however, turn out not to respect those balances. The balances should not, in other words, be left to the chances of technological possibility and business evolution. They should, rather, be established through a conscious policy response.

There are, I believe, three main principles that should guide us in the development of a successful policy response.

The first of those is neutrality to technology and to the business models developed in response to technology. The purpose of copyright is not to influence technological possibilities for creative expression or the business models built on those technological possibilities. Nor is its purpose to preserve business models established under obsolete or moribund technologies. Its purpose is, I believe, to work with any and all technologies for the production and distribution of cultural works, and to extract some value from the cultural exchanges made possible by those technologies to return to creators and performers and the business associates engaged by them to facilitate the cultural exchanges through the use of the technologies. Copyright should be about promoting cultural dynamism, not preserving or promoting vested business interests.

A second principle is comprehensiveness and coherence in the policy response. I do not think that there is any single magical answer. Rather, an adequate response is more likely to come from a combination of law, infrastructure, cultural change, institutional collaboration and better business models. Let me take each of those elements and comment on them briefly.

Law was for many decades, if not centuries, considered to be the way to make copyright policy. It must still be the final arbiter, but we know that it is a rather rigid and limited instrument in the digital environment. In that environment, the volume of traffic, the international or multi-jurisdictional nature of so many relationships and transactions and the loose regulation of the Domain Name System, which permits a large degree of anonymity, all make law a mere shadow of itself in the physical world, a weakened force. Its institutions and their reach are trapped in a territorial cage, whereas economic and technological behaviour burst out of that cage some time ago. In consequence, the culture of the Internet is such that platforms influence behaviour as much as, if not more than, law.

Recognizing the limitation of law, and its inability to provide a comprehensive answer, should not mean that we abandon it. There are many important legal questions to be addressed. Among them, I believe that the question of—and here I use, or misuse, advisedly a term from civil law—the responsibility of intermediaries is paramount. The position of intermediaries is key. They are at once, service providers to, as well as partners, competitors and even clones of creators, performers and their business associates; hence the difficulty that we have in coming to a clear position on the role of intermediaries.

As I have hinted, I believe that infrastructure is as important a part of the solution as law. Let us dare to say that the infrastructure of the world of collective management is out-dated. It represents a world of separate territories and a world where right-holders expressed themselves in different media, not the multi-jurisdictional world of the Internet or the convergence of expression in digital technology. This is not to say that collective management or collecting societies are no longer needed. But they need to re-shape and to evolve. We need a global infrastructure that permits simple, global licensing, one that makes the task of licensing cultural works legally on the Internet as easy as it is to obtain such works there illegally. Time does not permit me to go into detail here, but I would like to repeat two messages from recent conferences. First, I believe that an international music registry—a global repertoire database—would be a very valuable and needed step in the direction of establishing the infrastructure for global licensing. And, secondly, in order to be successful, future global infrastructure must work with the existing collecting societies and not seek to replace them. It should provide a means of linking them into a global system, much as the Patent Cooperation Treaty (PCT) links the patent offices of the world, rather than replacing them.

Beyond law and infrastructure, we have culture, and the Internet has, as we know, developed its own culture, one that has seen a political party, the Pirate Party, emerge to contest elections on the basis of the abolition or radical reform of intellectual property, in general, and copyright, in particular. The platform of the Pirate Party proclaims that "[t]he monopoly for the copyright holder to exploit an aesthetic work commercially should be limited to five years after publication. A five years copyright term for commercial use is more than enough. Non-commercial use should be free from day one."

The Pirate Party may be an extreme expression, but the sentiment of distaste or disrespect for intellectual property on the Internet that it voices is widespread. Look at the incidence of illegal down-loading of music. We may argue about the right methodology to use to measure that phenomenon, but we are all certain that the practice has reached alarming dimensions.

In order to effect a change in attitude, I believe that we need to re-formulate the question that most people see or hear about copyright and the Internet. People do not respond to being called pirates. Indeed, some, as we have seen, even make a pride of it. They would respond, I believe, to a challenge to sharing responsibility for cultural policy. We need to speak less in terms of piracy and more in terms of the threat to the financial viability of culture in the twenty-first century, because it is this which is at risk if we do not have an effective, properly balanced copyright policy.

The fourth element in a comprehensive and coherent design is institutional collaboration. This is a very delicate area, where any action may have a disproportionate influence on the battle for the hearts and minds of the public on the question of appropriate copyright policy. It is also a somewhat incoherent area, with different national approaches, some emphasizing action against offending consumers and others targeting intermediaries; some plurilateral approaches in the Anti-Counterfeiting Trade Agreement (ACTA); and some practical, industry actions or codes of self-regulation.

I believe that we need greater coherence if we are to make progress in this area. We need to define sensibly what objectives we share, starting in a modest manner. But we are very limited by the unwillingness of some countries to entertain any international discussion or action in this area.

The final element of a comprehensive and coherent design is better business models. This is undoubtedly happening now. But the story is not over and, for the future, we should constantly remind ourselves that the history of the confrontation of our classical copyright world with the digital environment has been more a sorry tale of Luddite resistance than an example of intelligent engagement.

Let me move to my final suggested guiding principle for a successful response to the digital challenge. I believe that we need more simplicity in copyright. Copyright is complicated and complex, reflecting the successive waves of technological development in the media of creative expression from printing through to digital technology, and the business responses to those different media. We risk losing our audience and public support if we cannot make understanding of the system more accessible. Future generations are clearly going to regard many of the works, rights and business agents that we talk about as cute artefacts of cultural history, much as the vinyl record has become in a very short space of time. The digital work is going to change dimensions. We see that happening with user generated content. We see it happening also with 3D printing or additive manufacturing, where the digital file is the manufacturing technology and factory. This is the realm of the blue sky, and I hope that this Conference can start to develop the tools for exploring that sky.

Francis Gurry
World Intellectual Property Organization (WIPO)

Preface

This book is a collection of papers on copyright law from wide and diverse perspectives.

It is designed to appeal beyond professionals in the copyright world to a wider interested audience. The papers have been selected to stimulate and inform.

The title of the collection itself illustrates the breadth of its survey. There are short and lengthy papers, some historical, many focusing on current issues, some with a policy and philosophical orientation and some with a more technical bent.

The collection contains perspectives which have not hitherto been the subject of much literature discussion. One paper discusses an Islamic perspective on intellectual property—that is, a perspective from one of the world's most significant legal systems—which has had little English language coverage. Other papers reflect the growing international voice of developing countries in debates over the future of copyright and intellectual property.

The collection canvasses current issues of controversy over the law and practice of copyright, such as

- the liability of internet service providers for infringement of copyright by its customers,
- the increasing use of the resources of the state via the criminal law as a vehicle to enforce copyright, rather than the resources of copyright owners, and the social impact of that change,
- questions raised by the digital age and internet publication, and
- the rapid growth in the practice of open content licensing.

While some of the chapters in this collection relate specifically to the law in Australia, the issues raised in most chapters pose questions presently faced by the vast majority of countries of the world.

The chapters in this collection are authored by distinguished professionals including Dr Francis Gurry, Director General of the World Intellectual Property Organization, Justice Emmett of the New South Wales Court of Appeal, Prof Ian Hargreaves from Cardiff University and Prof Brian Fitzgerald from the Australian

Catholic University. Prof Hargreaves, who led a review of intellectual property for the UK Government, published as *Digital Opportunity: A Review of Intellectual Property and Growth* in 2011, reflects on the future directions of copyright law reform in the afterword. Prof Hargreaves mentions the trend towards open access, the need for the improved licensing of material and the insufficient regard in general to the interests of users of copyright material in a digital context.

The Editors would like to thank Benedict Atkinson and Kunle Ola for their foundation work in developing this collection. The Editors also wish to thank the ARC Centre of Excellence for Creative Industries and Innovation (CCI) for their funding support of a number of the papers in this collection and the collection as a whole.

We hope you will be stimulated, provoked and stirred into further thinking about the future of copyright by reading the papers in this book.

27 December 2014   John Gilchrist
                                                                          Brian Fitzgerald

Contents

Chapter 1
Address of Victor Hugo to the International Literary Congress

Benedict Atkinson

1.1 Paris

1.1.1 Wednesday 17 June 1878

What makes this year so wonderful, so memorable, is that above the noise and clamour, to our astonishment, brooking no controversy, we hear the voice of civilization. This is a defining year. What should be done is being done. The old order is giving way to the new. Progress takes the place of war. Opposition is crumbling. Threats rumble around us but the friendship of nations makes us smile.

The achievements of 1878 will prove indestructible. They aren't temporary. We feel purpose in everything. This marvellous year announces, through the Paris

---

Victor Hugo (1802–1885), one of France's greatest poets and writers, author of *The Hunchback of Notre Dame* and *Les Misérables,* addressed the International Literary Congress in 1878 to rapturous acclaim. The Congress adopted resolutions including the principle of perpetual copyright, and called on the French Government to host an international conference to establish a convention to regulate use of literary property. The French Government did not respond but the call for a convention was a decisive step towards agreement of the Berne Convention. Hugo believed that literary property ought to extinguish on the author's death (with publishers entitled to publish the author's works post mortem subject to paying small royalties to direct heirs). He considered that authors' rights must not be allowed to restrict the public domain. He thought, however, that the grant of literary property assisted development of the public domain. This speech is only in part directly concerned with the question of literary property. In total, it is a triumphant statement of Hugo's belief in principles of freedom and emancipation, and his love of France. It is also a tender reflection on the feelings of the outcast and exile. Hugo lived in exile from France between 1852 and 1870.
Translation copyright Mary Atkinson and Ben Atkinson

B. Atkinson (⊠)
Thomas More Academy of Law, Australian Catholic University, 8-20 Napier Street, North Sydney, NSW 2060, Australia
e-mail: benedict_atkinson@bigpond.com

© Springer International Publishing Switzerland 2015
B. Fitzgerald, J. Gilchrist (eds.), *Copyright Perspectives,*
DOI 10.1007/978-3-319-15913-3_1

Exhibition,[1] unity of industry; in the centenary of Voltaire, philosophical unity; and in this Congress gathered today, literary unity. A vast federation of labour in all its forms. An awe-inspiring realization of human brotherhood, founded on the peasant and working man, and governed by thinkers.

Industry looks for what is useful, philosophy for what is true, and literature for the beautiful. This is the triple purpose of all human effort, the useful, the truthful and the beautiful; and the triumph of this sublime effort, gentleman, is civilization among peoples and peace among men.

You have gathered from all points in the civilized world to bear witness to this triumph. Yours are the elevated minds universally admired and respected, the talents everywhere recognised, the generous voices, yours the souls labouring for progress. You struggle for peace. You are men of fame and influence. You are ambassadors for the human spirit in this great city of Paris. We welcome you, authors, orators, poets, philosophers, thinkers, fighters. France salutes you.

Together, we are fellow citizens of a universal city. Together, hand in hand, let us reiterate our unity and allegiance. Together, let us enter the serene and noble realm of the absolute, which is justice, and of the ideal, which is truth. You are not here out of self-interest or necessity. You have come here to benefit others.

What is literature? It is the march of the human spirit. What is civilisation? It is an eternal discovery accompanying every step along the way, hence the term progress. We might say that progress and civilization are identical. People are judged by their literature. An army of two million men lives and dies, the *Illiad* remains. Xerxes' army lacks an epic and Xerxes vanishes, yet Greece, so small in size, is made immortal by Aeschylus. Rome is merely a town but through Tacitus, Lucretius, Virgil, Horace, and Juvenal, Rome becomes the world. If you mention Spain, Cervantes springs to mind. Speak of Italy and we think of Dante, of England, and behold, Shakespeare stands before us. France herself has her moments of genius, where the splendor of Paris is distilled in the sharp wit of a Voltaire.

Gentlemen you have a noble mission. You are a sort of literary parliament. You have the power to inspire laws, if not to enforce them. Speak justly, speak truth, and if by some mischance, no one listens, well, you will prove legislation wrong.

You are going to create a foundation for literary property. This is what is right, and you are going to embody it in law. I assure you that your suggestions and advice will be taken into account. You will persuade legislators seeking to confine the writer that literature has no boundaries. Literature is the mind leading humanity. Literary property is open to everyone. Royal decrees denied and still deny literary property. And why? For purposes of enslavement. The writer who owns his work is the writer who is free. Deny ownership and you deny him independence.

---

[1] The Universal Exposition of Paris, or World Fair, held in Paris May–November 1878, marked France's recovery from the trauma of invasion and defeat by the Prussian army in 1871. For Hugo, who suffered during the siege of Paris in 1870, when starvation threatened the population, the year 1878 could be seen as a turning point, one involving renunciation of war.

At least that's what is hoped. Hence the peculiar sophism that would be puerile if it were not so pernicious: thought belongs to everyone, thus it can't be owned. Therefore, literary property cannot exist. First of all, this is a strange confusion of the ability to think, which is general, with thoughts themselves, which are personal. Thoughts are the self. Next, thought, an abstraction, is confused with the material, that is, books. A writer's thoughts, as such, evade all attempts at capture. They fly from heart to heart. They have the power and gift of *virum volitare per ora* [spreading like wildfire].

But books are distinct from thought. Books are tangible and easily seized. So easily that they sometimes are seized. As a product of the printing press, the book belongs to industry, and, in all its manifestations, is central to a vast commercial process. It is bought and sold. It is property. It has material value. It is the author's contribution to national wealth, and, of course, from every standpoint, is the least controversial type of property.

This hallowed property is daily violated by tyrannical governments, which seize control of publication, hoping thereby to control the author. Hence the system of official patronage, which takes everything and gives next to nothing in return. Dispossession and subjugation of the author follow. First they steal from the him, then they try to profit from him. A useless endeavour all the same. The writer eludes them. He is impoverished but free. Who could buy the peerless conscience of a Rabelais, Moliere, or a Pascal? The attempt is made, however, and the result is dismal.

Monarchy is a terrible succubus on the vital forces of a nation. Historians endow kings with titles like 'father of the nation' or 'fathers of the arts and letters'. However, in the baleful machinery of monarchy, anything goes: as acknowledged by the sycophant Dangeau on the one hand, and Vaubant, strict and severe, on the other. For example, in the so-called Great Century,[2] the way kings behaved, these fathers of the nation and fathers of the arts and letters, led to these two grim facts: people going hungry and Corneille going shoeless. What an appalling end to the 'Great Reign'![3]

This is what happens, whether the burden falls upon the public or the author, when property born of labour is appropriated. Gentlemen, let us return to the principle: respect for property. Let us insist on literary property while at the same time fostering the public domain. Let us go further. Let us broaden our scope. The law should give publishers the right to publish any book after an author's death, provided they pay a small fee to his direct heirs, not more than 5 or 10 % of net profit. This very simple system, reconciling with the author's undeniable right to property, the equally undeniable rights of the public domain, was pointed out during the Commission of 1836 by the person addressing you now.

---

[2] 'Le Grand Siècle', broadly the seventeenth century, referring usually to the reign of Louis XIV (1643–1715).

[3] Of Louis XIV.

The development of this proposal may be traced in the Commission minutes published by the Ministry of the Interior. Let's not forget the twofold principle: a book, as such, belongs to the author, but the ideas in the book belong—without exaggeration—to all mankind. All minds have equal claim to them. If one of these two rights, that of the author, or that of humanity, had to be sacrificed, it would of course be the right of the author, because we are solely concerned with the public interest, and I declare that the public must take precedence. But, as I have just said, such a sacrifice is not necessary.

Light! Always light! Light everywhere! Everything needs light! Light is in books! Throw open the book and let it do its work! Whoever wants to cultivate, to animate, to refine, to soften, to soothe—encourage the spread of books! Teach, show, demonstrate, multiply schools. Schools are the shining lights of civilization!

You look after your towns. You want to be safe in your homes. The perils of dark unlit streets perturb you. Think of something even more perturbing—allowing darkness to overwhelm the human mind. Intellect is like a thoroughfare. People come and go, wayfarers with good or bad intentions. Some may be treacherous. A bad idea is like a thief cloaked in darkness. The soul has its enemies. Let's spread daylight everywhere. Don't let darkness fill the corners of the human mind, the places where superstition and error may flourish, and where lies lurk in wait. In the twilight of ignorance, evil roams about.

You may ponder the need for street lighting, but think, especially think, about bringing light to the mind. For this, we need light incalculable. France has been busy spreading light for 300 years. Gentlemen, allow me a filial word, one you hold in your hearts, as I do. Nothing prevails against the soul of France. France *is* the public interest. France is the light of nations. People cry out for enlightenment! Where there is enlightenment, there is France they say! It's amazing that anyone could be against France. Yet, even so, France has enemies. These are the enemies of civilisation, of books of freedom of thought, enemies of emancipation, of account-ability, of deliverance. The servants of dogma who want to enslave humanity forever. They're wasting their time! The past is past. Nations don't return to their vomit. Blindness comes to an end. Ignorance and error will not endure.

Do your worst you men of the past! We don't fear you. Go ahead, we watch with interest. Try your best. Insult the spirit of 1789. Overthrow Paris! Declare your hatred of freedom of conscience, freedom of the press, and of the courts, your hatred of civil law, of revolution and tolerance, your hatred of science, of all progress. Don't flag! Keep dreaming! You have as much hope of creating a suitable program for France, as you do of extinguishing the sun.

I do not want to end on a sour note. Let us return to the serene realm of thought. We began by supporting peace and harmony. Let's go on doing so proudly and calmly. I've said elsewhere, and I repeat, all human wisdom is contained in these two words: conciliation and reconciliation. Conciliating men and reconciling ideas. Gentlemen, today we are among fellow philosophers. Let us profit from the occasion. Don't be embarrassed. Speak out for truth. Here is one truth, and a terrible one: humanity suffers from a sickness, hatred. Hatred is the mother of war, frightful daughter of an iniquitous mother.

Give back, blow for blow. Hatred for hatred! War for war! Do you know the meaning of Christ's words, love one another? Universal disarmament, healing of mankind. True redemption is this, that we love one another. An enemy is more easily disarmed by offering him your hand rather than your fist. The advice of Jesus is a divine command. It is good and we accept it. We are for Christ! The writer is at one with the apostle. He who thinks with him who loves. Ah, let us proclaim civilization. No and no again! We want nothing to do with barbarians making war, nor with savages who murder and kill. We want nothing to do with war, pitting nation against nation, and man against man. All killing is not only horrific but senseless.

Brandishing the sword is absurd and the dagger imbecilic. We are warriors of the mind and our duty is to prevent physical conflict. Our purpose is always to throw ourselves between two armies, the spiritual and the material. The right to life is indisputable. We make no distinction between the great and the humble, between kings and men. It is through being merciful that we make peace. When the dread bell tolls, we beg kings to spare the lives of their people, and we beg republics to spare the lives of emperors.

It a beautiful day for the outcast when he implores a nation to pardon a prince or tries to obtain the grace of exile for an emperor.[4]

Yes, to conciliate and reconcile. Such is our mission oh philosophers. To my brothers in science, poetry and the arts, let us acknowledge the all-civilising power of thought. At every step that humanity takes towards peace, let us feel the deep joy of truth grow within us. Proudly embrace useful labour. Truth is one indivisible ray of light with one synonym only, justice. The light of truth is the light of reason.

There is only one way to be truthful, honest and reasonable. The *Iliad* shines with the same clarity as the *Philosophical Dictionary*. This pure beam spans the centuries, straight as an arrow, and as unsullied as the dawn. This ray overcomes the darkness of conflict and hatred. This is the miracle of literature. Nothing is more beautiful. Might, bewildered and confounded by right, war arrested by reason, this, oh Voltaire, is to tame violence with wisdom, this, oh Homer, is Achilles tangled in the hair of Minerva.

Now that I'm about to finish, allow me one wish, a wish intended not for one heart but all hearts.

Gentlemen, there was a Roman famous for one fixed idea: 'Carthage must be destroyed.' I too am obsessed by one thought and it is this. Hatred must be destroyed. If literature has a purpose, it is that. *Humaniores Litterae,* gentleman. The destruction of hatred is best achieved through forgiveness. Ah that this marvelous year should not end before lasting peace is declared. That it should not end before wisdom and friendship reign and wars, foreign and civil, cease. This is our souls' deepest desire.

---

[4] A tireless advocate against capital punishment, in 1867 Hugo, then in exile in Guernsey, asked Benito Juarez, President of Mexico to spare the life of the deposed Emperor Maximilian I, sentenced to death after civil war. Juarez refused requests for clemency.

At this hour, when France is showing her hospitality to the world, may she also show her clemency. Let us crown France with clemency. All celebrations are fraternal. Any celebration that does not offer forgiveness is not a celebration. Amnesty is cause for public rejoicing. May this sound the closing note for these solemn and admirable proceedings, the World Exhibition. Reconciliation! Reconciliation!

Of course it's wonderful to see here the marvels of human effort, industry and labour, the masterpieces jostling with each other. But even more wonderful is the sight of the exile hovering on the horizon whose homeland opens its arms to embrace him.[5]

---

[5] Presumably Hugo referred to himself. He returned from exile in 1870.

Chapter 2
Limitless Information

Benedict Atkinson and Brian Fitzgerald

2.1   Aaron Swartz

In the past three decades, since the ascendancy of the United States in the process of determining international copyright policy and rules, considerable bitterness has entered debate about copyright. Many individuals have objected to the attitude of the United States government to copyright legal infraction around the world. Many Americans have also protested at their government's vehement attitude to real or alleged copyright infringements of US citizens.

Anger swelled at the government's prosecution (2011–2013) of Aaron Swartz. Aaron Swartz was a programmer of prodigious ability, 'a kid genius',[1] and later advocate for public freedom from corporate or government oppression.[2] On 11 January 2013, he hanged himself in his Brooklyn apartment, aged 26.

Between September 2010 and January 2011, Swartz logged into the Massachusetts Institute of Technology's digital network to download millions of public

---

This chapter is taken from B. Atkinson and B. Fitzgerald, *A Short History of Copyright*, © Springer International Publishing Switzerland 2014, doi: 10.1007/978-3-319-02075-4_14, p. 129

[1] Lessig blog 12 January 2013, http://lessig.tumblr.com.

[2] Swartz became involved, aged 15, in the coding of Creative Commons. He was later known as a contributor to development of RSS and Reddit software. He advocated for open access in the *Guerilla Open Access Manual* (2008) and in 2010 he helped to found Demand Progress, an internet advocacy organisation dedicated to 'win[ning] progressive policy changes for ordinary people . . . '.

B. Atkinson (✉)
Thomas More Academy of Law, Australian Catholic University, 8-20 Napier Street, North Sydney, NSW 2060, Australia
e-mail: benedict_atkinson@bigpond.com

B. Fitzgerald
Thomas More Academy of Law, Australian Catholic University, 486 Albert Street, East Melbourne, VIC 3002, Australia
e-mail: Brian.Fitzgerald@acu.edu.au

© Springer International Publishing Switzerland 2015   7
B. Fitzgerald, J. Gilchrist (eds.), *Copyright Perspectives*,
DOI 10.1007/978-3-319-15913-3_2

domain academic articles from the JSTOR digital library. He connected remotely and by direct wire link. Download volumes exceeded guest user privileges and conventional download limits. In early January 2011, MIT recorded him entering and leaving a network wiring closet where he attached concealed a laptop for download. Notified by MIT, police arrested him.

Once Swartz supplied to JSTOR the hard drive cache of files downloaded, JSTOR declared itself uninterested in pursuing legal action against him. The US Attorney for Massachusetts, however, prosecuted under computer and wire fraud legislation. A 2011 Massachusetts Grand Jury indictment alleged six violations, increased in 2012 by nine felony counts.

After issuing of the first indictment, the US Attorney said in a press release that Swartz, 'faces up to 35 years in prison . . . restitution, forfeiture and fine of up to $1 million.' Before his death, her office offered Swartz a plea bargain of conviction and 6 months in a low security prison.

The tragic circumstances of his death did not obscure recognition of Swartz's talents and public contributions, and he swiftly became fixed in public memory as a quintessential figure, young, bold, expressing in his life his ideals about freedom, universality and the liberating use of technology. Among members of bisecting circles of people concerned by restriction of information access and political freedom, his death caused palpable public grief and anger. Some blamed the Justice Department for precipitating suicide by pursuing pre-trial tactics of intimidation and aggression.

Debate over the Justice Department's conduct[3] essayed the proposition that many or most prosecutors try to secure plea bargains by suggesting the likelihood of lengthy sentences for a convicted felon. By implication, the Justice Department acted towards Swartz as it does to most individuals accused of crimes. Even allowing a neutral attitude on the part of prosecutors, two questions linger: why was Swartz indicted for criminal offences, and what does his treatment suggest about broader government attitudes to future information regulation?

Prosecutors charged Swartz, under the wires and computer fraud legislation, for engaging (in substance) in fraudulent property appropriation. Conceptually, the authors of Swartz's indictment document hardly distinguish between abstract and tangible property. What matters above all is the crime of theft. The indictment states twice that Swartz acted to 'steal' from JSTOR. 'Property' is defined twice, once as 'real or personal' and a second time as JSTOR's collected articles. Choice of legislation to frame charges precluded consideration of the differing policies informing legal treatment of non-excludable and excludable property. Such consideration, had it occurred, must have led to focus on harm caused, and invited consideration of intent.

---

[3] A considerable number of Swartz's friends, including Cory Doctorow and Lawrence Lessig blogged and spoke about the Justice Department's actions. For a partial defence of the Justice Department's actions, pointing out that the Attorney and her officers acted consistent with usual departmental prosecutorial practice, see Orin Kerr in Volokh.com 16 January 2013. James Boyle replied to Kerr in http://Huffingtonpost.com 18 January 2013.

The focus on theft, or 'stealing' lies at the heart of bemusement at prosecutors' attitude to Swartz. Swartz, apparently, intended a gesture against enclosure of knowledge, even if the putative encloser is a not-for-profit disseminator like JSTOR. He presumably knew that his gesture would not be regarded as morally neutral. A person seeking to download material in a way that contravenes download conditions is aware of transgression: the omission (which may be a wrong) lies in acting without consent. Such a person, however, does not perceive correlation between unauthorised downloading and, for example, hijacking a cash transport van to steal its contents.

The peculiarity in prosecutors' analysis is that they seemed unable to distinguish between an act directed towards public welfare—Swartz's mammoth downloading for purpose of public dissemination—and any other act directed towards, or involving, public harm, such as hijacking a cash transport van.

To characterise Aaron Swartz, who intended public benefit, as felonious, to contemplate that his behaviour placed him in a cohort of people who might be bent against public good, is to repudiate an idea of public welfare with which he concerned himself in life. To call Swartz's downloading theft, punishable by decades of servitude, is to merge ideas about the material and transcendental. Investing academic articles, or any other kind of property, with sacerdotal value, and by extension, treating theft as sacrilege, is to distort reality.

Psychologically, Swartz's arraignment betrayed a sovereign's hatred at denial of its sovereignty. This supposition is illustrated by a blog entry in which Swartz unknowingly foretold his own unravelling in the teeth of sovereign power. After his indictment, a trial lawyer Max Kennerly suggested that Swartz read Franz Kafka's *The Trial*. A few months later, Swartz blogged about the book, 'I read it and found that it was precisely accurate – every single detail perfectly mirrored my own experience.'[4]

The Trial is a story about Josef K, who, arrested on his 30th birthday, for a year experiences waking life as if sojourning in the shadowlands of nightmare. Nothing makes sense. Nothing is explained. Power is unanswerable. The nightmare is inescapable. After fruitlessly trying to discover the reason for his arrest, K submits, on his 31st birthday, to execution.

In another play, Kafka's protagonist is condemned by his father with the words, 'I sentence you to death by drowning.' In Kafka's *Letter To His Father* (1919), he describes his father as despot, overshadowing his life. In *The Trial*, Kafka makes clear that K is murdered by inimical exercise of power that issues from a single source of authority—its own will. Kafka's father displays the same monstrous will. He does not propose his son's execution, but Kafka does not doubt that resistance to his will is a capital offence.

Parallels between the situation of Aaron Swartz and the literature of Kafka need not be laboured. At the same time, the death of Swartz, and his treatment by the

---

[4] See Litigation and Trial blog of Max Kennerly, 14 January 2011, and the 2011 *Review of Books* at http://www.aaronsw.com.

Justice Department, crystallise years of debate over the content and meaning of copyright policy and law. Aaron Swartz's downloads from JSTOR were intended to demonstrate the moral foolishness of refusing to share information. He acted boldly and found himself dragged, by authority of the United States, into a world of Kafka's devising.

His own country did not say, 'I sentence you to death by drowning.' Inimical power, exercised by the Justice Department, promised, in effect, to punish him for life. At the end of Swartz's review of *The Trial*, he observed, 'K . . . decides to stop fighting the system and just live his life without asking for permission. It goes well . . . for a while.'

If legal rules are permissive, in the sense that they permit humans to express the dignity of their natures, a 'life without asking for permission' is possible. Such a life is what Aaron Swartz appears to have wanted for everyone. The copyright system, as it has evolved to the present, appears to make difficult for its adherents thought of a world 'without asking for permission.'

2.2 Purpose

A decade of P2P cases, in which defendants consisted of music and film downloaders, producers of software that facilitated illegal downloading and ISPs that connected subscribers to the internet, shed little light on the question that occurred to internet users delighted by the seemingly miraculous utility of the internet: what is the purpose of copyright?

For more than 40 years preceding the end of the first decade of the twenty-first century, scholars examined the philosophy and economics of copyright, reaching conclusions mostly at odds with the premises adopted by government and judiciary. Non-legal analysis rarely accepted uncritically the favoured assertions of copyright apologists, that copyrights encourage production and dissemination, and the law balances the interests of producer and consumer. As a number of observers noted, these assertions were hypotheses, unvalidated by empirical evidence.

The courts in the P2P decade refrained from examining the question of purpose deeply and ignored derivative questions: Why is unauthorized downloading illegal? Why are copyright proprietors entitled to proscribe unauthorized copying that occurs outside a legally definable market? Do copyrights confer a right of automatic remuneration or a merely a right to negotiate for reward? Has any legislature or court ever settled these and other questions?

Arguments in P2P cases mostly followed conventional lines, complainants alleging harm caused by invasion of proprietary rights and defendants raising the defence of fair use (in the case of direct infringers) or innocent facilitation. Argument did not depart from interpretation of the scope and application of established doctrines, such as fair use, and adjudication, not surprisingly, focused on legal principle, not philosophical or theoretical exegesis.

Yet copyright law in the age of the internet could, from the perspective of internet users, hardly advance meaningfully unless legislature and courts could emancipate themselves from the restrictions of precedent-based legal reasoning. Digital technology called into question the presumptions of copyright law, and internet users, who rejected the validity of laws that constrained access, dissemination and use, increasingly rejected the pecuniary demands of proprietary interests and restrictions on supply of information (see Barlow 1994).

Those users expressed a public voice, a public volition, until now unheard and ignored by government or private interests. In a sense, the internet made copyright politics 'interactive', for whatever the law said, or politicians or corporations assumed, the diffuse public of internet users—including by necessity, inventive programmers—showed itself capable of flouting laws and doctrine, and finding new ways of securing access to information. Other users, such as writers of 'fan fiction'— a new genre involving creative segues from published works—present another challenge to precepts of copyright law, one that courts may not welcome.[5]

The rise of public access corporations confirmed the trend towards public insistence upon the individual right to what might be called freedom of information—or weightless information. As companies such as Google demonstrated, information is super-abundant, and consumers of information endlessly curious and inventive in its uses. The internet is destroying the old idea, which animated the copyright law for 300 years, that information is a scarce commodity to be protected with more and more extensive rights. This old idea persists in government thinking, in the discourse of copyright industries and in social precepts. Its disappearance is by no means inevitable so long as proprietary attitudes hostile to public access and freedoms—in short, the attitude of privatization—dominate society at large.

On the other hand, unless humankind discovers the means of deconstituting individuals and reconstituting them near-instantaneously in a new location—as depicted in science fiction fantasies such as Star Trek—it is difficult to imagine

---

[5] Although a case involving what could probably be better characterized as an example of derivative fiction, rather than fan fiction, *Salinger v. Colting*, 2010 WL 1729126, 9 (2d Cir. April 30, 2010) demonstrates judicial reluctance to permit creative appropriation of fictional characters and their back-stories. In Salinger, the Second Circuit Court of Appeals returned a copyright infringement case to the New York District Court to reconsider its finding of 'irreparable harm' (on which basis the district court granted an injunction against publication of a 'sequel' to the J.D. Salinger novel *The Catcher in the Rye*). The District Court found that the defendant, Frederick Colting, author of *60 Years Later: Coming Through the Rye*, breached copyright in J.D. Salinger's novel *The Catcher in the Rye*—and, more controversially, copyright in the character of Holden Caulfield, the protagonist of Salinger's work. *60 Years Later* imagined Caulfield as a man aged 76 ('Mr C'), escaped from his nursing home and wandering the streets of New York. In Salinger's novel, Caulfield is a 17 year old, expelled from school and wandering in New York. The District Court rejected arguments of fair use for the purpose of commentary and criticism (or parody). Though it vacated the lower court's decision, the appeals court found *60 Years Later* to be substantially similar to Salinger's novel. The Salinger trust was 'likely to succeed on the merits of his copyright infringement claim'. On fan fiction, and user-generated content, see Wong (2009), p. 1075.

invention of a more extraordinary mode of communication than digital storage and transmission. This means that the literal wonders of digital communication must invite more and more public participation and create burgeoning counterweight to the privatization impulse. This struggle between public and private will determine the future shape of copyright law and, ultimately, perhaps its existence.

2.3   Conclusion

That copyright law might cease to regulate information dissemination seems unlikely. The history of property relations is one of extending control over whatever is controllable. To some, last century's collectivist interregnum foretold abolition of property and emancipation from exactions of power and wealth. However, gulag, famine and murder extinguished belief in a society in which nothing is owned. In the twenty-first century, the regime of private property seems irreducible and illimitable, furnishing means to control the universe itself, should technology allow.

Why this should be so is nothing less than the story of politics, or the contest for sovereignty. Sovereignty is more than power to command. It is also power to possess and exclude, the constituents of ownership. Contest for sovereignty resulted almost invariably—until adoption, in the last 200 or more years, of the principle of equality—in shades of absolutism. Until some modern societies created a sovereignty of many, allocating rights of equality to their members, struggle for sovereign power ended in rule by tyrant or coterie.[6]

Copyright law created another tyranny, that of eternal market sovereignty. Copyright's span is finite. Yet monopolies that outlive populations may as well be called eternal. Since the time of the Stationers' monopoly, advocates repeated one article of belief: creative effort conjures varied and delightful fruit, which is easily plucked without licence, unless forever protected from pilfering. The copyright sovereign demands eternal sovereignty.

Belief in immutability is characteristic of sovereign power throughout history. Yet even everlasting sovereignties disappear. Some tyrannies may end suddenly, as if expunged by outraged nature. Others vanish slowly, and in part, like Roman monocracy, its traces imprinted in emerging patterns of feudalism. Always,

---

[6] In antiquity, political struggle created near universal tyranny, except in Athens and Rome. Citizens of the former city invented plebiscite democracy, permitting a small group of qualified men a right to vote. After a few decades, democracy of the few collapsed into tyranny. In Rome, aristocrats and people shared republican government for centuries, before aristocratic assertion of sovereignty resulted in ruinous civil wars, and finally tyranny of emperors. Feudalism established, in most of the world, control arrangements, conferring on small groups, emperors, kings and lords, control over land and labour. Until partial acceptance of the idea of popular sovereignty, all political systems assumed overlordship of one or a few. Even today, the vesting pattern of property rights suggests that popular sovereignty is unrealised. In all countries, ownership is highly concentrated.

contradiction becomes too much. Gross poverty contradicts gross wealth. Weakness contradicts power. Paraphrasing Marx, sovereignties produce their own gravediggers.[7]

Copyright's gravediggers, say its opponents, are millions of users of digital technology who circumvent, dissent, copy, upload, download, share, flout and jeer. A more accurate statement may be that if law reserves for the sovereign too much power, that sovereign, in this case the copyright system, is like a despot, and the day comes when the despot, refusing to share power, is hunted to terminus, a grave dug by those it declared lawless.

Problems arising from power concentration are not resolved without sharing. Sharing sovereignty, by grant of suffrage and other rights, erases its inimical character. No sovereign shares willingly. On the other hand, nothing commends a tyrant's recalcitrance. A fixed policy of proscription is usually fatal to the proscriber. The Bourbons proscribed and were proscribed. 'They had,' said Talleyrand, expert in accommodation, 'learned nothing, and forgotten nothing.'[8]

Comparison between Bourbons and copyright industries is faint speculation. A more concrete observation is that human freedom, object of the great formative constitutional documents of the United States and France, could become a motif for reform that helps copyright regulation to last. Copyright restricts human freedom to the extent that its prohibitions and punishments, and scope of rights, contradict ordinary expectation of what is legitimate.

In short, if copyright regulation is adapted to offer users freedom, akin to expressive political freedoms guaranteed in rights of free speech, communication and access to information, it may yet endure by consent. Consent may grow, if regulators continue to discuss, for reform purposes, the length of copyright monopoly. Regulation that reduced the central role of permission and control could not fail to win admiration in some quarters.

In 130 years since the Berne Convention, those who determine copyright policy and laws have shown small inclination to reduce scope of laws, once made. Regulation and deregulation alike begin as acts of executive will. The executive, however, proposes laws more prolifically than it seeks their repeal. The young will grow old before they see the light of Halley's Comet, or rejection of copyright precepts.

Thus legal code will enjoin, as before, preservation of sovereignty, not its diffusion. Identifying unlawful actions of tens or hundreds of millions of network users may be thought unfeasible. Crowds camouflage illegal acts. In reality, copyright prohibitions are more enforceable than many realise. Few hackers escape legal consequences if the executive—or industries—will their identification.

---

[7] Marx and Engels (1848), Chapter 1.

[8] Observation attributed to Charles Maurice de Talleyrand-Périgord, Minister of Foreign Affairs and Prime Minister of France. It is possible Talleyrand is not author of the saying. He is supposed to have made the statement after accession of Charles X, the last Bourbon, in 1824, or his deposition in 1830.

Those who argue that code will be used to preclude freedoms hitherto available to internet or software users emphasise the power of software writers to disable communications technology. According to internet pessimists, the possibilities offered by network communication will reduce as networks become restricted or controlled by surveillance gateways. Governments, may, for approved security purposes spy on private online activity. User records of network owners or managers may, with growing licence, be interrogated by security agencies, or inquirers investigating copyright infringement. Digital rights management software will circumscribe multifarious use. Laws will prohibit most unremunerated use.

This stygian future is possible if governments, industries, or other actors determined to control information supply, enlarge their sovereignty over supply. Such a future is perhaps growing unlikely, however, for two reasons. The first is that, as the rise of access corporations show, if digital technology creates means for inexhaustible information supply, supply finds demand. The second is that digital technology is agent of metamorphosis and new creation: in the internet's insterstices, injunctions of law or programming vanish.

If code is interdiction, it fails. The ganglions of digital creation are too numerous to be uprooted. As well forbid growth of sunflowers and dandelions, bursting in hues of yellow and gold. The argument that code is increasingly restrictive depends on the premise that statutory prohibitions are enforceable and software exclusions effective. Code has power to preclude digital uses. This premise is demonstrably correct, but only in part. Copyright laws are enforced to preclude piracy or unauthorised copying. Software programs prevent use of, or access to, digital material, unless the user complies with contractual terms specified by the supplier.

In due course, however, non-preclusion, dream and nightmare of science fiction may become reality. Non-preclusion means that code cannot preclude. Code is deprived of power to proscribe use or forestall decryption. In theory, software might develop autonomic generative function, that is, autonomous function, outside human control, responsive to voice command, anticipating human wishes, generating its own behaviour, and implementing its own repairs, modifications or improvements.

Autonomic generativity would create individual crypto-life-forms, subservient to human beings, and outside the jurisdiction of regulatory systems intended to govern human behaviour. Science fiction conceptions of machinery developing volition and personhood also posits that autonomic machines or systems must eventually face moral choices. More starkly, they must choose to do good or evil.

A more modest conception debars rational possibility of volition and moral choice, and asserts that while autonomic function is likely to place software systems outside jurisdiction, nothing prevents voluntary code replacing enforceable code, or co-operation substituting effectively for code-protected monopolies and exclusions.

At the very least, a future in which software code is, in function, permissive not restrictive, will more likely pertain than one in which a technology facilitating communicative emancipation is co-opted to limit expressive freedom. Global users of digital technology express support for the principle of non-preclusion by showing preference for what might be called permissive technology, specifically, communication devices that enable more untrammelled communication and use. Users may as well be revolutionaries rattling palace gates.

References

Barlow JP (1994) The economy of ideas: a framework for patents and copyrights in the digital age (everything you know about intellectual property is wrong). WIRED (2.03):1–13
Marx K, Engels F (1848) The communist manifesto. London
Wong M (2009) Transformative user generated content in copyright law: infringing derivative works or fair use? Vanderbilt J Entertain Technol Law 11(4):1075

Chapter 3
Roman Law, Private Property and the Public Domain: Lessons for Copyright Policy

Arthur R Emmett

3.1 Roman Law and the Common Law[1]

The greatest gift that the ancient Romans have left to posterity has been their law and legal principles. That law is derived from the *Code*, the *Digest* and the *Institutes* of Justinian, which are together generally referred to as the *Corpus Iuris Civilis*.

In AD 476, the city of Rome fell to the barbarians and there was no longer an emperor in the West. What remained of the Roman Empire was ruled from Constantinople, in the East. When Justinian became emperor in Constantinople in AD 527, he conceived the idea of re-establishing what he perceived to be the lost greatness of Rome. One of the pillars upon which Justinian intended to found the re-establishment of Roman greatness was an authoritative codification of Roman law.

Justinian's first step was to order the compilation of a collection of imperial enactments that were still relevant and in force. That first step was completed in AD 529, with the publication of the *Code*, which was updated in AD 534. The second step was the preparation of the *Digest*, which was to be a compilation of the writings of the classical Roman jurists. The *Digest* was published in accordance with Justinian's instructions in AD 533.

Together, the *Code* and the *Digest* were close to twice the size of the Bible. The nature of both compilations was such that, while they constituted authoritative reference works, only those already skilled in the law had the capacity to find a

---

[1] These notes were prepared in connection with "Blue Sky: Future Directions in Copyright Law", a conference organised by the Queensland University of Technology on 25 February 2011. In preparing the notes I drew on Vukmir (1991), Emmett (2001), Ver Steeg (2000), and Hyde (2010).

A.R. Emmett, BA LLB LLM LLD (hc) (Syd) (✉)
New South Wales Court of Appeal, Level 12 Law Courts Building, Queens Square, Sydney, NSW 2000, Australia
e-mail: justice_emmett@courts.nsw.gov.au

© Springer International Publishing Switzerland 2015   17
B. Fitzgerald, J. Gilchrist (eds.), *Copyright Perspectives*,
DOI 10.1007/978-3-319-15913-3_3

way through the material contained in them. Justinian perceived, therefore, that a textbook containing the first principles of all learning in the law would also be required in order to instruct students of law and to provide a map of the law. Accordingly, Justinian gave instructions for the preparation of a text book for students called the *Institutes*, which was published in AD 533.

At the end of the eleventh century, the law school of Bologna, the oldest university of Western Europe, began to teach the law of the *Corpus Iuris Civilis*. The fame of that law school spread throughout the whole of Europe in the centuries thereafter and, in consequence, the jurisprudence of the *Corpus Iuris Civilis* became the jurisprudential foundation of all modern European law systems.

By 1150, Roman law was being taught at the University of Oxford. Soon after, it was being taught at the University of Cambridge. At that time, Roman law was habitually cited in the law courts of England and relied upon by legal writers. Henry of Bracton's *De Legibus et Consuetudinibus Angliae*, published in 1256, was probably the first important book on English law. Bracton wrote in Latin and resorted extensively to the *Corpus Iuris Civilis* in compiling the work. Roman law supplied him not only with a framework under which his English subject matter could be fashioned into an articulated system of principles, but also with a precise technical vocabulary with which to describe and analyse the material. Bracton's treatise was very influential in many areas of Anglo-Norman jurisprudence, particularly after it was referred to favourably by William Blackstone.

During the time when the development of Anglo-Norman jurisprudence was in the hands of practitioners in the Inns of Court, the members of the Inns were often educated at Oxford and Cambridge. Henry VIII founded the Regius Chairs of Civil Law in both universities and the study of law at those institutions entailed, for the most part, the study of Roman jurisprudence. Accordingly, civil jurisprudence, founded on the *Corpus Iuris Civilis*, continued to affect Anglo-Norman jurisprudence through the universities.

Further, there was an international character attached to the dealings of merchants and mariners that gave rise to a need for universality in the principles of law governing their dealings. It was necessary that such principles be generally the same in the various countries visited by merchants and mariners. The law merchant developed out of that necessity. The growth of trade among the city states of Italy coincided with the rediscovery of the *Corpus Iuris Civilis*, which provided a convenient source of principles for the resolution of disputes involving merchants and mariners. While the law merchant was different from the ordinary law and was in fact administered by different courts, Edward I recognised the law merchant as part of the national law of England.

English jurists also had resort to Roman jurisprudence where there was no clear rule on a particular subject. For example, the law of easements, which developed in England and Wales in the early nineteenth century, was based entirely on Roman jurisprudence.

3.2 Copyright Today

Section 32 of the *Copyright Act 1968* (Cth) provides that copyright subsists in an original literary, dramatic, musical or artistic work that is unpublished, provided that the author has a relevant connection with Australia at the time when the work was made. Under s 22, a work is made when the work is first reduced to writing or to some other material form. Under s 10, "writing" means a mode of representing or reproducing words, figures or symbols in a visible form, and "material form", in relation to a work, includes any form of storage from which the work can be reproduced.

Section 31 provides that copyright, in relation to a work, is the exclusive right to do the things set out in s 31(1)(a), (b), (c) and (d). Under s 31(1)(a)(i), one of those acts is to reproduce the work in a material form. Under s 32(2), where an original, literary, dramatic, musical or artistic work has been published, copyright subsists in the work or, if copyright subsisted before its first publication, copyright continues to subsist in the work, if there is a relevant connection with Australia. The term of copyright in a work is 70 years after the death of the author or artist.

Under s 8, copyright does not subsist otherwise than by virtue of the *Copyright Act*. Further, copyright is not a proprietary right in an existing tangible thing. That is to say, it is not a right that can be enforced *in rem*. It can only be a right that is enforced *in personam*, to prevent reproduction or copying of a particular form of expression or to recover compensation where there has been an infringement. In that sense, it is an intangible or incorporeal interest. Thus, the right conferred by the *Copyright Act* gives no right in the physical medium on or in which a work is first recorded, expressed or embodied. Copyright is a right that is distinct from any property in the physical medium on or in which the subject matter of the copyright is recorded, expressed or embodied. The purchase of a physical medium on or in which a copyright work is recorded, expressed or embodied gives no copyright in the work, although it will give ownership of the physical medium. Ownership of a book or a manuscript or a canvas confers no copyright, in respect of the work recorded on that medium, to the owner of the medium.

If a literary, artistic literary or dramatic work is not written or recorded in some material form, being a form of storage from which it can be reproduced, copyright will not subsist in it. Accordingly, the work will be in the public domain, owned by the public at large. In addition, a work in which copyright does subsist can enter the public domain, by operation of law, when the copyright expires.

3.3 Roman Property Law

The Romans held that certain types of property, namely *res communes* and *res publicae*, were incapable of private ownership. *Res communes*, such as the air, the sea and the seashore, were things of common enjoyment available to all living persons by virtue of their existence.[2] *Res publicae* consisted of public roads, bridges, ports, market places, theatres, baths and rivers.[3] Persons enjoyed them as an inhabitant of the state. *Res communes* belonged to mankind as a whole, while *res publicae* belonged to the Roman people.

The Romans developed the concept of incorporeal property.[4] That is to say, they recognised a proprietary interest that could not be touched or handled. A book or a parcel of land is corporeal, or tangible, property. Each can be seen and possessed. Incorporeal, or intangible property, on the other hand, cannot be seen or possessed. An easement or a usufruct is incorporeal property. An easement or a usufruct is a *ius in rem*, albeit a right in someone else's property. An obligation, such as a debt or a claim for damages for wrongful conduct, is also intangible property. However, it is a *ius in personam*.

The Romans described usufruct as the right to the enjoyment and fruits of another person's property, with the duty to preserve its substance.[5] It is a right in a corporeal thing of another person. Thus, usufruct has to be split off from ownership. A usufruct could be for a fixed period or for life. In the latter case, it was similar to a life estate in the common law. The usufruct was a proprietary right enforceable *in rem*, because it was a right enforceable over the property, whoever happened to be the owner of the property. However, it could only be enforced by the person to whom the usufruct was granted. It was therefore described as an interest that was personal to the holder. The interest, however, could not be touched or possessed, although the interest could be exercised. The interest was incorporeal.

The Romans also treated an obligation owed by one person to another as incorporeal property. Such an obligation may arise out of contract or out of tort or wrong-doing, or delict as the Romans called it.[6] The person to whom the obligation is owed was treated by the Romans as owning incorporeal property. However, that type of property was treated by the Romans as a right enforceable *in personam*, rather than a right *in rem*. That is to say, it is a right enforceable against a person or persons. Infringement of copyright, as it is understood in modern law, would be, in effect, a statutory tort or wrong, or delict, if it existed in Roman law.

However, the Romans did not recognise an exclusive right to copy artistic or literary works. The Romans did not develop the notion of a proprietary interest in the result of literary or artistic effort. They did not recognise a right to exclude others from the result of literary or artistic effort. There was never any notion of ownership of the work itself.

Roman jurisprudence saw the question of ownership of a literary or artistic work only in terms of the physical material in which the work was recorded or evidenced. Roman jurisprudence did distinguish between the intangible work, on the one hand,

---

[2] *Institutes* 2.1.1.

[3] *Institutes* 2.1.2.

[4] See *Institutes* 2.2.

[5] *Institutes* 2.4 pr.

[6] *Institutes* 3.13.

and the physical medium or material form in which the work was expressed or embodied, on the other. However, they did not recognise a proprietary right in respect of the intangible work. Where the author was the owner of the medium, no question arose as to separate ownership of the medium and the work. It was only where the work was recorded on or embodied in a medium belonging to someone other than the author that Roman jurisprudence became interested.

The Romans dealt with that question under the rubric of *accessio*. Thus, writing on paper or parchment, even in letters of gold, accedes to, or becomes part of, the paper or parchment. If an author writes a poem or a history or a speech on your paper or parchment, you remain the owner of the paper or parchment. However, if the paper or parchment is in the possession of the author and you seek to recover it from the author, you will be required to compensate the author for the loss of the writing, assuming that the author acquired possession of the paper or parchment in good faith.[7] On the other hand, if you, as the owner, are in possession of the paper or parchment, the author has no claim against you.

Nevertheless, the obligation to give compensation as a condition of obtaining possession of your paper or parchment indicates that Roman jurists recognised some proprietary interest in the literary work recorded on the paper or parchment. However, there was nothing to stop the author from writing his poem, history or speech down on another paper or parchment. Nor of course was there anything to stop the owner of the paper or parchment from copying the work and distributing the copies by sale or otherwise. So far as the Romans were concerned, the work was in the public domain. No one owned the literary work as distinct from the material form in which it was embodied or on which it was recorded.

The position is different if someone paints a picture on your board or canvas. There was originally some jurisprudential disputation as to the consequence. A picture or painting by a famous artist was regarded as being of far greater value than the canvas or board on which it was painted. The Roman jurists regarded as it ridiculous to say that the paint acceded to the board or canvas, irrespective of the quality of the painting or picture. However, where the original owner of the canvas or board has possession of the painting or picture, and the painter claims return of his painting, the painter will be required to compensate the owner of the board for the value of the board or canvas. Even if the painter is in possession, the owner of the board or canvas is given an action to recover its value. Those principles, of course, apply only on the assumption that the painter painted on the board or canvas in good faith believing that it was his. If he knew he was not the owner, he would be liable for the theft of the board or canvas.[8]

The explanation for the difference between writing on somebody else's paper or parchment and painting a picture on somebody else's board or canvas is that the form of the painting or picture is unique, whereas the words of a poem, a history or a speech can be reproduced by the author. It is much harder to reproduce a picture or painting precisely, according to the technology available in Roman times.

---

[7] *Institutes* 2.1.33.

[8] *Institutes* 2.1.34.

The question of a sculptor who uses somebody else's bronze, silver or gold to make an artistic work was dealt with by the Romans under the rubric of *specificatio*, making a new thing or *species* out of different materials. If the maker owned the materials, no difficulty arose. However, when somebody else's materials were used, the position varied. The jurists dealt with such things as making wine from another's grapes, oil from another's olives or grain from another's corn, as well as making something from another's gold, silver or bronze. There was a juridical dispute in earlier times. One view was that the person who makes something from somebody else's materials should be the owner of the thing, subject to a right of compensation, similar to that applicable to paintings or pictures. The other view was that the owner of the materials was the owner of the new product. Justinian adopted a middle view. If the thing can be turned back into its materials, its owner is the one who owned the materials. If not, the maker is the owner. The completed pot, made from bronze, silver or gold, can be turned back into raw bronze, silver or gold. Hence, the owner of the materials is the owner of the pot. However, wine, oil or grain cannot be made back into grapes, olives or corn. Hence, the wine, oil or grain belongs to the maker, subject to rights of compensation.[9]

On the other hand, when the maker uses materials belonging both to himself and to someone else, the maker was regarded as the owner of the product, because he contributes not only his work but also part of the materials. Thus, the Romans recognised that the author or the maker of a thing had an interest in the product by reason of his effort in producing the product. However, that was not a proprietary right that could be alienated by the author, other than by alienation of the object on which the work was recorded or in which the work was embodied.

3.4 Copyright Rationale

Copyright is an exception to the law's general dislike of monopolies. The Romans disliked monopolies just as much as common lawyers. At the end of the fifth century, the Emperor Zeno provided that no one was to be permitted to monopolise the sale of certain common commodities. The provision also prohibited any agreement in any unlawful assembly that any kind of merchandise that was the object of commerce would not be sold for less than what was agreed upon by the parties in question. The measure provided that, should anyone practise monopoly, he would be deprived of all his property and sentenced to perpetual exile and that those who ventured to fix the prices of their merchandise or bind themselves by any illegal contracts of that kind would be punished by a fine. Any tribunal that did not enforce the laws as to monopolies was also to be punished by a fine.

Literary, dramatic, musical and artistic works are undiminished by use. Further, once they are published to the world at large, it is virtually impossible to make them

---

[9] *Institutes* 2.1.25.

private again. Thus, an infinite number of people can use or have possession of ideas, inventions, artistic works, literary works and the like, and consume them. On the other hand, if one person consumes a tangible thing or has possession of a tangible thing, no other person can. That is to say, even though a tangible thing is publicly available, others can easily be excluded from it. That is not the case with ideas, inventions, artistic works, literary works and the like, especially when there are devices like the printing press or the internet to disseminate them. Once an invention or a literary or artistic work is disclosed, it becomes part of human knowledge. It is only the intervention of the state, by imposing a monopoly in relation to an invention or creating a copyright, that prevents inventions, ideas, musical, artistic and literary works from being commonly available or in the public domain.

Several answers are traditionally given as to why a community might be motivated, *contra naturam*, to introduce a right to exclude. First, it is said that all creative people have a natural right to the fruits of their efforts. Where non-excludability makes it difficult to claim those fruits, society should intervene. Secondly, creative work is said to be a kind of extension into the world of the creator's personality and that the work therefore deserves the same respect and protection that is accorded to the person of an individual. The concern is with questions of honour, respect and reputation. Hence moral rights theory developed, which focuses on the individual creator.

The third answer is based on the needs of the community. If the community as a whole would benefit from a constant flow of useful and wonderful creations and if an exclusive right would motivate creators to create such things, the community may well offer that exclusive right. If such things are common by nature, then their very nature is an impediment to their production, so long as the creators or producers of the things need to earn a living. The principle that effort should have its reward arises in this context as well. However, the just reward for effort spent is not an end in itself but a means towards a broader utilitarian goal of providing the greatest good for the greatest number. Such a utilitarian or public benefit model can be divided into two versions, the commercial and the civic. The former shies away from trying to describe the good, trusting in market forces to reveal it. The latter nominates worthy ends then seeks to shape the offer of exclusive rights so as to achieve those ends. The point is that a utilitarian theory of exclusive rights of either version involves taking from the public domain in the short term so as to create a larger and richer public domain in the long term. It does not set the public interest against the private interest but seeks to leverage the private interest for the benefit of the public interest.

Copyright legislation strikes a balance between competing interests and competing policy considerations. Relevantly, it is concerned with rewarding authors of original literary works with commercial benefits, having regard to the fact that artistic, musical and literary works in turn benefit the public.[10] The purpose of

---

[10] *IceTV Pty Ltd v Nine Network Australia Pty Ltd* (2009) 239 CLR 458 at 471 [24] (French CJ, Crennan and Kiefel JJ).

copyright law is to balance the public interest in promoting the encouragement of literary, dramatic, musical and artistic works, by providing a just reward for the creator, with the public interest in maintaining a robust public domain in which further works are produced.[11] Thus, it is said that the true purpose of the grant of copyright is not to reward creators so much as to enrich the cultural or intellectual commons or public domain. That is illustrated by the historical development of copyright legislation.

It is often said that the invention of the printing press was the watershed date for the beginning of copyright as a practical concept. Printing technology is said to have provided the first realistic opportunity for authors to recognise the potential economic benefit from their work. In 1469, the Governors of Venice granted to John of Spira, a printer, the exclusive rights to publish both Cicero's and Pliny's letters for five years. Others in Venice and elsewhere quickly began seeking and securing the exclusive privilege to publish particular works in specific localities. The mid to late fifteenth century experienced a rise in the creation of copyright, taking the guise of an exclusive right granted by the state to a publisher.

By the early sixteenth century, the English Crown began granting to individual printers exclusive rights to publish specific books. In the sixteenth century, a Royal Charter gave to the Stationers' Company, which dominated all publishing in London at the time, exclusive and perpetual rights in books that were duly registered. Publishers thus enjoyed a state sanctioned monopoly over what appeared in print. However, the rights granted had nothing to do with rewarding authors. Rather, the grant was much more concerned with the control of the press by the Crown.

In that context, the Westminster Parliament enacted the *Statute of Anne*,[12] which came into force in 1710, giving the author or proprietors of books the sole liberty of printing and reprinting for the term of 14 years, renewable once if the author was still living. The privilege was not automatic. Authors and publishers had to apply for it, pay a fee and register the relevant work. The *Statute of Anne* is the significant forebear of English and, therefore, Australian copyright legislation. The *Statute of Anne* provided authors and publishers with remedies, which included stiff financial penalties for infringement. In addition to the remedies, however, the *Statute of Anne* stated that the term of exclusive rights was granted only for a specific, limited, period of time.

The exclusive right embodied in the *Statute of Anne* was an innovation of some significance. While it created a new monopoly, it put an end to the larger monopoly of the Stationers' Company, encouraging the release of work into the public domain. As publishing became more lucrative during the eighteenth century, more and more entered on the business of publishing. As a result, the limits and interpretation of the *Statute of Anne* were tested. A critical question that emerged was whether copyright was a perpetual right. The issue turned on whether copyright was considered a natural right that existed at common law, in which case, the right,

---

[11] *IceTV v Nine Network* at 485 [71] (Gummow, Hayne and Heydon JJ).

[12] (1710) 8 Anne, c. 19.

like most common law property rights, would be perpetual, or whether copyright was a grant from the Crown created by legislation, in which case, the legislation could limit its duration. *Donaldson v Beckett*[13] decided that the copyright of books exists only under the *Statute of Anne*, whereby the sole right of printing and disposing of copies is vested in the author, or the author's assigns, for 14 years from the first publication. As a result of *Donaldson's Case*, it was clear that booksellers could rely only on statutory copyright in published works.

The combination of a limited term and a registration requirement constituted a revolution in the history of the dissemination of knowledge. Even after 1710, most work remained unregistered and so became public as soon as it appeared. The books that were registered enjoyed only a limited run of exclusivity, after which they were automatically released to join the public domain.

Samuel Johnson observed that, for the general good of the world, whatever valuable work has once been created by an author and published should be understood as no longer in that author's power but as belonging to the public.[14] On the other hand, the author is entitled to an adequate reward. That should consist of an exclusive right to his work for a number of years. The question is how many years that should be. The *Statute of Anne* gave 28 years as a maximum. Johnson thought that the author's life plus 30 years would be reasonable.

There has always been some enclosure of intellectual material. Government documents and matters of state have never been fully available to the public. There has long been knowledge kept secret and there has long been some control of the press. The grant to John of Spira by the Governors of Venice excluded all others. The Royal Charter to the Stationers' Company was a form of enclosure and was so described. The *Statute of Anne* authorised enclosure, in that it created a right to exclude. The *Statute of Anne*, however, was seen to be laudable because it not only beat back the larger enclosure that was the character of the Charter given to the Stationers' Company, but also, by limiting the term of the grant, it established a way to feed new creations into the public domain. However, since 1710, the enclosure has been extended. The copyright law now grants very extensive private rights to almost every creative expression.

3.5 Copyright as Usufruct

An analogy can be drawn between the concept of copyright, as it exists under the *Copyright Act*, and the notion of a usufruct under Roman law. The author of a copyright work has the right to use and enjoy the work for the term of the statutory copyright. The work, however, is in the public domain and the public is the owner of the copyright subject to the usufruct. Under Roman law, a usufruct could be for a

---

[13] (1774) 2 Brown 129; 1 ER 837.

[14] Remarked in conversation in 1773. See Boswell J (1791) Boswell's Life of Johnson. Chapman RW (ed) (1953), Oxford University Press, Oxford.

fixed term or for life. Even if it was for a fixed term, the usufruct terminated on the death of the holder of the usufruct.

There is an anomaly in the term of copyright when considered against the term of the monopoly granted under the *Patents Act 1990* (Cth) in respect of an invention. The research and effort that is often required for an invention far exceeds the effort that is involved in the production of the vast majority of dramatic, literary, artistic and musical works that are the subject of copyright for a far greater term than is granted in respect of an invention. It may be that the time has come for a rethinking of the term of copyright. Rather than a fixed term after the death of the author or the composer or artist, irrespective of the nature of the work and the age of that author, composer or artist, it may be appropriate that there be variable terms.

Copyrightable works are ordinarily works that benefit society by providing entertainment or aesthetic enjoyment or communicating useful information such as educational materials. In modern systems, copyright is a trade-off. The state grants exclusive rights to authors and artists for a limited term. In return, the public benefits in two stages. In the first stage, the public has access to the work and may use it but must pay a royalty for that privilege. In the second stage, the public has unrestricted use. On one view, the difference between the current term of copyright and a perpetual copying is statistically trivial. The further away in time a sum is paid, the less that payment is worth in present values. The difference between such an increase and that of an infinite copyright term may be thought to be negligible.

Another anomaly is that an author, composer or artist who produces a work early in his or her lifetime will have a significantly greater return than a composer, author or artist who produces a work towards the end of his or her lifetime, when the experience and skill of the author, composer or artist would be expected to be worth much more than the competence and experience and skill at the beginning of a career.

If one begins with the proposition that a work, once published, belongs to the public, the enquiry should be as to the reasonable term for a usufruct in favour of the author, composer or artist. In an ideal world, that will not be a standard term ending 70 years after the end of the calendar year in which the author of the work dies.

The extension of the monopoly since the introduction of the *Statute of Anne* has been considerable, yet the term of the monopoly in respect of an invention has not changed significantly since the *Statute of Monopolies*,[15] which allowed patents to be granted for terms not exceeding 14 years. Perhaps the time has arrived for the standard term for the monopoly of copyright to be reconsidered. Works that are subject to copyright should attract the copyright monopoly for some period, as recognition of the contribution of the author or the composer or artist. Rather than a fixed term after the death of the author or the composer or artist, irrespective of the nature of the work and the age of that author, composer or artist, it may be appropriate that there be variable terms. However, perhaps there should be greater recognition of the notion that such works are in the public domain, subject to the limited usufruct of the author or the composer or artist.

---

[15] (1624) 21 Jac I, c. 3.

References

de Bracton H (1256) De Legibus et Consuetudinibus. In: Woodbine GE (ed) Publications of the Selden Society 1968–77, 4 vols (trans: Thorne SE). Harvard University Press, Cambridge

Emmett AR (2001) Roman traces in Australian Law. Aust Bar Rev 20:205

Hyde L (2010) Common as Air : Revolution, Art, and Ownership. Farrar, Straus and Giroux, New York

Ver Steeg R (2000) The Roman law roots of copyright. Maryland Law Rev 59:522

Vukmir M (1991) The roots of Anglo-American intellectual property law in Roman law. IDEA 32 (2):123

Chapter 4
Country of Origin and Internet Publication: Applying the Berne Convention in the Digital Age

Brian Fitzgerald, Sampsung Xiaoxiang Shi, Cheryl Foong, and Kylie Pappalardo

4.1 Introduction

It is increasingly common for copyright works to be made available to the public for the first time via the Internet. Online publication allows a work to be published simultaneously throughout the world to every country with Internet access. While this is certainly advantageous for the dissemination and impact of information and creative works, it creates potential complications under the Berne Convention for the Protection of Literary and Artistic Works ("Berne Convention"), an international intellectual property agreement to which most countries in the world now subscribe. The Berne Convention contains national treatment provisions, which require member countries to extend baseline rights and protections to foreign copyright works.[1] Rights accorded under the national treatment provisions may not be subject to any formality, such as registration requirements.[2] Member countries

---

[1] Article 5(1). Discussed in more detail below.

[2] Article 5(2). Discussed in more detail below.

B. Fitzgerald (✉) • K. Pappalardo
Thomas More Academy of Law, Australian Catholic University, 486 Albert Street, East Melbourne, VIC 3002, Australia
e-mail: Brian.Fitzgerald@acu.edu.au; kylie.pappalardo@gmail.com

S.X. Shi
East China University of Political Science and Law, Room 416, Chongfa Building, 555 Longyuan Rd., Songjiang District, Shanghai 201620, China
e-mail: sampsung@outlook.com

C. Foong
Curtin Law School, Curtin University, Building 407, Level 3, Kent Street, Bentley, WA 6102, Australia
e-mail: cheryl.foong@curtin.edu.au

© Springer International Publishing Switzerland 2015
B. Fitzgerald, J. Gilchrist (eds.), *Copyright Perspectives*,
DOI 10.1007/978-3-319-15913-3_4

are free to and some do impose formalities on the exercise of rights in relation to domestic copyright works. In the United States, for example, the *Copyright Act 1976* establishes a requirement that copyright owners register their work with the Copyright Office before they can commence a civil action for infringement of their work.[3] Additionally, the U.S. law limits the availability of certain remedies depending on when the work was registered.[4]

The Berne Convention contains "country of origin" provisions, which seek to assist member countries in determining whether copyright works are domestic or foreign for the purpose of applying Berne's protection for foreign works. Under the Convention, determining the country of origin of a published work is simply a matter of ascertaining where that work was first published or simultaneously published.[5] The rules provide that for works first published in a country of the Union, the country of origin will be that country.[6] For works published simultaneously in several countries of the Union which grant different terms of protection, the country of origin will be the country with the shortest term of protection, and for works published simultaneously in a country of the Union and a country outside of the Union, the country of origin will be the Union country.[7] Historically, determining the country of origin of a published work presented few challenges, because works were generally published physically—whether in print or otherwise—in a distinct location or few locations. However, publishing opportunities presented by new technologies mean that we now live in a world of simultaneous publication—works that are first published online are published simultaneously to every country in world in which there is Internet connectivity. These new opportunities present unique challenges and bring to the fore the apparent gaps in the Berne Convention's country of origin provisions. For example, as discussed further in Sect. 2.3 of this article, the Berne Convention fails to point to a distinct country of origin where a work is published simultaneously in multiple Union countries with the same term of protection.[8] This is exactly the kind of scenario that is likely to arise more frequently as Member countries seek consistency in the term of copyright protection accorded to copyright works[9] and as more and more works are first published online. In this situation, the Berne Convention

---

[3] *Copyright Act: 17 U.S.C.* § 411(a).

[4] *Copyright Act: 17 U.S.C.* § 412.

[5] "Simultaneous publication" is defined as within 30 days of first publication: Article 3(4). For unpublished works, the country of origin is the country of the Union of which the author is a national: Article 5(4)(c).

[6] Article 5(4)(a). Article 1 of the Berne Convention establishes a Union: "The countries to which this Convention applies constitute a Union for the protection of the rights of authors in their literary and artistic works".

[7] Article 5(4)(a) and (b).

[8] The language of Article 5 indicates that there should be only one country of origin of a work, though this is not entirely clear.

[9] The European Union recently extended its term of copyright protection from life of the author plus 50 years to life of the author plus 70 years, bringing it in line with the term granted in the United States of America, Australia, and a number of other countries around the world.

offers little guidance. This creates legal uncertainties for Member countries such as the United States in determining whether a work first published over the Internet is a domestic or foreign work for the purpose of applying national copyright formalities.

Two cases recently decided in the United States deal directly with this issue. In *Kernel Records Oy v. Timothy Mosley p/k/a Timbaland, et al.* ("*Kernel v Mosley*"),[10] the Florida Southern District Court of the United States ruled that first publication of a work on the Internet via an Australian website constituted "simultaneous publication all over the world," and therefore rendered the work a "United States work" under the definition in section 101 of the U.S. Copyright Act,[11] subjecting the work to registration formality under section 411. This ruling is in sharp contrast with an earlier decision delivered by the Delaware District Court in *Håkan Moberg v 33T LLC, et al.* ("*Moberg v 33T*").[12] The Delaware court held that the publication of a work via a German website did not render the work a "United States work" within the meaning of section 411 of the Copyright Act, and thus need not be registered in the U.S. in order for the copyright owner to bring suit for infringement. The conflicting rulings of the U.S. courts reveal the problems posed by new forms of publishing online and demonstrate a compelling need for further harmonization between the Berne Convention, domestic laws and the practical realities of digital publishing.

In this article, we argue that even if a work first published online can be considered to be simultaneously published all over the world it does not follow that any country can assert itself as the "country of origin" of the work for the purpose of imposing domestic copyright formalities. More specifically, we argue that the meaning of "United States work" under the U.S. Copyright Act should be interpreted in line with the presumption against extraterritorial application of domestic law to limit its application to only those works with a real and substantial connection to the United States. To be clear, we argue that the extraterritorial application of U.S. law at issue here is not the imposition of formalities at the point of enforcing copyright in courts within the United States (the "enforcement stage"), but the designation, via U.S. copyright legislation and the judicial interpretation of such, of all works first published online as "United States works" within the ambit of section 411 of the U.S. Copyright Act (the "designation stage"). We propose a number of factors that may be considered in assessing whether there is a "real and substantial connection" to the United States and assert that in most cases, the nationality, domicile or habitual residence of the author of the work should be the determinative factor in ascertaining the country of origin of the work. As discussed above, there are gaps in the Berne Convention's articulation of "country of origin" which provide scope for judicial interpretation, at a national level, of the

---

[10] 2011 U.S. Dist. LEXIS 60666 (S.D. Fla. June 7, 2011).

[11] The definition states that a work which is published simultaneously in the United States and another country is a "United States work" for the purposes of §411 of the Copyright Act. See further below.

[12] 666 F. Supp. 2d 415 (D. Del. Oct. 6, 2009).

most pragmatic way forward in reconciling the goals of the Berne Convention with the practical requirements of domestic law. We believe that the uncertainties arising under the Berne Convention created by new forms of online publishing can be resolved at a national level by the sensible application of principles of statutory interpretation by the courts. While at the international level we may need a clearer consensus on what amounts to "simultaneous publication" in the digital age, state practice may mean that we do not yet need to explore textual changes to the Berne Convention.

4.2 Country of Origin Under the Berne Convention

4.2.1 Essentials of the Berne Convention

One of the aims of the Berne Convention is "to help nationals of its member States obtain international protection of their right to control, and receive payment for, the use of their creative works".[13] For example, Article 5(1), under the title 'Rights Guaranteed', states that "Authors shall enjoy, in respect of works for which they are protected under this Convention, in countries of the Union other than the country of origin, the rights which their respective laws do now or may hereafter grant to their nationals, as well as the rights specially granted by this Convention".

In addition, the 1908 Berlin revision of the Berne Convention established a prohibition on the imposition of any governmental formalities by a Member country as a precondition for "the enjoyment and the exercise" of copyright in foreign works in that country. Today, this rule reads as follows in Article 5(2) of the Convention: "The enjoyment and the exercise of these rights shall not be subject to any formality". The Convention therefore purports to secure minimum rights for authors, which automatically arise without the need to obey formalities, in countries of the Union other than the country of origin of the work. Protection of works in their country of origin is governed by domestic law and may, in fact, be subject to formalities (as they are in the U.S. for enforcement of rights).[14] Therefore, a central object of the Convention is to guarantee that a foreign work will be protected in a Union country other than its country of origin without formality requirements.

---

[13] See World Intellectual Property Organization (WIPO), *WIPO Treaties – General Information*, http://www.wipo.int/treaties/en/general/. Note that in addition to protection in accordance with the principles of national treatment, the Berne Convention also sets out minimum standards of protection in relation to the works and rights to be protected, and the duration of the protection. See WIPO (1886).

[14] Berne Convention, Article 5(3).

4.2.2 The Notion and Place of Publication

The definition of "published works" set forth in Article 3(3) of the Convention is as follows:

> The expression "published works" means works published with the consent of their authors, whatever may be the means of manufacture of the copies, provided that the availability of such copies has been such as to satisfy the reasonable requirements of the public, having regard to the nature of the work. The performance of a dramatic, dramatico-musical, cinematographic or musical work, the public recitation of a literary work, the communication by wire or the broadcasting of literary or artistic works, the exhibition of a work of art and the construction of a work of architecture shall not constitute publication.

In addition, "simultaneous publication" is defined under Article 3(4): "A work shall be considered as having been published simultaneously in several countries if it has been published in two or more countries within thirty days of its first publication."

The definition of "published works" and the corresponding determination of the country of origin of a work are significant to the application of certain important clauses of the Convention. As highlighted by the Committees of Experts on a Possible Protocol to the Berne Convention, these clauses include "[the] application of the protection of the Convention to authors who are not nationals of one of the countries of the Union but whose works have been first published in one of those countries (Article 3(1)(b)); the comparison of terms of protection (Article 7(8)); and application of the Convention to works already in existence when their country of origin first joins the Convention (Article 18(1))."[15] In addition, whether or not protection under Articles 5(1), (2) and (3) comes into operation with respect to a work also hinges on this determination.

A modern enquiry, contemplated in both the *Kernel v Mosley* and *Moberg v 3TT* cases discussed below, is what happens under our assessments of "published" and "country of origin" where a work is first made available to the public online. Is the act of posting a work to the Internet enough to make the work a "published work" under the Berne Convention? And if so, given that the Internet is a globally distributed platform, how do we determine the country or countries of first (or simultaneous first) publication for the purpose of establishing the country of origin?

The general consensus appears to be that Internet dissemination is enough to render a work "published". A WIPO Committee of Experts has acknowledged as much, stating, "As far as the public is concerned, these new forms of publishing are functionally no different than the traditional forms: the works are available".[16] Under the abovementioned Article 3(3) of the Berne Convention, the dispositive factor in determining whether a work is published is "[that] the availability of such copies has been such as to satisfy the reasonable requirements of the public".

---

[15] WIPO (1996) at p. 16.
[16] *Id.*

We agree with the proposition that posting a work over the Internet may "easily satisfy this requirement".[17] Therefore, we contend that once a work is made available over the Internet the work will be published in every country with adequate access to the Internet. Nevertheless, it does not follow that the work will become a "work of every country"; or put differently, it does not mean that the country of origin of the work will be every country in the world.[18]

4.2.3   Identifying the Country of Origin

What then is the country of origin of a work first published online? Article 5(4) of the Convention sets out the rules for determining the country of origin as:

(a)   in the case of works first published in a country of the Union, that country; in the case of works published simultaneously in several countries of the Union which grant different terms of protection, the country whose legislation grants the shortest term of protection;

(b)   in the case of works published simultaneously in a country outside the Union and in a country of the Union, the latter country;

(c)   in the case of unpublished works or of works first published in a country outside the Union, without simultaneous publication in a country of the Union, the country of the Union of which the author is a national, provided that:

---

[17] *Id.*

[18] In December 1996, the WIPO Committee of Experts raised concerns about the potential impact of new technologies on the provisions of Article 3(3) and Article 5(4) of the Berne Convention. The Committee proposed the following solution:

Article 3 Notion and Place of Publication

(1) When literary or artistic works are made available to the public by wire or wireless means in such a way that members of the public may access these works from a place and at a time individually chosen by them, so that copies of these works are available, Contracting Parties shall, under the conditions specified in Article 3(3) of the Berne Convention, consider such works to be published works.

(2) When applying Article 5(4) of the Berne Convention, Contracting Parties shall consider works referred to in paragraph (1) of the present Article to be published in the Contracting Party **where the necessary arrangements have been made for availability of these works to members of the public**. [Emphasis in bold added.]

The Committee explained that "[t]he expression 'necessary arrangements' is intended to mean such steps as are an absolute *condition sine qua non* for the availability of the work. Mere linking or routing arrangements are not sufficient." While not perfectly clear, this approach suggests that the place of publication of a work would likely be the country where the work is first uploaded and made available online, or the country where the publication of the work is specifically targeted. However, the Committee's proposal was not adopted in the final text of the WIPO Copyright Treaty ("WCT").

See WIPO (1996), pp. 18–21.

(i) when these are cinematographic works the maker of which has his head-quarters or his habitual residence in a country of the Union, the country of origin shall be that country, and

(ii) when these are works of architecture erected in a country of the Union or other artistic works incorporated in a building or other structure located in a country of the Union, the country of origin shall be that country.

While these rules look comprehensive at first glance, they fail to address a number of probable scenarios. As a result, legal uncertainties may arise, particularly in the case of Internet publication. As Ricketson and Ginsburg have observed, certain situations are not directly covered by the rules in Article 5(4). These situations include where: (1) the country of origin of a Union author's published works is a different country from that of which they are a national; (2) a work is published simultaneously in several countries of the Union that have the same period of protection; and (3) a work is unpublished or first published in a country outside the Union and the work has several co-authors from different Union countries.[19]

In the digital era, it has become even more apparent that the rules in Article 5 (4) fail to cover the field. If a work is initially posted and made available to the public over the Internet, such publication "may be truly simultaneous, within seconds" to every corner of the world.[20] It is arguable that a work first made available online could be considered by any country in the world to be "first published" within that country and thus subject to domestic law (including any applicable formalities) as a "domestic work". Indeed, this was the position reached in relation to U.S. law in the *Kernel v Mosley* decision. As Professor Ginsburg noted,

> A Union member meets its Berne obligations if it accords protection consonant with Convention minima to *foreign*Berne-Union works. Arguably, with simultaneous universal publication via the Internet, every work of authorship could be considered a domestic work in each country of the Berne Union. In that event, ironically, Berne Convention minimum standards of protection might never apply, because there will be no foreign works.[21]

Alternatively, it is also arguable that under Article 5(4)(a) of the Convention, the work could be considered to be "published simultaneously in several countries" and the country of origin of the work should be "the country whose legislation grants the shortest term of protection". Then all works first published over the Internet will have whichever is the shortest term of protection in the world under the copyright laws in effect at that time.[22] "These anomalies", as Ginsburg points out, "suggest

---

[19] This will happen where an author who is a national of a Union country first publishes his work in another country of the Union. See Ricketson and Ginsburg (2006), pp. 283–286. See also, Ricketson (1987), pp. 214–215.

[20] Ricketson and Ginsburg (2006), at p. 285.

[21] Ginsburg (1998), p. 7. See also, Ginsburg (2009).

[22] See further Article 7(8) of the Convention, which provides as follows: "In any case, the term shall be governed by the legislation of the country where protection is claimed; however, unless

that the notion of Internet 'publication' should be limited to a single Berne Union country: but which one?"[23]

These uncertainties in the application of the Berne Convention become particularly relevant in suits for infringement of foreign works brought in the United States. The U.S. imposes a registration requirement before infringement actions can be brought with respect to U.S. works.[24] If a work first published online in any country in the world can be deemed a "U.S. work", then potentially all authors of the world, wherever they reside, must register their copyright with the U.S. Copyright Office before they can assert their copyright interests in U.S. courts. The difficulty in determining country of origin has been brought to light in two U.S. District Court cases involving works first made available online, *Kernel v Mosley*[25] and *Moberg v 33T*.[26] The courts had divergent views on what constituted a "United States work", which in turn led to two very different results.

4.3 "United States Works" in the U.S. Copyright Act

4.3.1 Defining "United States Works" for the Purpose of Section 411

Section 411(a) of the *Copyright Act 1976* of the United States provides that "no civil action for infringement of the copyright in any United States work shall be instituted until preregistration or registration of the copyright claim has been made". This means that in the U.S., domestic copyright owners must complete copyright registration or preregistration in order to bring a suit for infringement in federal court. This registration requirement only applies to "U.S. works", not foreign works. But copyright owners of non-U.S. works still must comply with registration requirements if they wish to seek statutory damages in court.[27]

---

the legislation of that country otherwise provides, the term shall not exceed the term fixed in the country of origin of the work."

[23] Ginsburg (1998), at p. 8.

[24] *Copyright Act: 17 U.S.C.* §411. Note that in limited circumstances, it may be possible to commence proceedings and subsequently obtain copyright registration. The plaintiff would have to amend the complaint and add the allegation that registration has been obtained, but good cause under the Federal Rules of Civil Procedure (Fed. R. Civ. P. 16) must be shown before a court will consider whether the amendment is proper under Fed. R. Civ. P. 15(a). To show good cause for an untimely amendment, the plaintiff must demonstrate diligence (see e.g. *Oravec v Sunny Isles Luxury Ventures, L.C.*, 527 F. 3d 1218, 1232 (11th Cir. 2008)). In *Kernel v Mosley* however, Justice Torres held that this was not satisfied because registration was sought and obtained *after* the Court had ruled for the Defendants.

[25] 2011 U.S. Dist. LEXIS 60666 (S.D. Fla. June 7, 2011).

[26] 666 F. Supp. 2d 415 (D. Del. Oct. 6, 2009).

[27] § 412 sets forth registration as prerequisite to certain remedies for infringement. Unlike § 411, the application of § 412 is not limited to "U.S. works". However, in a suit under § 411(c),

The removal of registration as a precondition to filing an infringement claim for non-U.S. works was one of the results of the *Berne Convention Implementation Act of 1988*[28] and the *WIPO Copyright and Performances and Phonograms Treaties Implementation Act of 1998*.[29] Furthermore, the U.S. Supreme Court has recently clarified in *Reed Elsevier, Inc. v Muchnick* that section 411(a) merely contains "claim-processing rules" rather than "jurisdictional conditions". Thus, the Court ruled that "[s]ection 411(a)'s registration requirement is a precondition to filing a claim that does not restrict a federal court's subject-matter jurisdiction."[30]

For the purposes of section 411, a full definition of "United States work" is set out in section 101. This definition provides:

For purposes of section 411, a work is a "United States work" only if—

(1) in the case of a published work, the work is first published—

(A) in the United States;
(B) simultaneously in the United States and another treaty party or parties, whose law grants a term of copyright protection that is the same as or longer than the term provided in the United States;
(C) simultaneously in the United States and a foreign nation that is not a treaty party; or
(D) in a foreign nation that is not a treaty party, and all of the authors of the work are nationals, domiciliaries, or habitual residents of, or in the case of an audiovisual work legal entities with headquarters in, the United States;

(2) in the case of an unpublished work, all the authors of the work are nationals, domiciliaries, or habitual residents of the United States, or, in the case of an unpublished audiovisual work, all the authors are legal entities with headquarters in the United States; or

(3) in the case of a pictorial, graphic, or sculptural work incorporated in a building or structure, the building or structure is located in the United States.

The legislative history of section 411 suggests a fairly strong correlation between the definition of "United States work" in the Copyright Act and the definition of "country of origin" in the Berne Convention.[31] The apparent intention

---

the copyright owner of a foreign work consisting of sounds, images, or both, the first fixation of which is made simultaneously with its transmission may obtain statutory damages without registering the work under certain conditions. See *Football Ass'n Premier League v. YouTube*, 633 F. Supp. 2d 159 (2009).

[28] Pub. L. No. 100-568, 102 Stat. 2853, 2854.

[29] Pub. L. No. 105-304, 112 Stat. 2860, 2861.

[30] *Reed Elsevier, Inc., et al., Petitioners, v. Irvin Muchnick, et al.*, 130 S. Ct. 1237 (2010).

[31] In *The Senate Statement on the Berne Convention Implementation Act of 1988* that appears on page S14544, Congressional Record (Daily Ed.) (1988), it was stated:

. . .

With regard to the specifics of the amendment on registration, the two-tier system is established by making three amendments to the committee-reported bill. First, the repeal of existing section 411(a) is eliminated, in favor of an introductory phrase to the existing provision which makes it inapplicable to "actions for infringement of copyright in Berne Convention works whose country of origin is not the United States." Secondly, in section

of the U.S. Congress was to parallel the relevant definitions in section 101 with those terms contained in Article 5(4) of the Berne Convention.[32]

Nevertheless, there are operative variations between the concepts of "U.S. works" and "country of origin". The definition of "country of origin" in the Berne Convention has a narrowing or pinpointing function—it seeks to determine, of all the countries in the world, the country from which a published work can be considered to have originated. The definition of "United States work" need not be so comprehensive. It seeks to determine only whether a work originates (i.e. is firstly or simultaneously published) in the U.S. or not for the purpose of imposing registration requirements. If the work does not originate in the U.S., then it has little relevance to the operation of section 411. As being emphasized in *The Senate Statement on the Berne Convention Implementation Act of 1988*, it is "not necessary in all cases to determine the precise country of origin of the work in order to know whether or not the registration prerequisite to suit applies".

Despite the relatively clear function of the section 101 definition of "United States work", it is not always easy to determine whether a particular work falls within the language of this definition. For example, it is uncertain (and unsettled) whether works that are first published online can be considered U.S. works for the purposes of section 411. This is because a work first published online is arguably published in all countries in the world with internet access, including the United States, which may bring the work within paragraph (1) (B) or (C) of the definition of "United States work" even if the work was not created or uploaded in the United States and the author is not a U.S. national, domiciliary or resident. As we have alluded to earlier, the following two cases considered this very issue of online publication and reached vastly different conclusions about whether the work was a U.S. work under section 411.

411(b), dealing with works such as live broadcasts that are first fixed simultaneously with transmission, the amendment inserts after the reference to post-broadcast registration of the work the phrase "if required by subsection (a)." Finally, the amendment inserts in the definitional section of the Copyright Act, 17 USC 101, a definition of "country of origin" of a Berne Convention work.

The definition of country of origin, while a new feature of U.S. copyright law, is a familiar principle to students of Berne. The definition contained in the amendment tracks the definition of this phrase contained in Article 5(4) of Berne. For the guidance of practitioners, and of the courts, the following observations may be in order.

. . .

[32] The *Berne Convention Implementation Act of 1988*, Pub. L. No. 100-568, 102 Stat. 2853, 2857, amended § 101 by adding the definition of "country of origin" of a Berne Convention work, for purposes of § 411. The *WIPO Copyright and Performances and Phonograms Treaties Implementation Act of 1998* Pub. L. No. 105-304, 112 Stat. 2860, 2861 amended that definition by changing it to a definition for "United States work," for purposes of § 411. See U.S. Copyright Office, *Copyright Law – Chapter 1* ('Chapter 1 Endnotes'), http://www.copyright.gov/title17/92chap1.html.

4.3.2   *Moberg v 33T*

Håkan Moberg, a professional photographer from Sweden created a series of photographs entitled "Urban Gregorian I-IX". These photos were first published in 2004 on a German website, blaugallery.com, which offered copies of the photos for sale as canvas prints. In late 2007, three websites began displaying the Moberg's Urban Gregorian images.

In September 2008, Moberg brought a complaint in the United States federal district court against the website proprietors for copyright infringement under the U.S. Copyright Act. The defendants argued that the court lacked subject matter jurisdiction because the work was a 'United States work', which had not been registered in accordance with s 411(a) of the Copyright Act.

Hillman J considered that the question of whether Moberg's photographs were 'United States works' involved two issues: (1) whether the posting of plaintiff's photographs on the Internet is considered "publishing," and, (2) if so, whether "publishing" on the Internet causes the photographs to be published only in the country where the Internet site is located, or in every country around the world simultaneously.[33]

In reaching its decision, the court focused on the broader purpose and policy rationale behind the Berne Convention. Regarding the issue (1), the court found that it need not "delve into yet another unsettled issue, because even assuming that the German website 'published' the plaintiff's photographs, [. . .] as a matter of U.S. statutory law the photographs were not published simultaneously in the United States". This reasoning was based on part of section 408(a) of the Copyright Act, which states that "registration is not a condition of copyright protection",[34] and the proposition in *Kuklachev v. Gelfman*[35] and *Muchnick v. Thomson Corp.*,[36] that "[u]nder the clear language of the statute, which refers only to 'any United States work,' foreign works originating in countries party to the Berne Convention need not comply with section 411."[37] The court concluded that the work was not a "United States work" for the purposes of section 411.

The court held that the acceptance of the defendant's contention that "publishing" on the internet would cause the work in question to become a United States work "would overextend and pervert the United States copyright laws".[38] To subject the copyright owner to the formalities of the copyright laws of every country would be "contrary to the purpose of the Berne Convention . . . [which] is

---

[33] 666 F. Supp. 2d 415, 421 (D. Del. Oct. 6, 2009).

[34] Note that § 408(a) only relates to "protection" of the work, and does not refer to a precondition to instituting a civil infringement action.

[35] 600 F. Supp. 2d 437, 473 (E.D.N.Y. 2009).

[36] 509 F.3d 116, 133 (2d Cir. 2007).

[37] 666 F. Supp. 2d 415, 423 (D. Del. Oct. 6, 2009).

[38] 666 F. Supp. 2d 415, 410 (D. Del. Oct. 6, 2009).

to provide protection to authors whose works will be published in many countries".[39] The court continued:

> [T]he United States copyright laws, in accord with the Berne Convention, provide for protection of foreign works in the United States without requiring the artists to undertake any formalities in the United States. . . .
>
> To require plaintiff to register his photographs in the United States prior to initiating suit against a United States company and the registrants of U.S.-based websites for their violation of United States law, which protects plaintiff's copyrights, would flout United States law and the international union the U.S. has joined voluntarily. Therefore, the Court finds that plaintiff's photographs are not "United States works," and, accordingly, his copyright infringement claims may stand without registration of the photographs.[40]

4.3.3   Kernel v Mosley

The dispute in *Kernel v Mosley*[41] arose from a sound recording of a composition entitled "AcidJazzed Evening" ("AJE") created by Glenn Rune Gallefoss. In 2007, Gallefoss transferred "all transferrable rights" to Kernel Records, a company registered in Finland. In 2009, Kernel alleged that the sound recording and musical arrangement of AJE had been copied into Nelly Furtado's song "Do It". It brought a claim for copyright infringement in the Florida Southern District Court against Timbaland (who wrote the composition and produced the recording), EMI Music and a few other recording and distribution companies. This dispute was initially tried and lost in Finland.[42] While the Finnish ruling remained pending on appeal in Finland, Kernel commenced the second duplicative action in Florida.

4.3.3.1   Online Publication

In Florida, Kernel alleged that Gallefoss first published AJE on a disk magazine (i.e. a computer disk containing a magazine) in Australia in August 2002. It argued that music file was only later made available online on 21 December 2002. Kernel also claimed that at least three whole months separated the first publication on the

---

[39] 666 F. Supp. 2d 415, 422–423 (D. Del. Oct. 6, 2009): "if the publishing of plaintiff's photographs on the German website simultaneously caused them to be published in the United States, and such publication transformed the work into a United States work, plaintiff would be subjected to the very formalities that the Berne Convention eschews. To hold otherwise would require an artist to survey all the copyright laws throughout the world, determine what requirements exist as preconditions to suits in those countries should one of its citizens infringe on the artist's rights, and comply with those formalities, all prior to posting any copyrighted image on the Internet. The Berne Convention was formed, in part, to prevent exactly this result."

[40] 666 F. Supp. 2d 415, 423–424 (D. Del. Oct. 6, 2009).

[41] 2011 U.S. Dist. LEXIS 60666 (S.D. Fla. June 7, 2011).

[42] See *Kernel Records Oy v. Mosley*, 2010 U.S. Dist. LEXIS 69424, 49 (S.D. Fla., July 5, 2010).

disk magazine and the online appearance of the music file. Further, Kernel argued that Gallefoss had not chosen the internet as the means to first publish his work.[43]

However, these submissions were not accepted by Justice Torress of the South Florida District Court. His Honour found that AJE was first published online via the so-called "disk magazine", which was held to be an online magazine. This finding of fact was largely due to Gellefoss's ambiguous oral testimony and Kernel's lack of evidence as to the nature of the alleged disk magazine.[44] Therefore, online publication had occurred.

The court further concluded that posting AJE on the internet was publication under section 101 of the Copyright Act. Although Justice Hillman in *Moberg v 33T* had deemed it unnecessary to delve into the issue of internet publication, Justice Torress in *Kernel v Mosely* stated, "We must address the issue".[45] His Honour reasoned that once a work is available for downloading and copying (as opposed to being merely viewable as was the case in *Moberg*), members of the public are able to obtain a possessory interest in the work. Hence, once the author has lost the physical ability to control the dissemination and enjoyment of the work and the work has been "acquired by the public", publication under section 101 of the Copyright Act has occurred.[46]

4.3.3.2 Simultaneous Publication

As to whether publishing on the Internet lead to simultaneous publication in the United States, the court expressly declined to follow the reasoning in the earlier persuasive (but not binding) Delaware District Court decision of *Moberg v 33T*.

The court held that the "Plaintiff's first publication of AJE on the Internet, an act tantamount to global and simultaneous dissemination of the work in question, constituted "publication" in the United States and around the world". Court accepted that *Moberg v 33T* is "the only other published opinion that has addressed this particular issue", but rebutted Justice Hillman's reasoning in *Moberg v 33T*:

> There can be little dispute that posting material on the Internet makes it available at the same time – simultaneously – to anyone with access to the Internet. There is nothing in the text of the statute to suggest that Congress intended to except works published on the Internet from the phrase "first published . . . simultaneously" or that certain works should be excluded from the definition of "United States work" based solely on the manner in which they are published.[47]

---

[43] See Response in Opposition re Defendant's Motion for Summary Judgment Statement of Undisputed Facts filed by Kernel Records Oy, 2009 U.S. Dist. Ct. Motions 337943; 2010 U.S. Dist. Ct. Motions LEXIS 52741, 2-3(S.D. Fla., June 21, 2010).

[44] 2011 U.S. Dist. LEXIS 60666, 11–13 (S.D. Fla. June 7, 2011).

[45] 2011 U.S. Dist. LEXIS 60666, 19 (S.D. Fla. June 7, 2011).

[46] 2011 U.S. Dist. LEXIS 60666, 22–24 (S.D. Fla. June 7, 2011). The court cites 1 *Nimmer on Copyright* S 4.07[A] at 4–43 and *Getaped.com v Cangemi*, 188 F. Supp. 2d 398 (S.D.N.Y. 2002) for this proposition.

[47] 2011 U.S. Dist. LEXIS 60666, 28 (S.D. Fla. June 7, 2011).

The court continued:

> Judge Hillman's objections to the proposition that publication on the Internet constitutes simultaneous global publication for copyright purposes are policy-driven. They reflect a deference to certain goals of the Berne Convention at the expense of clear statutory language.[48]

The court found no need to "spend much time examining the interrelationship between U.S. copyright law and the Berne Convention because a simpler approach is available and dispositive". In conclusion on this point, it stated:

> We respectfully decline to follow the reasoning of *Moberg*. As indicated in our prior Order, Judge Hillman's contextual and policy-driven analysis is reasonable and sound but is, in our opinion, wholly untethered to the actual statutory and treaty language that governs this dispute.[49]

4.4   Identifying "United States Works" in a Global Digital Publishing Market

The court's conclusion in *Kernel v Moseley* that a work created outside of the United States, uploaded in Australia and owned by a company registered in Finland was nonetheless a "United States work" by virtue of its being published online is somewhat concerning. Taken to its logical conclusion, this reasoning would hold every work first published online to be a "United States work" requiring registration before an action for infringement can be commenced in the United States. Arguably, this stretches the application of U.S. copyright law too far—to works with only tenuous connections to the United States—and draws into question the United State's compliance with Article 5(2) of the Berne Convention which prevents countries from imposing formalities on the exercise of rights with respect to foreign works.

In this section, we propose a limiting principle for reading the section 101 definition of "United States work". We argue that a broad interpretation of "United States work" results in the extraterritorial application of U.S. copyright law at the designation stage—i.e. at the point of deciding whether or not a work should be bound by U.S. copyright formalities. We believe that a narrower reading of "United States work" accords with U.S. jurisprudence supporting a principle of territoriality in legislative interpretation and ensures that the United States complies with its international obligations under the Berne Convention.

---

[48] 2011 U.S. Dist. LEXIS 60666, 31 (S.D. Fla. June 7, 2011).
[49] 2011 U.S. Dist. LEXIS 60666, 25 (S.D. Fla. June 7, 2011).

4.4.1 The Presumption Against Extraterritoriality

It is a "longstanding principle of American law 'that legislation of Congress, unless a contrary intent appears, is meant to apply only within the territorial jurisdiction of the United States.'"[50] This principle was famously applied in the *EEOC v Arabian Oil Co (Aramco)* case, and was recently cited with approval and applied by the United States Supreme Court in *Morrison v National Australia Bank* 130S. Ct. 2869 (2010). The *Morrison* court stated:

> This principle represents a canon of construction, or a presumption about a statute's meaning, rather than a limit upon Congress's power to legislate, see *Blackmer* v. *United States*, 284 U. S. 421, 437 (1932). It rests on the perception that Congress ordinarily legislates with respect to domestic, not foreign matters. *Smith* v. *United States*, 507 U. S. 197, n. 5 (1993). Thus, "unless there is the affirmative intention of the Congress clearly expressed" to give a statute extraterritorial effect, "we must presume it is primarily concerned with domestic conditions." *Aramco*, *supra*, at 248 (internal quotation marks omitted). The canon or presumption applies regardless of whether there is a risk of conflict between the American statute and a foreign law, see *Sale* v. *Haitian Centers Council, Inc.*, 509 U. S. 155, 173–174 (1993). When a statute gives no clear indication of an extra-territorial application, it has none.[51]

Similarly, the Court in *Aramco* stated:

> Our conclusion today is buttressed by the fact that 'when it desires to do so, Congress knows how to place the high seas within the jurisdictional reach of a statute.' *Argentine Republic v. Amerada Hess Shipping Corp.*, 488 U.S. 428, 440 (1989). Congress' awareness of the need to make a clear statement that a statute applies overseas is amply demonstrated by the numerous occasions on which it has expressly legislated the extraterritorial application of a statute.[52]

As a matter of policy, extraterritorial application of domestic law is contrary to the principle of democratic rule that has its basis in the idea of the consent of the governed.[53]

There is nothing in the section 101 definition of "United States work" that evinces a clear intention on the part of Congress that section 411 will have extraterritorial effect. Each of the paragraphs of subsection (1) (relating to published works) has a clear and explicit connection to the United States— (A) applies to publication *in* the United States, (D) requires, for works published outside of the United States, that *all* of the authors be nationals, domiciliaries or habitual residents of the United States, and (B) and (C) require that the work has been published in the United States simultaneously with its publication elsewhere. It is paragraphs (B) and (C) (the "simultaneous publication" provisions) that were at issue in the *Moberg* and *Kernel* cases. We argue that from a common-sense

---

[50] *EEOC* v. *Arabian American Oil Co.*, 499 U. S. 244, 248 (1991) *(Aramco)* (quoting *Foley Bros., Inc.* v. *Filardo*, 336 U. S. 281, 285 (1949).

[51] *Morrison v. National Australia Bank Ltd.*, 130 S. Ct. 2869 (2010), 2878.

[52] *EEOC* v. *Arabian American Oil Co.*, 499 U. S. 244, 258 (1991).

[53] *See further*, Gibney (1996), pp. 297, 305.

approach to and plain reading of the Act, it is not apparent that the intention of these provisions was to bring into the definition of "United States work" a huge expanse of foreign produced and owned works, thus subjecting them to registration requirements. Rather, it seems to us that the intention was to ensure that works with a sufficient connection to the United States were not excluded from the definition of "United States works" simply by virtue of them also being published (simultaneously) in foreign countries. Further, in the remaining subsections of the definition, relating to unpublished works and visual works incorporated into a building or structure, there is a clear requirement that all authors must be nationals, domiciliaries, or habitual residents of the United States (for unpublished works) or that the building or structure in which the work is incorporated be located in the United States. There is nothing in the language of any of the provisions of this definition that indicates an intent that the definition, or section 411, would have an extraterritorial effect.

Nor is there anything in the circumstances surrounding the inclusion of this definition in the Copyright Act to suggest an intention that section 411 would apply extraterritorially. The definition of "United States work" was inserted into the Copyright Act by the *Berne Convention Implementation Act* to give effect to the terms of the Berne Convention relating to country of origin.[54] Article 5 of the Berne Convention is clear that copyright in foreign works is to be recognised in all Member countries without being subject to formality requirements. A situation in which all works published online, regardless of where they are created or the nationality, domicile or habitual residence of the author, are subject to formalities under United States law does not sensibly accord with Article 5 of the Berne Convention, nor the purpose of implementing the Berne Convention within U.S. domestic law.

4.4.2   Interpreting "United States Works" Based on a Presumption Against Extraterritoriality: A Proposal

We propose that the country of origin of a work, including whether a work is or is not a "United States work" under the U.S. Copyright Act, should be determined (and confined) by reference to a "real and substantial connection" test. This test would ask: which is the jurisdiction with which the work has the most substantial connection, so as to reasonably conclude that the work originated from that jurisdiction?

---

[54] In fact, as explained above, the original definition inserted into the U.S. Copyright Act was for "country of origin"; this was later changed to "United States work" by the *WIPO Copyright and Performances and Phonograms Treaties Implementation Act of 1998,* Pub. L. No. 105-304, 112 Stat. 2860.

This test has parallels to the choice of law principles in United States law. The Restatement of the Law, Second, Conflict of Laws, §6, sets out the choice of law principles as:

(1) A court, subject to constitutional restrictions, will follow a statutory directive of its own state on choice of law.
(2) When there is no such directive, the factors relevant to the choice of the applicable rule of law include

   (a) the needs of the interstate and international systems,
   (b) the relevant policies of the forum,
   (c) the relevant policies of other interested states and the relative interests of those states in the determination of the particular issue,
   (d) the protection of justified expectations,
   (e) the basic policies underlying the particular field of law,
   (f) certainty, predictability and uniformity of result, and
   (g) ease in the determination and application of the law to be applied.

By analogy, the determination of the country of origin of a work can be assisted by reference to factors such as the needs of international systems, protection of justified expectations and certainty, predictability and uniformity of results. However, we argue that the one dominating factor in this analysis should be the nationality, domicile or habitual residence of the author of the work. This is the obvious factor in which to ground the origin of a work. In nearly all cases it will point to a clear and sensible point-of-origin for a work and in most cases it will effectively limit the extraterritorial application of domestic copyright law.

We can envisage some scenarios in which this factor would not conclusively indicate a country of origin for a work. One is where there are multiple co-authors of a work and each co-author resides in or is a national of a different country. These situations will not be the norm, however, and in these situations additional factors can be taken into account in ascertaining the country with the most substantial connection to the work, including where the work was created, where the work was uploaded, and the expectations of the affected parties.

We submit that this test would have helped to resolve the *Moberg v 33T* and *Kernel v Mosley* cases in a more sensible and legally foreseeable way. In *Moberg v 33T*, the country of origin of the work would be Sweden, the country of nationality and residence of the photographer of the work (Moberg). In *Kernel v Mosley*, the country of origin of the work would be Norway, the country of nationality and residence of the author of the work. The *Kernel* case is potentially more complicated in that the author claimed that the work was first published in an Australian disk magazine. If supported by sufficient evidence, it is arguable that the country of origin of the work should be Australia.

The critical point is that in neither of these cases is the United States logically or sensibly the country of origin of these works.

4.4.3   Nationality as a More Preferred Criterion in Networked Information Age

Our proposal for a nationality criterion is not a radical one.

As early as 1987, Samuel Ricketson argued that the country of origin of a work should, in most cases, be the country of the author's nationality. Referring to the Berne Convention, Ricketson wrote, "[this] concept of 'country of origin' is only really necessary in the case of non-Union authors, and there is little justification for its use in other cases, particularly when the application of the above rules often means that the country of origin of a published work will be different from the country of which the author is a national."[55] "In such cases," he suggested, "it is more logical that the [country of origin] of a work should be the country of which the author is a national."[56] As Ricketson highlighted, "[the country of origin] of a work is a concept which is linked directly to the criterion of territoriality ('the place of first publication') as the criterion for entitlement to protection under the [Berne] Convention".[57] However, the history at the time of making the Berne Convention indicates that there was a debate over the choice of "nationality" or "territoriality" as criterion for the protection of published works.[58] It was not until the ALAI Conference for the drafting of the Berne Convention in September 1883 that the territoriality approach triumphed.[59] It is likely that a key reason for selecting territoriality over nationality was that this criteria would maximize the chances of non-Union authors obtaining copyright protection for their works in different countries (particularly within Union nations) in later nineteenth and earlier twentieth centuries. At the time of drafting, the Convention had a very small number of Member countries and limited geographic coverage. Today there are 164 signatory nations of the Berne Convention out of about 192 countries and regions in the world.[60] However, only ten countries (Belgium, France, Germany, Great Britain, Haiti, Italy, Spain, Switzerland, and Tunisia) signed the Convention in 1886, and the number of member nations gradually expanded to 58 in 1970, 70 in 1980, 83 in 1990 and 147 in 2000.[61] The "territoriality" approach ensured that authors who were nationals of a non-Union countries could obtain copyright protection for their work in countries of the Union if their work was first published in a country of the Union or was published simultaneously in a Union country and non-Union country.

---

[55] Sam Ricketson (1987), p. 211.

[56] *Id.* See also, Ricketson and Ginsburg (2006), p. 280, which refers to "the country of which the author is a national or resident".

[57] Ricketson (1987).

[58] Ricketson and Ginsburg (2006), pp. 244–246.

[59] *Id.*, 245. For a history of the drafting of the Berne Convention, please see Blakeney (2003).

[60] A full list of contracting parties of the Convention can be found at WIPO's website—see WIPO, *Contracting Parties,*http://www.wipo.int/treaties/en/ShowResults.jsp?lang=en&treaty_id=15.

[61] WIPO, *Treaties Statistics,* http://www.wipo.int/treaties/en/statistics/StatsResults.jsp?treaty_id=15&lang=en. For a history of the signatory of the Convention, see United Nations (1970).

In December 1998, Professor Ginsburg prepared a document for WIPO in which she stated: "In effect, to determine the country of origin, we are seeking the country that has the most significant relationship to the act of making the work available to the public."[62] She suggested, therefore, that the country of the website's business establishment, the country where the author resides, or a country with significant contacts with the author should be considered as the country of origin, depending on the particular circumstances.[63] However, she also noted that this criterion "is not currently present in the Berne Convention".[64] Most recently, in 2006, Professors Ricketson and Ginsburg joined together to argue that where simultaneous publication is effected by means of digital communications such as the Internet, it made sense to designate the country of the author's nationality as the "country of origin" of the work.[65]

4.4.4 How Our Proposal Fits with the Language of the U.S. Copyright Act

Before our proposed text can be adopted, it is necessary to determine whether, as a matter of statutory interpretation, our test can be read into the determination of "United States work" under section 101 of the U.S. Copyright Act. We believe that it can. Justice Torres in *Kernel v Mosley* held:

> '[T]he starting point for interpreting a statute is the language of the statute itself.' *Consumer Product Safety Comm'n v GTE Sylvania, Inc.*, 447 U.S. 102, 108 (1980). 'As a basic rule of statutory interpretation, we read the statute using the normal meaning of its words.' *Consolidated Bank, N.A. v Office of Comptroller of Currency*, 118 F.3d 1461, 1463 (11th Cir. 1997)...We look beyond the plain language of a statute only when it is unclear or ambiguous, when Congress has clearly expressed a legislative intent to the contrary, or when an absurd result would ensue from adopting the plain language interpretation. *Id.* at 1463-64.[66]

His Honour went on to determine that "[a]bsent evidence of Congressional intent to the contrary, the term 'simultaneously' should be given its ordinary and plain meaning", that a work published online was published simultaneously in all countries with internet access, including the United States, and that this made the work a "United States work" for the purposes of section 411 of the Copyright Act.

---

[62] Ginsburg (1998), pp. 8–9.

[63] *Id.*, 8.

[64] *Id.*, 9.

[65] Ricketson and Ginsburg (2006), p. 285. The authors also presented an alternative: that the country of origin might be deemed the country with the most author-favourable domestic legislation.

[66] 2011 U.S. Dist. LEXIS 60666, 26–27 (S.D. Fla. June 7, 2011).

We do not believe that "United States work" can be so easily read to apply so broadly. The purpose of defining "United States works" is to determine which works will be subject to registration requirements under U.S. law—it therefore has a limiting function, not an expansive function. We do not believe that Congress intended that all works published online, wherever created and whether owned by foreign nationals or residents, would be considered U.S. works, and that the U.S. copyright law would, as a result, have such a broad, extraterritorial application. We believe that it is more sensible to read "first published... simultaneously in the United States and another treaty party or parties" and "first published...simultaneously in the United States and a foreign nation that is not a treaty party" to import a requirement that there be a proper (under our proposal: real and substantial) connection with the United States sufficient to reasonably render the work a "United States work" under U.S. law.

It is also worth noting that our proposal does not preclude foreign nationals from bringing their works within the definition of "United States work" under the U.S. Copyright Act. Foreign nationals who intend that their work be designated a United States work under section 411 can clearly exhibit this intention by first publishing their work in the United States, bringing it squarely within paragraph (1) (A) of the definition of "United States work".

4.4.5   How Our Proposal Fits with the Language of the Berne Convention

We also do not believe that our proposal has any negative impact on a reading of Article 5 of the Berne Convention. Our proposal is designed to assist a country in determining whether a particular work should be found to come within the scope of domestic copyright law, such that an exercise of the associated rights (including bringing an action for infringement) can be held to be dependent on certain formalities prescribed in domestic law. As argued above, adherence to the Berne Convention depends on a sensible interpretation of the requirements of the Convention at a national level. The Berne Convention provides little guidance as to country of origin in situations where a work is published simultaneously in multiple member countries with the same term of protection.[67] Such a situation will be increasingly common as more countries enact the same minimum term provisions (usually, life of the author plus 70 years) and more and more works are published online. In such situations, we need a means of determining the country of origin of a work that is logical, reasonable, and which respects the purpose behind Article 5 (2) of the Berne Convention in limiting the imposition of formality requirements for foreign works. We believe our proposal achieves this end.

---

[67] See further, Ricketson and Ginsburg (2006).

4.5 Conclusion

Justice Torres's interpretation of the "plain language" of the statute failed to appreciate the limiting function of the term "United States work", contrary to the intention of Congress. This interpretation was not in line with the presumption against extraterritorial application of U.S. law, and if applied widely, would mean that all works first published online would be subject to the U.S. registration requirement before an action for infringement could be commenced.

Many works are still physically published in select jurisdictions, and in those instances, the territoriality approach to determine whether a work is a "United States works" (or to determine if the United States is the Country of Origin) is still logical and relevant. However, the fact that many works are simultaneously published and made available online necessitates a sensible reading of the definition of "United States work" in section 411. This sensible reading calls for an enquiry into whether the works has a "real and substantial connection" with the United States—the dominating factor in this analysis being the nationality, domicile or habitual residence of the author. As we have discussed, this approach is consistent with both the U.S. Copyright Act and the Berne Convention, and reflects the changing pace of technology.

Acknowledgement We acknowledge the support of the Australian Research Council (ARC) Centre of Excellence for Creative Industries and Innovation (CCI). This chapter was first published in the (2011) NIALS Journal of Intellectual Property and is reproduced by kind permission of the publisher.

References

Books

Gibney MP (1996) The extraterritorial application of U.S. law: the perversion of democratic governance, the reversal of institutional roles, and the imperative of establishing normative principles. Boston Coll Int Comp Law Rev 19:297, 305
Ricketson S (1987) The Berne Convention for the protection of literary and artistic works: 1886–1986. Centre for Commercial Law Studies, Queen Mary College, London
Ricketson S, Ginsburg JC (2006) International copyright and neighbouring rights: the Berne Convention and beyond, 2nd edn. Oxford University Press, New York

Reports

Blakeney M (2003) The international protection of industrial property: from the Paris Convention to the TRIPS Agreement (WIPO/IP/CAI/1/03/2), prepared at the WIPO National Seminar on Intellectual Property, Cairo, 17–19 February 2003

Ginsburg J (1998) Private international law aspects of the protection of works and objects of related rights transmitted through digital networks (WIPO, GCPIC/2), 30 November 1998. http://www.wipo.int/meetings/en/doc_details.jsp?doc_id=926

The Senate Statement on the Berne Convention Implementation Act of 1988, on page S14544, Congressional Record (Daily Ed.), October 5, 1988 (Senate Legislative Day of Monday, September 26, 1988)

United Nations (1970) Yearbook of the International Law Commission 1968, vol. 2 (A/CN.4/SER. A/Add.1), United Nations, New York. Available at http://untreaty.un.org/ilc/publications/yearbooks/Ybkvolumes%28e%29/ILC_1968_v2_e.pdf

WIPO (1996) Basic proposal for the substantive provisions of the treaty on certain questions concerning the protection of literary and artistic works to be considered by the diplomatic conference (CRNR/DC/4), 30 August 1996. http://www.wipo.int/edocs/mdocs/diplconf/en/crnr_dc/crnr_dc_4.pdf

Webpages

Ginsburg J (2009) Borderless publications, the Berne Convention, and U.S. copyright formalities, The Media Institute, 20 October 2009. http://www.mediainstitute.org/new_site/IPI/2009/102009_BorderlessPublications.php

World Intellectual Property Organization (WIPO), Contracting parties.http://www.wipo.int/treaties/en/ShowResults.jsp?lang=en&treaty_id=15

WIPO (1886) Summary of the Berne Convention for the protection of literary and artistic works. http://www.wipo.int/treaties/en/ip/berne/summary_berne.html

WIPO, Treaties Statistics. http://www.wipo.int/treaties/en/statistics/StatsResults.jsp?treaty_id=15&lang=en

WIPO, WIPO Treaties – General Information. http://www.wipo.int/treaties/en/general/

Chapter 5
An Islamic Perspective on the Theories of Intellectual Property

Ezieddin Elmahjub

5.1 Introduction

The Islamic perspective on intellectual property (IP) is based on the sources of Islamic Shari'a. These sources mainly include the Qur'an, the traditions of the Prophet (pbuh)[1] known as Sunnah and the juristic mechanisms which used to deduce injunctions from the Qur'an and the Sunnah such as legal analogy (*qiyas*) and the consideration of public interest (*maslaha mursala*).[2] To varying degrees, the sources and principles of Islamic Shari'a affect culture and law-making in 57 counties worldwide.[3] Far from being an ancient faith system, it is an influential set of rules and philosophies, the scope of which extends beyond religious duties to regulating marriage and what to eat and wear. One of the fundamental domains of Islamic Shari'a is regulation of the process of law-making in Muslim societies. It can operate as a normative framework for law-making in different fields of law, including IP.

Virtually, all countries with dominant Islamic populations recognise and protect IP. Leading institutions in the Islamic world such as the Council of Islamic *Fiqh*

---

[1] Peace be upon him.

[2] Alzarqa (1998), p. 79 and Alboti (1965).

[3] According to the Organisation of Islamic Cooperation (OIC), Islam is the predominant religion in 57 countries around the world, OIC, Member States http://www.oic-oci.org/member_states.asp.

E. Elmahjub (✉)
Tripoli University in Libya, Tripoli, Libya

Thomas More Academy of Law, Australian Catholic University, 486 Albert Street, East Melbourne, VIC 3002, Australia
e-mail: Ez_m_elmahjub@yahoo.com.au

© Springer International Publishing Switzerland 2015
B. Fitzgerald, J. Gilchrist (eds.), *Copyright Perspectives*,
DOI 10.1007/978-3-319-15913-3_5

(Jurisprudence) Academy[4] and Al-Azhar*Fatwa* committee[5] issued Shari'a based opinions (*fatwas*) indicating that the sources of Shari'a promote the protection and enforcement of IP. However, very little has been written to establish the theoretical foundations of IP from an Islamic perspective.

The existing literature on IP and Islamic Shari'a is generally scarce. The available studies failed to efficiently and appropriately use the sources of Shari'a to introduce comprehensive theories on IP and Islamic Shari'a.

Islamic Shari'a along with the classic and modern Islamic jurisprudence can be used to provide more comprehensive theories on IP. In particular, they can be strongly linked to modern theories of IP as introduced in Western literature. The Islamic sources contain various principles which are relevant to the dominant theories of IP such as labour/fairness theory, utilitarianism and personality theory.

Introducing comprehensive justification for IP from an Islamic perspective is important for at least two reasons. First, it is important for comparative legal studies as it demonstrates the position of one of the world's largest legal and cultural systems towards IP. Secondly, this may help policymakers interested in making Shari'a-compatible IP system to understand the scope and limits of IP laws based on Islamic Shari'a.

This chapter is divided into two parts. The first part classifies the existing literature (both in Arabic and English) in terms of justifying IP from an Islamic perspective. This part critically analyses this literature in order to identify the proper scope for research. The second part of this chapter sets the foundations for introducing comprehensive theories on IP and Islamic Shari'a. This is done by showing that the sources of Shari'a greatly intersect with Western theories of physical property and IP, and by highlighting limits on IP from an Islamic perspective.

5.2   Intellectual Property in Islamic Literature

The concept of IP, its recognition and protection from an Islamic perspective has been a subject of debate amongst the contemporary commentators on Islamic Shari'a.[6] Generally, there are two different camps.[7] One contends that the sources

---

[4] International Islamic Fiqh Academy, Resolution No 43 (5/5) 1988 Regarding Incorporeal Rights, available online at: http://zulkiflihasan.files.wordpress.com/2009/12/majma-fiqh.pdf. The decision states that:

First: Business name, corporate name, trade mark, literary production, invention or discovery, are
     rights belonging to their holders and have, in contemporary times, financial value which can be
     traded. These rights are recognized by Shari'a and should not be infringed.
Second: It is permitted to sell a business name, corporate name, trademark for a price in the
     absence of any fraud, swindling or forgery since it has become a financial right.
Third: Copyrights and patent rights are protected by Shari'a. Their holders are entitled to freely
     dispose of them. These rights should not be violated.

[5] Al-azhar Fatwa Committee in a number of opinions issued on April 20, 2000 and August 16 2001 (cited in Raslan 2007, p. 503).

[6] Price (2009), p. 26.

[7] Raslan (2007), p. 502.

of Shari'a oppose, to different degrees, notions of IP, while the other camp argues that the sources of Shari'a strongly support IP. The following sections trace their arguments and critically analyse the integrity of these arguments.

5.2.1 Objections to Intellectual Property

The most extreme opinion on IP in Islamic literature holds that Shari'a does not accept IP as it is a tool imposed by the West, which would be of no benefit to the Muslim community.[8] An aspect of this approach was summarised by Mufti Taqi Usmani (who supports IP protection) as claiming that the primary sources of Shari'a and the juristic views of Muslim scholars have not supported the protection of intangible objects. Furthermore, knowledge in Shari'a cannot be subject to private ownership.[9] In that vein, the late Mufti of Pakistan, Sheikh Muhammed Shafe'e, issued a legal opinion *(fatwa)* stating that authorship and inventions are acceptable as a means of income, but it is not permissible to exclude others from using them, as they represent only an abstract right which is not protected according to Shari'a's rules.[10] However, as we traverse opinions objecting to IP, we will note that this opinion is the weakest and that the sources of Islamic Shari'a do not support it.

There are at least four objections to IP that can be identified from the relevant Islamic literature. These objections are based on the assumption that there are underlying inconsistencies between various injunctions within the Qur'an and Sunnah and notions of IP. These inconsistencies might affect the nature and scope of the protection afforded to some forms of IP.[11] This section examines these objections and considers whether they can be justified.

5.2.1.1 Intellectual Property and the Concealment of Knowledge

The Qur'an contains various *ayat* (verses) that disapprove of the concealment of anything that is good for society.[12] With regard to *ilm* (knowledge), it has been reported that the Prophet warned Muslims against the concealment of knowledge as it is the common property and the shared heritage of all humankind, the owner of

---

[8] Mahafzah et al. (2009), p. 464 and Raslan (2007), p. 501.

[9] Mufti T Usmani, *Copyright According to Shari'a* available online at: http://www.albalagh.net/qa/copyright.shtml. This opinion might be based on an old juristic view within the Hanafi School of Jurisprudence which restricts the ownership to tangible objects *(Al'Ayyan)* only. See Al-sarkhasi (1912), vol 11.

[10] Cited in Bakre (1986), p. 220.

[11] Jamar (1992), p. 1093.

[12] For instance see the following *ayat* (verses) in the Holy Qur'an, 2:42, 2:140, 2:174 and 371.

which is God.[13] The Prophet is reported to have said 'the one who conceals knowledge would appear on the day of resurrection as reined in a bridle of fire.'[14] A broad initial reading of this *hadith* (saying) suggests that every person who attains knowledge that would benefit other members of the society must disclose such knowledge and share it with them without any restrictions. This *hadith* is particularly relied upon by some scholars to reject copyright protection, as it might entail the concealment of knowledge.[15]

Moreover, Al-Mundhiri (d. 1258 CE) reports several *ahadith* (sayings) in which the Prophet encourages sharing and the dissemination of knowledge.[16] In one of these *ahadith* the Prophet considers knowledge which is being disseminated the best form of *saddaqah* (charity).[17]

Does IP fall within the prohibition of the concealment of knowledge according to the traditions of the Prophet (pbuh)? In other words, does the protection of knowledge underlying patents and copyright lead to the concealment of knowledge from an Islamic perspective?

The modern concept of IP is based on property rights over ideas or forms of expression that give the right holder time-limited monopolies.[18] These monopolies are embodied in the form of exclusive rights over the subject matter (which could be thought of as knowledge) to exclude others from using the intellectual products without permission or monetary compensation. According to some commentators this might contradict the Islamic prohibition of the concealment of knowledge.[19]

However it is inaccurate to conclude that IP leads to the concealment of knowledge in the meaning of the above-quoted *hadith* (saying of the prophet).[20] A closer look into the mechanisms of IP reveals that the overall structure and rules of IP does not lead to the concealment of knowledge which is prohibited under the *hadith*.[21]

---

[13] Azmi (1996a), p. 650.

[14] Nasr Al-din Al-albani, *Sahih al-Targhib wa al-Tarhib*, 29.http://al-mostafa.info/data/arabic/depot/gap.php?file=000558-www.al-mostafa.com.pdf.

[15] Abu Al-kher (1988), p. 1; Amanullah (2006), p. 303.

[16] Al-Mundhiri (2003), pp. 96*et seq* (it should be noted that this book was reviewed by the Islamic scholar Nasr Al-din Al-albani. Al-Albani maintains that some of the saying contained in this book in relation to the dissemination of knowledge are weak and unauthentic) 96–97.

[17] Ibid, 96.

[18] It is noteworthy that various prophetic *hadiths* (sayings) condemn the monopolisation of products and commodities which have public interest at heart. For examples of these *hadiths* please see Al-Mundhiri (2003).

[19] Price (2009), p. 27.

[20] Professor Azmi (1996a, p. 671) concludes that 'there are prophetic Hadith allowing a person to be selective of the recipient of information; therefore, a person has the right to control the disclosure and the audience of his work. In this respect, it is submitted that it is not the privatisation of ideas that leads to their monopolisation, but only the exclusive control of them'.

[21] Ibid, 653.

For instance, the basic forms of IP (copyright and patent) contain mechanisms that allow for knowledge to be disseminated in exchange for compensation to the rights holder for a limited period. Furthermore, in a wide range of circumstances, knowledge underlying IP rights can be disseminated without the consent of the rights holder and without any compensation.

With regard to copyright, there are various mechanisms within the copyright system that operate to prevent the type of concealment mentioned in the *hadith*. For instance:

- Copyright protects only forms of expression and does not protect the underlying idea,[22] so that any person could use any discovered idea without any restrictions. For example, if an author created software program, a third party could use the idea (knowledge) underlying the program to develop his or her own version;
- Where there is an overriding public interest in the dissemination of copyright knowledge, the copyright system neutralises the exclusive rights of the owner, and grants users the right to use the subject matter without permission. This is known in copyright systems as 'exceptions and limitations', such as use for educational purposes, reporting news, parody and satires, and fair use or fair dealing for various purposes including study or research[23];
- Exclusive rights over the copyright subject matter are not permanent. Generally, after the elapse of an extended period after the death of the author the subject matter enters into the public domain and can be freely used and exploited.[24]

On the other hand, the patent system has its own mechanisms which are supposed to ensure that the knowledge underlying the patent is disseminated. These include:

- The scope of patentability is limited by certain restrictions. Consequently not all knowledge can be subject to private ownership. For instance discoveries, scientific theories, laws of nature and mathematical methods are not patentable.[25]
- The patent system requires the inventor to fully disclose patent information; such disclosure is considered the main requirement for granting the inventor patent rights.[26]

---

[22] Fitzgerald and Fitzgerald (2004), p. 84.

[23] International conventions on copyrights, particularly the *Berne Convention for the protection of Literary and Artistic* Work enables its members the right to introduce limitations and exception into their domestic copyright legislations. Domestic copyright laws vary in relation to the scope of this exceptions and limitations. Some countries give open ended exceptions such as U.S fair use model, other provide specific list as is the case in the EU countries' copyright law. While other countries combine the two approaches. See for instance, *Australian Copyright Act*, 1968 sec 40*et seq.*

[24] Art 7 of *Berne Convention for the Protection of Literary and Artistic Works* (1886).

[25] Fitzgerald and Fitzgerald (2004), p. 282.

[26] See art 29 of the *TRIPS Agreement.*

- As in copyright, where there is an overriding public interest that necessitates using the patented invention, it may be used without permission from the owner.
- Also as in copyright, the exclusive monopoly of the patentee over the invention is not permanent, and normally ends after the expiry of 20 years from the application date.[27]

Individuals who use their intellect to write a software program or invent a machine should be entitled to benefit financially from their creations. And to do so, a certain degree of protection is required, to be able to prevent others from making use of the intellectual item in a way that prejudices the legitimate interests of the creator. However, this protection does not necessarily prevent others from accessing the relevant intellectual creation. Accordingly, the prohibition against the concealment of knowledge in Islamic Shari'a should not involve the prohibition of transactions involving knowledge[28] as it is possible to both disseminate knowledge and take money for it simultaneously.[29]

Nevertheless, this does not mean that the current regulation of IP is fully consistent with Islamic Shari'a principles, including those aspects related to the dissemination of knowledge. Islamic Shari'a's prohibition of the concealment of knowledge and encouragement of its dissemination may raise certain challenges for the current regulation of IP as laid down in its international framework.[30]

5.2.1.2   Islamic Shari'a and the Subject Matter of Intellectual Property

The scope of protectable subject matter under the international and Western IP systems is very broad when compared to what could be accepted as protectable subject matter according to Islamic Shari'a. Generally, the scope they provide for protectable subject matter is limited only by public order and morals[31] which in themselves are loose concepts, and substantially affected by the liberal understanding of personal freedom.[32] Islamic Shari'a has its own concept of morality, which may lead to reduce the scope for protection for various intellectual products.[33] This section examines the implications of Shari'a's sources on the subject matter of copyright, patent and trademark.

---

[27] See art 33 of the *TRIPS Agreement*.

[28] Azmi (1996b), p. 77.

[29] Amanullah (2006), p. 305.

[30] Elmahjub (2014).

[31] Not all the Western IP laws explicitly consider the public morality within its structure. For instance, *Australian Patents Act 1990 (Cth)* does not address this concept.

[32] For instance the *Berne Convention* does not specifically consider immorality as a barrier to granting copyright.

[33] Compare Azmi (1996b), p. 286.

Copyright

In their early days, copyright law was one instrument of State control over publication of works—a 'form of censorship'.[34] Courts denied copyright protection on the grounds of state morality; any works which were considered immoral were refused copyright protection and publication of them was proscribed. This historical attitude may no longer be relevant in the majority of jurisdictions.[35]

There are various copyright subject matters protectable according to the current international standards which raise problems when examined under the rules of Shari'a. For instance, literary works which contain what Shari'a deems as inappropriate language or pornographic content are not protectable as the ideas underlying them are not accepted in Islamic Shari'a.[36] Accordingly, the underlying ideas or forms of expression which contradict injunctions in the Qur'an or the teachings of the Prophet cannot constitute copyrightable subject matter in Islamic based IP system.[37]

Patents

The freedom to research and invent is very broad under the sources of Islamic Shari'a. However, these sources, and particularly the Qur'an, may lead to excluding certain intellectual products from the patentable subject, matter. In this regard, the Council of Islamic *Fiqh* (Jurisprudence) Academy stated:

> Islam does not set up any obstacle. . .to the freedom of scientific research that constitutes a means to discover the order established by God Almighty in His creation. Nevertheless, Islam stresses that the door cannot be left wide open, without restriction, to the generalised implementation, without limit, of the results of scientific research, without examining them closely in the light of Shari'a, so to authorise what is lawful '*halal*' and prohibit what is [unlawful] '*haram*'. It is not allowed to apply a discovery just because such an application is technically possible[38]

This confronts a belief held by some in the West, particularly in the United States that 'anything under the sun made by man can be patented'.[39] Certain discoveries and inventions will definitely fall within the scope of *haram* subject matter. According to the Qur'an, any modification to a living organism in a way that contradicts the order established by God Almighty is condemned.[40] In light of this, 'the human body or parts of human body must be excluded from patentability.

---

[34] Ibid.

[35] Ibid.

[36] Naser and Muhaisen (2008–2009), pp. 571 and 584.

[37] Abu Al-kher (1988), p. 36.

[38] *Resolutions and Recommendations of the Council of Islamic Fiqh Academy*, 1985–2000, 209.

[39] *Diamond v. Chakrabarty*, 447 US. 303 (1980).

[40] The Qur'an (Yusuf Ali trans) 4:119.

Inventions which involve processes for modifying the genetic identity of the human body must be excluded from patentability as they are contrary to the dignity of man'[41] from an Islamic perspective.[42]

Additionally, invented devices which promote activities that are contrary to the dictates of Shari'a, such as gambling,[43] will not be granted patent protection according to any Shari'a-compliant patent act.

In some Islamic countries, Shari'a's stance on the scope of patentability has been explicitly considered. The patent system of the Gulf Cooperation Council in Article 2 stipulates that for an invention to be patentable it should not contradict the rules of Islamic Shari'a.[44] Article 4 of *Saudi Patent Law*[45] and Article 2 of *Industrial Property Rights*[46] both carry provisions to the same effect.

Trademarks

The rules of Islamic Shari'a prohibit the consumption and trading of certain products and services such as alcoholic beverages,[47] pork[48] and casinos. In any Shari'a-compliant trademark law, the registration, and thus the protection, of any trademarks associated with any of these products would be denied.

It is common practice in Muslim countries in general and in some Gulf States in particular to reject the registration of trademarks or geographical indications relating to wines, spirits and other alcoholic beverages.[49] In Libya, the Implementing Regulations of Libyan Trademark Law exclude alcoholic beverages from the registrable trademarks.[50]

To sum up, the sources of Islamic Shari'a contain injunctions which lead to excluding various intellectual products from the scope of IP protection. Nevertheless, these injunctions do not demonstrate a conceptual contradiction between Islamic Shari'a and notions of IP. These injunctions lead only to reducing the scope of protectable subject matter in Shari'a-based IP system.

---

[41] Azmi (1996a), p. 670.

[42] *Australian Patent Act* of 1990 in s 18 (2) excludes from patentability "human beings, and the biological processes for their generation".

[43] See for example the Quranic injunction in relation to prohibiting gambling, the Qur'an (Sahih International 5: 90–91).

[44] Patent System (GCC) http://library.gcc-sg.org/Arabic/Books/ArabicPublish-116.htm.

[45] *Saudi Patent Law*, available online at: http://www.stplegal.com/Laws/SaudiArabia_P_Law.pdf (4 October 2011).

[46] *Industrial Property Rights and their Enforcement for the Sultanate of Oman* (Royal Decree No. 67/2008).

[47] The Qur'an (Sahih International trans) 5:90.

[48] The Qur'an (Sahih International trans) 5:3.

[49] Price (2009), p. 31.

[50] Libyan Ministry of Economy and Trade, *Implementing Regulations of Libyan Commercial Law* (as amended by *Decision no 86/2004*).

5.2.1.3 Intellectual Property and *Maysir*

The word *maysir is* derived from the word *yusr,* which literarily means easy.[51] The Qur'an encourages Muslims to gain their livelihood (*rizq*) through work. Therefore it prohibits acquiring money without labour, as in gambling.[52]

Some forms of intellectual creations could yield enormous revenues for the creator who might have spent little effort and time in making the relevant intellectual product. For example, a writer of a novel might spend a couple of months writing a novel which would bring hundreds of millions as revenues through the sale of books or from its derivative works. The same thing applies to an inventor of a machine or process who might acquire disproportionate profits to the initial investment made by the inventor through licensing or rent seeking practices.[53] The question which arises here, does the easy profit generated in situations such as these falls within the scope of *maysir?*

Some commentators observe that 'the prohibition against [*maysir*] may be relevant in IP transactions if the profit generated is significantly disproportionate to the time and money invested in developing and marketing the creation'.[54]

Nevertheless, it could be argued that the Qur'an encourages working to generate wealth and does not impose any restrictions on individuals so long as they seek profit through legitimate methods of income of which mental work is one as will be discussed below.[55] In the majority of cases the right holder of an intellectual creation does not generate income without incurring responsibility in the form of renewal fees, taxes, and compensation where their creations cause harm to others. It is also clearly established in Islamic scholarship that with certain degree of responsibility, the well-known rule of Islamic Shari'a *'al-kharaj bi al-dhaman'* (reward comes to those who could be held accountable) applies. One relevant aspect of this rule basically means that every person who assumes responsibility over something has the right to claim whatever benefits might come from the exploitation of that thing.[56] When applied to IP, this means that if the right holder could be held accountable for any harm that might be caused by his intellectual creation, he should benefit from the fruits of that creation regardless of the quantity of the generated benefits.

In addition, *mayser* should not negatively affect the recognition and protection of IP due to the existence of mechanisms within the IP system that could be used to control the dissemination of the product in a way that takes into consideration the

---

[51] Raslan (2007), p. 528.

[52] The Qur'an (Sahih International trans) 5:90: 'O you who have believed, indeed, intoxicants, gambling, [sacrificing on] stone alters [to other than Allah], and divining arrows are but defilement from the work of Satan, so avoid it that you may be successful'.

[53] Khory (2003), p. 188.

[54] Raslan (2007), p. 529.

[55] The Qur'an: 62:10.

[56] For information regarding this rule see: Al-sayouti (1983), p. 35.

public interest and the legitimate interests of the right holder to benefit from her or his creations. This includes, for instance, compulsory licenses and the rights of user of IP protected materials.

5.2.1.4 Indefiniteness (*Gharar*) and Intellectual Property

It is a fundamental rule within the system of civil transactions in Islamic Shari'a that the contracting parties must have complete knowledge of the countervalues (subject matter of the contract) to be exchanged in their transaction. The chief reason for establishing this rule is to protect the weak party in a contract against any exploitation that might occur by the strong party.[57]

Accordingly, Islamic Shari'a prohibits uncertainty (*gharar*) in contracts and requires that all transactions should be devoid of any speculation or risk. Nabil Saleh observes that to avoid, *gharar* in transactions should be no want of knowledge (*jahl*) regarding the existence of and the characteristics of the exchanged countervalues or the identification of their species or knowledge of their quantities or the date of future performance, if any. The parties also should have control over the exchanged countervalues.[58] The absence of these conditions would result in the transaction being invalid.[59] This strict approach, which requires complete certainty about the subject matter of the contract, might negatively affect the validity of certain transactions involving IP.

For instance, when licensing trade secrets, according to Shari'a the parties must have complete knowledge regarding the subject matter, which means that the licensor must disclose to the licensee all the relevant information. This would be problematic as the subject matter is the information itself, which, if disclosed, would have no value and might deter the potential licensee from concluding the contract.[60]

There is another example related to publication contracts. Abu Al-Hassan Al-Nadawi (a member of International Islamic *Fiqh* Academy) maintains that a publication contract falls within the prohibition of *gharar*.[61] In certain circumstances an author does not know in advance the exact monetary consideration that will be paid to her/him at the time of concluding the contract, as this is determined according to external factors such as the acceptance of the book in the market and

---

[57] Saleh (1992), 2nd edn, p. 62.

[58] Ibid, 66.

[59] Ibid, 70.

[60] Beltramitti (2009), p. 74.
  It should be stressed that the prohibition of *gharar* would only be problematic in contracts involving licensing trade secret so its effect should not be overstated as it will not hinder the licensing agreements in general. Raslan (2007), p. 530.

[61] Alnadawi (1977), p. 149.

the number of copies sold. This leads to uncertainty in relation the countervalues of the publication contract (copies to be sold and monetary compensation).[62]

A publication contract is a transaction which involves copyright. If there is *gharar* in such a transaction then the Islamic prohibition of *gharar* applies to that specific transaction and should not be generalised to be seen as objection to the IP system. This issue is dealt with below.

As is the case with *mayser*, *gharar* does not constitute a critical objection against Islamic Shari'a's recognition of IP. If a dispute arises with regard to *gharar* in a trade secrets or publication contract, the general principles of contract law in Islamic Shari'a should be applied on case by case basis.

It can be understood from the various objections to IP considered above that there is no serious conceptual conflict between Islamic Shari'a and the recognition and protection of IP.[63] However, there are certain injunctions and principles in Islamic Shari'a which may limit the scope of the protectable subject matter or invalidate certain transactions related to IP.

5.2.2 Support for The wordThe wordThe wordThe wordThe wordThe word Protection

The majority of contemporary Muslim scholars[64] argue that Islamic Shari'a recognises IP rights and 'there is nothing in [its rules] that enjoins or contravenes protecting and enforcing intellectual property'.[65] On the contrary, the principles derived from the Qur'an and Sunnah along with the non-textual sources of Shari'a seem to provide strong support for the recognition and protection of IP.

---

[62] Alnadawi argues that:

> [T]he author [in a publication contract] of a book is not compensated for its work with fixed amount of money; rather it is compensated according to the acceptance of its book in the market and the number of copies which were sold. Accordingly, the monetary consideration of the contract between the author and the publisher is unknown precisely at the time of concluding the contract. This ambiguity surrounding the consideration enters into gharar (sale by speculation or indefiniteness) and the Prophet (PBUH) strongly forbade sale by speculation. Ibid 155

[63] Cullen (2010), p. 15.

[64] Islamic websites are filled with legal opinions issued by Muslim scholars in the field of intellectual property; particularly copyright, stating that Islamic Shari'a recognises and protects intellectual property. It is noteworthy that even with religious knowledge, the scholars maintained the opinion that no form of expression should be infringed regardless of its nature. For more information see some of these opinions: http://guyanamuslims.org/viewtopic.php?f=59&t=439. http://www.bakkah.net/interactive/q&a/aamb080-copyrights-translations-intellectual-property.htm. http://www.islamqa.com/en/ref/52903.

[65] Raslan (2007), p. 502.

5.2.2.1   The Position of Intangible Property in Islamic Shari'a

The concept of *mulk* (property) under Islamic Shari'a includes both tangible and intangible assets. Since IP rights are intangible assets, they can be considered as *mulk* worthy of Islamic Shari'a's strict protection of private property.[66]

Several commentators have considered the position of intangibles (*manfa'ah*) within Islamic Shari'a.[67] Professor Al-dereni, who studied the four main schools of Islamic law (*Hanafis, Malikis, Hanbalis and Shafies*) asserts that the majority of those schools (*Malikis, Hanbalis and Shafis*) accept intangibles as a subject of ownership (*mulk*), as for tangible property.[68]

Only the classical scholars of the *Hanafi* School of law reject intangibles as a form of property. This is because they consider physical possession as a fundamental requirement to regard anything as property. Therefore, they only accept tangibles as *mulk*.[69]

Professor Al-Derini further argues that '[t]here is nowhere in the Holy Qur'an, the Sunnah, nor in any other source of Islamic Shari'a that you will find a text that states [in a direct or in indirect way] that intangibles are not a subject of property'.[70]

An example of the classic juristic acceptance of intangibles in Islamic Shari'a can be found in the writings of the distinguished Muslim scholar, Imam al-Qarafi (1260 CE), who states in one of the most comprehensive works of Islamic jurisprudence (*al-Furuq*) that the concept of *mulk* (property) includes intangibles.[71]

Husain Shalgammi argues that the opinion of the majority of Muslim scholars (which recognises intangibles as a form of property) is worthy of consideration as it can be extended to encompass IP rights.[72] This is because the intangible right of IP is a form of usufructuary right *(manfa'ah)*,[73] and since there is no authority in the sources of Shari'a denying protection for *manfa'ah*, legal analogy (*Qiyas*) could be used to encompass IP under the concept of *manfa'aa* and therefore recognises it as *mulk*.[74]

To sum up, the concept of *mulk* under Islamic Shari'a does not only include tangible assets, it also encompasses intangible assets. Therefore, extending Islamic

---

[66] Bakre (1986), p. 66.

[67] Khory (2003), p. 171.

[68] Alnadawi (1977), p. 20. The view held by the majority is supported by Prophetic approval that *Manfa'aa* could be *mal* as it has been reported that the Prophet approved teaching the Qur'an—usufructuary act—as a dowry and only *mal* (property) could be used as dowry which meant for many scholars that *Manfa'aa* is a form of property. Azmi (1996a), p. 660.

[69] Raslan (2007), p. 517.

[70] Alnadawi (1977), p. 42.

[71] Al-Qarafi (2010), 3rd edn, vol 3, p. 1009.

[72] Shalgammi (2004), p. 91.

[73] Azmi (1996b), p. 54.

[74] Ibid, 34.

Shari'a's recognition to IP based on its recognition of *manfa'ah* is 'methodologically correct'.[75]

5.2.2.2 Generation of Wealth

Through its main sources, Islamic Shari'a calls upon Muslims to work to create wealth and enhance the welfare of the community. The Qur'an advises Muslims to '*seek from the bounty of Allah*'.[76] The Prophet (PBUH) himself used to trade for his family and praised trade that leads to acquiring wealth for the benefit of all members of the society.[77] There were no limits to wealth generation except that it should come from legitimate sources and contribute to the good of all.

IP is granted to legal persons to ensure that any person who spends time and effort in developing something useful to humankind is given a chance to benefit from their creation. However, the ultimate aim is to ensure the innovation within the society is encouraged and boosted as it is fundamental to wealth generation in society. A certain level of IP protection is needed to create 'new technologies, products and services, describe new ways of doing things and expand the cultural richness of the society'.[78]

Accordingly, IP generally meets one of the highest objectives of Islamic Shari'a, that is, the preservation of wealth for humankind and maintaining the welfare of the community. This means that adequate protection for authors, inventors and trademark owners would be compatible with and encouraged by Islamic Shari'a.

5.2.2.3 Legitimate Labour in Islam and Intellectual Property

Islam's appreciation of labour (*aml*) has been used to justify the recognition of ownership over ideas.[79] Various verses in the Qur'an[80] and Sunnah encourage and praise labour.[81] In this context, the Prophet (pbuh) is reported to have said: 'No one

---

[75] Ibid, 71.

[76] The Qur'an: 62:10.

[77] Khory (2003), p. 165.

[78] Maskus (2000), p. 27.

[79] Azmi (1996b), p. 113.

[80] The Qur'an (Sahih International trans) 4:32; 35: 10; 16:97 and 9: 105.

[81] Azmi (1996a), p. 663 asserts that' Muslim scholars have developed the first acquisition theory into a labour theory, i.e. which holds that a man can only obtain what he strives for. According to this theory, the yardstick for economic gain is labour. She cites *Ibn Khaldon*, a leading Muslim scholar in social sciences (d. 1406 CE), where he states in his well know book of *al-Muqadema* 'the effort to (obtain sustenance) depends on God's determination and inspiration. Everything comes from God but human labour is necessary for every profit and capital accumulation. It has thus [became] clear that gains and profits, in their entirety or for the most part are value realised from human labour'.

ever ate better food than from the work of his own hands; and Allah's Prophet David used to eat from the work of his own hands'.[82] This appreciation of the work of the hand necessitates the protection of its fruits. Because labour is considered to be a legitimate source of acquiring property, the property which stems from labour should, accordingly, be respected. Does the concept of labour in Islam include mental labour?

Azmi contends that 'mental labour, in any case, should not be treated differently from any other kind of physical labour'[83] as the term labour in Islam is broad and flexible enough to include physical as well as mental exertions.[84]

The fact that the main sources of Islamic Shari'a do not directly or indirectly require the term 'labour' to be confined to physical effort supports this conclusion. In cases where there is no textual authority in a given issue, the Islamic jurisprudential rule of *al-asl fi al ashya al ibaha*[85] (permissibility is the default status in legal affairs) applies. Applied here, this rule would mean that labouring on ideas is permissible according to Islamic Shari'a and the fruits generated from such labour should be protected in the same manner as the products of physical labour. This provides additional support for the recognition and protection of IP.

5.2.2.4   Productivity in Islam and Intellectual Property

Islam recognises that the creative act of making something useful could be a means of acquiring ownership.[86] It is established in Islamic jurisprudence that if a person occupies an unclaimed piece of land for a certain period of time and spends effort and money to develop it and exploit it in a productive and fruitful manner; he or she will have the right of ownership over that land. This injunction finds its origin in a prophetic *hadith* (saying) which states that 'whoever revives a dead/vacant piece of land shall own it'.[87] The rules covering this means of ownership are comprehensively organised in the classical works of Islamic jurists under the title of *ihya al-mawat* (developing or improving vacant land). This concept (*ihya al-mawat*) reflects Shari'a's appreciation of all human endeavours that amount to create new things or develop and improve existing things for the benefit of humankind.[88]

Accordingly, creative individuals who apply their intellect to produce something unique or put their efforts into a copyrightable material, an invention or a trademark that distinguishes their products or services are no less worthy of legal protection

---

[82] Al-Maktabah Al-maqru'a, *sharh riyad al-salihin*, vol 3. http://www.ibnothaimeen.com/all/books/printer_18205.shtml.

[83] Azmi (1996a), p. 664.

[84] Beheshti (1988). Cited in Azmi (1996a), p. 664.

[85] For detailed account on this rule see Al-Sayouti (1983), p. 65.

[86] Jamar (1992), p. 1085.

[87] Al-Bahoty (1997), p. 398.

[88] Raslan (2007), p. 518.

than their counterparts who develop a vacant land. They are probably more worthy of protection than those who develop vacant land given the increasing importance of the information economy and the broader advantages of intellectual products over physical ones.

5.2.2.5   Islamic Shari'a Condemns Deceitful Practices

If the concept of *aml* (labour) in Islamic Shari'a is inclusive of mental and physical efforts then the fruits of one's mental labour should be respected. Accordingly, additional justification for the protection of rights over the products of intellectual effort can be found in direct injunctions within the Qur'an and the Sunnah which praise honesty and fairness in trade, and prohibit any deceitful acts or unjust commercial practices.[89]

One commentator has argued that '[v]arious verses of the Qur'an prohibit deceitful practices such as imitation and counterfeiting'[90] which by their nature fall also within the scope of 'unscrupulous acts' condemned by Islamic Shari'a. Examples of these verses include:

> Plead not on behalf of those that are unfaithful to themselves'[91]
> O you who have believed do not betray Allah and the Messenger or betray your trusts while you know [the consequence][92]
> "Indeed, Allah commands you to render trusts to whom they are due".[93]
> Surely Allah will defend those who believe; surely Allah does not love anyone who is unfaithful[94]

These verses illustrate Shari'a's condemnation of all kinds of unfair commercial practices in a traditional market. However, one commentator observes that the same verses could be broadly read to provide support from Islamic Shari'a for the protection of IP rights.[95] In linking the verses cited above and the Sunnah with IP, Al-ghamidi observes that violating an IP right would be:

> Cheating that contradicts religion, morals and honesty. It is condemned by many instructions and injunctions of Islamic Shari'a. Allah says [in the Qur'an] *'O ye who believe! betray not Allah and His messenger, nor knowingly betray your trust'* ... [t]he messenger of God is reported to have said [in Sunnah]'...he who cheats us, is not one of us'. ... Violating IP rights is prohibited by Shari'a because it is considered as cheating.[96]

---

[89] For the authentic *hadiths* relating to trade, see translation of Sunnah book of *Sahih Al-bukhary*. Available online at: http://www.Shariahprogram.ca/Hadith/Sahih-Bukhari/034.sbt.html.

[90] Khory (2003), p. 173.

[91] The Qur'an (M. M. Pickthall trans) 4:107.

[92] The Qur'an (Sahih International trans) 8:27.

[93] The Quran 4:58 (Sahih International).

[94] The Qur'an (Sahih International trans) 22:38.

[95] Raslan (2007), p. 524 and Khory (2003), p. 174.

[96] Alghamidi (2003).

Accordingly, any person who makes copies of a computer program and sells those copies as if they were authentic versions; a person who manufactures products using a patented invention without authorisation from the patent holder; or a trader who uses a trademark of other person to market counterfeited goods is committing an act that contradicts the general prohibition of deceitful practices in Islam. As a result, laws and regulations that prevent unfair 'free riding' on others' efforts and compensate any resultant damages are compatible with the main sources of Shari'a.

5.2.3   Evaluation of the Existing Literature on IP and Islamic Shari'a

Those who oppose IP protection from an Islamic perspective seem to lack a deep understanding of the diverse field of IP. Their objections deal only with limited aspects of the IP system. They have failed to provide convincing evidence to demonstrate a conceptual conflict between the sources of Islamic Shari'a and notions of IP. Their objections to IP are—at best—valid as grounds to introduce IP laws that are different from those implemented in the West, but they do not validate rejection of IP by Shari'a. For instance, the objection raised against IP subject matter may lead to excluding subject matters that contradict certain injunctions in the Islamic sources. Likewise, objection based on *gharar* only leads to nullifying certain transactions involving IP, but it is not a valid ground to exclude IP protection altogether.[97]

With regard to the proponents of IP, their arguments are stronger and reveal that the principles contained in the textual sources of Islamic Shari'a unequivocally support the recognition and protection of IP rights. For instance, the theoretical concept of *mulk* in Islamic Shari'a is broad enough to encompass intangible property. Islamic Shari'a recognises mental labour as a method of making a livelihood and it strictly condemns 'free-riding' or obtaining an advantage without paying for it or earning it.

Nevertheless, the analysis introduced by the proponents of IP protection from an Islamic perspective is not deep enough. This is evident from the following two gaps, which were not addressed.

First, the sources of Islamic Shari'a were not used to introduce general theories of IP, despite the fact that the Qur'an and the Sunnah as well as classic and modern Islamic jurisprudence can be relied upon to establish Islamic theories for IP similar to those dominant in the West.

Second, the existing literature also failed to—at least—highlight the existence of principles in the sources of Islamic Shari'a that may be relevant to placing limits to individual IP rights. Concepts of ownership in Islamic Shari'a, its prohibition of

---

[97] As for the objection about IP and concealment of knowledge, I will discuss its ramification in the concluding part of this paper.

concentration of productive resources, and its encouragement for the wide dissemination of knowledge may be seen as grounds for limiting, modifying, and otherwise affecting the existence or the scope of individual IP rights.

At this stage, I would like to emphasise the fact that I am not arguing that Islamic Shari'a will create new theories for IP, but I am simply arguing that there are concepts and principles in the sources of Islamic Shari'a that provide broader theoretical framework to justify IP from an Islamic perspective and also to place limits on IP from an Islamic perspective. The next section will discuss in detail the origins of these concepts and principles, and how they are relevant to modern theories of IP.

5.3 An Islamic Perspective on the Dominant Theories of IP

The dominant theories of IP, at least in the West, are based on fairness, utilitarianism and personality theories used in justifying the right to physical property. This section starts by briefly tracing these theories. After that, it identifies profound similarities between Western and Islamic theories of property. This section ends by arguing that as much as IP can be justified according to Western theories, it can also be justified according to Islamic theories of physical property.

5.3.1 Justification of Property in the West

Generally, the right to physical property is justified in the West by reference to the writings of theorists such as John Locke (d. 1704), Immanuel Kant (d. 1804) and Georg Hegel (d. 1831).

In Chapter 5 of his *Two Treatises of Government*,[98] Locke justifies the right to private property based on fairness. In sections 25, 26 and 34 Locke maintains that '*God gave the world to men in common*', (emphasis added)[99] and that the resources of nature are available for all people.[100] In Locke's theory on property, each individual owns 'the labour of his body and the work of his hands ... Whatsoever then he removes out of the state that nature hath provided, and left it in, he hath mixed his labour with, and joined to it something that is his own, and thereby makes it his property.'[101] Thus, 'no man but he can have a right to what that is once joined

---

[98] John Locke, *The Second Treatise of Civil Government* (1690) available online at: http://www.constitution.org/jl/2ndtreat.htm.

[99] Sec 34.

[100] Sec 27.

[101] Sec 27.

to, at least where there is enough, and as good, left in common for others.'[102] From this assumption comes the exclusionary nature of the contemporary Western right of private property.

The most prominent example in Locke's Treatises is the private ownership of land (sections 32, 37 and 43). An individual, who tills, plants, improves and cultivates a piece of land,[103] has 'added something to [it] more than nature ... and so [it] became his private right'.[104] 'Thus, labour ... [gives] a right of property, whenever anyone was pleased to employ it upon what was common'.[105]

Moreover, according to Locke, it is not only fairness that may justify private ownership, public interest also does. The American philosopher Albert Brogan maintains that "Locke formulated the basic theses of early or eighteenth-century Utilitarianism".[106] Based on the utilitarian account, private property should be protected because protection is in the public interest of society at large. Failing to protect private property will lead to making people losing incentive to labour on the resources held in common. This, in turn, will reduce value in society and impede progress. In this sense, recognising and protecting private property secures the good for all.

Hegel, on the other hand, argues that *'man has by nature the impulse to right [and] the impulse to property'* (emphasis added).[107] On that basis Hegel proposes his so-called personality theory. According to personality theory, property can be justified as an expression of the self. What creates ownership is the will of an individual. This takes place, for instance, when that will interacts with the external world at various levels of activity. According to Hegel's philosophy, intellectual processes such as realisation, remembering, contemplation, classification and constructive imagination 'can be viewed as appropriations of the external world by the mind',[108] and since the will of an individual represents his or personality, the right to private ownership over what has been appropriated by the will should be considered as a fundamental prerequisite for satisfying natural human urges.[109]

---

[102] Ibid, the language of sec 44 carries meaning to the same effect.

[103] Sec 32.

[104] Sec 28.

[105] Sec 45.

[106] Brogan (1959), p. 79.

[107] Hegel (2001), p. 41.

[108] Hughes (1988), p. 30.

[109] Fisher (2001), p. 5, online version available at: http://cyber.law.harvard.edu/people/tfisher/iptheory.pdf.

5.3.2 Justification of Property in Islamic Shari'a

The theories of both Locke and Hegel have strong parallels in the theoretical framework of private property in Islamic Shari'a. For instance, the theological premise of Locke (sec 34) is emphasised throughout the Qur'an:

> It is He (Allah) who created for you (humankind) all of that which is on the earth.[110]

> And He has subjected to you whatever is in the heavens and whatever is on the earth - all from Him. Indeed in that are signs for a people who give thought.[111]

As is the case in the Western philosophy, fairness is used to justify private property in Islamic Shari'a. Muslim scholars define the resources held in common as *mubah*.[112] From an Islamic perspective, the *mubah* includes vacant land (*al-ard al-jardaa*), marine life (*al-hayate al-bahriyya*), animals (*hayawanat*), plants (*nabatat*) and mines (*ma'adin*).[113] Generally, the appropriation from *mubah* grants title (*mulkiyya*) to the appropriator.[114] This takes place through labour that leads to possession of some of the resources that are held in common (*ihraz al-mubah*).[115]

As is the case in Locke's Treatises, the example of land is widely used in the jurisprudence of Islamic Shari'a to justify granting title over resources held in common (*ihraz al-mubah*). As we have seen above, this is known as *ihyaa al-mawat* (reviving the death), and relies on a *hadith* of the Prophet (pbuh) that implies whoever labours on an unclaimed piece of vacant land will have the right to own that land.[116]

Ali al-Khafif and Muhammad Abu Zahra have studied the meaning of '*ihyaa al-mawat*' according to the opinions of *Hanafi* (d 767 CE), *Maliki* (d 796 CE), *Shafie* (d 820 CE) and *Hanbali* (d. 855 CE) jurists.[117] What appears from their work is that the term '*ihyaa*' resembles the concept of labour in Locke's Treaties. Ali al-Khafif contends that ownership of vacant land cannot be recognised without productive labour that adds something to the land which makes it more beneficial than its original or natural condition.[118] Abu Zahra gives examples for the kind of labour that qualifies for the ownership of the vacant land, which could be

---

[110] The Quran (Sahih International trans) 2:29.

[111] The Quran (Sahih International trans) 45:13.

[112] See for instance Abu Zahra (1977), p. 55.

[113] Alzarqa (1998), p. 336 and Shalabi (1985), p. 381.

[114] Sayeed (2002), p. 60.

[115] Shalabi (1985), p. 38.1.

[116] This *hadith* was narrated in different forms by Imam Al-Termidi. It is also reported in Sahih Albukhari from Aisha the wife of the Prophet. Ali (1996), p. 58; see also Mansour Kashaf al-Qina ann matn al-Iqna'a y (1997), p. 398.

[117] Alkhafif (1996), p. 249; Abu Zahra (1977), pp. 125–126.

[118] Alkhafif (1996), p. 249.

understood to include the examples that were given by Locke in sec 32: tilling, improving and cultivating.[119]

Based on the concepts of *ihraz al-mubah* and the concept of *ihyaa al-mawat*, Muslim scholars developed 'labour theory' to justify ownership of God-given resources. For instance, Abu-Bakr ibn Abi Al-Duniyya, (d. 894 CE) in his book *Islah al-Mal* (maintenance of wealth) traced the texts of Islamic Shari'a and found that productive labour justifies private property.[120] What is more, the Muslim jurist, philosopher and sociologist Abdul Rahman ibn Khaldun (known as Ibn Khaldun) who died in 1406 CE (298 years before John Locke) in his highly acclaimed book *al-Muqaddimah* (the Prolegomena) developed an advanced Islamic theory of labour resembling that of Locke.

In the fifth chapter of the first volume of *al-Muqaddimah*, Ibn Khaldun refers to several verses from the Qur'an which illustrate that *Allah* has given the world with all its natural resources for the benefit of humankind.[121] He maintains that 'hands of humans' have equal opportunities to appropriate those resources, and once an individual exerts his or her labour on a certain object, it becomes his/her own property and thus 'cannot be taken without remuneration'.[122] This could be understood as recognition for exclusive right from an Islamic perspective.

As is the case in Western philosophy, Islamic legal philosophy also supports a utilitarian account for the right to private property. Two leading scholars in this field, al-Ezz Ibn Abd Alsalam (1261 CE) and Imam Al-Shatibi (1388 CE), conclude that it is evident through induction from the Qur'an and Sunnah that the ultimate purpose of Islamic Shari'a is to promote the welfare of the community and prevent harm from being inflected upon it.[123] Scholars have developed the concept of *maslaha mursala* (consideration of public interest), which operates as a mechanism to adopt emerging legal institutions and scientific issues so long as they promote the overall public interest of society.[124]

Here as well, it can be argued that protecting property rights promotes the welfare of the society as such protection will provide people (at least in many cases) with the incentive to develop natural resources into useable products. In this context, Ibn Khaldun argues that 'human labour is a prerequisite for wealth accumulation' (which is necessary to welfare), and that 'profits and gains, in their entirety or in the majority of cases, are value realised from human labour'.[125] He notes that 'welfare and prosperity of a society is dependent on the magnitude of

---

[119] Abu Zahra (1977), p. 125.

[120] Abu-Bakr Ibn Abi Aldunnya, *Islah al-Mal*, this book was authenticated in a study prepared by Mustafa. M. Alghatat (Al-wafa Publications, 1990), p. 84.

[121] Ibn Khaldun (2005), vol 2, p. 259.

[122] Ibid, 259.

[123] Izz Ibn Abd Alsalam (2003) and Al-shatebi (1997), vol 2, p. 7.

[124] Alboti (1965).

[125] Ibid, 260–261.

labour in that society'[126] which means that those societies which respect the fruits of human labour and reward it, shall flourish, and those who do not respect human labour will suffer adverse consequences.[127]

Moreover, as is the case in Hegel's personality theory, in which Hegel affirms that having private property is innate, Muslim scholars submit that the texts of the Qur'an and Sunnah pertaining to property illustrate that having private property is a natural disposition of human beings.[128] For instance, the Qur'an says:

And you (humans) love wealth with immense love.[129]

And indeed he (human being) is, in love of wealth, intense.[130]

As for the Sunnah of the Prophet Muhammed (pbuh), he is reported to have said: 'If the son of Adam were to possess two valleys of riches, he would long for the third one'.[131]

The main sources of Islamic Shari'a recognise that it is part of human nature to desire the ownership of wealth. It is widely stressed in Islamic jurisprudence that Islamic Shari'a does not aim at undermining natural dispositions of humans, but rather to regulate them. Accordingly, the recognition provided in the Islamic sources for ownership as being a human natural need, must have a normative implication, that is, providing some sort of protection for ownership acquired through legitimate means, especially labour. Protection for the right to property means essentially giving the owner the right to prevent others from making use of her property without compensation or permission. In this vein, Mustafa al-Zarqa concludes that *mulkiyyah*, under Islamic Shari'a, is a private right that permits owners to exclude others from using the subject matter,[132] and that it encompasses tangible and intangible assets.[133]

Once property rights are recognised according to Islamic Shari'a, the state is obliged to protect them and allow the owner to practise their rights. In this regard, the renowned Hanafi scholar, Abu Yusuf (d. 798 CE), wrote to Harun al-Rashid (d. 809 CE) the head of Islamic State (*Caliphate*):

Neither according to the religion nor according to the law can the sovereign [*Imam*] concede to anyone what belongs to another Muslim or to a person under the protection of the Muslims. Nor can he deprive them of anything they possess, except when he has a legal claim against them. In this case, he may exact from them that to which he has a right.[134]

---

[126] Ibid, 262.

[127] Ibid.

[128] See for instance, Abdallah. M. Younes, *Athar al-Tandeem al-Islami li al-Mulkeyyah* (Dar Al-shimaa Publications) 31 and Al-Mosleh (1982), pp. 35–36.

[129] The Quran (Sahih International trans) 89:20.

[130] The Quran (Sahih International trans) 100:08.

[131] Translation of Sahih Muslim, Hadith no 2281, available online at: http://www.iium.edu.my/deed/hadith/muslim/005_smt.html.

[132] Alzarqa (1998), p. 333.

[133] Ibid, 334.

[134] Ibrahim (1884), p. 34, cited in Habachy (1962), p. 455.

In summary, the general framework of *mulkeyyah* as prescribed in the sources of Islamic Shari'a, and the writings of Islamic scholars, is consistent with the general framework of property as developed in Western philosophical thought. How does this relate to IP?

5.3.3 'Common Terms'

The sources of Islamic Shari'a support the general framework of theories of fairness, utilitarianism and personality as introduced in the writings of classic Western philosophers such as Locke or Hegel. It follows that so much as IP can be justified according to these theories; it can also be justified under the sources of Islamic Shari'a.

Justin Hughes, William Fisher and Robert Merges conducted intensive research to articulate theories of IP on the basis of the classical theories of real property as expounded in the works of Locke and Hegel discussed above.

Hughes argues that private ownership of ideas can be justified under Locke's approach according to three propositions. First, the state of nature or the 'common' in Locke's words can be imagined as the realm of ideas. Second, the production of useful ideas generally requires labour by the individual. Third, ideas can be made property and, yet, there will be 'enough, and as good, left in common for others' as Locke's proviso of non-waste suggests.[135]

In the same context, Merges asserts that Locke's theory 'applies ... well ... to intellectual property'[136] because '[the] stock of public domain information from which individual creators draw fits closely with Locke's conception of a vast realm of common resources',[137] so 'the claiming of intellectual property rights out of the public domain follows the same logic as the emergence of property rights from the state of nature'.[138] Merges further argues that the importance of labour in Locke's theory has significant bearing on the world of IP:

---

[135] Hughes (1988), p. 8. Elsewhere Hughes argues that intellectual property systems, however, do seem to accord with Locke's labor condition and the 'enough and as good' requirement. In fact, the 'enough and as good' condition seems to hold true *only* in intellectual property systems. Hughes (1988), p. 27.

[136] Merges (2011), p. 32. Professor Merges defended the applicability of Locke's theory of IP against criticisms from the leading philosophers, Robert Nozic and Jeremy Waldron. See Merges (2011), pp. 43–46.

[137] Ibid, 33.

[138] Ibid. Similarly Hughes argues that: 'It requires some leap of faith to say that ideas come from a 'common' in the Lockean sense of the word. Yet it does not take an unrehabilitated Platonist to think that the 'field of ideas' bears a great similarity to a common. The differences between ideas and physical property have been repeated often. Physical property can be used at any one time by only one person or one coordinated group of people. Ideas can be used simultaneously by everyone. Furthermore, people cannot be excluded from ideas in the way that they can be excluded from physical property.' Hughes (1988), p. 18.

[N]ontrivial creations presumably requiring significant effort are often said to be at the heart of IP law. Although labour is relevant in establishing some real property rights, it is a much larger, and much more prominent, part of the IP landscape. So Locke is more pertinent to IP.[139]

The Islamic concept of *mubah* carries identical features to the concept of the commons, from which real property is appropriated. Likewise, the concept of *mubah* could be extended to the stock of public domain information, from which individual creators draw ideas for artistic and innovative products.[140] These products could be perceived as private property according to Islamic Shari'a so long as they meet the general criteria of private ownership as discussed above, which requires productive effort (*amal*) that adds value to resources held in common (*mubah*).

Additionally, Fisher inferred from Locke's theory the existence of a utilitarian approach in IP that riddles American Law; starting from US Constitution through to legislation, judgments and legal argument.[141] According to the utilitarian interpretation of Locke's theory, intellectual labour should be rewarded by granting those who labour the exclusive right to exploit their respective creations, as through this channel, lawmakers will ensure the maximisation of social welfare. Contrariwise, failing to allocate such exclusive rights 'will deter creators from making socially valuable intellectual products in the first instance' and thereby creating an 'economically inefficient outcome'.[142]

Under Islamic Shari'a a utilitarian justification for IP can be established as well. If the texts of the Qur'an and Sunnah aim to promote the overall public interest of society, it is arguable that they would support IP. This is because IP would lead to promoting (at least in many cases) innovation and progress by incentivising the creation of more intellectual products. Several commentators on Islamic Shari'a and IP used utilitarian accounts to justify IP protection from an Islamic perspective.[143] For instance, the widely renowned Muslim scholar Professor Wahba Al-zohili issued a *fatwa* (legal opinion) in 1977 in favour of 'Islamic protection' for copyright. That *fatwa* was explicitly based on utilitarian accounts. Professor Al-zohili stated that:

> Copyright, which enters under a new legal concept, the intellectual right, is protected under Islamic Shari'a [and] the basis for such protection would be *Istislah or maslaha mursala* (the consideration of public interest). This is because any work that brings prevailed interest or obviates damage and evil is legitimate under Islamic Shari'a.[144]

---

[139] Merges (2011), p. 33. Fisher argues in the same direction, Fisher (2001), p. 4.

[140] A similar opinion is held by Azmi (2004), p. 202.

[141] Fisher (2001), p. 8, Fisher refers at the begging of his research to the utilitarian approach as a separate from Locke's theory; however, Justin Hughes presents the utilitarian approach as a potential interpretation of Locke's labour theory. See Hughes (1988), p. 6. It should be noted that Professor Fisher has wrote on the theories in 1988 see, Fisher (1988), pp. 1755 et seq.

[142] Fisher (2001), p. 2.

[143] See for instance Raslan (2007), p. 526; Beltramitti (2009), pp. 80–81, and Shalgammi (2004).

[144] Al-Zohili (1977), p. 188.

As for the personality theory's justification for IP, Islamic sources, particularly the Qur'an and Sunnah, support the understanding that the need for private ownership is a natural disposition of human beings. Such understanding is in line with Hegel's personality theory.[145] Based on the latter theory Fisher and Merges imply that granting IP rights could be looked at as 'crucial to the satisfaction of some fundamental human needs'[146] or as fulfilling 'human instinct' which is bound with the existence of an individual's will.[147] This holds true especially in the field of artistic creation, where an artist represents his or her will in a novel or painting.[148] The reflection of personality theory is evident in the generous protection of moral rights in the European countries. Brian Fitzgerald refers to the influence of the personality theory in shaping the recognition of moral rights in Article *6bis* of the *Berne Convention.*[149]

By way of conclusion, as is the case in Western philosophy, fairness, utilitarianism and personality theories can be used to justify the right to property from an Islamic perspective. Therefore, from an Islamic perspective it is fair, beneficial and satisfying to own IP rights.

5.4   Limitation to IP Rights from an Islamic Perceptive

Justifying IP rights, from an Islamic perspective, as being fair, beneficial and satisfying does not mean that they are without limits. The way in which we design our IP laws and policies has significant impact on the rights and freedoms of the members of society, as well as on the progress of the society in relation to economic, social and cultural domains. Therefore, setting limits on the IP rights is part of their fabric.

Generally, there is a strong case in international IP scholarship against the dominant IP systems for focussing overly on owners' exclusive rights while giving insufficient weight to the interests of users of intellectual products, and also for being highly restrictive in allowing efficient utilisation and allocation of knowledge resources.[150] In particular, a substantial part of the current IP scholarship, led by prominent scholars and experts, argues that IP laws and policymaking on an

---

[145] Although Professor Justin Hughes in his mentioned article did not refer to the influence of Kant on shaping the personality theory, Kant's contribution is mainly recognised by Fisher and Merger, see respectively, Fisher (2001), p. 5 and Merges (2011), p. 72.

[146] Fisher (2001), p. 5.

[147] Merges (2011), p. 72.

[148] Hughes (1988), p. 28.

[149] Fitzgerald (2003), p. 182.

[150] See for instance: Lessig (2004); Boyle (2003), p. 140, Litman (2011); Patry (2011); Netanel (2008) Boldrin and Levine (2002). For insightful critic of the international copyright system and particularly with regard to its insufficient consideration for distributive justice concerns see Chon (2007). See also Drahos (2004).

international are negatively linked to the overall public interests in developing countries in areas such as public health, access to food, access to education and overall economic growth.[151]

The scope of this paper does not allow—and is not intended—to introduce a comprehensive critique for the dominant IP systems. I just wanted to make the reader bear in mind that justifying the ownership of IP rights, based on fairness or efficiency is one thing and the regulation of those rights is another thing. Accepting the principle of ownership of intellectual assets must be accompanied with limits to ensure that IP rights serve the overall public interest of society by, among other things, promote fair distribution of resources within society and by not impinging on the rights, activities, freedoms and basic needs of others.

In this section, I identify four principles based on the Islamic sources which operate as a balancing normative framework to limit the scope and breadth of IP rights in favour of considerations of society—wide fairness and the overall public interest. The sources of Islamic Shari'a, particularly the Qur'an and the teachings of the Prophet, emphasise principles on stewardship (*khilafa*), non-concentration of wealth, limits to property rights and encouragement for the dissemination of knowledge. These principles can be the subject of an entire book. Therefore, I will very briefly introduce them and highlight their normative implications for the overall design of IP infrastructure.

5.4.1 *Stewardship* (Khilafah)

Stewardship (*Khilafah*) is a fundamental aspect of the Islamic perspective on the regulation of society, including the regulation of property rights in both tangible and intangible assets. *Khilafah* can be used to place limits on IP rights and ensure that the regulation of IP takes into consideration the broader public interest and not only the exclusive rights of IP holders.

According to this concept, the ultimate ownership of resources and end products should be considered for *Allah* who created these resources and created humans who labour on these resources. The concept of *Khilafa* is stressed throughout the Qur'an.[152] Several verses support the assumption that resources include knowledge as well.[153] In one verse the Qur'an says:

> Believe in Allah and His Messenger and spend out of that in which He has made you successors. For those who have believed among you and spent, there will be a great reward[154]

---

[151] See for instance: Drahos and Mayne (2002); Yu (2008), p. 365; Okidiji (2006), p. 32.

[152] See for instance: The Quran (Sahih International trans) 7: 69 and 57:5.

[153] The Quran (Sahih International trans) 96: 4–5; 21: 80; 2:32.

[154] The Quran (Sahih International trans) 57:7.

Read! And your Lord is the Most Generous. Who has taught by the pen. He has taught human that which he/ she knew not.[155]

The concept of *Khilafa* in the Qur'an is linked to the concept of accountability '*then We made you successors in the land after them* (stewardship) *so that We may observe how you will do* (accountability).'[156] Humans are accountable to exploit the property given to them by Allah in conformity with the dictates of Islamic Shari'a, which aim at full and efficient utilisation of resources for the general welfare of society.[157] In order to do that, those who hold property under the Islamic concept of *Khilafa* are requested to accept laws, regulations and instructions which pursue the objective of fair redistribution or reallocation of resources for the benefit of the community (*ummah*).[158]

In this context, Al-Zamakhshari (d. 1144 CE) states that: the ultimate ownership of all assets, which are under the possession of individuals, is for Allah who created these assets. Allah grants those assets to humankind as trustees with permission to enjoy the fruits of these assets. Therefore, believers are called to spend from these assets with ease in the cause of public interest, as if they were granted permission to spend from another person's wealth.[159] Imam Al-Qarafi (d. 1260 CE) and Imam Al-Shatibi (d. 1388 CE) argue to the same effect.[160]

Whenever there is evidence which shows that IP rights contradict the principle of *Khilafa* by, for example, restricting efficient access to and utilisation of knowledge resources needed to promote welfare, the principle of *Khilafa* can be invoked to support policy measures and legislative reforms to allow such access. This can come in form, for example, of protecting and expanding the public domain of ideas and expressions or redefining the scope of the exclusive rights of the IP holder to make them account more for society's interest.

5.4.2   Non-concentration of Wealth (Tadawu)

Allah's ultimate ownership as prescribed in the Qur'an lays the foundations for constraints on private property.[161] Among these constraints lies the general prohibition of the hoarding of wealth, deemed a fundamental principle of Islamic economic policy.[162]

---

[155] The Quran (Sahih International trans) 96: 4–5.

[156] The Qur'an (Sahih International trans) 10:14.

[157] Bashir (2002), pp. 75–91 and 77.

[158] Al-Qaradawi (1995), pp. 47–50.

[159] Alzamakhshari (1998), vol 6, p. 43.

[160] Kamal (1990), p. 153.

[161] Behdad (1989), p. 193.

[162] Qutb (1993), 13th edn, p. 92.

Islam strictly condemns the concentration of wealth in the hands of few members of society: '*and those who hoard gold and silver and spend it not in the way of Allah - give them tidings of a painful punishment.*'[163] Muhammed Al-Ghazali argues that Islam encourages the circulation of wealth among all sectors of society and does not accept that any particular group should hold a monopoly over such wealth.[164]

By analogy, the Islamic prohibition for the concentration of tangible assets, can be extended to prevent IP laws and policies that lead to concentrating the control of knowledge and culture in the hands of a few.

Strong exclusive rights for IP holders without sufficient consideration for fair distribution of intellectual products and the right of others to engage in the re-creation of these products can lead to the concentration of knowledge and cultural resources in the hands of few IP holders. For instance, Lawrence Lessig refers to statistics showing that in 2001 ownership of American culture in literary and artistic works was concentrated in less than 20 firms[165] and observes:

> Never in our history have fewer exercised more control over the development of our culture than now ... Never has the concentration been as significant as it is now.[166]

In particular, Islam does not approve of institutional arrangements that lead to circulating wealth and especially productive resources in the hands of the few. There is evidence from the history of implementing Islamic sources which shows that the concentration of productive resources has received particular prohibition. The second *Caliph* (head of state), Umer Ibn Al-khatab (d. 644), used to make sure that lands under Muslims' possession were used to their full operational capacity and, as head of state, he used to redistribute lands if the owners of these lands did not meet the condition of 'full operational capacity'.[167] In this context, Sohrab Behdad argues that whenever a person does not exploit a productive resource to its fullest operational capacity, it could be regarded as hoarder. This justifies state intervention to appropriate the unused productive resources.[168]

IP laws that *highly restrict* the circulation of intellectual goods contradict the non-concentration principle in Islamic Shari'a. It is widely accepted that the mindset of policymakers is prone to tailoring legislative and administrative policies on IP which in the main follow the unproven economic assumptions and underlying protocols of the big corporates.[169] They grant IP holders more rights on the use and re-use of knowledge and cultural products. In most cases, this leads to an excessive concentration of private powers and exclusion of users from the cultural and

---

[163] The Qur'an (Sahih International trans) 9:34.

[164] Al-ghazali (2005), 4th edn, p. 95.

[165] See Lessig (2001), pp. 116–119.

[166] Lessig (2004), pp. 8–9.

[167] For an example of such tradition please see Al-Qaradawi (1995), p. 168.

[168] Behdad (1989), p. 194.

[169] Butler and Ribstein (2011), p. 463; Patry (2011), p. 52.

knowledge domains.[170] The more-rights-approach resulted in overlooking vital issues for the larger global community, particularly with regard to access to food, medicine, education and overall economic development.

Applying the non-concentration principles derived from Islamic sources opens possible avenues for the reorientation of IP policymaking towards the fairer and more open distribution of knowledge resources. The scope and breadth of the exclusive rights should be designed so as to enable other members of the society to widely use knowledge and cultural products and also participate in their creation to achieve overall economic, social and cultural development. This cannot be done by only focusing on the rights of the IP holder, but also and equally by protecting and expanding the public domain of ideas and expression through conceptualising, developing and further enhancing the functions, capacities and legal rights of users within IP system.[171]

5.4.3 Doctrine of the Abuse of Rights in Islamic Shari'a

Under the concept of *Khilafah*, absolute ownership is not recognised in Islamic Shari'a. Rather, it is tied to the concept of accountability. The most relevant and direct implication for the concept of accountability is Islamic Shari'a's constraints on the exercise of property rights when they result in harm to public or legitimate private interests. These restrictions are contained in the Islamic Shari'a's doctrine of abuse of rights (*su isti'mal al-haq*). The basic rule of the doctrine is that when the exercise of a right impinges on the public interest, it should be considered as an abuse. When the exercise of a right is considered as an abuse, limits on that right should be decided.

Contemporary scholar Fathi Al-Dereni was among the first modern Muslim scholars to introduce comprehensive analysis for the doctrine by relying on interpretations of the Qur'an, the Sunnah and Islamic jurisprudence.[172] Al-Dereni put forward the following argument:

Allah is the source of all rights. The main objective of Islamic Shari'a is preventing harm and securing the interests of society. The exercise of rights (including property rights) should not run afoul of that objective. When the exercise

---

[170] Ibid.

[171] The implementation of the non-concentration principle may contribute to striking a more appropriate balance between the IP holders and IP users as it may be relied upon to promote the rights of users. In a similar context, Julie Cohen argues that an appropriate balance of interests can be achieved only if the interests of users, in addition to those of authors, are accommodated in the theoretical foundations of copyright. Cohen (2005), pp. 347–348.

[172] Al-Derini (1988), 4th edn, pp. 92–176. Among the important sources used by Al-Darini to articulate the theory of abuse of rights from Islamic perspective is the Shari'a principle which dictates that 'harm must be eliminated', which is based on Prophetic *hadith*, where the prophet is reported to have said 'harm may neither be inflicted nor reciprocated' at p. 117.

of property rights conflicts with the public interest (e.g. education, public health and economic competition) the public interest takes precedence.[173]

A thoughtful application of the doctrine of abuse of rights in Islamic Shari'a would assist in striking a balance between the exclusive rights of the IP holder and the public interest, and thereby contribute to an IP system that is more responsive to the sources and objectives of Islamic Shari'a.

If we are convinced that current system of IP does not adequately serve the public interest due to its rights-centric approach which leads to blocking needed access to educational material and essential medicine and slows the economic growth of developing nations, then this rights-centric approach should be rethought using the doctrine of abuse of rights. Implementation of the doctrine can occur through various balancing measures such as doctrines of patent and copyright misuse, rethinking prohibition against the exclusive rights of IP holders and promoting fair uses of IP protected materials, particularly in relation to education, research, national trade and public health.[174]

5.4.4 Encouragement for the Dissemination of Knowledge

Islamic Shari'a's prohibition of the concealment of knowledge discussed above may not be a valid ground for arguments against IP protection. However, it can be relied upon to support limits on excessive IP rights and also as grounds to encourage initiatives to disseminate knowledge and protect public domain.

It is established in the Islamic sources and traditions that the dissemination of knowledge is highly encouraged. For instance, it has been reported by Ibn Majah (d. 887 CE) that the Prophet said[175]:

1. The best of charity is when a Muslim man gains knowledge, then he teaches it to his Muslim brother[176];and
2. The rewards of the good deeds that will reach a believer after his/her death are: Knowledge which he taught and spread . . .[177]

---

[173] Ibid, 40, 80–82.

[174] If the exercise of exclusive rights leads the IP holder to misuse his patent or copyright by employing anti-competitive practices (delay in exploitation of IP subject matters, refusal to license others to use the subject matter on reasonable commercial terms, selling IP subject matter at excessively high prices, etc) or to impinge on legitimate uses for educational and public health purposes, the doctrine can be used to justify state intervention to curb the exclusive rights as the public interest dictates. Compare Azmi (1996b), pp. 289, 290 and 301.

[175] See also Sunan aAl-Tirmidhi*hadith* no 2685 on the dissemination of knowledge, Al-tirmidhi, Al-jami' Al-sahih,http://ahadith.co.uk/sunanaltirmidhi.php.

[176] Majah (2007), p. 232.

[177] Ibid, 233.

The companions of the Prophet (pbuh) used to unconditionally disseminate whatever knowledge they had obtained from him.[178] Scholars of Islam, in different eras, promoted the dissemination of religious knowledge by allowing their students to copy and disseminate their books free of charge.[179] In the ancient Islamic libraries of Cairo, Baghdad and Cordoba, knowledge was freely circulated and the dissemination of knowledge was even encouraged by the state.[180] This might be considered an application of the principle of *Khilafah*, by which ownership of knowledge is attributed to Allah, and humankind are considered as trustees. Ida Abdul Ghani Azmi argues that

> [D]issemination of knowledge is encouraged, and in certain circumstances compulsory in Islam. [Therefore] there is a need to mediate between control of and access to ideas. . . thus . . . any calls for the limitation of property rights over ideas on the basis of efficiency, justice and education as postulated by Lessig, Boyle, Netanel and several others. . .merit serious consideration by Muslim scholars.[181]

As a starting point, applying Shari'a's prohibition of the concealment of knowledge and its encouragement for the dissemination of knowledge to IP law and policymaking leads to limit the unduly locking of knowledge and cultural resources by excessive IP rights and promoting initiatives that lead to openness in using and re-using these resources. This can be done by shifting the mindset of law and policymaking from focusing only on building the infrastructure for IP rights to considering the protection and the expansion of the public domain and the support of A2K and open source modalities of knowledge and cultural production.

5.5 Conclusion

Islamic Shari'a recognises private ownership. This recognition can be extended to IP. The sources of Shari'a and its jurisprudence can offer comprehensive perspective on the theories IP rights. The general framework of the theories of fairness, utilitarianism and personality used to justify IP rights in Western literature in consistent with notions derived from the sources of Islamic Shari'a.

However, a comprehensive study of IP and Islamic Shari'a has to consider not only providing justifications for Shari'a's recognition of ownership of ideas but also the scope of such recognition. It must consider how the sources, principles and objectives of Islamic Shari'a view the effects of IP rights on the interests of society in areas such as education, public health and economic growth.

There are various principles derived from the sources of Shari'a that may assist in defining the scope of IP rights. These principles place significant emphasis on

---

[178] Al-Qaradawi (2001), p. 79.

[179] Ibid, 84.

[180] Elmahjub (2014).

[181] Azmi (2004), p. 203.

third parties' interests against those of the IP owner. The principles of stewardship (*khilafa*), non-concentration of wealth, abuse of rights and the encouragement for the dissemination of knowledge under Islamic Shari'a can be employed as a normative framework to design an IP system and policies that are not necessarily similar to their dominant counterparts. These principles, if integrated into the fabric of future law and policymaking, will not only promote the recognition and protection of more exclusive rights for the IP holders. They will contribute to reducing the concentration of private power to expand the public domain, empowering users of intellectual products and contributing to greater openness and distribution of cultural and knowledge resources.

References

Books (Arabic)

Abu Al-kher A-S (1988) al-Haq al-Mali li al-Mowalef fi al-Figh al-Islami wa al-Qanun al-Mesri. Wahba Library, Cairo
Abu Zahra M (1977) al-Mulkeyyah wa Nazareyat al-Aqd fi al-Shari'a al-Islameya. Dar Al-Fikre Al-Arabi, Cairo
Al-Derini F (1988) Nazariyat al-Ta'asuf fi isti 'mal al-Hagg. Muassasah al-Risalah, Beirut
Al-ghazali M (2005) al-Islam wa al-Manahej al-Ishtirakeya. Nahdat Misr, Cairo
Alkhafif A (1996) al-Mulkeyyah fi al-Shari'a al-Islameya. Dar al-Fikre al-Arabi, Cairo
Al-Mundhiri AA (2003) al-Targhib wa al-Tarhib. Maktabat Al-Ma'aref, Alexandria
Al-Qaradawi Y (2001) al-Rasul wa al-Ilm. Dar Al-Sahwa, Cairo
Al-Qaradawi Y (1995) Dawr al-Qiyam wa al-Akhlaqq fi al-Iqtisad al-Islami. Maktabat Wahba, Cairo
Al-Qarafi (2010) al-Furuq. Dar Al-Salam, Cairo
Al-Sayouti JA (1983) al-Ashbah wa al-Naza'er. Dar al-Kotob al-Elmeya, Beirut
Al-Shatebi (1997) al-Muwfaqat. Dar ibn Affan, El-Gîza
Alzamakhshari (1998) al-kashaf. Maktabat al-Abikan, Riyadh
Alzarqa M (1998) al-Madkhal al-Fiqhi al-A'am. Dar al-Qalam, Damascus
Ibn Khaldun (2005) al-Muqadema. Bait al-Ulum wa al-Funun wa al-Addab, Morocco
Izz Ibn Abd Alsalam (2003) Qaw'aid al-Ahkam fi Islah al-Anam. Dar ibn Hazm, Cairo
Kamal Y (1990) al-Islam wa al-Madhaheb al-Iqtisadeyya al-Mu'assera. Dar Al-Waffa, Cairo
Qutb S (1993) al-Adalah al-Ijtima'eya fi al-Islam. Dar al-Shorouq, Cairo
Sayeed RM (2002) al-Mal, Mulkkeyatuh, Istithmaruh wa Infaqoh. Dar al-Wafa, Cairo
Shalabi MM (1985) al-Fiqh al-Islami: Tarekhuhu wa Madarisahu wa Nazareyatuhu: al-Mulkeyyah wa al-Aqd. Al-Dar al-Jame'eya, Beirut

Books (English)

Boldrin M, Levine KD (2002) The case against intellectual property. Michele University of Minnesota and UCLA, Minnesota
Drahos P, Mayne R (eds) (2002) Global intellectual property rights: knowledge, access and development. Oxfam

Fitzgerald A, Fitzgerald B (2004) Intellectual property in principle. Lawbook, Sydney
Hegel GWF (2001) Philosophy of right (trans: Batoche D). Books Kitchener, Ontario
Lessig L (2001) The future of ideas: the fate of the commons in a connected world. Random House
Lessig L (2004) How big media uses technology and the law to lock down culture and control creativity. Penguin Books, New York
Merges RP (2011) Justifying intellectual property. Harvard University Press, Boston
Netanel N (2008) Copyright paradox. Oxford University Press, Oxford
Patry W (2011) How to fix copyright? Oxford University Press, Oxford
Price D (2009) the development of intellectual property regimes in the Arabian Gulf States: infidels at the gates. Routledge, London
Saleh NA (1992) Unlawful gain and legitimate profit in Islamic law. Graham and Tortman, UK

Book Chapters (Arabic)

Alnadawi AA (1977) Al-Ister'ad al-Fighi li haqq al-Taleef wa al-tiba'a. In: Fathi A (ed) Haqq al-ibtikar fi al-fiqh al-islami al-moqaren. al-Resala Foundation, Beirut

Book Chapters (English)

Butler HN, Ribstein LE (2011) Legal process and the discovery of better policies for fostering innovation and growth. In: Kauffman task force on law, innovation, and growth, rules for growth: promoting innovation and growth through legal reform. Ewing Marion Kauffman Foundation
Fisher W (2001) Theories of intellectual property. In: Munzer SR (ed) New essays in the legal and political theory of property. Cambridge University Press, Cambridge

Journals

Amanullah M (2006) Author's copyright: an Islamic perspective. J World Intellect Prop
Azmi I (1996a) Basis for the recognition of intellectual property in light of the Shari'ah. Int Rev Ind Prop 27
Azmi I (2004) The philosophy of intellectual property rights over ideas in cyberspace: a comparative analysis between the western jurisprudence and the Shari'ah. Arab Law Quarterly
Bashir AHM (2002) Property rights and institutions and economic development: an Islamic perspective. Humanomics 18(3):75–91
Behdad S (1989) Property rights in contemporary Islamic economic thought: a critical perspective. Rev Soc Econ 47(2)
Beltramitti S (2009) The legality of intellectual property rights under Islamic law. Prague Yearb Comp Law 56
Boyle J (2003) The second enclosure movement and the construction of the public. Law Contemp Probl
Brogan A (1959) John Locke and utilitarianism. Ethics 69(2):79 (University of Chicago Press)
Chon M (2007) Intellectual property 'from Below' copyright and capability for education. U C Davis Law Rev 40

Cohen JE (2005) The place of the user in copyright law. Fordham Law Rev

Cullen CM (2010) Can TRIPS live in harmony with Islamic law? An investigation of the relationship between intellectual property and Islamic law. SMU Sci Tech Law

Drahos P (2004) Securing the future of intellectual property: intellectual property owners and their nodally coordinated enforcement pyramid. Case W Res J Int Law 36

Fisher WW (1988) Reconstructing the fair use doctrine. Harv Law Rev

Fitzgerald B (2003) Theoretical underpinning of intellectual property: 'I am a pragmatist but theory is my rhetoric. Can J Law Jurisprudence 16(2)

Habachy S (1962) Property, right and contract in Muslim law. Colum Law Rev

Hughes J (1988) The philosophy of intellectual property. Geo Law J

Jamar S (1992) The protection of intellectual property under Islamic law. Cap Univ Law Rev 21

Khory A (2003) Ancient and Islamic sources of intellectual property protection in the middle east: a focus on trademarks. IDEA J Law Technol 43

Lessig L (2004) Creative commons. Mont Law Rev 65

Litman J (2011) Readers' copyright. J Copyright Soc USA

Mahafzah Q et al (2009) The perspective of moral and financial rights of intellectual property in Islam. Arab Law Q 23

Naser MA, Muhaisen WH (2009) Intellectual property: an Islamic perspective. J Copyright Soc USA 56

Raslan H (2007) Shari'a and the protection of intellectual property, the example of Egypt. Intellect Prop Law Rev

Yu PK (2008) Access to medicines, BRICS alliances, and collective action. Am J Law Med 365

Others

Al-bahoty M (1997) Kashaf al-Qina ann matn al-Iqna'a. a'lem al-kutub

Alboti SM (1965) dawabit al-maslaha fi al-Shari'a al-islameya. PhD Thesis, Faculty of Shari'a Al-Azzhar University

Alghamidi NM (2003) Himayat al-mulkeyyah al-fikreyah fi al-fiqh al-Islami. Third International Conference on Islamic Economy/University of Umm Al-Qura Saudi Arabia. http://uqu.edu.sa/lib/ar/66911

Ali A (1996) Ihya al-Aradhi al-Mawat fi al-Islam. The League of the Islamic World

Al-mosleh A (1982) al-Mulkeyyah al-Khassa fi al-Shari'a al-Islameyah. The International Association of Islamic Banks

Al-sarkhasi AI (1912) al-Mabsut. Dar al-sa'a d'a

Al-zohili W (1977) Haq al-Ta'aleef wa al-Nasher wa al-Tawzi. Resala Foundation

Azmi IMBTAG (1996b) Intellectual property laws and Islam in Malaysia. PhD Thesis Submitted to the Intellectual Property Law Unit of the Centre of Commercial Law Studies, Queen Mary and Westfield College, London

Bakre AZA (1986) mulkyaat al-taleef tareekhan wa hukman. J Int Islamic Fiqh Acad 2(2)

Beheshti (1988) Ownership in Islam. (trans: Reza A Afghani Foundation of Islamic Thought Tehran)

Elmahjub E (2014) Protection of intellectual property in Islamic Shari'a and the development of the Libyan intellectual property system. PhD Thesis Submitted to Queensland University of Technology, Law School, Brisbane

Majah SI (2007) English Translation by Nasiruddin Al-Khattab. Darussalam

Mansour Kashaf al-Qina ann matn al-Iqna'a y (1997) kashaf alqina; ann matn aliqna'a. A'lem Al-kotob

Maskus KE (2000) Intellectual Property Rights in the Global Economy. Institute for International Economics

Okidiji RL (2006) The international copyright system: limitations, exceptions and public interest considerations for developing countries. International Centre for Trade and Sustainable Development (ICTSD), 32

Shalgammi HH (2004) wasa'el hemayat al-mulkeya al-fekreya fi al-fiqh al-islami wa al-qanon al-waddi. PhD Thesis, Al-Azhar University

Yaqub ibn Ibrahim (1884) Kitab al-Kharaj

Chapter 6
IP and Development: A Road Map for Developing Countries in the Twenty-First Century

Rami Olwan and Brian Fitzgerald

6.1 Introduction

The value of an intellectual property (IP) regime to a developing country is the subject of increasing debate. On one side IP evangelists argue that IP laws can stimulate untold innovation and provide a foundation for economic progress. On the other side IP sceptics or abolitionists question whether IP laws really incentivise innovation or simply represent an unforeseen burden on social and economic development. The reality for many countries is that while theoretical debates are important they do not provide immediate solutions. For this reason, we want to put the polarising debates to one side and focus on how developing countries can utilise and sensitize IP to their development needs. In order to do this in the following pages, we outline current thoughts on development theory, how it informs IP law and practice and then produce same practical suggestions about ways in which developing countries can grow and implement IP regimes that are more supportive of their needs.[1]

---

[1] Professor Madhvai Sunder note that:

> Intellectual property is essential to development, not just in the narrow sense of efficiency, but in this broader view of expanding capability for central freedoms. Surely, copyright and patents determine our access to basic needs, from educational material to lifesaving medicines. What is less obvious is that failure to be recognised as an author or inventor may impede one's access to these essential life goods by diminishing one's material wealth

R. Olwan (✉)
College of Business Administration, Sharjah University, Sharjah, 27272 United Arab Emirates (UAE)
e-mail: ramiolwan@yahoo.com

B. Fitzgerald
Thomas More Academy of Law, Australian Catholic University, 486 Albert Street, East Melbourne, VIC 3002, Australia
e-mail: Brian.Fitzgerald@acu.edu.au

© Springer International Publishing Switzerland 2015
B. Fitzgerald, J. Gilchrist (eds.), *Copyright Perspectives*,
DOI 10.1007/978-3-319-15913-3_6

85

6.1.1 The Meaning of Development

"Development" is a contested term between scholars, organizations and development experts in developed and developing countries. Nevertheless, it is one of the most important challenges facing the international community, and has been widely acknowledged in many international conventions and forums.[2] It is understood to mean improving the lives of people socially and economically. It encapsulates the improvement of individuals' lives through providing greater education, skills development, income and employment.

There is no single international definition of what is meant by the term "developing countries". The UN organizations divide developing countries into several groups of countries based on their income, education, healthcare and life expectancy.[3] The following criteria have been used to determine if a country is a developing country:

- Small Gross National Product (GNP) relative to the major players in the trade arena;
- limited domestic resources;
- exports are concentrated in terms of products and trading partners;

---

and the capability for living a full life. Stated differently, the implications in intellectual property rights go well beyond incentives for innovation: these rights are related to questions of cultural relations, social development, and GDP growth.

Sunder (2009), pp. 453 and 470.

Professor James Boyle note that:

Intellectual property laws are the legal sinews of the information age; they affect everything from the availability and price of AIDS drugs, to the patterns of international development, to the communications architecture of the Internet.

See James Boyle, *A manifesto on WIPO and the Future of Intellectual Property,* http://www.movimientos.org/foro_comunicacion/show_text.php3?key=3400

[2] These include: the United Nations Millennium Summit in 2000, the United Nations Declaration on the Right to Development of 1986, the United Nations Millennium Development Goals of 2001, the São Paulo Consensus of 2004, the Plan of Implementation agreed at the World Summit on Sustainable Development (WSSD), the Declaration of Principles of the first phase of the World Summit on the Information Society (WSIS), the Doha Declaration of 2005, the Programme of Action for the Least Developed Countries (LDCs) for the Decade 2001–2010, the Monterey Consensus, and the Johannesburg Declaration on Sustainable Development.

[3] The World Bank classified countries in 2015, according to their gross national income (GNI) per capita, into the following categories of countries:

- low income ($1,045 or less);
- lower middle income ($1,045–$4,125);
- upper middle ($4,125–$12,746); and
- high income ($12,746 or more).

World Bank, *How We Classify Countries,* http://data.worldbank.org/about/country-and-lending-groups

- high average trade barriers; and
- economic and political dependence on developed countries.[4]

Within the term of "developing countries", one might also distinguish between "Least Developing Countries" (LDCs)[5] and "emerging economies" or "newly industrialized countries".[6] According to the United Nations Conference on Trade and Development (UNCTAD), there are currently 33 countries in Africa, 14 in Asia, 1 in Latin America and the Caribbean that are considered as LDCs.[7]

It is worth mentioning that the concept of developing countries is highly controversial, IP commentators Shamnd Basheer and Annalisa Primi argue that there is a need to move away from an antiquated developed-versus-developing-countries classification and differentiate developing countries according to their technological and innovative proficiencies.[8] The problem with such a proposal is the difficulty in agreeing on the criteria used to assess and classify countries according to their technological or innovative capabilities.

6.1.2 The Theory of IP and Development

There are various theories on development formulated particularly in the 1960s suggesting that a system of IP protection is a necessary part of the evolution of states from being "under-developed" to becoming "developed".[9] Over time, European

---

[4] See Horn and Mavroidis (1999) Remedies in the WTO dispute settlement system and developing countries interests. http://www.econ-law.se/Papers/Remedies%2009990611-1.pdf.

[5] The UN uses the following three criteria for the identification of LDCs:

1. a low-income estimate of the gross national income (GNI) per capita;
2. a weak human assets as measured through a composite of Human Assets Index; and
3. a high degree of economic vulnerability as measured through a composite Economic Vulnerability Index.

See UN-OHRLLS, http://unohrlls.org/about-ldcs/criteria-for-ldcs

[6] "Emerging economies" can be defined as 'countries that are restructuring their economies along market-oriented lines and [that] offer a wealth of opportunities in trade, technology transfers, and foreign direct investment'. These countries can also be called Newly Industrialized Countries (NICs). According to the World Bank, the five biggest emerging markets are China, India, Indonesia, Brazil and Russia.

One World Nations Online, *Countries of the Third World,* http://www.nationsonline.org/oneworld/third_world.htm

[7] See UN-OHRLLS, LDCs, http://www.un.org/en/development/desa/policy/cdp/ldc/ldc_list.pdf

[8] Basheer and Primi (2009), pp. 100 and 102.

[9] See Gana (Okediji) (1996), pp. 315 and 331.

countries have required that many of their colonies in Asia, Africa and Latin America to adopt IP laws[10] to help them in their social and economic development.[11]

Scholars working in the field of IP have different views on the effect of development within the context of IP. Some agree that development could be achieved through the introduction of IP systems in developing countries whilst others are doubtful whether such systems would be sufficient to support development.[12]

It is argued that IP systems will not bring social and economic development of developing countries without the support of proper development policies. In pursuing economic development, developing countries must address a range of activities including efficient and effective government, coherent economic policies, political stability, human capital, technical infrastructure and the rule of law.[13]

It is important for the drafters of IP laws in developing countries to increase their understanding as to how IP can affect their economies and how to connect it with the economic realities of their countries. While IP may bring Foreign Direct Investment (FDI), technology transfer, domestic innovation, and Research and Development (RD) to developing countries, economic development will not occur simply through the introduction of IP laws. Policy makers in developing countries need to consider broader development initiatives in the structuring of their IP system. To this end, every provision that is introduced into the IP law should be studied and examined as a part of the broader development plan for the country.[14]

In 2004, Brazil and Argentina presented a comprehensive proposal on behalf of developing countries to establish the Development Agenda in the World Intellectual Property Organisation (WIPO). They put forward a view that IP laws in their current form are not helping those countries in their development, as is constantly being suggested by developed countries, and that there is a need to rethink the international IP system and the work of WIPO.[15] In 2007, WIPO member States

---

[10] See Gana (Okediji) (2003), pp. 315 and 324–325; Yu Peter (2009), pp. 466 and 470.

[11] Yu (2007b), pp. 1 and 4; Peter Drahos, *An Alternative for the Global Regulation of Intellectual Property Rights*, 9 http://cgkd.anu.edu.au/menus/PDFs/DrahosAustrian%20JDS%20-%20Alterna tive%20IPv2.pdf; Carolyn Deere, *Developing Countries Perspectives on Intellectual Property in the WTO: Setting the Pre- TRIPS Context*, 1–26 (1), http://papers.ssrn.com/sol3/papers.cfm? abstract_id=1405430.

[12] Gana (Okediji) (1995), p. 109; Chon (2006), pp. 2813 and 2877; Keith E. Maskus, *Intellectual Property and Economic Development* http://www.colorado.edu/Economics/mcguire/ workingpapers/cwrurev.doc. See also Odagiri et al. (2010), pp. 420 and 427.

[13] See Maskus (2008), p. 504; Maskus and Reichman (2005), p. 6; Yu (Yu 2007a), p. 214; Lee (2006), p. 160.; See Gana (1996), pp. 315, 335 and 341; Schiappacasse (2003–2004), p. 166; Beattie (2007), p. 28. Sherwood (1990); Primo Burga (1989), p. 259.

[14] Olwan (2013), p. 352.

[15] The WIPO Development Agenda proposal noted:

[T]he need to integrate the "development dimension" into the policy-making on intellectual property protection and called for, among other things, the establishment of a new subsidiary body within WIPO to examine technology transfer; a new treaty to promote access to the results of publicly-funded research in developing countries; fair enforcement of IP rights; and more development-oriented technical cooperation and assistance. The proposal concludes by

made a historic decision for the benefit of developing countries, to establish a WIPO Development Agenda[16] to ensure that IP rights are not considered in isolation, but within a broader picture of economic, social and public interests.[17] WIPO approved the Development Agenda and established a Committee on Development and Intellectual Property (CDIP) to manage its implementation.

As a consequence, research on IP and development has gained renewed momentum.[18] Many scholars and international organizations are critical of the failure of the international IP system to assist developing countries and argue that it needs to be changed to meet the development ambitions and objectives of these countries.[19]

Arguably, we have reached a critical point in history where the credibility of the international IP system is being seriously challenged. This has provided a window of opportunity for developing countries to advocate for a more accountable, transparent and humane IP system.

6.1.3 The Practice of IP and Development

In pursuing any plan for development, developing countries need to be aware of how they can tailor their IP system to their needs. In the following pages, we suggest some practical measures that we consider developing countries should explore with the aim of getting better return from their IP systems.

---

saying that "a vision that promotes the absolute benefits of intellectual property protection without acknowledging public policy concerns undermines the very credibility of the IP system. Integrating the development dimension into the IP system and WIPO's activities, on the other hand, will strengthen the credibility of the IP system and encourage its wider acceptance as an important tool for the promotion of innovation, creativity and development".

WIPO, *The Proposal by Argentina and Brazil for the Establishment of a Development Agenda for WIPO*, http://www.wipo.int/edocs/mdocs/govbody/en/wo_ga_31/wo_ga_31_11.pdf.

[16] The World Health Organization (WHO) has also launched its own development agenda with the intergovernmental Working Group on Public Health, Innovation and IP (IGWG), which is tasked with preparing a 'global strategy and plan of action', aimed at '[s]ecuring an enhanced and sustainable basis for needs-driven, essential health research and development relevant to diseases that disproportionately affect developing countries'. Lerner (2008), p. 296.

[17] See the WIPO Development Agenda, http://www.wipo.int/ip-development/en/agenda/

[18] Maskus (2008); De Beer (2009); Netanel (2009); Wong and Dutfield (2011); Melendez-Ortiz and Roffe (2010); Odagiri et al. (2010); Rizk and Shaver (2010); Shaver (2010); Chon (2006), p. 2821, http://www.abifina.org.br/arquivos/encontros/Margaret_Chon.pdf; Chon and Borges (2008), p. 71 http://papers.ssrn.com/sol3/papers.cfm?abstract_id=1081366; Margaret Chon, *Intellectual Property from Below: Copyright and Capability for Education*, 818, http://papers.ssrn.com/sol3/papers.cfm?abstract_id=971294; Sunder (2006) http://papers.ssrn.com/sol3/papers.cfm?abstract_id=897753.

[19] Professor Margaret Chon calls for the adoption of an "IP from below" approach for IP and development, See Chon (2006), pp. 2813, 2821 and 2877, http://papers.ssrn.com/sol3/papers.cfm?abstract_id=894162.

6.1.3.1   Educate Policymakers and the Public on IP and Development Issues

It is critically important to educate policy makers and those involved in the drafting of IP laws in developing countries on IP and its relationship to development theory.[20] IP can no longer be seen as a tool that is used for the sole benefit of inventors and intellectual creators, but rather it is important for many people in developing countries, as it impacts on their lives in a wide range of issues including education, innovation, creativity and health.[21]

It is important to undertake studies to evaluate the economic and cultural impacts of industries that rely on IP, in developing countries. Such studies should help understand the needs of various sectors of the economy and how they can be encouraged by IP systems. These studies would aid the drafting of appropriate IP laws which correspond with the economic and cultural needs of developing countries.

Many of the IP government organizations (such as copyright and patent offices) in developing countries need to be structured in a way to meet the needs of those countries and to help in their development. These government organizations should not only work (or be seen to be working) to promote the IP rights of foreign corporations or to increase their portfolio of IP registrations, but should also work closely with local inventors and creators, especially those who are keen to protect local culture and indigenous knowledge. This will require them to educate the public on how to use IP for the benefit of the domestic economy. They should also advise governments on the proper policies that need to be implemented in order to gain maximum benefits under the international IP systems.

Developing countries should also spread awareness among IP offices, IP scholars, international organizations and others in developing countries, of the importance of the WIPO Development Agenda and the implications that it might have on the practice of IP in those countries and beyond.

Finally, it is also important to teach people in developing countries about IP from the perspective of development. This means that IP scholars in those countries should teach IP to students in a balanced way that takes into consideration the needs of businesses as well as consumers and the general public. IP scholars in developing countries should also make sure that appropriate educational materials reflecting this approach are made available for the benefit of the students and the greater community.

---

[20] The following is a primary reading list:

- Sen (1999)
- Chang (2003); and
- Odagiri et al. (2010).

[21] See Sunder (2009), pp. 453 and 470.

6.1.3.2 Revise IP Laws and Adopt a Pro Development Perspective

As suggested before, most developing countries already have IP laws and are not in a position to repeal those laws. However, developing countries need to re-examine these IP laws to ensure that such laws are in fact of assistance to them and are not impeding their social and economic development. Such IP laws need to be structured in a way that is 'pro-development', by understanding the circumstances for each developing country, its international obligations and its local needs, and by structuring an IP system that correlates with those needs and obligations and which assists in its development. IP laws will also need to be amended from time to time to adapt to the changing needs of each developing country as it grows.

It is argued that it is important to move beyond the view that only owner centric IP laws are essential for developing countries. This could happen by adopting a more balanced view of IP that does not favour only IP owners, but also gives an equal importance to users and the public. Instead of drafting "stronger IP laws", it is more important to have appropriate laws that correspond with the needs of both IP owners and their community.[22] Furthermore, IP laws should be structured in a way that supports public policy objectives such as those relating to the transfer of technology, public health and the environment.[23]

IP laws should not be looked upon as an end in itself, but as one of a range of possible tools that developing countries can use to promote innovation, creativity, technological capacity and development.[24] It is also important to recognise IP not only from an economic perspective, but also from a cultural perspective. This requires developing countries to design IP systems that not only promote economic development, but which also promote local culture and boost local innovation.

The internet is a powerful tool and a source of opportunities that should be used by developing countries to further their development. Accordingly, it is important to make sure that IP laws in developing countries are structured in a way that does not unreasonably interfere with their citizens' usage of the internet, and to ensure that such usage contributes to their country's social and economic development. IP laws in developing countries therefore need to facilitate access to knowledge and allow citizens to develop their educational capabilities.

Finally, it is critical to acknowledge the importance of having liberal and generous limitations and exceptions in the IP laws of developing countries,[25] as

---

[22] Mary S Wong, *The Next Years in Copyright Law: An Asian Perspective*, http://papers.ssrn.com/sol3/papers.cfm?abstract_id=1017144#PaperDownload

[23] Ahmed Abdel Latif, 'A Perspective on Reform in Arab Countries' in Melendez-Ortiz and Roffe (2010), p. 53.

[24] UNCTAD, *Towards Development–Oriented Intellectual Property Policy: Advancing the Reform Agenda* http://www.iprsonline.org/unctadictsd/bellagio/docs/Bellagio2_Report.pdf

[25] For example in the field of copyright, It is also important to permit proper limitations and exceptions for students officially enrolled in a course, regardless of their physical location, and to clarify the library limitations and exceptions to cover any possible electronic use of a work in order to permit effective research, gathering and organizing information. Adequate limitations and

they are an essential part of achieving a balance between private and public rights.[26] There are many flexibilities set out in international IP agreements, including the *TRIPS Agreement*[27] that could be used to the advantage of developing countries.

6.1.3.3   Consider Seriously Alternative Approaches to IP

Some observers think that IP laws are overly restrictive when applied in the internet context. They argue that we should be looking for ways to reduce impediments to the use and reproduction of information over internet networks. This approach has not yet been fully explored in many developing countries by academics and researchers interested in IP. It is important to consider alternative approaches to managing IP including open source software, sui generis protection, public domain, open content licensing and Access to Knowledge (A2K). These alternatives could be helpful in assisting social and economic development in developing countries.

It is submitted that developing countries generally should commit resources towards launching a public awareness campaign to educate people on how best they (particularly students, teachers, archivists, academics and librarians) can access and capitalize on copyrighted materials, which they are legally entitled to access freely.[28]

It is imperative for developing countries to understand and know how to use open code and content licensing systems (voluntary mechanisms) such as Free and Open Source Software (FOSS) and Creative Commons (CC).

---

exceptions for libraries, archives and museums (including provisions for accessing and providing information; digitization; preservation and digital creation (including migration to new technologies as they change)) must be included in the copyright laws of developing countries.

See Azmi (2009), pp. 273–274.

[26] Shaver (2010), p. 68.

The Gowers Review of Intellectual Property was concerned that "the limitations in developing countries are too narrow and this may result in stunning new creators from generating and producing new works". The Gowers Review of Intellectual Property (November 2006) http://www.hm-treasury.gov.uk/d/pbr06_gowers_report_755.pdf.

Professor Margret Chon argued also that:

There is a lot of "room for manoeuvre" both for intellectual property protection in the form of copyright, on the one hand, and for limitations and exceptions to copyright in order to access knowledge goods for essential education, on the other.

Chon (2006), p. 2813, http://papers.ssrn.com/sol3/papers.cfm?abstract_id=894162

[27] A study conducted by the organization, Consumers International, has found that a number of developing countries and emerging economies including Cambodia, China, Indonesia, Malaysia, Mongolia, and the Philippines have not benefited from the flexibilities available under international copyright conventions.

See Consumers International (CI), *The CI Study on Copyright and Access to Knowledge* (2006) http://www.consumersinternational.org/media/303356/copyright%20and%20access%20to%20knowledge%20-%20full%20report%20(pdf).pdf

[28] Ibid.

According to Professor Steven Weber, FOSS could be an important tool in helping developing countries in their social and economic development,[29] especially when it has been localised for the benefit of the people working in the government, business and education sectors.

CC is also helpful for enabling developing countries to increase access to educational materials and research. It allows researchers in developing countries to legitimately access scientific and educational materials through CC licensed materials from researchers and public institutions in the developed world. This does not solve all A2K problems in developing countries, but can help these countries to access works available under permissive licences.

CC can be used by internet users, bloggers and others for encouraging wider debates and spurring innovation, remixing culture and development through the Internet.[30] There are a large number of digital works that are licensed under CC copyright licensing systems including materials available through Flickr, Massachusetts Institute of Technology Open Courseware (MIT Open Courseware), Public Library of Science: PLOS, Wikipedia and Aljazeera. Scholars, researchers and government officials in developing countries should also be encouraged to explore the use of CC "licensing out" their work to the general public especially when it is publicly funded. This would allow others to access their work and build on it.

---

[29] As Professor Steven Weber has noted that:

> Of course information technology and open source in particular is not a silver bullet for longstanding development issues; nothing is. But the transformative potential of computing does create new opportunities to make progress on development problems that have been intransigent.

The advantages of adopting FOSS in developing countries are not only economic. As Professor Steven Weber has noted:

> The potential leverage on development comes not from software itself, but from the broad organizational changes that the open source process, as a way of making software, will drive. FOSS should not be used to make up for lack of sufficient legal and economic infrastructure, or replace institutions by installing internet connections. But there are interesting possibilities for building systems of distributed innovation within emerging developing countries and emerging economies that lead to autonomous innovation. This could have a significant impact on development prospects

Weber (2004), p. 254.

[30] On 26 April 2010, CC submitted the following statement to WIPO Committee on Development and Intellectual Property (CDIP 5) in Geneva:

> We also strongly believe that Creative Commons offers developing countries opportunities to legitimately access scientific and educational materials released under a Creative Commons licence by researchers and public institutions in the developed world, something that is already taking place. We are aware that this does not solve digital divide access issues, but we believe that making the works available under permissive licences is a step in the right direction.

Tecnoliama, *CC Statement at WIPO CDIP*, http://www.technollama.co.uk/creative-commons-statement-at-wipo-cdip

6.1.3.4   Other Suggested Practical Measures

Developing countries need to be open about their development plans and should express their views and engage widely with their citizens, especially in relation to IP and development. It is also important for developing countries to work closely with international organizations working in the field of IP and development. These include Consumers International,[31] working in the field of access to knowledge; Knowledge Ecology International,[32] working in the field of IP and health; CopySouth[33] working in the field of copyright; South Centre,[34] working in global trade for development, and innovation and access to knowledge; and Electronic Information for Libraries (EIFL)[35] working for public access and libraries. Developing countries should follow the work of these international organizations and solicit their opinions in relation to IP in their jurisdictions. They should also be regular participants in any of the events and conferences that these organizations hold in the future.

It is important for any developing country that is considering entering into a Free Trade Agreement (FTA) with the US, EU or any developed country, to prepare its own strategy to deal with the consequences of signing that FTA. Any developing country that is considering entering an FTA should ask itself a number of questions. What are the social, economic, and cultural implications of signing the FTA? Does signing the FTA serve or impede social and economic development?

IP provisions should be considered to be an important part of any FTA that is signed by any developing country this is because those provisions can have a major effect on the law and practice of law in the developing country. It is important to study carefully the legal, health, educational, social and cultural implications of the IP provisions that are to be introduced in the FTA. If the FTA puts more IP obligations on the developing country than are required in the international IP treaties that it has actually signed, it should seriously consider not introducing such provisions or at least negotiate less restricted provisions that do not go beyond its international obligations.

Government institutions in the various developing countries should work together much more closely, especially in terms of sharing their experiences on how best to run their offices. Developing countries which are close to each other could develop mechanisms that allow them to achieve that coordination. For example, in relation to Traditional Knowledge (TK), a number of developing countries could work together to establish a TK database that would allow them to share their registration information. Developing countries also need to work with

---

[31] Consumers International, http://www.consumersinternational.org/

[32] Knowledge Ecology International, http://keionline.org/

[33] CopySouth, http://www.copysouth.org/portal/

[34] South Centre, http://www.southcentre.org

[35] EIFL, http://www.eifl.net/

international organizations (WIPO) and even with developed countries which offer various programs that could boost the experiences of their IP offices.[36]

To guarantee against the misuse of the IP system by any powerful corporation or owner, and to make sure it used for the benefit of the citizens and the economy, it is important for developing countries to put in place strong competition laws that support the proper use of the IP system. The competition laws should be carefully drafted to ensure that they are aligned with the country's economic circumstances and the requirements of local industry.[37]

IP laws should not simply be transposed from laws introduced in another country, even where that other country is also a developing country. The legislation should be drafted specifically for the particular developing country and should take into account the country's stage of economic development, including the extent of knowledge of IP law and its application. The laws should also be reviewed on a regular basis and revised as necessary to ensure that they meet the country's changing economic and industrial needs. A committee of legal experts and economists should be established to meet regularly to discuss the effects of competition laws on the development of the economy and to make sure that the laws are amended when required.[38]

6.1.4 Conclusion

Some of the examples of IP laws in developing countries leave a lot to be desired. If IP is a reality of daily life, developing countries need to manage it and consider how it fits with other elements needed for their development. This will require developing countries to consider their IP systems as a part of their visions for development. This article has suggested various practical measures and recommendations that developing countries could implement to ensure IP systems work in their best interests.

References

Books

Basheer S, Primi A (2009) The WIPO development agenda: factoring in the "Technologically Proficient." developing countries. In: De Beer J (ed) Implementing the world intellectual property organization's development Agenda. Wifrid Laurier
Chang HJ (2003) Kicking away the ladder-development strategy in historical perspective. Anthem
De Beer J (2009) Implementing the world intellectual property organization's development agenda. Wifrid Laurier
Lee Y-S (2006) Reclaiming development in the world trading system. Cambridge University

---

[36] Olwan (2013), pp. 351–357.

[37] Ibid.

[38] Ibid.

Maskus K (2008) Incorporating a globalized intellectual property rights regime into an economic development strategy. In: Maskus K (ed) Intellectual property, growth and trade. Elsevier

Maskus K, Reichman JH (2005) The globalisation of private knowledge goods and the privatization of global public goods. In: Maskus KE, Reichman JH (eds) International public goods and transfer of technology under globalized intellectual property regime. Cambridge University

Melendez-Ortiz R, Roffe P (2010) Intellectual property and sustainable development. Edward Elgar

Netanel NW (ed) (2009) The development agenda- global intellectual property and developing country. Oxford University

Odagiri H et al (2010) Intellectual property rights, development and catch up. Oxford University

Olwan R (2013) Intellectual property and development: theory and practice. Springer

Rizk N, Shaver L (2010) Access to knowledge in Egypt. Bloomsbury

Sen A (1999) Development as freedom. Oxford University

Shaver L (ed) (2010) Access to knowledge in Brazil. Bloomsbury

Sherwood RM (1990) Intellectual property and economic development. West View

Sunder M (2009) Intellectual property and development as freedom. In: Netanel NW (ed) The development agenda- global intellectual property and developing country. Oxford University

Weber S (2004) The success of open source software. Harvard University

Wong T, Dutfield G (2011) Intellectual property and human development. Cambridge University

Yu Peter K (2007) Intellectual property, economic development, and the China puzzle. In: Gervais D (ed) Intellectual property, trade and development-strategies to optimize economic development in a TRIPS plus era. Oxford University

Articles

Azmi IMAG (2009) Institutional repositories in Malaysia: the copyright issues. Int J Law Inform Technol 17(3):273

Barbosa D, Chon M, Borges D (2008) Slouching towards development in international intellectual property. Mich State Law Rev 2007:71

Beattie P (2007) The (Intellectual property law &) economics of innocent fraud: the IP & development debate. Int Rev Intellect Prop Competition 38(1):28

Chon M (2006) Intellectual property and the development divide. Cardozo Law Rev 27:2813

Lerner J (2008) Intellectual property and development at WHO and WIPO. Am J Law Med 34:296

Okediji R (1995) Has creativity died in the Third World? Some implications of the internationalisation of intellectual property. Denver J Int Law Policy 24:109

Okediji R (1996) The myth of development, the progress of rights: human rights to intellectual property and development. Law Policy Law J 18

Okediji R (2003) The international relations of intellectual property: narratives of developing country participation in the global intellectual property system. Singapore J Int Comp Law 7:315

Primo Burga CA (1989) The economics of intellectual property rights and the GATT: a view from the south. Vanderbilt J Transnatl Law 22:259

Schiappacasse M (2003–2004) Intellectual property rights in China: technology transfers and economic development. Buffalo Intellect Prop Law J 3:166

Sunder M (2006) IP3. Stanford Law Review 59(2)

Yu Peter K (2007) The international intellectual property regime complex: international enclosure, the regime complex, and intellectual property Schizophrenia. Mich State Law Rev 2007:1, 4

Yu Peter K (2009) Dean's lecture series: a tale of two development agendas. Ohio North Univ Law Rev 35:466

Chapter 7
Evolution and Future Trends of Copyright in Nigeria

Kunle Ola

7.1 Introduction

7.1.1 Creativity

Creativity gives expression to the ideas in the human soul. Every culture reveals an intrinsic part of itself through the creativity of her people. The Director of the Museum of Fine Arts in Boston commenting on some Nigerian artistic works said "These objects are the Benin Kingdom's legacy to the world and a testament to the brilliance and creativity of its artists".[1] The works he referred to were 34 in number, 28 made of bronze and 6 of ivory and are currently displayed at the Benin Kingdom Gallery of the Museum of Fine Arts in Boston.[2] These works include what the gallery describes as "Horseman, Battle Plaque, Double Gong, and Oba Dominating Leopards".[3]

This chapter was first published in the (2014) Journal of Open Access to Law Vol 2, No 1 and is reproduced by kind permission of the publisher.

[1] MFA (2013a).

[2] MFA (2013b).

[3] Sowole (2013).

K. Ola (✉)
Thomas More Academy of Law, Australian Catholic University, 486 Albert Street, East Melbourne, VIC 3002, Australia

Nigerian Copyright Commission, Abuja, Nigeria
e-mail: kunle.ola@acu.edu.au

© Springer International Publishing Switzerland 2015   97
B. Fitzgerald, J. Gilchrist (eds.), *Copyright Perspectives*,
DOI 10.1007/978-3-319-15913-3_7

7.1.2 Iyoba

Seating in another Museum outside the shores of Nigeria is a bone ivory sculpture known as the Queen Mother Pendant Mask-"Iyoba". Iyoba is a sculptured work of Idia, who was the Queen mother of Oba Esigie, an ancient monarch of the Bini's now part of the people of Nigeria and located in Edo State in the mid-western part of Nigeria.[4] The sculptured work dates back to the sixteenth century and its presence at the Metropolitan Museum in London serves as a reminder to the world of the creative genius of Nigerians.[5]

7.1.3 Nigeria

Nigeria is a country with over, one hundred and sixty (160) million people, 500 ethnic groups, two hundred and fifty (250) local languages (however, English is the official language), thirty-six (36) states, a Federal Capital Territory (Abuja) and seven hundred and seventy four (774) local government councils. It is the most populous African nation and the seventh most populous in the world.[6] It has a dual mixed culture, one from its traditional background and the other from its British colonial heritage. Her people are distinct in culture, tradition, belief and religion and it is these differences that bring about an enriched cultural diversity and a uniqueness in the expression of her creativity.

Nigeria's rich cultural diversity plays a key role in the creative expressions of her people and has a strong influence on the copyright based works created by Nigerians. The rise in the Nigerian entertainment industry, popularly known as Nollywood has put Nigeria on the limelight both in the music and film industries. It is therefore not surprising that Nigeria's film industry has been rated as the third largest in the world after Hollywood of the United States and Bollywood of India.[7] These creative works continue to lay credence to the creative capabilities of Nigerians and underscores the need to encourage further creativity by putting in place a strong and viable copyright system.

Creativity is the bedrock of every civilization and it encourages the transform-ation of ideas into tangible products such as articles, books, pictures, films, drawings, music, poems and drama amongst several other things. Appreciation of the value of

---

[4] The Bini's are now referred to Benin's of the Federal Republic of Nigeria and this should not be confused with Benin Republic.

[5] Metropolitan Museum of Arts, *Queen Mother Pendant Mask: Iyoba. On Display in Gallery 352., available at* http://www.metmuseum.org/collections/search-the-collections/318622.

[6] Federal Republic of Nigeria, *About Nigeria, available at* http://www.nigeria.gov.ng/2012-10-29-11-05-46.

[7] Assessing the participation of domestic SMEs in the international production chain: The case of Nu Metro in Nigeria (2010). Available at http://unctad.org/en/Docs/diaeed20095_en.pdf.

these tangibly expressed ideas often lead to commercialisation of the products. This was the situation that occurred in the United Kingdom when printers were enabled by the invention of the printing press to commercialise the writings of popular authors.[8] This practice by printers to commercially exploit the literary works of authors must have been due to the fact that printers recognised an appeal by the general public to some works and that such works if mass produced could be commercially viable. The challenge was that commercialisation of these works meant reproduction of the works and this was done without the consent of authors and apparently, with no financial benefits accruing to them. This practice gave rise to complaints and agitations which brought about the introduction of the first copyright law to protect the rights of authors to their literary works by the grant of exclusive rights to the work, for a specified period of time.[9]

Since the passage to law of the first copyright legislation, the Statute of Anne,[10] many copyright laws have been passed by national governments and the international community.[11] These laws underscore the importance of copyright and rights related to copyright also referred to as neighbouring rights to national and socio-economic development. Nigeria is one of the nations with copyright legislation[12] and plays her role within the international copyright system.

7.2 What Is Copyright?

7.2.1 Definition

Before venturing into the historical perspective of how copyright began, it would be useful to understand the term copyright. Copyright is a legal system that protects the creative outputs of authors by granting them exclusive rights to control the use of their creations for a limited time, subject to certain limitations, exceptions and statutory licensing arrangements allowing use and exploitation without the author's consent. Copyright is one of the two major heads of the field known as Intellectual Property and Intellectual Property has been defined by the World Intellectual Property Organisation (WIPO) as "creations of the mind: inventions, literary and artistic works, and symbols, names, images, and designs used in commerce".[13] Whereas, inventions, symbols, names and designs used in commerce are majorly

---

[8] Chris Butler, *FC74: The invention of the printing press and its effects at* http://www.flowofhistory.com/units/west/11/FC74.

[9] Olukunle (2013), pp. 6–7.

[10] Statute of Anne, 8 Anne c. 19 (1710).

[11] WIPO, *WIPO Administered Treaties, available at* http://www.wipo.int/treaties/en/. WIPO provides a comprehensive list of all national and international copyright legislation.

[12] Nigerian Copyright Act, Cap C28 (2004).

[13] WIPO, *What is Intellectual Property, available at* http://www.wipo.int/about-ip/en/.

under the other head of Intellectual Property known as Industrial property; copyright covers literary, artistic, musical and dramatic works. It also covers under a copyright related rights regime, broadcast, sound recording and cinematograph film works.

7.2.2 Purpose

Two purposes will be considered, economic and moral. With regards to the economic purpose, copyright encourages creativity and provides a legal regime for recouping investments put into products of creativity by granting authors exclusive rights to control the exploitation of these products for a specified period of time.[14] On the moral side, copyright protects the integrity of the created work by giving the author the right to object to any distortion, mutilation or other modifications which would be prejudicial to his honour or reputation.[15]

In achieving the economic and moral purposes of copyright, the copyright system as a whole strives to provide balance between the interest of the author and that of the user. Copyright therefore aims to ensure that the public has some form of access to the products that have been created. After all, the whole essence of externally expressing an inward idea is for public appreciation, maximal utility of the expressed idea and for the betterment of mankind.[16] Copyright is therefore meant to play some form of balancing role; that is, balancing the proprietary economic interests of the author in exploiting his created works against that of the public, to wit, accessibility to such created works by the public.

7.2.3 No Formality Required

Once a work is created, copyright is automatically conferred and its enjoyment and exercise is not subject to any form of formalities. This no formality standard for conferment of copyright stems from a series of meeting which resulted in the Berne Convention, where it was agreed that no formality requirement be placed on the exercise and enjoyment of copyright.[17] In other words, once a work has been created, it ought to enjoy the protections conferred by copyright without the need

---

[14] Section 6 (1) Cap C28 (2004). where it states "copyright … shall be the exclusive right to control the doing in Nigeria of the following…".

[15] Id. at Section 12 (b).

[16] Fitzgerald et al. (2006), p. 80. Where it was noted that "the whole purpose is information is to be shared as the purpose of bread is to be eaten".

[17] Section 5(2) Berne Convention for the Protection of Literary and Artistic Works, September 9, 1886, amended last on September 28, 1979 (September 9, 1886).

to comply with formality such as registration. It is however important to note that certain countries practice some form of registration or recordation systems for copyright but none of them make it a prerequisite for the conferment of copyright.[18]

7.2.4 Recordation System & Notification Scheme

The United States Copyright Law has a recordation system which requires registration of copyright, but it clearly notes that registration does not prevent automatic conferment of copyright once a work has been created.[19] However, in the event of copyright infringements, works originating in the United States but which have not been registered cannot be filed in respect of an infringement suit and are therefore not eligible for enforcement except they are registered.[20]

Nigeria also has a recordation system called the Notification Scheme.[21] It is not a mandatory registration scheme but rather a platform to enable authors give notice of the existence of their work in which copyright subsists. Unlike the recordation system in the United States, failure by a copyright owner to notify the Nigerian Copyright Commission through the notification scheme on the existence of a work does not affect the right of a copyright owner to commence an action in respect of an infringement suit requiring enforcement. This scheme takes its source from one of the mandates of the agency responsible for regulating and administering copyright in Nigeria.[22] The Nigerian Copyright Commission (NCC), established by virtue of Section 34 of the Nigerian Copyright Act is responsible among other things for maintaining an effective data bank of authors and their works. The Notification Scheme is the mechanism through which records of authors and their works are received and through which the databank is maintained. The Commission's Notification Scheme will be discussed later in the chapter.

7.2.5 Idea Expression Dichotomy

Copyright does not protect ideas and discoveries but may protect the form in which they are expressed. For a work to be eligible for copyright protection it must show

---

[18] WIPO, *Copyright Registration and Documentation*, *available at* http://www.wipo.int/copyright/en/activities/copyright_registration/.

[19] Section 408 The Copyright Act of 1976 Title 17 of United States Code (1976).

[20] Id. at Sections 411 and 412.

[21] NCC, *General Information on Copyright Notification Scheme*, *available at* http://www.copyright.gov.ng/index.php/regulatory-schemes/copyright-notification.

[22] See Section 34 (3) eCap C28 (2004). Section 34 in general provides for the establishment of the Nigerian Copyright Commission.

that sufficient effort has been expended on making the work to give it an original character. The work must also be in a fixed and definite form.[23]

7.3 Historical Perspective

7.3.1 King Diarmund & Statute of Anne

The history of copyright law cannot be told without reference to the Statute of Anne and truly the Statute is an important reference point to the legal expression of copyright but in reality copyright predates the Statute of Anne and has a longer historical origin than 1710. The Declaration by King Diarmund while passing judgement in respect of the dispute between Finnanin and Columcille in the sixth century in Ireland is said to have ushered copyright into the world.[24] The issue that lead to the declaration was that Finnanin accused Columcille of copying his Bible without his permission and requested that Columcille return the copied work to him. Columcille pleaded in defence that the copy made from the original copy did not take anything away from the original copy and hence no wrong could have been done. In making his decision, King Diarmund declared that "to every cow her calf; and to every book its copy".[25] This declaration set in motion the principles that protect works of creativity and established that creative works and in this case, a book had the right to enjoy protection against unauthorized exploitation. This same principle has provided guidance in the development of copyright through the ages even to this present day.

7.3.2 English Copyright Act 1911

Nigeria's copyright history is deeply connected to that of the United Kingdom because of the colonial linkage. Nigeria's copyright history can be traced from two perspectives. The first traces the history to economic and political interests by the United Kingdom which could have been linked to the growing dependence by Nigerians on literary, artistic, musical and other copyright related works originating from the west. During Britain's colonial rule over Nigeria which lasted for 60 years,[26] a new copyright law replacing the Statute of Anne was passed and by

---

[23] Section 1(2) a&b, id. at.

[24] Francis (2013).

[25] *Royal Irish Academy*, MS 24, 25. See also, Cahill (1995), pp. 14 and 170.

[26] World History, *History of Nigeria, available at* http://www.historyworld.net/wrldhis/plaintexthistories.asp?historyid=ad41.Nigeria was under British Colonization from 1900 till 1960 when she gained her Independence. British interests in Nigeria however predates 1900.

virtue of the extension order in council of 1912 of the English Copyright Act of 1911, the English copyright law became applicable in the Southern Protectorate of Nigeria. The introduction of the English copyright Law to Nigeria represents the first perspective. The second is of the opinion that copyright has been and is an intrinsic part of the customs and traditions of the people of Nigeria. This view points to the practice where dancers and singers pay homage to their ancestors and predecessors in the trade before they commence their performances. The intent for acknowledgement is the traditional believe that if the current performers desire to succeed, homage must be paid to their ancestors and predecessors in the trade and such homage will attract the requisite blessings. They also point to the practice where money, gifts, refreshment and other forms of remuneration is given to the performers in appreciation and recognition of their performances.[27] All these practices go to the root of the modern copyright concepts of moral and economic rights. Both perspectives support the importance of respect, appreciation and some form of remuneration for the efforts of those who have produced creative works. It is without contention however that the extension of the English Copyright Act of 1911 to Nigeria in 1912 introduced into Nigeria's legal system, a copyright legal framework.

The introduction of the English Copyright Act of 1911 (hereinafter referred to as CA 1911), in Nigeria made very little impact on the ordinary Nigerian's day to day life and this was probably due to cultural differences between the people that originated the CA of 1911 and those to whom it was now being applied in Nigeria. At the time of the enactment of the CA 1911, writing had become a way of life in the United Kingdom, expressing ideas be they original or non-original in fixed tangible forms had become the general mode of communication and constituted important elements in the 'fixation and originality' requirements for what would qualify as a copyright work.[28] In Nigeria however, the predominant mode of communication at the time was through verbal and non-written modes. Information was passed down from one generation to the other verbally, that is through word of mouth. Songs were composed and given life not by being written down but by it being sung. Many a times, singers pick up their inspiration while performing and songs are delivered extempore. The audience is the only living evidence that the songs exist. Excluding sculptures and other artistic works which were naturally expressed in fixed form, musical and dramatic works were expressed verbally and were rarely expressed as literary works.[29]

Furthermore, the Nigerian tradition that favours communal ownership and encourages the spirit of camaraderie and free sharing was at variance with the individualistic and proprietary nature of the modern concepts of copyright. In the eyes of the ordinary person, the laws did not exist and would have been regarded as just another administrative process introduced by the colonial masters. The Act

---

[27] Adewopo (2012).

[28] Davis (2008), p. 28. Particularly at 2.12, 2.14 & 2.15.

[29] Asein (2012).

however provided the first legislative framework for Nigeria's administration of a copyright system and provided the basis for further development of copyright laws in Nigeria. This Act continued in force through independence in 1960 until 1970 when the first indigenous Copyright Act was promulgated.

7.3.3 The Copyright Act, 1970

The 1970 Act was passed as a decree on the 24th day of December in 1970 under the then General Gowon led military government of Nigeria. The legislation had twenty (20) sections and three (3) schedules. It provided for works eligible for copyright, conferment of copyright, nature of copyright in certain works, first ownership, assignment and licensing, infringement and actions for infringement. The Act provided powers for the appointment of a competent authority to resolve copyright licensing conflicts but the said powers were never activated throughout the life of the legislation.[30] Nigeria being a party to the Universal Copyright Convention (UCC)[31] provided for reciprocal extension of protection and placed restrictions on importation of printed copies. Reliance on copyright deriving its source from common law rights were abrogated and the enactment allowed for the making of regulations to fill any lacuna which the enactment left out or which may arise. The sections providing for repeals, transitions and saving provisions as well the interpretations and citation sections were the last three sections.

The First Schedule to the Act provided for the term of copyright and interestingly reduced the term of copyright from 50 years after the death of the author as reflected in the earlier CA 1911 legislation to 25 years for literary, musical and artistic works. For photographs it provided for 25 years after the end of the year in which the work was first published in contrast to that of the CA 1911 which provided for 50 years from the making of the original. That amounted to a 25 years reduction.

The Copyright Act 1970 being the first indigenous act was expected to protect the Nigerian interest and be reflective of the peculiarities of her people as well as their culture and traditions. This may have accounted for why it cut down the term of copyright to 25 years from 50 years, after all the Nigerian traditional culture is more disposed to a culture of sharing as opposed to the proprietary system. The cut down has however been viewed as a negative move in that the Nigerian copyright owners expected to have retained at least the same rights provided by a non-indigenous legislation and that the indigenous legislation would provide enhanced and more favourable rights, instead it cut down on the term of copyright and was in general terms a watered-down version of the English Copyright Act of 1911. The Act while making provisions on copyright failed to designate any particular

---

[30] OLA, Copyright Collective Administration in Nigeria Lessons for Africa 28, Springer 2013.
[31] UNESCO (1952).

authority to oversee copyright issues in Nigeria. The legislation was basically a lame duck and at this time the local copyright based industry in Nigeria was beginning to grow and required a firm policy structure to support this local industry from a local and international perspective.[32] Concerns about the lacuna in the 1970 Act led to agitation in the copyright based industries which eventually led to the 1988 Copyright Act. Okoroji captured the frustration succinctly when he said

> The very weak provisions of Decree No 61 of 1970, the copyright law then in force, was identified as the major obstacle to effective confrontation of the copyright problem. The civil provisions were cumbersome and had many loop holes... The criminal sanctions... were laughable. There was no provision for any imprisonment. There was therefore very little legal deterrent against piracy... It became very clear that the most important and urgent task ... was to get an effective copyright law promulgated in Nigeria.[33]

7.3.4   The 1988 Copyright Act

The end of the Nigerian civil war in 1970 coincided with Nigeria's oil boom which brought immense wealth to Nigeria. With lots of money to spend and people needing to get back their lives, entertainment offered comfort and further developed into an important industry in Nigeria. Highlife was in high demand and the likes of Sir Victor Uwaifo, Osita Osadebe, Victor Olaiya, Cardinal Rex, Jim Lawson and Celestine Ukwu met these entertainment needs through life performances and productions with Philips Ijora Causeway studios in Lagos Nigeria. Philips which later became phonogram was not the only point of production at the time, there was also Polygram which later became Premier and then EMI which changed to Ivory, DECCA and then Afrodisia. Popular Nigerian artists such as Fela Anikulapo Ransome-Kuti known for his Afro-beat Music, Sunny Okosun for his popular singles "Fire in Soweto"[34] and Mother & Child", Bongos Ikwue for "Beautiful woman" all produced with EMI. EMI also sold foreign produced works, such as those of Bob Marley, Peter Tosh, Jimmy Cliff and Jonny Nash amongst several others. Indigenous producers were also thriving and made big hits. Homzy Sounds produced the popular "Love Nwantinti" performed by Nelly Uchendu. Another indigenous producer was Rogers All stars who produced what may be regarded as one of Nigeria's most impacting songs "Sweet Mother" performed by Prince Nico Mbarga and the Rocafil Jazz Orchestra.[35] In the midst of all these developments in the entertainment industry, technological development enabled the invention of the cassette player and cassettes which further brought about cheaper and easier copying. A proliferation of facilities to mass produce works on cassettes brought

---

[32] Wikipedia, *Music of Nigeria, available at* http://en.wikipedia.org/wiki/Music_of_Nigeria#The_1950s.2C_.2760s_and_.2770s.

[33] Okoroji (2008).

[34] Author, *Fire in Soweto* (Youtube).

[35] Okoroji (2008).

about piracy challenges in the entertainment industry. Producers, authors and performers were all concerned about the high level of piracy.[36] The same effects were being felt in the publishing industry as well. This led to setting up an Anti-Piracy Vanguard made up of the music and publishing industries.[37] Despite several anti-piracy raids and collaborations with the police, piracy was on the rise and the copyright law which had been recently passed had no teeth to bit and therefore did not deter the pirates from their acts. The Nigerian copyright industry frustrated and agitated identified legislative reform as one of the cardinal issues in combatting the challenges posed by piracy. After series of meetings and lobbying the 1988 copyright legislation was passed and became a part of the Nigerian legal system.

The Act was promulgated under a military administration and was therefore passed as a decree. The Act has been amended twice, firstly in 1992 and secondly in 1999. In 2004, the laws were re-codified under the laws of the federation of Nigeria. The recodification changed the numbering of the sections but its contents are still the same. The Act when passed in 1988 had 41 sections but the combined effect of the recodification and the amendments to the Act has moved the number of sections to 53 sections while retaining the original number of parts and schedules, that is, four parts and five schedules.

The four parts provide for the following:
Part I: Copyright,
Part II: Neighbouring rights,
Part III: Administration of copyright and
Part IV: Miscellaneous.
The five schedules to the act cover the following:
First Schedule: Terms of copyright,
Second Schedule: Exceptions from copyright control
Third Schedule: Special exceptions in respect of a sound recording of a musical work respectively.
Fourth Schedule: Compulsory licences for translation and reproduction of certain works
Fifth Schedule: Translation and savings provisions.

7.3.5 Works Eligible for Copyright Under the Act

Works eligible for copyright the world over are generally similar but there exist some differences depending on the jurisdiction. Under the Nigerian Copyright Act, six works are particularly mentioned as eligible for copyright. They are as follows: **literary, musical and artistic works; cinematograph films, sound recordings**

---

[36] Nigerian Copyright Commission (2008). See the foreword at page v.

[37] Okoroji (2008).

and broadcasts.[38] The first three works form the core of copyright while the last three, are bye products of the first three. They are the economic and commercial end of the first three and are referred to as neighbouring or related rights. Therefore in the discussions on copyright in this section, the focus will be on the first three (literary, musical and artistic) and when reference is made to the last three (cinematograph films, sound recordings and broadcasts), it is in respect of neighbouring rights.

For a work to be eligible for copyright under the act, sufficient effort must have been expended on the work to give it an original character and it must have been fixed in a definite medium directly perceivable or perceivable with the aid of any device or machine.[39] The fact that the making of a work involved some form of copyright infringement would not alone constitute grounds for ineligibility.[40]

7.3.6 Conferment of Copyright

Once a work is eligible for copyright, copyright may be conferred on such a work through a number of channels.

   i. **By virtue of nationality or domicile**: The author(s) is a citizen of or is domiciled in Nigeria or an organisation/company duly registered under the laws of Nigeria.[41]

   ii. **By reference to country of origin**: The work was first published or made in Nigeria.[42]

   iii. **In Works of government, State authorities and International bodies**: The work is made under the direction of the government, a state authority or an international body.[43]

   iv. **Reference to International agreements**: The work is made by a person who on the date of the first publication of the work, such person was a citizen of a country or domiciled in a country to which Nigeria is a party to an obligation in a treaty or other international agreement; or where the work was first published in a country where Nigeria has treaty obligations, or where it was first published in either of the following organisations, the United Nations or any of its specialised agencies, the African Union or the Economic Communities of West African States.[44]

---

[38] Section 1 (1) (a)–(f) Cap C28 (2004).

[39] Id. at Section 1 (2) (a) & (b).

[40] Id. at Section 1 (4).

[41] Id. at Section 2.

[42] Id. at Section 3.

[43] Id. at Section 4.

[44] Id. at Section 5.

7.3.7 Powers of a Copyright Owner

The author of a copyright work or the owner of copyright enjoys certain exclusive rights. These rights operate as restrictive rights in that the author is empowered by copyright to control the doing of certain actions and without his consent or authorization, such works may not be carried out. The doing of any of such works without consent amounts to an infringement of the right of the author or the copyright owner. Sections 6–9 of the Act provides for the general nature of copyright and provides for the exclusive actions that the author/copyright owner controls. These exclusive actions include reproducing, publishing, performing, translating, making any cinematograph film or a record in respect of the work, distributing to the public for hire or for commercial purpose copies of the work, communicating to the public and making an adaptation of the work. The doing of any of the afore-mentioned actions amounts to copyright infringement which carry consequence both in the civil and criminal realms.

7.3.8 Infringement of Copyright

An important part of the legislation are the infringement provisions of the Act which provide for both civil and criminal actions which may be instituted simultaneously.[45] The Act specifically states amongst other things when prescribing copyright infringement that

> Copyright is infringed by any person who without the licence or authorisation of the owner of the copyright
> (a) does or causes any other person to do an act, the doing of which is controlled by copyright; (b) imports or causes to be imported into Nigeria any copy of a work which, if it had been made in Nigeria would be an infringing copy under this section of this Act;. . .[46]

In the event of an infringement, the copyright owner, assignee or exclusive licensee may bring an action before the Federal High Court and may claim for damages, injunctions and/or accounts. Ignorance is a defence to copyright infringement, but it must be proved that at the time of the infringement the defendant was actually unaware and had no reasonable grounds to suspect that copyright subsisted in the work. In such situations plaintiffs are not entitled to damages but rather account for profits in respect of the infringement.[47]

The Act criminalises copyright infringement with Section 20 of the Act providing conviction or fine and conviction and fine punishment to those found guilty. It provides that where a person is found guilty of making or causing to be made for sale, hire or other commercial purposes any infringing copy, or imports or causes to

---

[45] Id. at Section 24.

[46] Id. at Section 15 (1).

[47] Id. at Section 16 (3).

be imported into Nigeria a copy of any work which if it had been made in Nigeria would be an infringing copy, or makes, causes to be made or has in his possession, any plate, master tape, machine, equipment or contrivances, for the purpose of making any infringing copy of any such work, such a person shall be liable to a fine of an amount not exceeding N1,000 for every infringing copy or a term of imprisonment not exceeding 5 years, or to both such fine and imprisonment. The criminal provisions with stiff penalties have been tested in the courts and have in many ways served as deterrence to further copyright infringements.

7.3.9 Court Convictions

In the cases of **NCC V Godwin Kadiri**,[48] **NCC V Michael Paul**[49] **and NCC V Emordi Henry Chukwuma**[50] all on charges infringing broadcast rights, the defendants were all found guilty. In the case of NCC V Godwin Kadiri, which held in the Benin judicial division, the defendant was sentenced to serve a 6½ years jail term with no option of fine and is being made to serve two jail terms. In NCC V Emordi Henry Chukwuma and NCC V Micheal Paul which were heard in the Abuja and Lafia jurisdictions of Nigeria, they were both sentenced upon conviction to pay fines of N10,000 and 5,100 respectively. Convictions have been made with regards to infringements of other works. In **NCC V Nwoke Isreal**,[51] the Lagos judicial division of the Federal High Court, convicted and sentenced the defendant to 1 year imprisonment without the option of fine for infringing upon literary rights. In **NCC V. Anoke Celestine** on charges bordering on infringements of sound recording and cinematograph film rights, the Benin judicial division of the federal high court sentenced the defendant to 10 months imprisonment.

7.4 Nigerian Copyright Commission

7.4.1 Establishment

The 1999 amendment to the Act amongst other things established a body responsible for all matters affecting copyright in Nigeria known as the Nigerian Copyright Commission.[52] Although the Nigerian Copyright Act was passed in 1988, it was not

---

[48] NCC V GODWIN KADIRI, FHC/B/43C/2010 (Federal High Court, Benin-City. 17/12/2012).

[49] NCC V MICHAEL PAUL, FHC/LF/CR/2/2013 (Federal High Court, Lafia 3/10/2013).

[50] NCC V EMORDI HENRY CHUKWUMA, FHC/ABJ/CR/90/2013 (Federal High Court, Abuja. 19/06/2013).

[51] NCC V NWOKE ISREAL, FHC/L/159C/2013 (Federal High Court, Lagos 6/05/2013).

[52] Cap C28 (2004). Section 34.

until August 1989 that the Nigerian Copyright Council was established by virtue of Decree No. 47 of 1988 and in 1996 government approved that it become the Nigerian Copyright Commission. The 1999 Amendment to the Act gave legislative effect to the government's earlier approval. The Nigerian Copyright Council has it then was, was only saddled with copyright administrative responsibilities but with the amendments to the Act, its mandate was extended to cover enforcement and it became a full-fledged enforcement agency with perpetual succession.[53] The Commission was given certain powers such as powers to grant compulsory licenses,[54] approval of organisations desirous of operating as collecting societies,[55] powers to make regulations subject to the approval of the Minister[56] and powers to appoint copyright inspector inclusive of all police powers.[57] The combined effect of these provisions upgraded the status of the Commission from an administrative agency to an enforcement agency.

In addition to the responsibility provided in Section 34 (3) a, that is, to administer all matters affecting copyright in Nigeria, Section 34 (3) b–f of the Act provides for other functions of the Commission as follows:

b) monitor and supervise Nigeria's position in relation to international conventions and advise government thereon;
c) advise and regulate conditions for the inclusion of bilateral and multilateral agreements between Nigeria and any other country;
d) enlighten and inform the public on matters relating to copyright;
e) maintain an effective databank on authors and their works;
f) be responsible for such other matters as relate to copyright in Nigeria as the Minister may from time to time direct.

7.4.2 Strategies

In carrying out the above functions, the Commission over time has adopted several strategies. In 2005, the Commission launched the Strategic Action Against Piracy (**STRAP**) which had three core components namely, mass enlightenment, rights administration and enforcement. This strategy also entailed an alternative dispute resolution (ADR) component tagged Copyright Litigation and Mediation Programme (**CLAMP**) which enable out of court settlements in the event of misunderstandings.[58] The focus of STRAP when launched was to reduce the menace

---

[53] Nigerian Copyright Commission NCC, *About NCC Historical Background, available at* http://www.copyright.gov.ng/index.php/about-us/ncc-historical-background.

[54] Cap C28 (2004). Section 37.

[55] Id. at Section 39 (1).

[56] Id. at Section 45.

[57] Id. at Section 38. This section was introduced into the Act through the 1992 Amendment to the Act as Section 32A.

[58] Nigerian Copyright Commission NCC (2008).

caused by piracy through strategic engagement with the general public and with stakeholders through targeted enlightenment programs, effective rights administration and where necessary through enforcement. The current administration of the Commission has re-adapted STRAP into what is now called a Medium Term Corporate Plan and Strategy (**MTCPS**) 2012–2014 and has the following ten critical goals:

1. Improving the Policy and Legislative Framework for copyright Protection
2. Enhancing copyright Awareness and Education
3. Promoting Effective Rights Management and Regulation of copyright Industries
4. Proactive Enforcement Interventions
5. Strengthening Prosecutorial Activities
6. Strengthening Human and Institutional Capacity for Better Service Delivery
7. Deepening Strategic Engagement with Stakeholders
8. Expanding International Cooperation
9. Strong Public Private Partnership
10. Enhancing the Funding Profile of the Commission

The objective of the Commission either through STRAP, CLAMP or MTCPS is to harness and maximise the creative genius of Nigerians for national development and global influence through dissemination of copyright knowledge, effective rights administration and protection of rights.[59]

7.4.3 Public Enlightenment

Enlightenment in any society is crucial because it provides requisite information and empowers ordinary citizens with the knowledge required to interact in the society. The esoteric nature of copyright makes it somewhat complex for the ordinary person to comprehend or appreciate what copyright is, what it does and how it works. Many copyright owners do not understand what it is and how it works and hence do not know what rights they have and what users can do without the need for authorization. When copyright is infringed, right owners need to know what to do, who and where to go to. Similarly, if users feel cheated or do not understand certain issues regarding copyright, they ought to know where to go to seek relevant information and to get some sense of fairness and justice.

Under STRAP and now vigorously pursued under MTCPS, the Commission in furtherance of its vision to disseminate copyright knowledge set up the training arm of the Commission called the Nigerian Copyright Institute which is responsible amongst other things for training both the members of staff and the general public on issues of copyright. The institute carries out regular training programs for staff members, agencies of government, the judiciary, stakeholders, Intellectual Property

---

[59] NCC (2012). See page 3 where it mentions the vision, mission and strategies of the Commission.

lawyers and the general public.[60] The Commission has also embarked on several enlightenment campaigns in furtherance of one of her core mandates as contained in Section 34 (2) d of the Act, that is to "enlighten and inform the public on matters relating to copyright;". Below is a list of some activities the Commission has been involved in as noted in its 2012 Annual Report.

1. Developed and placed Nigerian Copyright Commission's anti-piracy jingle on DSTV Channels 114 and 118
2. Sustained periodic engagement with the press. Ten (10) press briefings were organized and several press releases issued on the state of copyright enforcement and administration in Nigeria.
3. Effectively implemented an interactive website that is constantly updated with information on the Commission's activities and relevant issues on copyright.
4. Dissemination of copyright information at the 2012 edition of the Creativity Week co-organised with the Federal Ministry of Culture and Tourism.
5. Issuance of press release, production and distribution of posters to raise public awareness on copyright during this year's commemoration of World Intellectual Property Day on 26th April 2012. The World Intellectual Day is aimed at drawing attention to the phenomenal contributions of intellectual property to fast-tracking the pace of development of the knowledge-driven economies of our modern world.
6. Celebration of the World Book and Copyright Day through issuance of press release and distribution of leaflets to raise public awareness on copyright. The World Book and Copyright Day is celebrated every 23rd April to acknowledge the significance of books and pay tribute to authors.
7. Produced a variety of publicity materials on "Copyright System in Nigeria"; "Copyright Administration in Nigeria"; and a "Stop Piracy Now" slogan.
8. Conducted anti-piracy sensitization campaigns at different piracy endemic markets across south-south and south-east geo-political zones in Nigeria, namely Alaba International Market Lagos; Ochanja Market Onitsha and Ariara Market, Aba. It entailed a sensitization talk on the Commission's zero tolerance for piracy and distribution of publicity materials.
9. Organized a "Basic Copyright Training for the Media" for the staff of African Independent Television (AIT) on 6 June 2012.
10. Carried out anti-piracy sensitization exercises against book piracy in Zaria, Central Market, Chang Chang Market, Kakuri and Sabo Market, Kaduna in September 2012. The public enlightenment focused on the ills of book piracy in the socio-economic growth and development of our country
11. Organized an induction training and sensitization workshop on copyright for students at the Nigerian Law School campuses in Abuja and Lagos in November 2012. The workshop exposed students to the basics of copyright.[61]

---

[60] Nigerian Copyright Commission NCC, *Nigerian Copyright Institute*, *available at* http://www.copyright.gov.ng/index.php/2013-02-10-16-11-10/nigerain-copyright-institute-nci.

[61] NCC (2012), pp. 10–11 where the activities where listed under the heading "Enhancing Copyright Awareness and Education".

7.4.4 Rights Administration

When the 1988 copyright legislation was passed, the agitations leading to the legislation was centred on the outcry for greater protection of the rights of copyright owners.[62] To ensure protection of these rights, the Commission has been saddled with the responsibility for all matters affecting copyright in Nigeria and this responsibility is both symbolic and significant. It is symbolic because the Commission has been made the designated reference point for all copyright matters in Nigeria and it is significant because whilst the Commission protects the rights of copyright owners, it simultaneously must protect the rights of user. It must therefore carry out this very sensitive role of maintaining an uncertain balance and must at the same time avoid delving into the arena of conflict. To achieve this symbolic and significant role, the Commission has been involved in and has also developed a number of mechanisms to administer copyright in Nigeria. These mechanism include administration of the following:

7.4.4.1 Copyright (Reciprocal Extension) Regulation 1972

This regulation was issued to enable the extension of copyright protection in works protected under the Act to countries to which Nigeria shares treaty obligations. The regulation was issued on the 1st of February 1972.[63]

7.4.4.2 Copyright (Security Devices) Regulation 1999

Advancement in technology has enabled the invention of machines such as the photocopiers, printers, cassette recorders and other recording machines. These machines have made it much easier to reproduce contents and a lot of these contents are copyright protected. Section 21 of the Nigerian Copyright Act empowers the Commission to prescribe the use of any anti-piracy device for use on any work in which copyright subsists. The intention is dual; first of which is to help the general public identify genuine products and secondly to curb the menace of piracy thereby providing authors an additional incentive for further creativity and for copyright owners to recoup their investments. In view of the above, the Commission issued the Copyright (Security Devices) Regulation 1999 which majorly focused on the issuance of hologram stamps.[64] The regulation was issued on the 7th of September 1999.[65]

---

[62] NCC, About NCC Historical Background.

[63] Nigerian Copyright Commission NCC (1972).

[64] Adewopo (2011), p. 186.

[65] Nigerian Copyright Commission NCC (1999a).

7.4.4.3   Copyright (Video Rental) Regulations 1999

As the hiring and renting of video cassettes, cd's and dvd's became common in most parts of Nigeria, the need to consider the issue of sells, rentals and hiring of cinematograph films became imperative. The practice amongst those involved in video rental was to buy one video cassette, cd or dvd, reproduce the single copy into multiple copies and then rent them out to as many people as were willing to rent or hire them. To the ordinary mind, this meant that the general public appreciated the films and that the actors were becoming famous. On the contrary, what was happening was that illegal reproduction, sells, rentals and hiring of cinematograph (audio–visual) works was taking place. These acts by virtue of the Nigerian copyright laws constitute infringement of copyright.[66] In addressing these new challenges, the Commission came up with the Copyright (Video Rental) Regulations. The regulations prescribed the issuance of a rental copy, which copy was meant to be produced by the copyright owners and would be purchased by the rental shops.[67] The intention was that hiring, rentals, leasing or distributing in the public for commercial purposes would be regulated by the use of rental copies. A task force to monitor the rental shops would ensure compliance. This regulation was issued on the 7th of September 1999.[68] The major challenges to the regulation remain the failure of the industry to produce the prescribed rental copies. Another challenge is that the cost of purchasing cinematograph films in Nigeria have become very cheap due to competitions between optical discs manufacturing plants, Asian importation of pirated films and multiple cinematograph films on a single disc.

7.4.4.4   Copyright Notification Scheme

The notification scheme of the Commission is the mechanism through which a national copyright databank of authors and their works are kept.[69] This scheme is not a mandatory registration system and does not confer any additional right than what copyright already confers. The scheme operates by encouraging authors to notify the Commission of the existence of copyright in their creative endeavours or the transfer of such copyright. The advantage of the scheme is that one's work is in the databank of the commission and in the event of litigation or uncertainty, it could constitute prima-facie proof of the date of the existence of the work. Works eligible for notification include, literary, musical, artistic, cinematograph films, sound recording and computer programmes and may be filed by the author, the copyright

---

[66] See Section 20 (2) a, b, c & d. Cap C28 (2004).

[67] Regulation 5(1&2) Nigerian Copyright Commission NCC (1999b).

[68] Id. at.

[69] S.34 (2) e Cap C28 (2004).

owner, an assignee, a licensee, an agent or a transferee. The Copyright Notification Scheme was introduced in 2005.[70]

7.4.4.5 Copyright (Optical Disc) Regulation 2006

This regulation became imperative to address the issue of piracy from the point of production.[71] The discovery of two pirate plants in 2004 and 2005 necessitated the regulation. Prior to the discovery of the plants, works in which copyright subsists and embedded on optical discs were imported into Nigeria from Asia. The aim of the regulation was therefore to identify the sources of production and provide a legal regime for optical disc manufactures and producers to operate within a regulated legal framework. The regulation which requires all manufactures, importers and producers of optical discs and production parts to be registered with the Commission was issued on the 15th of December 2006.[72]

7.4.4.6 Copyright (Collective Management Organisation) Regulations 2007

Authors all over the world create works which users enjoy. Works made by authors find their way around the world and users continue to discover new works and use them. Considering that the human race is currently above seven billion and the number is still on the increase, all seven billion humans are potential users as well as potential creators of copyright works. Creative works enjoy copyright protection and except use of such works fall under some form of limitation and exception, the current legal regime for copyright requires that authorisation be obtained from the copyright owner prior to use. However, considering the vast number of copyright owners and users, it is impracticable to expect every user to track down every copyright owner and obtain the requisite authorisation.[73] To address the above challenge, collective management organisations (CMO) exist to negotiate on behalf of copyright owners and grant licences to users as well as to collect payments from users and distribute royalties on an agreed rate to copyright owners. CMO's could therefore be considered as a one stop shop for clearing copyright contents in the interest of both copyright owners and the user publics.

---

[70] Nigerian Copyright Commission NCC (2005).

[71] Adewopo (2011).

[72] Nigerian Copyright Commission NCC (2006).

[73] OLA, Copyright Collective Administration in Nigeria Lessons for Africa 8. 2013. "The rationale for this system of management arises from the impracticability of managing these activities individually, namely the inability of the individual right owner to personally monitor and enforce all of his rights in every situation".

Considering the above and that Nigeria has a growing creative industry, the need for collective management organisations to serve both the copyright owner and the user community cannot be overemphasized. In 1993, the first regulation in this regards was issued and more recently, the Copyright (Collective Management Organisation) Regulations 2007 was issued which repealed the earlier regulation.[74] Two organisations are currently approved as collective management organisations, Reprographic Rights Organisation of Nigeria (REPRONIG) for the literary industry and Copyright Society of Nigeria (COSON) for the music industry.

7.4.4.7 Copyright (Levy on Materials) Order 2012

This is the most recent regulation issued by the commission. It takes its route from the provisions of the Act in Section 40 which provide for levies on copyright materials and more directly mandates the payment of a levy on any material capable of being used to infringe copyright in a work. The intendment of the regulation is to create a platform where right-owners are able to receive some form of remuneration for the exploitation of their work however through a compulsory licensing methodology. The order prescribes levies payable in respect of materials used or capable of being used to infringe copyright. The rationale for the scheme lies in the need to ensure that right owners are properly remunerated for their works whilst at the same time enabling users exploit the work without any fear of contravening the legal provisions of any Law(s). The regulation was issued in 2012.[75]

7.4.5 Enforcement

In addition to public enlightenment and rights administration, the Commission uses enforcement mechanisms in tackling the challenges in the industry. It does this in collaboration with the traditional enforcement agencies in the country such as the Nigerian Police Force (NPF), the Nigerian Customs Services (NCS), the Economic and Financial Corruptions Commission (EFCC) and other non-enforcement sister agencies. The Commission shares information with other agencies and maximizes available platforms. The Commission embarks on regular anti-piracy raids, arrests and prosecution of pirates. These raids are conducted in conjunction with sister organisations and cover notorious areas such as well-known markets where the products are usually trafficked and the borders through which the products are known to be brought in or taken out.

---

[74] Nigerian Copyright Commission NCC (2007). The earlier regulation was called Copyright (Collecting Societies) Regulation 1993.

[75] Nigerian Copyright Commission NCC (2012).

In the discharge of the Commission's enforcement mandate, the Commission carries out its operations through Copyright Inspectors who are empowered by Section 38 of the Act to enter, inspect and examine any premises they reasonably believe is being used for infringing activities. They are also empowered to seize items which they reasonably suspect to be infringing items as well as to arrest any person who they reasonably believe has committed an offence as stipulated by the Act.

In the Commission's 2012 annual report, successful enforcement activities were listed some of which are provided here-under as follows:

1. Conduct of over sixty (60) anti-piracy surveillances by the operatives of the Commission in piracy endemic locations across the country.
2. Carrying out of fifty-five (55) strategic anti-piracy operations against book, software, broadcast and audio-visual piracy in different piracy hotbeds across Nigeria, including Alaba International Market, Ojuelegba and Ijora in Lagos; Ariara Market Aba; Onitsha; Kano; Benin City and so on.
3. Arrest of 84 suspected pirates
4. Removal of 3,621,787 quantities of assorted pirated copyright works, comprising of books, software, DVDs, CDs etc from different piracy outlets and seaports across Nigeria with an estimated market value of four billion, three hundred and seventy-nine million, four hundred and thirty-one thousand Naira (N4,379,431,000).
5. Unprecedented confiscation of a total of thirteen (13) containers at different seaports across Nigeria in collaboration with the Nigerian Customs Service. Whereas, eleven (11) of the containers were stacked with pirated books of Nigerian and foreign authors, the remaining two (2) contained pirated musical and film works of local and foreign titles.
6. Drastic reduction in the activities of pirates, resulting in an over 50 % increase in the profit margin of genuine investors in the copyright-based industries, creation of employment and a boost in the tax earnings of government from the industry practitioners. For instance, the Copyright Society of Nigeria (COSON), a collecting society for music and sound recordings shared a total of one hundred million Naira (N100,000,000) to their members as royalty paid for the use of music of its members. Distribution of such an amount of money is unprecedented in the annals of a collecting society in Nigeria.
7. Robust and enhanced monitoring of optical disc plants manufacturing outlets to ensure compliance with relevant extant laws and generate revenue for government. More specifically, three (3) inspections of optical disc replicating plants were conducted in the replicating facilities of ECOMAX, Dalla Music, Transerve Disc, Chronotec, Nasinma, Hoperising, Mediapro, Skymedia, Nira Sound Laboratories, Infobright Ltd and Alfa Magnetics within the period under review.
8. Public burning of 722 million units of pirated works and contrivances estimated at N6.5 billion, comprising literary, musical, film works and contrivances, including those from the broadcast industries, which were confiscated between

2007 and 2011. The purpose was to demonstrate the Commission's commitment to its zero tolerance policy on piracy and to send out a warning signal that piracy would no longer be a profitable venture.[76]

7.5 The Future of Copyright in Nigeria

As noted at the beginning of this chapter, Nigeria is a nation rich in creativity. The pre-colonial era provides evidence of this in the artistic works seating in the museum in the western parts of the world. Today, Nigeria's Nollywood, the third largest film industry in the world is also evidence of Nigeria's rich and ingenious creativity. Nigeria's collective management organisation in music, copyright society of Nigeria (COSON) in 2011 and 2012 distributed royalties of 25 million naira in 2011 and 100 million naira in 2012 to members of the society.[77] The legal framework covering copyright in Nigeria has been instrumental to these developments as well as the STRAP and now MTCPS strategies adopted in carrying out mandates on copyright administration in Nigeria. The future of Nigeria like any other country is intrinsically tied to its ability to harness the potentials in her people as the world has since moved from dependence on an industrial based economy to a knowledge based economy with structural frameworks protected under the laws of intellectual property of which copyright is a core component. If Nigeria must play a significant role in this new frontier, there is the urgent need for strategic repositioning to ensure maximal benefits in today's global knowledge based economy and tomorrow's dynamic technologically driven market.

7.5.1 Internet Treaties

In 1996, the World Intellectual Property Organisation passed the WIPO Copyright Treaty and the WIPO Phonogram and Phonographic Treaty, both referred to as the Internet treaties. The treaties were to bring international copyright issues in tandem with the growing use of the internet and technological advancements. Nigeria has since signed these treaties but is yet to domesticate them. If Nigeria will play a leading role in the emerging economy, there is the need to strategically domesticate these laws to enable copyright owners and the general public maximize the opportunities created by the advancements in technology. The whole idea of strategic domestication is to ensure that whatever laws are enacted should be primarily focused on favouring national development and on a secondary level should accommodate the interests of the wider global community. The general observation

---

[76] NCC (2012). See pp. 6–9.

[77] Vanguard (2013).

has been that many developing countries enact legislation which do not favour the nationals but rather favour the developed countries.[78] Such engagement with legislations cannot promote national development, hence the need for Nigeria to strategically domesticate the legislation.

7.5.2 TRIPS & Flexibilities

The Uruguay round negotiations that produced in 1996, the Agreements on Trade Related Aspects of Intellectual Property (TRIPS) upgraded international copyright protection and places on all parties to the agreement obligations to provide certain minimum standard of protection to copyright works. Nigeria as a developing country has complied with most of these requirements but it is important to note that these requirements are majorly in the interest of developed and not developing countries. Articles 7 and 8 of the agreement provides some flexibilities to developing countries. Understanding these flexibilities and maximizing them in the interest of Nigeria's creative industry and copyright legislation will enable her play a stronger role in the present and coming economies. Nigeria's copyright future must therefore be one of strategic engagement for the development of the Nigerian creative industry through appropriate legislative reforms, strengthening international negotiation in the interest of Nigeria's creative industry and encouraging further development of creativity from the cradle to the grave.

7.6 Open Access and the Future of Copyright Law

7.6.1 Copyright and Open Access

In situating copyright in today's technologically enabled and driven society, there is the need to create some kind of synergy between copyright as a system and the open culture that favours free, online, unrestricted and immediate dissemination of information (Open Access). Whereas the current copyright system is restrictive by default, the open culture seeks ways to change that default. The underpinning for this change is the inability to access requisite information due to certain factors hindering access; factors which have been identified as "price, permission and technical".[79] Price in the form of subscription costs by publishers as well as pay

---

[78] Deere (2009), p. 232. "…the world's poorest countries adopt some of the world's highest IP standards at an earlier date than TRIPS required".

[79] Suber (2012), pp. 4–5; See also, Budapest Open Access Initiative, *Ten years on from the Budapest Open Access Initiative: Setting the default to open, available at* http://www.opensocietyfoundations.org/openaccess/boai-10-recommendations.

per view by specialised vendors. The obstacle created by permission is directly connected to the exclusive rights granted to copyright owners which restricts access to copyright materials except permission has been obtained.[80] Technology provides the opportunity for right owners to place technologically enabled measures for protection on devices carrying their copyrighted contents as well as to monitor the use of such contents. By means of these measures, right owners are able to block access to their copyright materials and are also able to manage the use of their copyrighted contents. These technical possibilities may actually prove to be beneficial to right-owners but at the same time constitutes a hindrance to access; access to knowledge, access to information and access to peer-reviewed literature. In a global context access restriction constitutes hindrance to knowledge be they peer-reviewed, educational, public sector information or purely entertainment information. For purposes of this chapter, access to information which are purely for entertainment purposes such as music, films and novels are not the focus because they can be considered as luxuries, non-necessities for fundamental development. On the other hand, access to peer-reviewed literature, educational resources and public sector information is cardinal for the development of any society.

7.6.2 Changing the Default from Closed to Open

Whereas the default setting for protecting knowledge under the current copyright regime is closed (no access without permission), a movement seeks to change this default from closed to open for purposes of empowering the general public with access to peer-reviewed literature, access to educational resources, access to public sector information to the end that the general public will be properly equipped to make the best from available knowledge. Prior to the great exit of Nelson Mandela he noted that Education is the greatest tool for changing lives.[81] But what is the value of education when the knowledge required to gain education cannot be accessed? It is now commonly known that knowledge is power and that we live in a knowledge based economy.[82] Impact in this generation and probably the next will have a lot to do with knowledge. Acquiring knowledge is therefore imperative for development and the currency to acquiring knowledge is access. No knowledge no development, no access, no knowledge.

To ensure maximal utility of created knowledge, highest impact on such knowledge and greatest visibility to such knowledge amongst other things, the open access movement has concerned herself with shifting the access default from closed to open. In recognition of the importance of the current Copyright system, which

---

[80] OLA, Copyright Collective Administration in Nigeria Lessons for Africa 4. 2013.

[81] Strauss (2013).

[82] World Bank (2012). Where the World Bank Group President Robert Zoellick said "knowledge is power".

empowers the copyright owner to restrict all others (except those falling under some form of limitation or exception) from exploiting copyright protected works without prior consenting having first been obtained, the movement relies on this right of the Copyright owner but this time not in a restrictive manner but rather in an enabling manner. It achieves this through open licensing systems which grants prior consent to prospective users. This system has been very successful in the software industry through the free open source software licenses such as GNU GPL.[83] In the content industry, there are several licenses but the creative commons licences appear to be the most popular.[84]

In Nigeria's copyright future, embracing the open culture will be very instrumental to her development. However in adopting this culture, there is the need for proper understanding of the concepts though enlightenment and to adopt policies that would encourage further creativity within the Nigerian creative industry. This is very important because the open culture has the tendency of opening developing countries to become mere consumers and non-contributors to the world library. In order to benefit from the open access movement, Nigeria needs to strategically engage with the open culture for purposes of empowerment and not mere consumption. A mentality or attitude of mere consumption may seem to provide an easy win at the beginning but will eventually kill creativity and could no doubt bring about the eradication of the Nigerian culture and may produce the next dispensation of colonization. Proper engagement with the open culture will afford the opportunity to share the knowledge of the poor with the rich and the rich with the poor; it will also afford the highest level of visibility to works by Nigerian authors and allow for the possibility of global impact on locally generated works. The sharing culture typified by "Open" is the now and future for all form of content.

7.7 Conclusion

When the British carted away our creative works prior to our independence it may have seemed that our creativity had been stolen. The reality is that creativity is deeply rooted in the people and their culture and it will take more than carting away a few items to steal ones national creativity. The passage into law of the 1970 Copyright Act signalled Nigeria's first domestic copyright law but it did not provide much in the opinion of Nigerian copyright owners and it led to the current 1988 Copyright Act which has been amended twice to reflect the changing and dynamic nature of copyright. The several regulations that have been issued by the Commission and the different strategies adopted by the Nigerian Copyright Commission have in no small way helped in the administration of copyright in Nigeria. The heightened convictions on copyright infringement will hopefully continue to serve

---

[83] Richard Stallman, *The GNU Project at* http://www.gnu.org/gnu/thegnuproject.html.

[84] Fitzgerald (2007).

as deterrence to others who think flagrant disregard for copyright is acceptable. The future of copyright for Nigeria will however lie in the ability of Nigeria to strategically engage with the international community in domesticating legal instruments and negotiating issues of interest for the development of Nigeria's creative industries. Cardinal to the development of copyright in Nigeria will be her ability to embrace the open culture by first understanding the concepts and taking steps to put in place policies that would enable the freedoms required for development. If the open culture is not embraced, copyright may be suffocated and relegated to a place of insignificance.

References

Adewopo A Intellectual property regime and the global financial crisis: lessons from Nigeria. (2011) J Money Laundering Control 14

Adewopo A (2012) Nigerian Copyright System: principles and perspectives. Odade Publishers, Lagos.

Asein J (2012) Nigerian copyright law and practice, 2nd edn. Books and Gavel Limited, Abuja.

Assessing the participation of domestic SMEs in the international production chain: the case of Nu Metro in Nigeria (2010)

Author, Fire in Soweto (Youtube)

Berne Convention for the Protection of Literary and Artistic Works, September 9, 1886, amended last on September 28, 1979 (September 9, 1886)

Budapest Open Access Initiative, Ten years on from the Budapest open access initiative: setting the default to open. Available at http://www.opensocietyfoundations.org/openaccess/boai-10-recommendations

Cahill T (1995) How the Irish saved civilization. Anchor Books, Doubleday/New York

Chris Butler, FC74: The invention of the printing press and its effects at http://www.flowofhistory.com/units/west/11/FC74

Davis J (2008) Intellectual property law, 3rd edn. In: Padfield N (ed) Oxford University Press, New York.

Deere C (2009) The TRIPS Agreement and the global politics of intellectual property reform in developing countries. Oxford University Press, London

Federal Republic of Nigeria, About Nigeria. Available at http://www.nigeria.gov.ng/2012-10-29-11-05-46

Fitzgerald B (2007) A short overview of creative commons. Sydney University Press, Sydney.

Fitzgerald B et al (2006) OAK LAW PROJECT NO. 1: creating a legal framework for copyright management of open access within the Australian Academic and Research Sector (Report for the Department of Education and Science and Training (DEST))

Francis G (2013) Re-thinking the role of intellectual property. WIPO, available at <http://www.wipo.int/export/sites/www/about-wipo/en/dgo/speeches/pdf/dg_speech_melbourne_2013.pdf>

Metropolitan Museum of Arts, Queen mother Pendant mask: Iyoba. On display in gallery 352. Available at http://www.metmuseum.org/collections/search-the-collections/318622

MFA (2013) Museum of fine arts, Boston, opens Benin kingdom gallery showcasing Robert Owen Lehman collection of rare West African art. Available at http://www.mfa.org/news/benin_kingdom

MFA (2013) Benin Kingdom Gallery Gallery 172, Museum of fine arts Boston. Available at http://www.mfa.org/collections/featured-galleries/benin-kingdom-gallery

NCC 2012 Annual Report (2012)

NCC, General information on copyright notification scheme. Available at http://www.copyright. gov.ng/index.php/regulatory-schemes/copyright-notification

NCC V EMORDI HENRY CHUKWUMA, FHC/ABJ/CR/90/2013 (Federal High Court, Abuja. 19/06/2013)

NCC V GODWIN KADIRI, FHC/B/43C/2010 (Federal High Court, Benin-City. 17/12/2012).

NCC V MICHAEL PAUL, FHC/LF/CR/2/2013 (Federal High Court, Lafia 3/10/2013)

NCC V NWOKE ISREAL, FHC/L/159C/2013 (Federal High Court, Lagos 6/05/2013)

Nigerian Copyright Commission (2008) Survey of copyright piracy in Nigeria. Management Review Limited

Nigerian Copyright Commission NCC (1999a) Copyright (Security Devices) Regulation 1999. Available at http://www.copyright.gov.ng/images/downloads/Copyright%20Security%20devices%20regulation%201999.pdf

Nigerian Copyright Commission NCC (1999b) Copyright (Video Rental) Regulation 1999. Available at http://www.copyright.gov.ng/images/downloads/Copyright%20Video%20rental%20regulation%201999.pdf

Nigerian Copyright Commission NCC (2005) Copyright notification scheme. Available at http://www.copyright.gov.ng/index.php/regulatory-schemes/copyright-notification

Nigerian Copyright Commission NCC (2006) Copyright (Optical Discs Plants) Regulation 2006. B 697-711. Available at http://www.copyright.gov.ng/images/downloads/Optical%20Disc%20Regulation.pdf

Nigerian Copyright Commission NCC (2007) Copyright (Collective Management Organisation) Regulation 2007. Available at http://www.copyright.gov.ng/images/downloads/CMO%20Regulation%202007.pdf

Nigerian Copyright Commission NCC (2008) STRAP and CLAMP – Nigeria Copyright Commission in Action. WIPO magazine September 2008

Nigerian Copyright Commission NCC (2012) Copyright (Levy on Materials) Order 2012. Available at http://www.copyright.gov.ng/images/downloads/REVISED%20DRAFT%20LEVY%20ON%20COPYRIGHT%20MATERIALS%20ORDER.pdf

Nigerian Copyright Commission NCC, About NCC historical background. Available at http://www.copyright.gov.ng/index.php/about-us/ncc-historical-background

Nigerian Copyright Commission NCC, Nigerian Copyright Institute. Available at http://www.copyright.gov.ng/index.php/2013-02-10-16-11-10/nigerain-copyright-institute-nci

Nigerian Copyright Commission NCC, Copyright (Reciprocal Extension) Regulation 1972(1972). Available at http://www.copyright.gov.ng/images/downloads/Copyright%20Reciprocal%20Extension%20Order%201972.pdf

Nigerian Copyright Act, Cap C28 (2004)

Okoroji T (2008) Copyright neighbouring rights & the new millionaires (the twists and turns in Nigeria. Tops Limited, Lagos

Olukunle OLA (2013) Copyright collective administration in Nigeria lessons for Africa. Springer, Berlin Heidelberg

Royal Irish Academy, MS 24

Sowole T (2013) U.S. Museum splits Benin Royal House. The Guardian, 29 September 2013

Stallman R, The GNU Project at http://www.gnu.org/gnu/thegnuproject.html

Statute of Anne, 8 Anne c. 19 (1710)

Strauss V (2013) Nelson Mandela's famous quote on education. The Washington Post

Suber P (2012) Open access. MIT Press, Cambridge, Massachusetts

The Copyright Act of 1976 Title 17 of United States Code (1976)

UNESCO, Universal Copyright Convention, with Appendix Declaration relating to Article XVII and Resolution concerning Article XI. Geneva, 6 September 1952. Available at http://www.unesco.org/eri/la/convention.asp?KO=15381&language=E

Vanguard (2013) COSON to Distribute 2013 copyright royalties. Available at http://allafrica.com/stories/201312121381.html

Wikipedia, Music of Nigeria. Available at http://en.wikipedia.org/wiki/Music_of_Nigeria#The_
    1950s.2C_.2760s_and_.2770s
WIPO, WIPO administered treaties. Available at http://www.wipo.int/treaties/en/
WIPO, What is intellectual property. Available at http://www.wipo.int/about-ip/en/
WIPO, Copyright registration and documentation. Available at http://www.wipo.int/copyright/en/
    activities/copyright_registration/
World Bank (2012) World Bank announces open access policy for research and knowledge,
    launches open knowledge repository, Press Release No: 2012/379/EXTOP
World History, History of Nigeria. Available at http://www.historyworld.net/wrldhis/
    plaintexthistories.asp?historyid=ad41

Chapter 8
Copyright, Fair Use and the Australian Constitution

Kylie Pappalardo and Brian Fitzgerald

8.1 Introduction

There has been much debate over recent years about whether Australian copyright law should adopt a fair use doctrine.[1] In this article we argue by pointing to the historical record that the incorporation of the term 'copyrights' in the Australian Constitution embeds a notion of balance and fair use in Australian law and that this should be taken into account when interpreting the Australian *Copyright Act 1968*.

In an era where copyright issues have become foundational to everyday life it is inevitable that lawyers, as they have done in other countries, will resort to the supreme law of the land in looking for guidance. In Australia, to this point in time, there has been limited judicial consideration of how the Constitution and copyright law intersect.[2] Our focus is on the (concurrent) constitutional power to make legislation "with respect to copyrights, patents of inventions and designs, and trade marks" (hereinafter called the "copyright power").[3] In short, we believe that

---

[1] See the ALRC Report 122, Copyright and the Digital Economy (tabled 13 Feb 2014), which recommended that Australia adopt a fair use defence. http://www.alrc.gov.au/publications/copy right-report-122.

[2] See, e.g., *Australian Tape Manufacturers Association Ltd v Commonwealth* (1993) 176 CLR 480; [1993] HCA 10; *Nintendo Co Ltd v Centronics Systems Pty Ltd* (1994) 181 CLR 134; [1994] HCA 27; *Copyright Agency Limited v State of New South Wales* (2008) 233 CLR 279; [2008] HCA 35 (briefly, at [57], [69] (Gleeson CJ, Gummow, Heydon, Crennan and Kiefel JJ)).

[3] The Australian Constitution enacted by the British Parliament in 1900 and through time accepted by the people as a supreme law creates a federal system wherein legislative power is shared between the Commonwealth/Federal government and the State governments. Section 51 of the Constitution lists concurrent heads of legislative power upon which the Commonwealth and the

K. Pappalardo (✉) • B. Fitzgerald
Thomas More Academy of Law, Australian Catholic University, 486 Albert Street, East Melbourne, VIC 3002, Australia
e-mail: kylie.pappalardo@gmail.com; brian.fitzgerald@acu.edu.au

© Springer International Publishing Switzerland 2015
B. Fitzgerald, J. Gilchrist (eds.), *Copyright Perspectives*,
DOI 10.1007/978-3-319-15913-3_8

the use of the word "copyrights" embeds in the Australian Constitution a fundamental notion of copyright that took definition from copyright law as it stood at 1900 and as it has evolved since.[4]

When one looks to the English law (and beyond) underpinning copyright law when the *Commonwealth of Australia Constitution Act 1900* (Imp) was enacted, it is clear that owners of private rights of copyright did not have an unlimited power to prevent copying; they had a power to prevent *infringing* copying. Asked in 1900 what stood outside the realm of infringing copying, the copyright lawyer would no doubt have responded: copyright law protects expression not ideas,[5] requires infringement to involve the taking of a "substantial part",[6] runs for a limited time[7] and allows for a margin of productive reuse or what the English courts at

---

states can enact legislation, although s 109 Constitution provides that where there is inconsistency the Commonwealth law shall prevail. Section 51 (xviii) provides that The Parliament shall, subject to this Constitution, have power to make laws for the peace, order, and good government of the Commonwealth with respect to copyrights, patents of inventions and designs, and trade marks.

[4] As will be set out later in this article, the definition of "copyright" as it stood in 1900 was developed primarily by the legislature and courts of England, including in the Statute of Anne. It was also informed, however, by the *Berne Convention for the Protection of Literary and Artistic Works* (1886), the US Constitution, and by developments in the courts of the United States and in the legislation of colonial Australia.

[5] See Copinger (1870), pp. 5–6: "Ideas, being neither capable of a visible possession nor of sustaining any one of the qualities or incidents of property, inasmuch as they have no bounds whatsoever, cannot be the subject of property... They are of a nature too insubstantial, too evanescent, to be the subject of proprietary rights. When, however, any material has embodied those ideas, then the ideas, though that corporeity, can be recognized as a species of property by the common law. The claim is not to ideas, but to the order of words, and this order has a marked identity and a permanent endurance."

[6] See Copinger (1870), p. 37 (referring to *Bramwell v Halcomb* 3 My. & Cr. 737, where Lord Cottenham said, "It is not only quantity, but value, which is looked at"), 84–86, 95–96 (for an early expression of the principle of substantial part: "The quantity of matter subtracted cannot in all cases be a true criterion of the extent of the piracy, for a work may be a piracy upon another, though the passages copied are stated to be quotations, and are not so extensive as to render the piratical work a substitution for the original work. If so much is taken that the value of the original is sensibly diminished, or the labours of the original author are substantially, to an injurious extent, appropriated by another, that is sufficient, in point of law, to constitute a piracy *pro tanto*": at 95).

[7] See Copinger (1870), pp. 56–57: "[Some have] argued... that the concessionary allowance of a perpetuity in copyright would encourage publication, and tend greatly to the promotion and furtherance of science and literature. But, admitting that learning and science should be encouraged, that everything tending or conducible to the advancement of knowledge, and consequently to the happiness of the community, should be favoured and tenderly cherished by the legislature, and that the labour of every individual should be properly recompensed, it does not follow that the same or a similar end might not be obtained by different and less objectionable means. If the individual is a gainer by the existence of perpetual copyright, society is a loser. The absurdity of the assertion that authors are alone inclined to make known their works from the specific benefit arising from an absolute perpetual monopoly, is manifest." See also *Donaldson v Beckett* (1774) 1 ER 837, where the House of Lords found that the Statute of Anne extinguished common law copyright, thereby rejecting the argument that perpetual copyright could exist in published materials. For additional sources and discussion on limited term, see Fitzgerald and Atkinson (2008), p. 253, note 75.

least up until 1900 called "fair use".[8] As the High Court of Australia reiterated in the recent *Ice TV* decision,[9] copyright law is premised on a balance between the bestowal of private property rights to incentivize creativity and production and the right of the public to receive and access culture and knowledge.[10]

The essence of copyright for the last 300 years has been to enable an owner of private rights (copyright) to prevent infringing copying. We submit that the word "copyrights" in the Australian Constitution, a subject matter upon which legislation can be made, in essence refers to the notion of infringing copying.[11] The purpose of this article is to investigate how this notion should inform the interpretation of the *Copyright Act 1968*.

It is important to be clear from the outset that we do not seek to claim that the *Copyright Act 1968* is unconstitutional. Rather, we believe that the Copyright Act can be read in a way that gives effect to the constitutional notion of copyrights as regulating only those forms of copying that produce infringing copies.

This argument has two dimensions. Firstly, we look to s. 15A of the *Acts Interpretation Act 1901* (Cth), which embeds in statute the longstanding principle that "Every Act shall be read and construed subject to the Constitution." We submit that although the *Copyright Act 1968* is constitutional as enacted, if read and applied too broadly the Act could operate outside of constitutional bounds. We argue that the Act must be read generally as being subject to a constitutional notion of "copyright" that regulates only infringing copying.

The second dimension looks to the specific wording of the Copyright Act and argues that the Australian Constitution forms part of the relevant extrinsic material that may be consulted to confirm the ordinary meaning of those words in accordance with s. 15AB of the *Acts Interpretation Act 1901*. In particular, we submit that the infringement test is included within the *Copyright Act 1968* in s. 36(1) and s. 101(1), which define infringement as the doing (or authorising) of "any act comprised in the copyright".[12] This is the point at which the Act sets its sights on

---

[8] The principle of fair use is discussed throughout this chapter.

[9] *IceTV Pty Limited v Nine Network Australia Pty Limited* (2009) 239 CLR 458; [2009] HCA 14 (22 April 2009).

[10] "The 'social contract' envisaged by the Statute of Anne, and still underlying the present Act, was that an author could obtain a monopoly, limited in time, in return for making a work available to the reading public": (2009) 239 CLR 458; [2009] HCA 14 (22 April 2009), 471 [25] (French CJ, Crennan and Kiefel JJ). This statement was quoted by Crennan and Kiefel JJ in *Phonographic Performance Company of Australia Limited v Commonwealth of Australia* [2012] HCA 8 (28 March 2012) [96].

[11] We acknowledge that current copyright law goes beyond the notion of reproduction and dealing with copies to include things such as public performance and communication to the publication. For the purposes of this chapter it is sufficient to make our argument by reference to copying as that was the dominant paradigm in copyright up until the twentieth century, the historical cases we rely on deal with copying and the Australian case study we use deals with copying.

[12] *Copyright Act 1968* (Cth) s 36(1) provides, "Subject to this Act, the copyright in a literary, dramatic, musical or artistic work is infringed by a person who, not being the owner of the copyright, and without the licence of the owner of the copyright, does in Australia, or authorizes

regulating infringing copying while excluding non-infringing copying.[13] We therefore argue that the ordinary meaning of "act comprised in copyright" encompasses the constitutional notion of infringing copying.

The following pages outline our argument in greater depth as we focus on one particular aspect of this discussion, namely, the development of a notion of productive or fair use in English law and how it contributes to the meaning of infringing copying. Section 8.2 of this article explores the development of the doctrine of fair use in the early English and U.S. case law, beginning with the case of *Gyles v Wilcox* in 1740 and ending with *Walter v Steinkopff* in 1892, just before the enactment of the copyright power in the Australian Constitution in 1900. In Sect. 8.3, we examine the copyright power in light of the *Grain Pool of Western Australia v Commonwealth* case and argue that the principle of fair use is one of the essential characteristics of the meaning of "copyrights" as it appears in the Australian Constitution. In Sect. 8.4, we consider how the *Copyright Act 1968* gives effect to the principles of balance and fair use. We canvass past efforts to give greater emphasis to fair use in the test for substantial part. But most importantly, we examine how sections 36(1) and 101(1) can incorporate the core "copyright balance" which is maintained by regulating infringing copies and excluding non-infringing copies such as productive or fair uses. Sections 36(1) and 101(1) define what an infringement is under the *Copyright Act 1968*. These sections and the associated tests that help us to interpret and apply the Act—especially, for the purposes of copying, the test for objective similarity—should be read in line with the Constitutional understanding of "copyrights" as a mechanism of balance. We conclude, in Sect. 8.5, with a case study that demonstrates how a constitutional understanding of "copyrights" can inform the operation of the *Copyright Act 1968* in practice.

8.2 Early Development of Fair Use in England and the United States

In this part, we consider the development and treatment of fair use as a doctrine in early English case law. We undertake this task in order to show that fair use is a key element of the notion of "copyrights" that was imported into the Australian

---

the doing in Australia of, any act comprised in the copyright." Section 101(1) provides, "Subject to this Act, a copyright subsisting by virtue of this Part is infringed by a person who, not being the owner of the copyright, and without the licence of the owner of the copyright, does in Australia, or authorizes the doing in Australia of, any act comprised in the copyright."

[13] For a detailed discussion of what does and does not fall within the ambit of infringing copying, see Greenleaf and Bond (2013), pp. 111–138.

Constitution at federation and, as such, may legitimately form a part of judicial reasoning in Australia.[14]

The fair use doctrine codified in section 107 of the United States Copyright Act (as amended) provides:

> Notwithstanding the provisions of sections 106 and 106A, the fair use of a copyrighted work, including such use by reproduction in copies or phonorecords or by any other means specified by that section, for purposes such as criticism, comment, news reporting, teaching (including multiple copies for classroom use), scholarship, or research, is not an infringement of copyright. In determining whether the use made of a work in any particular case is a fair use the factors to be considered shall include—
>
> (1) the purpose and character of the use, including whether such use is of a commercial nature or is for nonprofit educational purposes;
> (2) the nature of the copyrighted work;
> (3) the amount and substantiality of the portion used in relation to the copyrighted work as a whole; and
> (4) the effect of the use upon the potential market for or value of the copyrighted work.
>
>   The fact that a work is unpublished shall not itself bar a finding of fair use if such finding is made upon consideration of all the above factors.[15]

The U.S. case of *Folsom v Marsh*[16] is often cited as the origin of the fair use doctrine, and it is generally accepted that the factors codified in §107 are based upon Justice Story's articulation of the doctrine in that case.[17] In reality, however, the principles underpinning fair use were developed significantly earlier than 1841 in a series of cases in the United Kingdom dealing with fair abridgements.[18] As William Patry observes in his treatise on fair use:

> [T]he basic foundations and rationale [of fair use] were established remarkably early. In the century from 1740 to 1839, English judges developed a relatively cohesive set of principles

---

[14] In this chapter we have focused on the historical case law giving rise to the doctrine of fair use in UK precedent. We have focused on the position in the UK prior to 1900 because the Commonwealth of Australia Constitution Act 1900 was an Imperial Act, influenced by the current state of the law in England at that time. Additionally, fair use was a concept developed in the case law. For these reasons, we have not looked to the colonial copyright Acts in Australia in this article.

[15] 17 U.S.C. §107.

[16] 9 F. Cas. 342 (C.C.D. Mass. 1841).

[17] See, for example, *Campbell v Acuff-Rose Music*, 510 U.S. 569 (1994) (per Souter J delivering the opinion of the court: "In *Folsom v Marsh*, Justice Story distilled the essence of law and methodology from the earlier cases...Thus expressed, fair use remained exclusively judge made doctrine until the passage of the 1976 Copyright Act, in which Story's summary is discernible"); Leval (1989–1990), pp. 1105–1136 at 1105 ("In *Folsom v Marsh*, in 1841, Justice Story articulated an often-cited summary of how to approach a question of fair use...The 1976 Copyright Act largely adopted his summary."); House Judiciary Committee, Copyright Law Revision, H.R. Rep. No. 94-1476, 94th Cong., 2d Sess. 66 (1976) ("Section 107 is intended to restate the present judicial doctrine of fair use, not to change, narrow or enlarge it in any way."); Reese (2006), pp. 259–297 at 292.

[18] This part describes those early cases. As well as consulting the primary judgments, we found exceptionally useful and have drawn heavily from William Patry's excellent treatise: Patry (1985).

governing the use of a first author's work by a subsequent author without the former's consent.[19]

Beginning with *Gyles v Wilcox*[20] in 1740, the English courts developed the principle that an abridgment of a first author's work would not be an infringement if it were "real and fair" and if it involved "invention, learning and judgment".[21] In other words, the courts considered whether the second author had engaged in a productive use.[22] In *Gyles v Wilcox*, the plaintiff sought an injunction to restrain the printing of an allegedly infringing legal treatise. Lord Chancellor Hardwicke referred the case to a Master, who found that the defendant had copied 35 pages of the plaintiff's 275-page work. Lord Chancellor Hardwicke found for the defendant, holding,

> Where books are colourably shortened only, they are undoubtedly within the meaning of the act of Parliament, and are a mere evasion of the statute, and cannot be called an abridgment. But this must not be carried so far as to restrain persons from making a real and fair abridgement, for abridgements may with great propriety be called a new book, because not only the paper and print, but the invention, learning, and judgment of the author is shewn in them, and in many cases are extremely useful, though in some instances prejudicial, by mistaking and curtailing the sense of an author.[23]

Subsequently, *Tonson v. Walker*[24] also highlighted the relevance of whether a defendant had engaged in a productive use. In that case, the plaintiff had produced a compilation of Milton's poems which contained 1,500 notes from various authors. The defendant copied the plaintiff's work and attached a further 28 notes. Lord Chancellor Hardwicke granted an injunction against the defendant, holding that this was not a fair abridgment but a mere evasion.[25]

Later cases emphasised other attributes of a fair abridgment—*Dodsley v Kinnersley*[26] considered whether the defendant's copy would prejudice the market for the original, and *Macklin v Richardson*[27] found it important that the defendant's work should not supersede the original.[28] These are the very same attributes that we

---

[19] Patry (1985), p. 3.

[20] (1740) 2 Atk. 141 (No. 130).

[21] *Gyles v Wilcox* (1740) 2 Atl. 141, 143 (No. 130).

[22] See Patry (1985), p. 6. See also, Kaplan (1967), p. 17; Tehranian (2004–2005), pp. 465–508 at 474, 475, 479.

[23] *Gyles v Wilcox* (1740) 2 Atl. 141, 143 (No. 130).

[24] (1752) 3 Swans. (App.) 672.

[25] See further, Patry (1985), pp. 7–8 (arguing that this case demonstrates that a passive use of another's work (i.e. an unproductive use) was insufficient for a claim of fair abridgment); Alexander (2010), p. 172: "Over the course of his years as Lord Chancellor, Lord Hardwicke's views on infringement evolved to the point of developing the principle that a 'fair abridgement' would not be considered to fall foul of the Statute of Anne."

[26] (1761) Amb. 403 (No. 212); 27 ER 270.

[27] (1770) Amb. 694 (No. 341); 27 ER 451.

[28] Isabella Alexander has done an excellent job of charting the rhetoric of public interest in nineteenth century copyright law and policy. She argues that in the early nineteenth century, the

see informing the concept of fair use today.[29] In *Dodsley v Kinnersley*, plaintiffs were assignees of Samuel Johnson. They published a two-volume work of his fiction, from which the defendant printed one-tenth in a magazine. The court held for the defendant.[30] The court was less influenced by the small quantity taken than the fact that the plaintiffs had previously published an abstract of their work in a newspaper. The court thought that this demonstrated that the market for the original would not be prejudiced by the availability of abstracts. In *Macklin v Richardson*, the plaintiff was the creator of an unpublished two-act play. The defendant hired transcribers to attend a performance of the play and he then published the first act in his monthly magazine with a notice that the second act would be published in the next issue. The plaintiff sued and the defendant claimed fair abridgment or fair review. The court held that this was an infringement. Lord Commissioner Smythe stated, "This is not an abridgment, but the work itself."[31] William Patry has argued, "Without articulating it, *Macklin* provides the foundation for the principle that a review may not supplant the market for the work itself, a concept repeated many times in subsequent decisions."[32]

In 1803 in *Cary v Kearsley*,[33] a case that became known as an important decision in this area,[34] the court used language that could be interpreted to apply more broadly than just to fair abridgement cases. In fact, Patry has asserted, "we find here the origins of fair use, as opposed to fair abridgment."[35] *Cary v Kearsley* concerned the defendant's copying of the plaintiff's work, *The Book of Roads*, which was an itinerary that the plaintiff had composed by taking surveys of various roads. To evidence infringement, the plaintiff pointed to various errors in his work that had appeared verbatim in the defendant's work. Lord Ellenborough did not consider that proof of errors transmitted into the defendant's work amounted to proof of

---

fair abridgment doctrine was influenced by the principle that an abridgement was a "new work" and that it was in the public interest that new works be produced and circulated to the reading public. According to Alexander, however, this public interest consideration waned during the course of the nineteenth century, as courts began to pay greater attention to the effect that the copying would have on the market for the original work. Thus, copyright law became, in a sense, a law about unfair competition: see Alexander (2010), Chapter 6. The doctrine of fair use, as it was developed in the nineteenth century and as it is understood today, is consistent with Alexander's account of the development of copyright law in the nineteenth century. Fair use incorporates market-based considerations, by asking whether the defendant's work prejudices or supersedes the market for the original work.

[29] See factor (4) in 17 U.S.C. §107.

[30] See also Alexander (2010), p. 171: "Clarke MR appeared to treat it as settled that a 'fair abridgment' would not be considered a piracy."

[31] *Macklin v Richardson*, (1770) Amb. 694, 696 (No. 341); 27 ER 451.

[32] Patry (1985), 9.

[33] (1803) 4 Esp. 168.

[34] See Copinger (1870), p. 92; Leval (1989–1990), pp. 1105–1136 at 1110.

[35] Patry (1985), p. 10. He continues: "Lord Ellenborough is here referring to fair use in the sense in which it was subsequently utilized – the use by a second author of a first author's work for the promotion of science."

infringement, stating that the defendant was authorised to make extracts of another's work in his own and that "mistaking the names and descriptions, and taking such detached parts, was only using an erroneous dictionary."[36] On the contrary, His Honour considered that where the defendant's work contained additional observations or *corrections* of mistakes, this was likely to be evidence that the work was not an infringing copy. He said, "[W]hile I shall think myself bound to secure every man in the enjoyment of his copyright, one must not put manacles upon science."[37] Lord Ellenborough observed:

> That part of the work of one author is found in another, is not of itself piracy, or sufficient to support an action; a man may fairly adopt part of the work of another: he may so make use of another's labours for the promotion of science, and the benefit of the public: but having done so, the question will be, Was the matter so taken used fairly with that view, and without what I may term the *animus furandi*?[38]

Animus furandi, in law, generally means "the intention to steal".[39] Our understanding of the role of *animus furandi* in copyright law is that the presence or absence of *animus furandi*—or bad faith—may be a helpful indicator of infringement, though it will not be determinative in itself. Copyright infringement is actionable per se; a defendant does not need to intend to infringe to be liable. However, a bad faith intention may be reflected in the *way* that the defendant has copied—a copy made in bad faith is less likely to be transformative or to contain an original contribution from the defendant. Rather, a defendant with *animus furandi* is more likely to copy the plaintiff's work verbatim or very closely. *Animus furandi* may point to infringement, therefore, not because the intent of the defendant is relevant in itself but because the intent can influence the *type* of copying engaged in by the defendant.[40] Thus, William Patry contends that in the sense it is used in *Cary*

---

[36] (1803) 4 Esp. 168, 169.

[37] *Cary v Kearsley* (1803) 4 Esp. 168, 170.

[38] Ibid.

[39] See Black's Law Dictionary, http://blackslawdictionary.org/animus-furandi/ (accessed 7 February 2012), citing to *Gardner v. State*, 55 N.J. Law, 17, 20 Atl. 30; *State v. Slingerland*. 19 News 135. 7 Pac. 280.

[40] While nowadays this may seem to be an obscure and outdated term, Justices Gummow, Hayne and Heydon considered the existence or absence of *animus furandi* to be relevant to the question of substantial taking in *IceTV Pty Ltd v Nine Network Australia Pty Ltd* (2009) 239 CLR 458, 512; [2009] HCA 14 [171]; see also 512–515 [172]–[184]. In that case, the circumstances of the defendants' use seemed to indicate that the use was a productive use and that there was a lack of *animus furandi*; however, the Justices did not reach a conclusion on this point because they had already determined that the part taken was insubstantial: (2009) 239 CLR 458, 516; [2009] HCA 14 [186]. Cf. *EMI Songs Australia Pty Limited v Larrikin Music Publishing Pty Limited* [2011] FCAFC 41 (31 March 2011) [221], where Jagot J argued that the references to *animus furandi* in *IceTV* are relevant only in the context of a compilation case where the distinction between information (not protectable) and the way in which information is expressed (protectable) is unclear. In these circumstances, "the intention of the alleged infringer may take on considerable significance".

v Kearsley, *animus furandi* "involves both a moral inquiry and an examination of the defendant's creative effort."[41]

Lord Ellenborough concluded *Cary v Kearsley* with a description of his directions to the jury:

> I shall address these observations to the jury leaving them to say, whether what [was] so taken or supposed to be transmitted from the plaintiff's book, was fairly done with a view of compiling a useful book for the benefit of the public, upon which there has been a totally new arrangement of such matter, – or taken colourably, merely with a view to steal the copyright of the plaintiff?[42]

Kathy Bowrey has cited an earlier case, *Sayres v Moore*,[43] as the "earliest expression of fair use".[44] The case involved the copying of four sea charts into one large map. The court found that there had been "very material errors" in the plaintiffs' charts, which the defendant had corrected in his map. Chief Justice Mansfield directed to the jury:

> If an erroneous chart be made, God forbid it should not be corrected even in a small degree, if it thereby become more serviceable and useful for the purposes to which it is applied. But here you are told, that there are various and very material alterations. This chart of the plaintiffs' is upon a wrong principle, inapplicable to navigation. The defendant therefore has been correcting errors, and not servilely copying. If you think so, you will find for the defendant; if you think it is a mere servile imitation, and pirated from another, you will find for the plaintiffs.[45]

The jury found for the defendant. As with *Cary v Kearsley*, the focus of the court here was on whether the defendant's use delivered a public benefit, in terms of correcting errors or promoting science. Both cases involved the copying of maps and neither act of copying could be accurately described as an abridgment, but this was not the primary concern of the courts. Therefore, it can be said that both cases contemplated whether the defendant engaged in a fair *use* as opposed to a fair *abridgment*.[46]

---

[41] Patry (1985), p. 11.

[42] *Cary v Kearsley* (1803) 4 Esp. 168, 171. The reported judgment notes that the counsel for the plaintiff consented to be nonsuited.

[43] (1785) 102 ER 139.

[44] Bowrey (2008).

[45] *Sayres v Moore* (1785) 102 ER 139 at 140.

[46] Interestingly, Alexandra Sims has remarked: "It is curious that *Cary v Kearsley* is considered by some to represent the beginning of the fair dealing exception. It may well be that Lord Ellenborough's reference to 'used fairly' has caused some confusion. On the one hand, the term 'fair' had been used extensively in the abridgment cases and as we have seen the courts recognised that criticism and review was non-infringing. On the other hand, arguably 'fair' was being used in a different and more general sense in *Cary v Kearsley*. In contrast to the early abridgment cases, which dealt with the reduction of one large work to a smaller work, the defendant in *Cary v Kearsley* was compiling a new book...*Cary v Kearsley*, therefore, represents the beginning of a judicial recognition of fairness in relation to the use of factual materials in the creation of new works, but not fairness in the sense of using materials for the purpose of review and criticism or even quotation." Sims (2011), pp. 3–27 at 21.

Wilkins v Aiken[47] followed a similar approach to *Cary v Kearsley*. In that case, the plaintiff alleged that the defendant had copied several drawings and pages from his book on the antiquities of Greece; the defendant claimed that this use was a fair abridgment or a fair quotation. Lord Eldon characterised the question before the court as "whether this is a legitimate use of the plaintiff's publication in the fair exercise of a mental operation, deserving the character of an original work."[48] Copinger has described this case as one in which "[the] actual use is avowed and the only question is, whether it is a fair use."[49]

Sayres v Moore, *Cary v Kearsley* and *Wilkins v Aiken* all focused on the use made by defendant of the plaintiff's work, giving weight to the transformativeness of the use and the original contributions of the defendant.[50] Additionally, *Sayres v Moore* and *Cary v Kearsley* considered whether the use made by the defendant provided public benefit and promoted "science". This approach mirrors, to some extent, current U.S. jurisprudence, where the fair use doctrine is considered an important safeguard against copyright monopolies in promoting the public's interest in free expression, including expression made through iterative creative processes and transformative works.[51] The important point here, as Oren Bracha notes, is that by undertaking these assessments of whether the defendant made a new intellectual contribution and whether the defendant's use was fair, "[t]raditional English doctrine...allowed ample breathing space to abridgements, translations, imitations and other derivative uses."[52]

In *Lewis v Fullarton*,[53] a case involving an alleged infringement of *The Topographical Dictionary of England*, the defendant argued that his use his was lawful because he had "made only a fair use of a former publication on the subject of his own subsequent work."[54] Although the court held for the plaintiff, finding that "in a large proportion of the Defendant's work, no other labour has been applied than in copying the Plaintiff's work",[55] it is significant that the court posed no objection to defendant's framing of his defense as a "fair use".[56]

---

[47] (1810) 17 Ves. (Ch.) 422.

[48] Ibid 426.

[49] Copinger (1870), p. 94.

[50] On the importance of focusing on the defendant's originality in assessing infringement (as well as the plaintiff's in determining subsistence) see Bowrey (2008).

[51] See further, Sect. 8.3.

[52] Bracha (2008). Citing to Kaplan (1967), pp. 9–12.

[53] (1839) 2 Beav. 6; 48 ER 1080.

[54] *Lewis v Fullarton* (1839) 2 Beav. 6, 8; 48 ER 1080, 1081 (defendant's arguments as recounted by Lord Langdale M.R.).

[55] *Lewis v Fullarton* (1839) 2 Beav. 6, 9; 48 ER 1080, 1081.

[56] William Patry cites *Lewis v Fullarton* as the first U.K. case in which the term "fair use" is applied to extracting: Patry (1985), p. 16.

Lewis v Fullarton was decided in 1839. This, then, was the state of the law in the United Kingdom immediately before *Folsom v Marsh* was decided in the United States in 1841.

Folsom v Marsh[57] concerned biographies of George Washington, both of which contained copies of Washington's original letters. Jared Sparks wrote and compiled a biography that amounted to 12 volumes (around 7,000 pages). The first volume was an original biography of Washington written by Sparks, and the remaining volumes constituted Washington's private and public letters, which Sparks had acquired from Washington's estate along with permission to publish them. The volumes were printed by the publishing house, Folsom, Wells and Thurston.[58] Many of the letters included in the biography had not been previously published. Subsequently, Charles Upham published a two-volume biography of Washington, which ran to 866 pages. The biography was intended for use in schools and was published by Marsh, Capen, Lyon and Webb as part of their Massachusetts School Library series.[59] Upham's intention was to tell Washington's story through Washington's own words in his writings and letters. The Master in the case found that 356 pages of Upham's work corresponded identically to passages in Sparks' work and that of those pages, 319 pages were letters first published by Sparks.[60] Upham argued that he had the right to "quote, select, extract, or abridge from another, in the composition of a work essentially new."[61]

Justice Story cited to the U.K. cases of *Dodsley v. Kinnersly* and *Tonson v. Walker* for the proposition that a fair and bona fide abridgement was not an infringement.[62] Referring to *Gyles v Wilcox*, he stated that the requirement for such an abridgment was: "There must be real, substantial condensation of the materials, and intellectual labor and judgment bestowed thereon; and not merely the facile use of the scissors; or extracts of the essential parts, constituting the chief value of the original work."[63] He held that Upham's use could not properly be regarded as an abridgment because "[i]t is a selection of the entire contents of particular letters, from the whole collection or mass of letters of the work of the plaintiffs."[64] In finding for the plaintiffs, Justice Story seemed to conclude that defendant's use was closer to a "facile use of the scissors" than a result of intellectual labor and judgment.

---

[57] 9 F. Cas. 342 (C.C.D. Mass. 1841) (No. 4, 901).

[58] See Bracha (2008).

[59] Ibid. For further background information on this case, see Reese (2006), pp. 259–297 at 259–275 and Patry (1985), pp. 19–25.

[60] *Folsom v Marsh* 9 F. Cas. 342, 345 (C.C.D. Mass. 1841).

[61] *Folsom v Marsh* 9 F. Cas. 342, 344 (C.C.D. Mass. 1841).

[62] Ibid 345 citing to *Dodsley v Kinnersley*, 1 Amb. 403; *Whittingham v. Wooler*, 2 Swanst. 428, 430, 431; *Tonson v Walker*, 3 Swanst. 672–679, 681.

[63] *Folsom v Marsh* 9 F. Cas. 342, 345 (C.C.D. Mass. 1841), citing to *Gyles v Wilcox*, 2 Atk. 141.

[64] *Folsom v Marsh* 9 F. Cas. 342, 348 (C.C.D. Mass. 1841).

Then, Justice Story uttered his famous proclamation:

> In short, we must often, in deciding questions of this sort, look to the nature and objects of the selections made, the quantity and value of the materials used, and the degree in which the use may prejudice the sale, or diminish the profits, or supersede the objects, of the original work.[65]

Folsom v Marsh had a strong effect on fair use jurisprudence in the United Kingdom as well as in the United States.[66] In the English case of *Scott v Stanford*,[67] decided in 1867, Vice-Chancellor Wood quoted from Justice Story's opinion with approval. *Scott v Stanford* concerned primarily factual information. The plaintiff was the registrar of the coal market for London, and published statistics showing the quantity of the imports of various collieries. The defendant "took the names of collieries, rearranged them in alphabetical order, placed the figures from the collieries opposite their name and summarized the whole of the information contained therein."[68] The defendant argued that there was an absence of *animus furandi* because he had honestly acknowledged the source from which the information was taken and he had acted "in good faith, for purely scientific purposes, and without any intention of making a profit, or superseding the sale of the original work."[69] Vice-Chancellor Wood couched the inquiry as "what is a fair commentary or fair use for scientific purposes of the labours of another man[?]".[70] He continued, "The general principles guiding the Court in cases of this description could hardly be found better stated than in the following words, used by Mr. Justice Story in *Folsom v. Marsh*..."[71] He then quoted in full the statement set out above (see footnote 65). The court ultimately held for the plaintiff because, despite the defendant's good intentions, "the great bulk of the Plaintiff's publication – a large and vital portion of his work and labour – has been appropriated and published in a form which will materially injure his copyright".[72] The court was primarily influenced by the fact that "[a] great deal of time and labour must have been

---

[65] Ibid. Justice Story had made a similar statement 2 years earlier in *Gray v. Russell,* 10 F. Cas. 1035, 1038 (C.C.D. Mass. 1839) (no. 5,728): "The question, in such a case, must be compounded of various considerations; whether it be a bona fide abridgement, or only an evasion by the omission of some unimportant parts; whether it will, in the present form, prejudice or supersede the original work; whether it will be adapted to the same class of readers; and many other considerations of the same sort."

[66] See further, Yankwich (1954–1955), pp. 203–215.

[67] L.R. 3 Eq. 718 (1867).

[68] Patry (1985), p. 32.

[69] *Scott v Stanford* L.R. 3 Eq. 718, 721 (1867).

[70] Ibid 722.

[71] Ibid.

[72] Ibid 723. This approach accords with our framing of the application of *animus furandi*, being that intention is not determinative in and of itself but, in some circumstances, bad intent may be relevant to the *type* of copying engaged in by the defendant. Here, the Court rightly focused on the type of copying to find that, despite the defendant's good intention, the copying was too close to the form and content of the original work and was likely to harm the market for the original.

spent in [the plaintiff's] compilation",[73] whereas the defendant had operated "by the mere use of paste and scissors, and without the exercise of any of that labour which the Plaintiff has had to encounter in extracting his materials from the mass of daily returns."[74] However, Vice-Chancellor Wood was also swayed by the difference in price between the two publications. The defendant's work was being sold more cheaply than the plaintiff's work, which prejudiced the plaintiff's market.[75]

Scott v Stanford was not Vice-Chancellor Wood's first fair use decision. Previously, but still after *Folsom v Marsh*, he had decided *Jarrold v Houlston*,[76] in which he stated,

> The really difficult question in cases of this description, where it must be admitted that the matter is not original, is how far the author of the work in question can be said to have made an unfair or undue use of previous works protected by copyright? As regards all common sources, he is entitled to make what use of them as he pleases; but, as Lord Langdale said in *Lewis v. Fullarton* (2 Beav. 6), he is not entitled to make any use of a work protected by copyright which is not what can be called a fair use.[77]

In 1870, 3 years after *Scott v Stanford*, Walter Copinger's landmark treatise on *The Law of Copyright* was published.[78] There, Copinger recites the same statement of Justice Story in *Folsom v Marsh* that Vice-Chancellor Wood quoted in *Scott v Stanford*.[79] Further, he describes the test for copyright infringement in the following terms:

> So entirely must each case be governed and regulated by the particular circumstances attending it, that any general rules on the subject must be received with extreme caution. Regard must be had to the value of the work, and the value of the extent of the infringements; for while, on the one hand, the policy of the law allows a man to profit by all antecedent literature, yet, on the other, the use made of such antecedent literature may not be so extensive as to injure the sale of the original work...[80]

Finally, for the purposes of our discussion, *Walter v Steinkopff* was decided in 1892.[81] There, the defendant, publisher of the *St James' Gazette*, published extracts

---

[73] *Scott v Stanford* L.R. 3 Eq. 718, 723 (1867).

[74] Ibid 724.

[75] Ibid 723–724.

[76] 3 K & J 708 (1857). This case involved the copying of an educational text that compiled, in question and answer format, instruction on science. The court found for the plaintiff. The court stated that the defendant and plaintiff could refer to common sources and use public domain sources in common, and that the defendant could refer to the plaintiff's work to see if he had forgotten anything in his own compilation. However, the court found that the defendant's copying went beyond these uses and purposes. The court was strongly influenced by the defendant's flat denial of any copying, which given that copying was evident the court found to be indicative of *animus furandi*.

[77] 3 K & J 708, 714–715 (1857). Vice-Chancellor Wood continued: "As regards the question of fair use of the Plaintiff's work, the Defendant to a great degree prevents inquiry. He says broadly in his affidavit, 'I deny that I copied or took any idea or language from the work of Dr. Brewer.' Upon a broad statement of that description that question of fair use is almost excluded."

[78] Copinger (1870).

[79] Ibid 96.

[80] Ibid 84.

[81] *Walter v Steinkopff* [1892] 3 Ch. 489.

from articles in the plaintiff's newspaper, the *Times*. In arguing their case for infringement, counsel for the plaintiffs stated (citing to earlier cases including *Scott v Stanford* and *Wilkins v Aiken*):

> The considerations on which the Court acts in granting or refusing an injunction are the nature and objects of the selections made by the copyist, the quantity and value of the material used, and the degree in which the use may affect the sale or supersede the objects of the original work, and whether the Defendants have applied in these selections what the Court can regard as real intellectual legitimate labour, or merely copied.[82]

Thus, the plaintiff's lawyers used the exact language set down by Justice Story in *Folsom v Marsh* in framing the question of infringement and whether the remedy of an injunction should follow. Justice North, delivering the opinion of the Court, took up this approach, quoting Lord Eldon in *Wilkins v Aiken*: "The question upon the whole is whether this is a legitimate use of the plaintiff's publication in the fair exercise of a mental operation deserving the character of an original work."[83] Justice North concluded, "In the present case what the Defendants have had recourse to is not a mental operation involving thought and labour in producing some original result, but a mechanical operation with scissors and paste, without the slightest pretention to an original result of any kind; it is the mere production of a 'copy' without trouble or cost."[84]

U.K. case law developed a complex but consistent doctrine in the eighteenth and nineteenth centuries that copyright infringement did not occur where the defendant's use was a fair use. The principle began with fair abridgments, but over time it broadened to include other derivative uses as well. Fairness was demonstrated by a use that did not prejudice or supersede the market for the original work. Courts generally found fair use where the defendant made a productive use that did more than colourably shorten or alter the original work for the purpose of evading liability (i.e. was more than a mere "scissors and paste" approach) and where the defendant had made an original contribution to the resulting work. The factors set down by Justice Story in *Folsom v Marsh* in 1841, which were essentially codified in the U.S. Copyright Act in 1976, were adopted without controversy by English courts determining infringement disputes in the late nineteenth century. The principle of fair use remained a central part of English copyright jurisprudence up to the turn of the century, which is where our historical inquiry ends.[85] In 1900, the UK

---

[82] Ibid 493.

[83] Ibid 495, quoting from *Wilkins v Aikin*, (1810) 17 Ves. (Ch.) 422, 426 (Lord Eldon).

[84] *Walter v Steinkopff* [1892] 3 Ch. 489, 495.

[85] Alexandra Sims has also tracked the legislative developments in England at the turn of the century, which generally support our argument that fair use was an established part of the copyright landscape at that time. For example, she writes that the UK Copyright Commission in 1878 noted that questions frequently arose as to "what is a fair use of the works of other authors" and concluded that these questions were in general best provided by the courts because the legislature was unable to lay down a principle to cover every example that might occur: see Sims (2011), pp. 3–27 at 21. She further notes that the Copyright Bill 1900, cl. 4(5), provided that "copyright shall not be infringed by a person making a copy, abridgment or translation of a book

Parliament enacted the *Commonwealth of Australia Constitution Act*,[86] which contained, in section 9, the Constitution of the Commonwealth of Australia and which granted to the Australian Parliament the power to make laws with respect to copyrights.[87] At the time of including the copyright power in the Constitution, the general legal understanding of "copyrights" would have included the notion of fair use as it had been established in U.K. precedent.

8.3 The Australian Constitution and the Copyright Power

In Sect. 8.2, we sought to show that fair use was an important concept in nineteenth century UK copyright jurisprudence. In this part, we focus on the Australian Constitution and discuss how the copyright, patent and trade mark power may incorporate this concept that a fair use does not infringe copyright.

Section 51 of the *Commonwealth of Australia Constitution Act 1900* provides:

> The Parliament shall, subject to this Constitution, have power to make laws for the peace, order, and good government of the Commonwealth with respect to: ... (xviii) copyrights, patents of inventions and designs, and trade marks.

Unlike the Intellectual Property Clause of the United States Constitution,[88] the power to make laws with respect to copyright in the Australian Constitution is not

---

for his private use...or otherwise fairly dealing with the contents of the work." The Copyright Bill 1910 contained a similar provision. Notably, these Bills did not limit the exempted use for only prescribed purposes. The UK Parliament finally codified the fair dealing exceptions in the *Copyright Act 1911*. No explanation was given for the enumerated fair dealing purposes (for criticism and review etc.). Sims observes that this is odd, particularly given the Parliament's stated intention that the provision was intended to merely reflect the common law position at that time: see Sims (2011), pp. 3–27 at 22–23. The fifth edition of Copinger's treatise, published in 1915, queries why prescribed circumstances were set out in the fair dealing provision of the 1911 Act, "for fair dealing for other purposes has always been...permitted and, presumably, it was not intended to cut down the rights of fair user previously enjoyed under the old law": Copinger (1870), p. 144, cited by Sims (2011), pp. 3–27 at 4.

[86] *Commonwealth of Australia Constitution Act 1900* (UK).

[87] Burrell and Coleman have considered the role of fair use in early Australian legislative developments. They argue that the *Copyright Act 1905* (Cth) "provided for a fair use defence in unambiguous terms": Burrell and Coleman (2005), p. 257. Section 28 of that Act provided that copyright would not be infringed by a person "otherwise fairly dealing with the contents of the book for the purpose of a new work". The *Copyright Act 1912* (Cth) (adopting the UK 1911 Copyright Act) replaced the 1905 Act and replaced "Australia's statutory fair use defence with the fair dealing provision", though the fact that this change did not draw any attention "suggests that no one at the time thought that the 1911 Act marked a break with the past as regards fair use": Burrell and Coleman (2005), pp. 257–258. Burrell and Coleman also refer to the fifth edition of *Copinger on Copyright* (1915), in which the author, J.M. Easton, "was happy to cite pre-1911 fair use cases as if they continued to be good law": Ibid 258.

[88] Constitution of the United States of America, Article 1, Section 8, Clause 8 gives Congress the power "To promote the Progress of Science and the useful Arts, by securing for limited Times to Authors and Inventors the exclusive Right to their respective Writings and Discoveries".

limited by express requirements that, for example, exclusive rights must be secured only for "limited Times" and to promote "Progress". Nevertheless, we would argue that the word "copyrights" in the Australian Constitution is infused with particular meaning that incorporates certain fundamental principles relating to the scope, operation and limits of copyright law. These principles maintain the important balance between private property rights to incentivize production and the public's right to access knowledge and culture, by preserving the distinction between infringing copying and non-infringing copying. The notion that non-infringing copying includes a productive or fair use of a copyrighted work is one which, we submit, is included within the meaning of "copyrights" in the Australian Constitution.

Although the Australian Constitution has a special status in Australian law, it was nonetheless enacted as part of an Imperial statute in the *Commonwealth of Australia Constitution Act 1900* (UK) s. 9. The Constitution, therefore, is to be interpreted according to the ordinary principles of statutory interpretation.[89] The words of the Constitution should be given the ordinary and natural meaning that they had at the time of federation, though it must be kept in mind that the Constitution is intended to endure.[90] Historical materials may be considered when construing the provisions of the Constitution to determine the background circumstances surrounding those provisions.[91]

In *The Grain Pool of Western Australia v Commonwealth* (2000) 202 CLR 479, [2000] HCA 14, the High Court considered the scope of the power in s 51 (xviii) in determining whether it supported the enactment of the *Plant Variety Rights Act 1987* (Cth) and the *Plant Breeders' Rights Act 1994* (Cth) as laws with respect to "patents". The majority judges adopted the approach of Higgins J in his dissenting judgment in *Attorney General for NSW v Brewery Employees Union of NSW*,[92] a case concerning trade marks. Justice Higgins held that while it was necessary to ascertain the meaning of "trade marks" in 1900 when the Constitution was enacted, that meaning "gives us the central type; it does not give us the circumference of the power".[93] The majority judges in *Grain Pool* determined that "it would be wrong to regard the legislative grant of monopoly rights in new plant varieties as being, in 1900, outside the 'central type' of the subject matter of

---

[89] See *McGinty v Western Australia* (1996) 196 CLR 140, 230 (McHugh J).

[90] See *Attorney General (NSW); Ex rel Tooth & Co Ltd v Brewery Employees' Union (NSW) (Union Label Case)* (1908) 6 CLR 469; *Singh v Commonwealth* (2004) 222 CLR 322; [2004] HCA 43 [159]–[160] (Gummow, Hayne and Heydon JJ).

[91] See *Singh v Commonwealth* (2004) 222 CLR 322; [2004] HCA 43 [12]–[21] (Gleeson CJ); *Wong v Commonwealth* (2009) 236 CLR 573; [2009] HCA 3 [18]–[21], [52], [60] (French CJ and Gummow J), [172] (Hayne, Crennan and Kiefel JJ), [262]–[265] (Heydon J); *Williams v Commonwealth* (2012) 86 ALJR 713; [2012] HCA 23 at [346], [348] (Heydon J).

[92] (1908) 6 CLR 469 (the *Union Label Case*).

[93] *Attorney General for NSW v Brewery Employees Union of NSW* (1908) 6 CLR 469, 610–611. See *Grain Pool of Western Australia v Commonwealth* (2000) 202 CLR 479, 493–494; [2000] HCA 14 [19] (Gleeson CJ, Gaudron, McHugh, Gummow, Hayne and Callinan JJ).

patents of inventions", noting that legislation to grant patent rights for plant-related inventions had been proposed in the United States as early as 1892 and that views in support of this legislation "would have been at the time apposite to the position of Australia wheat breeders such as William Farrer, whose Federation cultivar of wheat was named in 1901".[94]

The majority judges dismissed the plaintiff's assertion that the constitutional concept of a patentable invention is one that displays elements of both novelty and inventiveness, and that legislation which grants a patent right without requiring both novelty and inventiveness is unconstitutional.[95] The judges held that this requirement could not be said to have formed part of the constitutional understanding of "patent" because "the distinction later drawn between prior publication or lack of novelty and obviousness or lack of invention or of subject-matter was not fully developed in the case law as it stood in 1900."[96]

In a concurring opinion, Justice Kirby stated that the "ultimate criterion [is] not pre-Federation legal understandings, but a search for the 'essential characteristics' of the words used in the Constitution."[97] He referred to the judgment of Justice Isaacs in the *Union Label Case*:

> Isaacs J insisted that the search was ultimately not for the procedural or substantial incidents of "trade marks" as they had developed in England up to 1900. Instead, it was for something more fundamental and enduring (and therefore released from such a reference point). He described it as a search for the "really essential characteristics", the "universal element", the "fundamental conception" or the "essential particulars".[98]

The *Grain Pool* case concerned the question of what subject matter fell within the scope of the "patents" power. Our inquiry with respect to copyrights does not concern subject matter, but rather is an investigation into the very meaning of "copyrights" or, in other words, the "essential characteristics" of "copyrights" as it appears in the Constitution.

The fundamental conception of copyright, as envisaged originally by the Statute of Anne[99] and later by the Australian Constitution, is that copyright grants to an author of an original work exclusive rights in the exploitation of that work in exchange for the author making that work available to the public. This understanding of copyright as a balance between private rights and public rights endures to this day—the High Court in the 2009 *IceTV* case noted as such:

---

[94] *Grain Pool of Western Australia v Commonwealth* (2000) 202 CLR 479, 496; [2000] HCA 14 [26] (Gleeson CJ, Gaudron, McHugh, Gummow, Hayne and Callinan JJ).

[95] Ibid [48].

[96] Ibid [49].

[97] Ibid [103] (Kirby J).

[98] Ibid [123] (Kirby J), referring to the reasons of Isaacs J in *Attorney General for NSW v Brewery Employees Union of NSW* (1908) 6 CLR 469, 560, 572, 577, 581 (Isaacs J).

[99] The long title of the Statute of Anne was "An Act for the Encouragement of Learning, by Vesting the Copies of Printed Books in the Authors or Purchasers of such Copies, during the Times therein mentioned." See further, Leval (1989–1990), pp. 1105–1136 at 1108–1109.

The "social contract" envisaged by the Statute of Anne, and still underlying the present Act, was that an author could obtain a monopoly, limited in time, in return for making a work available to the reading public.[100]

Thus, copyright seeks to balance the monopoly interests of an author with the public's interest in gaining access to new works of creative authorship.[101] The public interest is promoted through essential characteristics of the copyright doctrine, including that copyright protection is granted for a limited time,[102] that copyright protects only expression and not ideas,[103] that copying an insubstantial part will not be a copyright infringement,[104] and, we argue, that a productive or fair

---

[100] *IceTV Pty Limited v Nine Network Australia Pty Limited* (2009) 239 CLR 458, 471; [2009] HCA 14 (22 April 2009) [25] (French CJ, Crennan and Kiefel JJ). This statement was quoted by Crennan and Kiefel JJ in *Phonographic Performance Company of Australia Limited v Commonwealth of Australia* [2012] HCA 8 (28 March 2012) [96].

[101] Australian courts have highlighted the centrality of authorship to copyright law: see *Telstra Corporation Limited v Phone Directories Company Pty Ltd* [2010] FCA 44 [20]–[21] (Gordon J) (stating: "The centrality of authorship is self evident." Also: "Original works emanate from authors... Authorship and originality are correlatives"), [45], [343]–[344]. *Affirmed in Telstra Corporation Ltd v Phone Directories Co Pty Ltd* [2010] FCAFC 149, see particularly [57], [90] (Keane CJ), [100], [104]–[105], [119], [127] (Perram J), [133]–[134], [137], [143] (Yates J). Both cases followed *IceTV Pty Limited v Nine Network Australia Pty Limited* (2009) 239 CLR 458, 471; [2009] HCA 14. The requirement of authorship can also serve as a limit on the scope of copyright protection, especially in relation to computer generated works. Although we do not deal with authorship in any great detail in this article, we note its importance in promoting balance within the copyright doctrine.

[102] *IceTV Pty Limited v Nine Network Australia Pty Limited* (2009) 239 CLR 458, 471; [2009] HCA 14 (22 April 2009) [25] (French CJ, Crennan and Kiefel JJ). (Note the judges inclusion of "limited in time" in relation to the copyright monopoly).

[103] See, for example, *IceTV Pty Limited v Nine Network Australia Pty Limited* (2009) 239 CLR 458, 472; [2009] HCA 14 (22 April 2009) [28] (French CJ, Crennan and Kiefel JJ): "That facts are not protected is a crucial part of the balance of competing policy considerations in copyright legislation. The information/expression dichotomy, in copyright law, is rooted in considerations of social utility. Copyright, being an exception to the law's general abhorrence of monopolies, does not confer a monopoly on facts or information because to do so would impede the reading public's access to and use of facts and information. Copyright is not given to reward work distinct from the production of a particular form of expression." The Justices cite, as authority, *MacMillan & Co Ltd v K & J Cooper* (1923) 93 LJPC 113, 117–118 (Lord Atkinson). For an older source, see Copinger (1870), pp. 5–6: "Ideas, being neither capable of a visible possession nor of sustaining any one of the qualities or incidents of property, inasmuch as they have no bounds whatever, cannot be the subject of property...They are of a nature too unsubstantial, too evanescent, to be the subject of proprietary rights...When, however, any material has embodied those ideas, then the ideas, through that corporeity, can be recognised as a species of property by the common law. The claim is not to ideas, but to the order of words, and this order has a marked identity and a permanent endurance."

[104] See, for example, *IceTV Pty Limited v Nine Network Australia Pty Limited* (2009) 239 CLR 458, 470; [2009] HCA 14 (22 April 2009) [21] (French CJ, Crennan and Kiefel JJ): "If there were no reproduction of a substantial part from any of the individual works, the conclusion must be that there was no infringement of copyright in any of the works"; see also 472–473 [28]–[29], [31]: "This principle has a long provenance"—citing to *Scott v Stanford* (1867) LR 3 Eq 718, 723, 724 (Page Wood VC); *Bradbury v Hotten* (1872) LR 8 Exch 1, 7 (Pigott B); *Leslie v J Young &*

use of a copyrighted work is not an infringing copy capable of being regulated by copyright law. A fair use of a work, provided it contains an original contribution of the defendant, is almost certain to enhance the public interest aspect of copyright's social bargain in encouraging the production and dissemination of new works for the learning and advancement of the public. These essential characteristics together promote a robust public domain and an appropriately delineated copyright doctrine. The U.S. Supreme Court has expressly characterised the idea/expression dichotomy and fair use as important free speech safeguards[105] which ensure that "copyright itself [is] the engine of free expression" despite its grant of monopoly rights.[106]

Further, as was demonstrated in Sect. 8.2 of this paper, the concept of fair use was one that had been fully considered and sufficiently developed by the time that the Australian Constitution was enacted in 1900. In the United States, the fair use factors laid out by Justice Story in *Folsom v Marsh*[107] in 1841 remained sufficiently static for the US Congress to codify them in the 1976 Copyright Act.[108] *Folsom v Marsh* was considered in *Scott v Stanford*,[109] one of the prominent English cases that formed part of the legal precedent in Australia at the turn of the nineteenth century.[110] By the time the Australian Constitution was enacted, the UK courts had established a doctrine that copyright infringement did not occur where the defendant made a productive use that included an original contribution and that did more than colourably alter the copyrighted work.[111] Thus, fair use can be easily distinguished from the concept that a patentable invention must be both novel and inventive because, unlike that concept, it *was* fully developed as a doctrine in 1900.

Sons [1894] AC 335, 341 (Lord Herschell LC); and *Cooper v Stephens* [1895] 1 Ch 567, 572 (Romer J). See also *IceTV* at 487 [75] (Gummow, Hayne and Heydon JJ): "The notion of substantial appropriation as sufficient to constitute infringement is found also in the pre-1911 case law"—citing to *Bradbury v Hotten* at 7 and *Cooper v Stephens* at 572.

[105] See *Harper & Row v. Nation Enterprises,* 471 U.S. 539, 558 (1985); *Eldred v Ashcroft,* 537 U.S. 186, 219 ("built-in First Amendment accommodations"), 221 ("copyright's built-in free speech safeguards") (2003).

[106] *Harper & Row v. Nation Enterprises,* 471 U.S. 539, 560 (1985); *Eldred v Ashcroft,* 537 U.S. 186, 219, 220 (2003).

[107] *Folsom v Marsh,* 9 F. Cas. 342 (C.C.D. Mass. 1841). Although Story J did not use the term "fair use" (Cohen et al. have noted that this term first appeared in *Lawrence v Dana,* 15 F. Cas. 26, 60 (C.C.D. Mass. 1869): Cohen et al. 2010, pp. 530–531), U.S. courts continued to look to the factors set out by Story J in resolving fair use cases until these factors were codified in 1976.

[108] 17 U.S.C. §107.

[109] L.R. 3 Eq. 718 (1867). *Scott v Stanford* was referred to by Finkelstein J in *TCN Channel Nine Pty Ltd v Network Ten Pty Ltd (No 2)* [2005] FCAFC 53 at [8] and [11].

[110] Australian courts habitually followed English court precedent until the passage of the *Australia Act 1986* (UK) and the *Australia Act 1986* (Cth), which terminated all appeals from Australian courts to the Privy Council in England (section 11 of both Acts). In *Cook v Cook* (1986) 162 CLR 376, Mason, Wilson, Deane and Dawson JJ said (at 390): "Subject, perhaps, to the special position of decisions of the House of Lords given in the period in which appeals lay from this country to the Privy Council, the precedents of other legal systems are not binding and are usually only to the degree of the persuasiveness of their reasoning."

[111] See Sect. 8.2.

To use the words adopted by Justice Kirby in the *Grain Pool* case,[112] we submit that fair use is a "fundamental" and "enduring" aspect of copyright law which goes to the "central type" of the copyright power in the Australian Constitution.

8.4   Balance and the Copyright Act

In line with our submission that the meaning of "copyrights" in the Australian Constitution includes the notion of fair use, we argue that the *Copyright Act 1968* (Cth) has sufficient scope to incorporate the principle that a productive use—or a fair use—of a copyrighted work is not an infringement. It can do this through the provisions that distinguish between infringing copies and non-infringing copies, in particular sections 36(1) and 101(1), which contain the phrase "any act comprised in the copyright".

It is clear from the examination of the older English cases in Sect. 8.2 that the understanding of UK copyright law in 1900 and underpinning our constitutional notion of "copyrights" was not that of an unlimited power to prevent all copying. Rather, the essence of copyright law was balance. Copyright distinguished between infringing and non-infringing copying and granted to the copyright owner only the power to control the former.[113] We argue that copyright law today, which finds expression in the *Copyright Act 1968*, must draw the same distinction and regulate only infringing copying.

While we do not suggest that the *Copyright Act 1968* is unconstitutional as enacted, we do argue that it must be read to operate within constitutional bounds. This position has judicial support. In *FCT v Munro; British Imperial Oil Co Ltd v FCT*, Justice Isaacs said, "There is always an initial presumption that Parliament did no intend to pass beyond constitutional bounds. If the language of a statute is not so intractable as to be incapable of being consistent with this presumption, the presumption should prevail."[114] In *Attorney-General (Vic) v Commonwealth ('the Pharmaceutical Benefits Case')*, Justice Dixon stated:

> In discharging our duty of passing upon the validity of an enactment, we should make every reasonable intendment in its favour. We should give to the powers conferred upon the Parliament as ample an application as the expressed intention and the recognised implications of the Constitution will allow. We should interpret the enactment, so far as its

---

[112] See discussion above; *Grain Pool of Western Australia v Commonwealth* (2000) 202 CLR 479, [2000] HCA 14 [123] (Kirby J), referring to the reasons of Isaacs J in *Attorney General for NSW v Brewery Employees Union of NSW* (1908) 6 CLR 469, 560, 572, 577, 581.

[113] For a detailed discussion of what does and does not fall within the ambit of infringing copying, see Greenleaf and Bond (2013), pp. 111–138.

[114] *FCT v Munro; British Imperial Oil Co Ltd v FCT* (1926) 38 CLR 153 at 180 per Isaacs J. This statement was endorsed in *Lim v Minister for Immigration, Local Government and Ethnic Affairs* (1992) 176 CLR 1, 14 (Mason CJ) and *Minister for Immigration and Multicultural and Indigenous Affairs v Al Masri* (2003) 126 FCR 54; 197 ALR 241.

language permits, so as to bring it within the application of those powers and we should not, unless the intention is clear, read it as exceeding them.[115]

These statements accord with section 15A of the *Acts Interpretation Act 1901* (Cth), which provides, "Every Act shall be read and construed subject to the Constitution".[116]

The constitutional notion of copyright focuses on balance, which is achieved through the essential characteristics of limited term, substantial part, material form (relating to the idea/expression dichotomy) and productive or fair use. This focus on balance is evident in present-day copyright law in Australia, in a number of sections of the *Copyright Act 1968*. For example, the notion of limited term is apparent in sections 33, 34 and 93–96, which relate to duration of copyright in works and subject matter other than works. The requirement that an infringing copy involves the taking of a substantial part appears in section 14(1), which provides, "In this Act, unless the contrary intention appears: (a) a reference to the doing of an act in relation to a work or other subject-matter shall be read as including a reference to the doing of act in relation to a substantial part of the work or other subject matter."

We submit that the *Copyright Act 1968* can also be read to give effect to fair use notwithstanding that the fair use doctrine is not *expressly* incorporated into Australian copyright legislation.[117] This lack of express incorporation is not necessarily surprising. As Jessica Litman has argued, copyright law traditionally granted very narrow rights and "aimed its proscriptions at commercial and institutional entities", leaving ordinary uses such as reading, listening and viewing unconstrained.[118] The Statute of Anne was directed towards those who caused to be "Printed, Reprinted or Imported" books without the consent of the proprietor[119]—acts which were necessarily outside the reach and abilities of ordinary citizens because of the constraints of technology and the printing press at the time. Because copyright law was concerned with regulating printers and publishers, it did not concern itself with the activities of ordinary citizens, nor did it need to. These ordinary activities—

---

[115] *Attorney-General (Vic) v Commonwealth ('the Pharmaceutical Benefits Case')* (1945) 71 CLR 237, 267 (Dixon J). This statement was endorsed in *Lim v Minister for Immigration, Local Government and Ethnic Affairs* (1992) 176 CLR 1, 14 (Mason CJ) and *Minister for Immigration and Multicultural and Indigenous Affairs v Al Masri* (2003) 126 FCR 54; 197 ALR 241.

[116] See also *Lim v Minister for Immigration, Local Government and Ethnic Affairs* (1992) 176 CLR 1, 14 (Mason CJ).

[117] Cf. *Collier Constructions v Foskett* (1990) 19 IPR 44; [1990] FCA 392 at [54]–[63], where Gummow J rejected the argument that there was a defence to copyright infringement grounded in the public interest. His Honour rejected this defence on the basis that it sprang from the general law with no grounding in statute and that the English authority giving rise to the defence lacked consideration of "fundamental principle" and failed to demarcate the limits of the defence. In this article, we seek to demonstrate how the principle of fair use or productive use is firmly established in UK precedent and how it can be incorporated within statute. We therefore submit that fair use can be distinguished from the defence considered by Gummow J in *Collier Constructions v Foskett*.

[118] Litman (2007), pp. 1871–1920 at 1882. See also, Atkinson (2007).

[119] The Statute of Anne, 1710.

which we might deem "fair uses"—"functioned as historic copyright liberties, implicit in the copyright statutory scheme and essential to its purpose."[120]

In the United States, copyright law evolved so that the scope of protection expanded and the doctrine of fair use was included as a statutory defence in §107 of the Copyright Act 1976. Thus, while the *Folsom v Marsh* case was originally understood in US jurisprudence as "describing the boundaries of a prima facie claim of infringement" it gradually came to be treated as a precedent for the fair use defence now enshrined in copyright legislation.[121] In fact, some US scholars have argued that it was *Folsom v Marsh* itself that casually flipped the copyright paradigm and began the US on the march towards a system of copyright law that treats virtually every copy as an infringement subject only to statutory defences. For example, John Tehranian has argued that whereas the early Anglo-American fair abridgment and fair use cases "viewed acts of borrowing, if they were sufficiently transformative, as simply *non-infringing* uses",[122]*Folsom v Marsh* subtly altered the infringement inquiry by focusing on what was taken from the copyrighted work rather than what was produced by the defendant. Tehranian claims that it is because of this conceptual shift in applying the infringement test that US cases subsequent to *Folsom* began, over time, to treat fair use as a defence.[123]

In Australia, the law has not developed to the point that fair use is treated as a defence to infringement, whether based in common law or statute. Nonetheless, fair use forms part of the complex tapestry of the copyright law. We submit that fair use can be incorporated in the *Copyright Act 1968* through sections 36(1) and 101(1), which we argue distinguish between infringing and non-infringing copies with the phrase "any act comprised in the copyright". We make this argument more fully below in Sect. 8.4.1.

We further seek to demonstrate how the principle of fair use can be used to interpret and apply the tests for infringing copying under the Australian Copyright Act. To prove that infringing copying has occurred, a plaintiff must generally show that there has been (1) copying (2) of a substantial part of the copyrighted work. Copying has two elements—there must be a causal connection and there must be an objective similarity between the two works.[124] The tests of causal connection and

---

[120] Litman (2007), pp. 1871–1920 at 1882.

[121] Reese (2006), pp. 259–297 at 293, see generally 287–293, 297. See also Bracha (2008); Patterson (1998), pp. 431–452; Tehranian (2004–2005), pp. 465–508.

[122] Tehranian (2004–2005), pp. 465–508 at 483.

[123] "Under *Folsom* and its progeny, once the copyright holder made a *prima facie* showing that the alleged infringer borrowed the protected work, the burden then shifted to the alleged infringer to demonstrate that his use was excusable": Tehranian (2004–2005), pp. 465–508 at 483. See also Patterson (1998), pp. 431–452; Reese (2006), pp. 259–297 at 293; Bracha (2008).

[124] See Sam Ricketson and Chris Creswell, *The Law of Intellectual Property: Copyright, Designs and Confidential Information* (Thomson Reuters) (updated April 2012) [9.85] Infringing reproduction: the need for causal connection and objective similarity (accessed 14 May 2012). See also, *EMI Songs Australia Pty Limited v Larrikin Music Publishing Pty Limited* [2011] FCAFC 41 (31 March 2011) at [51] (Emmett J), citing to *Francis Day & Hunter Ltd v Bron* [1963] 1 CH 587, 614.

objective similarity are not statutory tests set out in the Act, but they are used by courts to assist in interpreting the Act and determining infringement. The doctrine of fair use can inform this interpretative process, by helping courts to distinguish between infringing and non-infringing copying both within the objective similarity test and the substantial part requirement of the Act. In the follow sections, we address the role of fair use in relation to each of the following in turn: (1) the term "an act comprised in copyright" in sections 36(1) and 101(1) of the Act; (2) the objective similarity test; and (3) the substantial part requirement in s. 14 of the Act.

8.4.1 An Act Comprised in Copyright

Sections 36(1) and 101(1) of the *Copyright Act 1968* set out what it means to infringe copyright under Australian law. Sections 36(1) and 101(1) are virtually identical, though the former relates to Part III works and the latter relates to Part IV subject matter other than works. Section 36(1) provides,

> Subject to this Act, the copyright in a literary, dramatic, musical or artistic work is infringed by a person who, not being the owner of the copyright, and without the licence of the owner of the copyright, does in Australia, or authorizes the doing in Australia of, any act comprised in the copyright.

This defines copyright infringement under Australian law as the doing, without licence, of an *act comprised in the copyright*. The term "act comprised in the copyright" is significant, because by its construction it necessarily contemplates that there may be acts undertaken that are *not* comprised in the copyright.

What exactly does "any act comprised in copyright" mean? Section 13 (1) provides:

> A reference in this Act to an act comprised in the copyright in a work or other subject-matter shall be read as a reference to any act that, under this Act, the owner of the copyright has the exclusive right to do.

In relation to s. 36(1), this points us to section 31(1), which sets out the exclusive rights of copyright owners of original works.[125]Section 31 (1)(a)(i) gives the copyright owner, in relation to a literary, dramatic or musical work, the exclusive right to reproduce the work in a material form.

We know, however, that the Copyright Act does not give a copyright owner unlimited power to prevent all copying of her work, despite the broad language in s. 31.[126] For example, we know that a copyright owner cannot prevent people

---

[125] The exclusive rights in section 31 are (for literary, dramatic and musical works) the rights to: reproduce the work in a material form; publish the work; perform the work in public; communicate the work to the public; and make an adaptation of the work. For artistic works, the exclusive rights are the rights to reproduce the work in a material form; publish the work; and communicate the work to the public.

[126] See also the corresponding language in ss. 85–88 in relation to subject matter other than works.

copying the ideas contained in her work if they do not also copy the expression, and she cannot prevent people copying an insubstantial part of her work. Nor can she (or her estate) prevent people copying her work once the period of copyright protection has expired and the work has moved into the public domain. Importantly, these exclusions operate as limits on the infringement test and not as exceptions or defences to infringement once infringement has been established. Thus, copying an idea is a *non-infringing act*, not an act of infringement that has been excused under a defence or exception in the Copyright Act.[127] Likewise, copying an insubstantial part is a *non-infringing act*.

Read together, sections 36(1), 101(1) and 13(1) incorporate the infringement test into the Copyright Act by distinguishing "act[s] comprised in the copyright" (i.e. acts that the copyright owner has the exclusive right to do) from acts understood to be non-infringing. These sections are the touchstones in the *Copyright Act 1968* for the notion of an infringing copy; they mark the point at which the Act sets its sights on regulating infringing copying while excluding non-infringing copying.

It is our submission that a fair use of a work is also a non-infringing act at the point of applying the infringement test. We take our understanding of fair use from the U.K. case law surveyed in Sect. 8.2, which established a principle that a fair use of a copyrighted work was not an infringing copy prohibited by law. Fair use was generally demonstrated by a productive use that did more than colourably alter the original work for the purpose of evading liability and where the defendant had made some kind of original contribution to the resulting work. It was also important that the fair use did not supersede the original work or prejudice the market for the original work. This was the state of the law at the time that the right to make laws with respect to copyright was included in the Australian Constitution—it was accepted that just like the use of an idea or public domain work, a fair use of a work was not an infringement. It is through the principle of fair use and the other essential features of copyright such as substantial part, limited term and the idea-expression dichotomy, that copyright law preserves the important balance between owner and public by distinguishing infringing copying from non-infringing copying.

Justice Leval, in this 1990 *Harvard Law Review* comment, highlighted the role played by fair use in maintaining balance within copyright law:

> Fair use is not a grudgingly tolerated exception to the copyright owner's rights of private property, but a fundamental policy of the copyright law. The stimulation of creative thought and authorship for the benefit of society depends assuredly on the protection of the author's monopoly. But it depends equally on the recognition that the monopoly must have limits. Those limits include the public dedication of facts (notwithstanding the author's efforts in uncovering them); the public dedication of ideas (notwithstanding the author's creation); and the public dedication of the right to make fair use of material covered by the copyright.[128]

---

[127] For the defences and exceptions to infringement in the Copyright Act, see *Copyright Act 1968* (Cth), ss. 40–73 and ss. 103A–112E.

[128] Leval (1989–1990), pp. 1105–1136 at 1135–1136.

If fair use is a fundamental part of the constitutional notion of copyrights, as we argue it is, then Australian copyright law must provide space for fair use of copyrighted works. We submit that this space is built into the *Copyright Act 1968* through sections 36(1) and 101(1). Our claim is that a fair use of a work does not produce an infringing copy and so a fair use is not an "act comprised in the copyright" under s. 36(1) or s. 101(1), just as copying of insubstantial parts, ideas or public domain works are not "acts comprised in the copyright".

We further argue that this position accords with the ordinary meaning of the words used in sections 36(1) and 101(1), in particular the term "any act comprised in the copyright". There is nothing in the text of Act, including sections 13 and 31, which contradicts our position. Section 15AB(1)(a) of the *Acts Interpretation Act 1901* provides that extrinsic materials may be used to "confirm that the meaning of the provision is the ordinary meaning conveyed by the text of the provisions taking into account its context in the Act and the purpose or object underlying the Act". It is our submission that the Australian Constitution and the constitutional notion of "copyrights" are extrinsic materials that may be consulted to confirm that the ordinary meaning of "act comprised in the copyright" in sections 36(1) and 101 (1) is a reference to *infringing* copying. The constitutional notion of copyrights further helps to confirm that the purpose of these provisions in the Copyright Act is to exclude from regulation certain non-infringing uses, such as use of an idea, use of an insubstantial part and productive or fair uses. These uses, including and especially fair uses, are *not* acts comprised in the copyright.

Section 15AB(2) of the *Acts Interpretation Act 1901* sets out a list of materials which may be consulted to confirm the ordinary meaning of a provision, including explanatory memorandum relating to the Bill, speeches made to a House of Parliament, international agreements and reports of Royal Commissions and Law Reform Commissions. For our purposes, it is important to note that the list in s. 15AB(2) is non-exhaustive and, furthermore, the rule at common law is that any relevant extrinsic material may be considered.[129] It is our contention that the Australian Constitution—and therefore, logically, the constitutional notion of "copyrights"—can therefore form part of this relevant extrinsic material.

Given our emphasis on infringing copying, we now turn to consider how courts today recognise infringing copying in the cases that come before them. Over the years, courts have developed various tests to aid in understanding when an infringing copy has been made. For example, the causal connection test helps to distinguish copying from independent creation. The objective similarity test, examined more closely below, is designed to help courts determine when infringing copying has occurred by holding that copying should, by its very nature, result in evident similarity between two works. These are tests developed to assist courts in interpreting the *Copyright Act*, however, and should not be given independent significance beyond the Act itself. The tests must correspond to the Act and stay

---

[129] *CIC Insurance Ltd v Bankstown Football Club Ltd* (1997) 187 CLR 384, 408 (Brennan CJ, Dawson, Toohey and Gummow JJ).

within its scope, and the Copyright Act, in turn, must correspond to the Constitution and stay within the scope of the constitutional power to make laws with respect to "copyrights".[130] This means that the tests designed to help courts understand sections 36 and 101 must also be applied in ways that facilitate fair use. In the section below, we examine how the test for objective similarity can be applied to give effect to an understanding of copyright that incorporates the doctrine of fair use.

8.4.2 Objective Similarity

To succeed in a copyright suit, a plaintiff must prove that the defendant has made an infringing copy of the plaintiff's original work. To prove copying, the plaintiff must show that there is objective similarity between her work and the defendant's work.[131] Establishing objective similarity is not always an easy task, particularly where the allegedly infringing work is not an exact reproduction but instead is an adaptation or a composite work such as a remix or mash-up. This can implicate the idea/expression dichotomy and requires the plaintiff to show that there is objective similarity between the *expression* of the two works and not merely the *ideas* behind them.[132] The *Copyright Act 1968* does not prescribe how objective similarity is to be determined, but generally the two works are compared side-by-side.

In *EMI Songs Australia Pty Ltd v Larrikin Music Publishing Pty Limited*, Justice Jagot affirmed that the correct approach to determining infringement was to deal with objective similarity first and substantial part second.[133] However, we would argue that this sequential approach to the steps of the infringement inquiry has been confined too narrowly by the courts so that objective similarity is often treated as an easy-to-establish threshold test: a mere formality that is established by *any* apparent similarity, no matter how remote or minor. Instead, courts should require clear similarity between the two works in question, *within the appropriate context of the taking*. This approach would take into account the features of the fair use doctrine established in the early English case law, including whether the defendant has engaged in servile imitation (infringement) or a productive use (fair).

---

[130] For a discussion of the difference between factual determinations and legal tests, and the primacy of statute, see *Network Ten Pty Ltd v TCN Channel Nine Pty Ltd & Ors* [2005] HCATrans 842 (7 October 2005).

[131] See Sam Ricketson and Chris Creswell, *The Law of Intellectual Property: Copyright, Designs and Confidential Information* (Thomson Reuters) (updated April 2012) [9.85] Infringing reproduction: the need for causal connection and objective similarity (accessed 14 May 2012).

[132] Ibid.

[133] *EMI Songs Australia Pty Limited v Larrikin Music Publishing Pty Limited* [2011] FCAFC 41 (31 March 2011) [197]–[198] (Jagot J), referring to *Metricon Homes Pty Ltd v Barrett Property group Pty Ltd* (2008) 248 ALR 364; [2008] FCAFC 46 [23] and *Elwood Clothing Pty Ltd v Cotton On Clothing Pty Ltd* (2008) 172 FCR 580; [2008] FCAFC 197 [41]. See also at [66] per Emmett J.

The early English cases considered the defendant's use of the copyrighted parts within the context of the contributions made and labour invested by the defendant in creating a substantially new work. Where the defendant had done more than merely "copy and paste" from the original work, the courts generally found that there had been a fair or non-infringing use. There is scope for courts today to make similar determinations when assessing objective similarity.

A consequence of a more contextual approach to objective similarity is that the defendant's work *as a whole* should be compared to the plaintiff's work *as a whole* when assessing whether the works are sufficiently similar. Justice Jagot in the *Larrikin* case stated that "[t]he test is not whether, considered overall, [the defendant's work] Down Under is similar to [the plaintiff's work] Kookaburra."[134] She further stated, "For the trial judge to have done otherwise and adopted the approach of the EMI parties and Mr. Hay of determining objective similarity by reference to the whole of Down Under, would have involved a departure from established principle."[135] However, it is not clear that this "established principle" is as clear-cut as her Honour makes out. There have been cases in Australian law where courts have assessed similarity by reference to the whole of the works. One example is *Zecolla v Universal City Studios Inc.*,[136] a case addressing whether a film about a man-eating shark (*Great White*) infringed the copyright in the film, screenplay and novel of *Jaws*. There, the primary judge watched the film, *Jaws*, and the allegedly infringing film one after the other to determine whether there was objective similarity between the two as entire works.[137] This was not held to be erroneous on appeal.[138] A similar assessment was undertaken in *Telstra Corp. Ltd. v Royal & Sun Alliance Insurance Ltd.*,[139] where the court decided that similarities apparent in two commercial advertisements related to ideas and concepts rather than protectable expression.[140] This decision was reached by comparing the script of one advertisement with the script and film of the second advertisement, and the series

---

[134] *EMI Songs Australia Pty Limited v Larrikin Music Publishing Pty Limited* [2011] FCAFC 41 (31 March 2011) [186] (Jagot J), referring to *Dixon Investments Pty Ltd v Hall* (1990) 18 IPR 490, 497.

[135] *EMI Songs Australia Pty Limited v Larrikin Music Publishing Pty Limited* [2011] FCAFC 41 (31 March 2011) [199] (Jagot J). See also [224]–[225], where Her Honour argues the comparing the whole works is only appropriate when dealing with compilations where originality is low or the idea/expression dichotomy is implicated (referring to *Leslie v Young & Sons* [1894] AC 335 at 411, which concerned railway timetables).

[136] (1982) 46 ALR 189.

[137] See *Zecolla v Universal City Studios Inc.* (1982) 46 ALR 189, 194.

[138] Ibid 194, where Lockhart J (delivering a joint judgment with Fitzgerald J) stated, "No doubt numerous factors, including differences of sequence and of dialogue, aspects of idea or theme which lack originality and various other matters were all properly to be considered, at least subconsciously, but only as part of a process of forming an overall impression as to the originality of the respondent's novel, screenplay and film, the originality of the appellant's film, the extent of similarity or dissimilarity and whether or not there was copying."

[139] (2003) 57 IPR 453.

[140] *Telstra Corp. Ltd. v Royal & Sun Alliance Insurance Ltd.* (2003) 57 IPR 453, 466–468 (Markel J).

of dramatic events recorded in the first advertisement with the series of dramatic events recorded in the second advertisement.[141]

To apply an objective similarity test that compares only small parts of the works in question—as Justice Jagot suggests—risks reducing the test to a state of pointlessness.[142] It is possible to fragment a defendant's work so much that objective similarity between the fragmented parts of the defendant's work and the fragmented parts of the plaintiff's work will almost *always* be found.[143] This, however, runs counter to the policy of encouraging the production of new works and to the reality that all works draw upon and are influenced by other works. Conversely, comparing the two works in their entireties provides a clear and distinctive opportunity for courts to take into account the context and nature of the defendant's use—in particular, whether the defendant has engaged in a productive or transformative use. Critically, where the defendant has made original contributions to the part taken from the copyrighted work sufficient to create a new and altogether different work, then a court may find that objective similarity is lacking.

For example, in *Joy Music v Sunday Pictorial Newspapers*,[144] an early parody case, the transformative nature of the defendant's use was central to the Court's determination that there had been no infringement of copyright. The facts of that case were as follows. Plaintiffs owned copyright in the words and music of a song called "Rock-a-Billy". Defendants printed the *Sunday Pictorial* newspaper, which published an article on the sporting activities of Prince Philip. The article was entitled, "Rock-a-Philip Rock! Rock!" and contained a parody of the plaintiffs' song. The plaintiffs objected, alleging copyright infringement. The legislation governing the parties' dispute, the *Copyright Act 1956* (UK), did not contain a fair dealing exception for parody.[145] Nevertheless, Justice McNair found for the defendants, stating, "Although it is clear that the article in the 'Sunday Pictorial' had its origin in 'Rock-a-Billy', it was produced by sufficient independent new work by Mr. Boyle to be in itself, not a reproduction of the original 'Rock-a-Billy', but a new work derived from 'Rock-a-Billy'."[146] His Honour considered the earlier case of *Hanfstaengl v Empire Palace*,[147] which concerned whether the defendant's

---

[141] "Dramatic events" here related to the original parts of the plaintiff's advertisement said to comprise a "dramatic work". See *Telstra Corp. Ltd. v Royal & Sun Alliance Insurance Ltd.* (2003) 57 IPR 453, 466 (Markel J).

[142] Crosthwaite H (2012) Laughing Objectively: The Objectively Similar Test in Larrikin Music Publishing Pty Ltd v EMI Songs Australia Pty Ltd (unpublished manuscript on file with authors).

[143] For example, the trial judge in the *Larrikin Music* case compared "the flute riff in Down Under when it plays the fourth bar of Dr Ford's Example D, and the second bar of Kookaburra, and, second, the flute riff in Down Under when it plays the second and fourth bars of Dr Ford's Example E, and the first and second bars of Kookaburra": see *EMI Songs Australia Pty Limited v Larrikin Music Publishing Pty Limited* [2011] FCAFC 41 (31 March 2011) [198] (Jagot J).

[144] [1960] 1 All ER 703.

[145] See *Copyright Act 1956* (UK), s. 6, available at http://www.legislation.gov.uk/ukpga/1956/74/section/6/enacted.

[146] *Joy Music v Sunday Pictorial Newspapers* [1960] 1 All ER 703, 708.

[147] [1894] 3 Ch. 109.

sketches were infringing reproductions of the plaintiff's work. There, Lindley LJ had concluded, "The amusing sketches in 'Punch' of the pictures in the Royal Academy are not, in my opinion, infringements of the copyrights in those pictures, although probably made from the pictures themselves."[148] McNair J opined, "There it seems to me the learned judge is saying: 'These are not infringements judged by the purpose and intention with which they had been produced'."[149] He further observed, "Lindley LJ decided that, on his appreciation of the facts, no unfair use had been made of the plaintiff's original copyright, and that there had been no substantial taking."[150] Justice McNair also quoted from *Glyn v Weston Feature Film Co*,[151] where Younger J had referred to "the principle" that "no infringement of the plaintiff's rights take place where a defendant has bestowed such mental labour upon what he has taken and has subjected it to such revision and alteration as to produce an original result".[152]

Joy Music v Sunday Pictorial Newspapers considered the transformative nature of the defendants' parodic use to find that the use was non-infringing, notwithstanding that there was no statutory exception to infringement for parody. Justice McNair grounded his decision in substantial part, finding that because the defendants had produced the parodic song by "sufficient independent labour to make it an original work" they had not reproduced a substantial part of the plaintiffs' song.[153] As we discuss below, it may be appropriate to consider fair use within the substantial part test in many cases. However, it is our view that Justice McNair's analysis would have worked just as well, if not better, as part of the objective similarity assessment. Since the objective similarity test can compare the defendant's work as a whole with the plaintiff's work as a whole, it potentially provides better scope for courts to observe and take into account the changes and additions that the defendant has made to the plaintiff's work, such as the incorporation of parodic or satirical elements (in the *Joy Music* case).

8.4.3 Substantial Part

In Australia, where the *Copyright Act* has been interpreted to give effect to the principle of fair use, this has usually occurred within the context of the test for substantial part. Courts assess substantial part by reference both to the quantity of what was taken from the original work as well as the quality of what was taken.

---

[148] *Hanfstaengl v Empire Palace* [1894] 3 Ch. 109, 130.

[149] *Joy Music v Sunday Pictorial Newspapers* [1960] 1 All ER 703, 707.

[150] Ibid.

[151] [1916] 1 Ch. 261.

[152] *Joy Music v Sunday Pictorial Newspapers* [1960] 1 All ER 703, 708 (McNair J), quoting from *Glyn v Weston Feature Film Co*, [1916] 1 Ch. 261, 268 (Younger J).

[153] *Joy Music v Sunday Pictorial Newspapers* [1960] 1 All ER 703 at 703, 708.

In fact, courts have noted that it is the qualitative aspect of substantial part that is the critical consideration.[154] The quality of what is taken is determined contextually— how important is that part to the copyrighted work as a whole, taking into account the type of work concerned. Fair use has some bearing on this analysis. In *Folsom v Marsh*, Justice Story stated that courts must look to "the nature and objects of selections made [and] the quantity and value of materials used", and the current statement of fair use in §107 of the US Copyright Act directs courts to consider "the amount and substantiality of the portion used in relation to the copyrighted work as a whole." This language fits squarely within the test for substantial part under Australian law. Where a defendant has acted in a way that seems fair, by taking only a small amount (in quantity) of the copyrighted work or by taking a part of the work that does not go to its core originality or value,[155] courts are more likely to find that the part taken was insubstantial and thus not infringing.[156] In this way, a fair use analysis can help to define and confine our understanding of "substantiality" in the context of a taking, by incorporating notions of what is a "fair" amount for the defendant to have used.

One of the most significant Australian cases to consider substantial part through the lens of fair use is *TCN Channel Nine Pty Ltd v Network Ten Pty Ltd (No 2)*.[157] There, Justice Finkelstein noted that to determine whether a substantial part of a (Part III) copyrighted work has been taken, the first step is to compare the part taken with the original work as a whole.[158] Often, Finkelstein J observed, it will be obvious from a visual or oral comparison of the allegedly infringing work with the copyrighted work whether a substantial part has been taken.[159] However, sometimes a straightforward comparison between the two works will not clearly show whether the part taken is substantial, particularly if the part is small in terms of quantity.[160] In these more complex cases, other factors must be considered, including the economic significance of what was taken and the use that the defendant made of the copied part.[161] "An unfair use, as when the defendant intends

---

[154] *Ladbroke (Football) Ltd v William Hill (Football) Ltd* [1964] 1 All ER 465, 469; *SW Hart & Co Pty Ltd v Edwards Hot Water Systems* (1985) 159 CLR 466, 474; *Autodesk Inc. v Dyason (No 2)* (1993) 176 CLR 300, 305; *TCN Channel Nine Pty Ltd v Network Ten Pty Ltd (No 2)* [2005] FCAFC 53 [9], [49]; *IceTV Pty Ltd v Nine Network Australia Pty Ltd* (2009) 239 CLR 458, 473, 509; [2009] HCA 14 [30], [155].

[155] See *Ladbroke (Football) Ltd v William Hill (Football) Ltd* [1964] 1 All ER 465, 473; *IceTV Pty Ltd v Nine Network Australia Pty Ltd* (2009) 239 CLR 458, 474, 480; [2009] HCA 14 [32], [52].

[156] See, for example, *IceTV Pty Ltd v Nine Network Australia Pty Ltd* (2009) 239 CLR 458, 481 (French CJ, Crennan and Kiefel JJ), 512 (Gummow, Hayne and Heydon JJ); [2009] HCA 14 [56] (French CJ, Crennan and Kiefel JJ), [170] Gummow, Hayne and Heydon JJ).

[157] [2005] FCAFC 53; 216 ALR 631.

[158] *TCN Channel Nine Pty Ltd v Network Ten Pty Ltd (No 2)* [2005] FCAFC 53 (26 May 2005) [4], [8] (Finkelstein J). See also [27] (Finkelstein J).

[159] Ibid [9] (Finkelstein J).

[160] Ibid [10] (Finkelstein J).

[161] Ibid [10], [11], [13] (Finkelstein J). When discussing the economic significance of what has been taken as an important factor, Finkelstein J referred to a number of historical cases including *Scott v Stanford* (1867) LR 3 Eq. 718 at 723 (described in Sect. 8.2 of this paper).

to go into competition with the plaintiff, may be a determining factor."[162] Justice Finkelstein stated,

> The effect of the authorities seems to be this. The test of substantiality – that is the notion of quality – is not confined to an examination of the intrinsic elements of the plaintiff's work. The test of substantiality may involve a broader enquiry, an enquiry which encompasses the context of the taking.[163]

The additional factors articulated by Finkelstein J—the economic significance of the part taken and whether the use is competitive—echo the fair use doctrine's preoccupation with the impact of the subsequent work on the market and objects of the original work. Indeed, in discussing these factors, His Honour not only cites older English authorities including the fair use case, *Scott v Stanford*,[164] but he quotes directly from Justice Story's judgment in *Folsom v Marsh*,[165] stating that "this whole area is neatly summed up by Story J".[166]

---

[162] *TCN Channel Nine Pty Ltd v Network Ten Pty Ltd (No 2)* [2005] FCAFC 53 (26 May 2005) [13] (Finkelstein J), referring to *Bradbury v Hotten* (1872) LR 8 Ex 1 at 6.

[163] Ibid [15] (Finkelstein J). Justice Finkelstein, here, is discussing Part III works. In assessing substantial part for Part IV subject matter, His Honour looked to the case of *Nationwide News Pty Ltd v Copyright Agency Ltd* (1996) 65 FCR 399. There, Justice Sackville had said that "the quality of what is taken must be assessed by reference to the interest protected by copyright": 65 FCR 399, 418. In applying this test to broadcast copyright, Finkelstein J asked whether the part taken constituted an "essential part", the "heart" or the "core" of the broadcast program, such as the best scenes, the highlights, or the "most valuable and pertinent portion" of the program: [2005] FCAFC 53 (26 May 2005) [20]. In framing his inquiry, Finkelstein J referred to a number of US cases. In the hearing for special leave to appeal, Justice Kirby in the High Court expressed some misgivings with Justice Finkelstein's approach to the test for substantial part of a television broadcast and with his reliance on the US sources. Justice Kirby's concern was directed purely to Justice Finkelstein's reliance on US authority in defining the "heart" or "core" or "essential part" of a Part IV subject matter in paragraph [27] of the Full Court judgment; it is worth noting that Justice Finkelstein's references to *Folsom v Marsh* and other fair use authorities were not criticised by the High Court. The *Nationwide News* case was also criticised by the High Court in *IceTV Pty Limited v Nine Network Australia Pty Limited* (2009) 239 CLR 458, 483, 509; [2009] HCA 14 (22 April 2009) [62]–[64], [155]–[157] (Gummow, Hayne and Heydon JJ).

[164] (1867) LR 3 Eq. 718. See further, Sect. 8.2.

[165] *Folsom v Marsh* 9 F Cas 342, 348 (Mass, 1841) (Story J):

> It is certainly not necessary, to constitute an invasion of copyright, that the whole of the work should be copied, or even a large portion of it, in form or in substance. If so much is taken, that the value of the original is sensibly diminished, or the labors of the original author are substantially to an injurious extent appropriated by another, that is sufficient, in point of law, to constitute a piracy pro tanto ... Neither does it necessarily depend upon the quantity taken ... [i]t is often affected by other considerations, the value of the materials taken, and the importance of it to the sale of the original work ... In short, we must often, in deciding questions of this sort, look to the nature and objects of the selections made, the quantity and value of the materials used, and the degree in which the use may prejudice the sale, or diminish the profits, or supersede the objects, of the original work.

[166] *TCN Channel Nine Pty Ltd v Network Ten Pty Ltd (No 2)* [2005] FCAFC 53 (26 May 2005) [14] (Finkelstein J). Justice Finkelstein had also quoted from *Folsom v Marsh* 2 years previously, in *Kabushiki Kaisha Sony Computer Entertainment v Stevens* [2003] FCAFC 53 [224].

For the idea that a use may be "unfair" if it harms a copyright owner's financial interests in her work,[167] Finkelstein J referred to the Australian case of *Blackie & Sons Ltd v Lothian Book Publishing Co Pty Ltd*,[168] in which Starke J said that the question of infringement was whether "the defendant, to use the words of the statute, reproduced a substantial part of the plaintiff's book...or...has an unfair or undue use been made of the work protected by copyright?"[169] The statement in *Blackie & Sons* reflects the earlier English cases discussed in Sect. 8.2 of this article, particularly *Jarrold v Houlston* where Vice-Chancellor Wood said, "The really difficult question is...how far the author of the work in question can be said to have made an unfair or undue use of previous works protected by copyright."[170]

An unfair use, in this sense, may indicate that the part taken by the defendant is substantial in relation to the original work from a qualitative perspective. Quality is assessed contextually, and where the context of the taking indicates that the defendant has taken enough that her use is likely to prejudice the market for the original work, then the use is likely to be infringing. A substantial part inquiry that encompasses the context of the taking should consider, in line with English authority and the Australian constitutional notion of "copyrights", the extent to which the defendant has engaged in a productive use and the extent to which the use is likely to prejudice the market for the original work.

This broader approach to substantial part was adopted by Justices Gummow, Hayne and Heydon in the High Court in the *IceTV* case.[171] In deciding whether IceTV took a substantial part of Channel Nine's television guides, their Honours considered not only *what* was taken but also *how* it was used.[172] Gummow, Hayne and Heydon JJ looked at the significant efforts undertaken by IceTV *not* to make an infringing copy, including generating their own broadcast time information from watching television for lengthy periods of time, "predicting" programming schedules for future weeks based on their own viewing records, and writing their own

---

Additionally, in that case he referred to "the substantial body of English case law" which, prior to the Copyright Act 1911 (UK), "had developed an analogous doctrine of fair use" (referring specifically to *Gyles v Wilcox*): [2003] FCAFC 53 (26 May 2005) [224] (Finkelstein J).

[167] *TCN Channel Nine Pty Ltd v Network Ten Pty Ltd (No 2)* [2005] FCAFC 53 (26 May 2005) [15] (Finkelstein J).

[168] (1921) 29 CLR 396.

[169] *TCN Channel Nine Pty Ltd v Network Ten Pty Ltd (No 2)* [2005] FCAFC 53 (26 May 2005) [15] (Finkelstein J), quoting from *Blackie & Sons Ltd v Lothian Book Publishing Co Pty Ltd* (1921) 29 CLR 396, 402–403 (Starke J).

[170] 3 K & J 708, 714–715 (1857).

[171] *IceTV Pty Limited v Nine Network Australia Pty Limited* (2009) 239 CLR 458; [2009] HCA 14 (22 April 2009).

[172] Ibid [171] (Gummow, Hayne and Heydon JJ): "Thirdly, it is important to ask whether IceTV acted as it did in preparing the IceGuide with animus furandi, to take from the Aggregated Guides the time and title information to save itself from effort on its part. This invites further attention to the business plan and methods adopted by Ice and to the matter of 'predictions'." (Citations omitted)

synopses for the IceTV guide.[173] In these circumstances, the Channel Nine guides were used and copied only to correct mistakes or to update the IceTV guides in response to scheduling changes.[174] For this reason and because the Channel Nine guides had very low levels of originality, Their Honours concluded that IceTV had not taken a substantial part of Channel Nine's television guides.[175] The judgment of Justices Gummow, Hayne and Heydon reflects a focus on preserving balance in the application of the *Copyright Act*; indeed, earlier in their judgment their Honours state:

> A safer, if necessarily incomplete, guide when construing Pt III of the Act is the proposition that the purpose of a copyright law respecting original works is to balance the public interest in promoting the encouragement of 'literary', 'dramatic', 'musical' and 'artistic works', as defined, by providing a just reward for the creator, with the public interest in maintaining a robust public domain in which further works are produced.[176]

The *IceTV* court did not consider fair use directly. Justices Gummow, Hayne and Heydon did, however, emphasise the importance of balance in copyright law and they applied the test for substantial part in a way that took into account how the defendants had used the parts taken from the plaintiff's work. This more flexible and considered approach to the tests establishing infringement is consistent with our argument that the copyright law can and should be applied in such a way as to provide sufficient scope to permit fair and productive uses of works.

8.5 Case Study: The Kookaburra Case

In this section, we use a case study to demonstrate how the principle of fair use can form part of a court's interpretive process when deciding a copyright infringement case. The case study we use is the recent Full Federal Court case, *EMI Songs Australia Pty Limited v Larrikin Music Publishing Pty Limited* ("the Kookaburra case" or "*Larrikin*").[177]

---

[173] *IceTV Pty Limited v Nine Network Australia Pty Limited* (2009) 239 CLR 458, 512–515; [2009] HCA 14 (22 April 2009) [172]–[184] (Gummow, Hayne and Heydon JJ).

[174] Ibid.

[175] Ibid [185] (Gummow, Hayne and Heydon JJ). See also [167]–[170] (Gummow, Hayne and Heydon JJ). Their Honours' decision was also based on the conclusion that the copyrighted guides exhibited very little originality and contained many facts which cannot be protected by copyright. There was therefore a heavy burden on the plaintiffs to show that the defendants had copied a substantial part of *protected expression* and not mere facts. The plaintiffs did not meet this burden to the satisfaction of the Court. See also [30]–[44], [49]–[56] (French CJ, Crennan and Kiefel JJ).

[176] *IceTV Pty Limited v Nine Network Australia Pty Limited* (2009) 239 CLR 458, 485; [2009] HCA 14 (22 April 2009) [71] (Gummow, Hayne and Heydon JJ), criticizing the approaches to copyright that focus on "misappropriation" of skill and labour to the detriment of balance.

[177] [2011] FCAFC 41 (31 March 2011).

The Kookaburra case concerned the reproduction by the Australian band, Men at Work, of two bars of music from the children's folk melody, "Kookaburra Sits in the Old Gum Tree" ("Kookaburra"). Men at Work had reproduced two bars of Kookaburra as a flute riff in their song, "Down Under", to inject "Australian flavour" into the song. The similarity between the two works went unnoticed for over 20 years.[178] The Full Court of the Federal Court of Australia found that Down Under reproduced a substantial part of Kookaburra and, accordingly, found infringement. Justice Emmett, although finding for the copyright owner, expressed "some disquiet" about the outcome of the case.[179] His Honour stated:

> [O]ne may wonder whether the framers of the *Statute of Anne* and its descendants would have regarded the taking of the melody of Kookaburra in [Down Under] as infringement, rather than as a fair use that did not in any way detract from the benefit given to Ms. Sinclair for her intellectual effort in producing Kookaburra.[180]

Men at Work had used two bars from Kookaburra, a four bar musical work. Notwithstanding the nature of Kookaburra as a round—meaning that in practice it actually formed a seven bar musical number—it is difficult to argue that this was not a substantial taking from a quantitative perspective.[181] The Full Federal Court found that Men at Work had reproduced a substantial part of Kookaburra both quantitatively and qualitatively.[182] However, it is possible that the qualitative inquiry undertaken was not complete. There are fair use factors that could have been considered more fully both as part of the qualitative inquiry of substantial part and, pertinent in this case, as part of the objective similarity test.

Despite his expressed reservations, Emmett J adopted an objective similarity approach that focused narrowly on an aural perception of similarity between the works separate from context. At [86], his Honour held:

> A similarity between part of Kookaburra and the flute phrase is clearly perceptible. True it is that that similarity went largely unnoticed for in excess of 20 years, notwithstanding that each work is said to be an iconic Australian work. Nevertheless, the question is one of objective similarity. The aural resemblance need not be resounding or obvious. The relevant test is not the effect upon a casual listener of the whole of the versions of Down Under in the Impugned Recordings. Sensitised though the primary judge may have been to

---

[178] It was not detected until the resemblance was pointed out in the course of a popular television program, *Spicks and Specks,* in 2007: see *EMI Songs Australia Pty Limited v Larrikin Music Publishing Pty Limited* [2011] FCAFC 41 (31 March 2011) [26] (Emmett J), [153]–[154] (Jagot J).

[179] *EMI Songs Australia Pty Limited v Larrikin Music Publishing Pty Limited* [2011] FCAFC 41 (31 March 2011) [98] (Emmett J).

[180] Ibid [101] (Emmett J).

[181] The primary judge had focused quite heavily on the quantitative aspects of the copying. On appeal, defendants argued that the primary judge had erred by failing to consider the taking in the context of Kookaburra as a round (meaning that in practice it was longer than four bars). Justice Emmett accepted these arguments in relation to the quantity of what was taken, but still found that a substantial part had been taken when assessed according to both quantity and quality: see *EMI Songs Australia Pty Limited v Larrikin Music Publishing Pty Limited* [2011] FCAFC 41 (31 March 2011) [15], [58], [67], [74]–[75] and [88]–[89] (Emmett J).

[182] See *EMI Songs Australia Pty Limited v Larrikin Music Publishing Pty Limited* [2011] FCAFC 41 (31 March 2011) [84] and [88]–[89] (Emmett J), [226] (Jagot J), [367] (Nicholas J).

the similarity, it is not erroneous to direct oneself to the relevant parts of the works, to listen to the works a number of times, and to accept the assistance of the views of experts, in determining the question of objective similarity.[183]

Yet there were a range of contextual factors present in this case which may have altered the analysis.[184] We argue that an approach to the infringement inquiry that had at its forefront the goal of preserving balance in the copyright system would have given these factors greater weight. This analysis would incorporate the factors established in early UK precedent which examine whether the defendant had made a productive use of the plaintiff's work and which remain relevant to our constitutional understanding of "copyrights".

Firstly, in line with the UK authorities, an analysis informed by fair use would highlight the original contributions made by Men at Work in creating a new and independent work in Down Under. Men at Work independently developed the lyrics, vocal melody, chords and bass line of Down Under.[185] The bars taken from Kookaburra were used only in part of a flute riff, and only in 5 of the 93 bars of Down Under.[186] Each bar from Kookaburra was separated from the others by original material.[187] As such, the music was used in an entirely different way to how it operates in Kookaburra, which is structured as a round.[188] The basic hook of Down Under "owed nothing to Kookaburra".[189] Of course, the fact that the part taken comprises only a minimal portion of the defendant's work is not itself conclusive that the defendant's use is non-infringing.[190] However, it can, in context, support the claim that the defendant has engaged in a productive and transformative use. In this sense, it is important to have regard to the whole of the defendant's work and to compare the whole of that work with the whole of the plaintiff's work.[191] In the *Larrikin* case, such a comparison highlights the

---

[183] Ibid [86] (Emmett J). See also [202], [213] ("There is no principle that the ordinary reasonably experienced listener may not hear a work or part of it more than once. Nor do the cases suggest that the trial judge was not entitled to have regard to the expert evidence when determining objective similarity"), [218], [226] ("Accordingly, while it may be accepted that there is not a 'ready' aural perception of the bars of Kookaburra in the flute riff of Down Under, the bars are there and, as the trial judge found, can be heard once attention is directed to them") (Jagot J).

[184] Justice Emmett acknowledged many of these factors but did not apply the kind of comprehensive, fair use-informed analysis advocated in this article.

[185] *EMI Songs Australia Pty Limited v Larrikin Music Publishing Pty Limited* [2011] FCAFC 41 (31 March 2011) [19] (Emmett J).

[186] Ibid [25] (Emmett J).

[187] Ibid [25], [94] (Emmett J).

[188] Ibid [88] (Emmett J).

[189] Ibid [79] (Emmett J).

[190] Ibid [82] (Emmett J), [190] (Jagot J) (referring to *Designers Guild Ltd v Russell Williams (Textiles) Ltd (trading as Washington D.C.)* [2000] 1 WLR 2416 at 2425 (in the context of substantial part)).

[191] See Sect. 8.4 for our argument that the objective similarity test should compare the defendant's work *as a whole* with the plaintiff's work *as a whole*. See also Justice Emmett's statements in *EMI Songs Australia Pty Limited v Larrikin Music Publishing Pty Limited* [2011] FCAFC 41 (31 March 2011) [82] with respect to substantial part: "In the light of the legal principles summarised above,

differences between the two works and the significant original contributions of Men at Work. This was clearly far more than an exercise in "cutting and pasting". As Emmett J acknowledged:

> There are limited features of similarity between Kookaburra and Down Under in terms of key, harmony, tempo and rhythm. Kookaburra was written in a major key. The relevant bars in the Impugned Recordings appear as part of an overall work in a minor key. The harmony in Kookaburra arises both from its character as a round, and the implied harmonies suggested by casting its melody in a specific key. The versions of Down Under in the Impugned Recordings have a highly distinctive harmony, arising from the voice of Mr. Hay, singing very different lyrics, and the mix of instruments.[192]

Additionally, a fair use analysis would consider the purpose of the defendant's use. Here, Men at Work gave evidence that they used the parts taken from Kookaburra to "inject [Down Under] with Australian flavour"[193] and to give tribute to Kookaburra, an iconic Australian folk song.[194] Their purpose was not to compete with the original copyrighted work or to appropriate the original creator's efforts. On the strength of these submissions, Justice Emmett found that there was no *animus furandi* on the part of the defendants.[195] He held that there was no evidence that the defendants "took any part of Kookaburra with the intention of taking advantage of the skill and labour of Ms. Sinclair in composing Kookaburra,

---

the question is whether the evidence established that, having regard to Kookaburra as a whole, there was a reproduction of a substantial part of it in the particular use made in the Impugned Recordings of two of its phrases, without either lyrics or any relationship in the nature of a round. It is important to have regard to the part said to have been taken from Kookaburra, not only as it appears in Kookaburra as originally published, but also in the context in which it appears in the Impugned Recordings. Regard must be had to the whole of each work in making that assessment, and attention must be given to what it was that constituted Kookaburra as an original work."

[192] See *EMI Songs Australia Pty Limited v Larrikin Music Publishing Pty Limited* [2011] FCAFC 41 (31 March 2011) [90] (Emmett J); see also [226] (Jagot J). In concluding that Down Under was nonetheless infringing, Justice Emmett was influenced by a series of older cases dealing primarily with musical works. These cases, prominent among which was *D'Almaine v Boosey* (1835) 1 Y & C Ex 288, distinguish between the books that were the subject of the fair use cases examined in Sect. 8.2 and musical works. In *D'Almaine v Boosey*, Lord Chief Baron stated (after referring to the fair abridgment doctrine), "[T]he subject of music is to be regarded upon very different principles.": (1835) 1 Y & C Ex 288 at 301. However, he later said, "Now it appears to me that if you take from the composition of an author all those bars consecutively which form the entire air or melody, *without any material alteration*, it is a piracy; though, on the other hand, you might take them in a different order or broken by the intersection of others, like words, in such a manner as should not be a piracy": (1835) 1 Y & C Ex 288 at 301 (emphasis added). This seems to be a restatement of the principle that a use which is sufficiently productive or transformative, going beyond mere "cutting and pasting", will not be an infringement, as extended to musical works. Interspersing the bars taken with original material is, also, exactly what Men at Work had done (although the judges concluded that this was not enough to make Down Under a non-infringing work: see *EMI Songs Australia Pty Limited v Larrikin Music Publishing Pty Limited* [2011] FCAFC 41 (31 March 2011) [94] (Emmett J), [152], [192]–[194] (Jagot J)).

[193] *EMI Songs Australia Pty Limited v Larrikin Music Publishing Pty Limited* [2011] FCAFC 41 (31 March 2011) [19] (Emmett J) [134], [155], [219] (Jagot J).

[194] Ibid [67], [95], [99] (Emmett J).

[195] Ibid [95], [99] (Emmett J). Though cf. Jagot J at [221] (concluding that *animus furandi* was not relevant in the context of this case).

in order to save effort on their part."[196] As noted in Sect. 8.2, the presence or absence of *animus furandi* may be reflected in the *way* that a defendant has copied a plaintiff's work. Where *animus furandi* is present, the defendant is more likely to have copied verbatim or closely enough that the use may supersede the plaintiff's work or prejudice the market for the plaintiff's work. By contrast, where the defendant lacks *animus furandi* then she is more likely to have used the work, or attempted to use the work, fairly, by transforming the work or including her own contributions. Thus, a lack of *animus furandi* may indicate, though not prove, fair use. The way in which the defendant has used the work is relevant to the qualitative aspect of the substantial part inquiry and may also be relevant to the objective similarity test where the resulting work is dissimilar to the copyrighted work because of the new work's divergent purpose.

Finally, a fair use analysis would consider the impact on the market for the original work from the defendant's use. In *Hawkes & Son (London) Ltd v Paramount Film Service Ltd,*[197] one of the musical works cases considered by Emmett J in his reasoning, Lord Justice Slesser (one of the three appellate judges hearing that case) found infringement on the basis that a substantial part of the plaintiff-appellant's work had been taken by the defendant-respondent. Slesser L.J. then said, "[I]t is clear to my mind that a fair use has not been made of it; that is to say, there has been appropriated and published in a form which will or may materially injure the copyright, that in which the plaintiffs have a proprietary right."[198] Justice Emmett relied on this case for the notion that, when assessing substantial part, it is appropriate to consider "whether or not the amount of the copyright musical work that is taken is so slender that it would be impossible to recognise it", or, conversely, whether what was taken "constitutes the principal air or melody of the copyright work", which anyone would recognise as such.[199] His Honour might have equally had regard to the fact that Slesser L.J. considered fair use and found that the defendant's use was unfair because it was likely to *materially injury* the copyright of the plaintiff. In *Larrikin*, it was held that "the works do not represent similar musical genres or styles. Kookaburra is a folk melody, children's song or nursery rhyme, while Down Under was characterised as a rock anthem, and is influenced by ska and/or reggae. There is no similarity between the respective natures and objects of the works."[200] The significant differences between the style, nature and objects of the works strongly indicate that the defendant's work would not supersede the plaintiff's work. It also warrants, we argue, greater inquiry into whether Men at Work's use had harmed or was likely to harm the markets for the plaintiff's work.

---

[196] *EMI Songs Australia Pty Limited v Larrikin Music Publishing Pty Limited* [2011] FCAFC 41 (31 March 2011) [95] (Emmett J).

[197] [1934] 1 Ch. 593.

[198] *Hawkes & Son (London) Ltd v Paramount Film Service Ltd* [1934] 1 Ch. 593, 606–607.

[199] See *EMI Songs Australia Pty Limited v Larrikin Music Publishing Pty Limited* [2011] FCAFC 41 (31 March 2011) [49] (Emmett J), referring to *Hawkes & Son (London) Ltd v Paramount Film Service Ltd* [1934] 1 Ch. 593, 604, 609.

[200] *EMI Songs Australia Pty Limited v Larrikin Music Publishing Pty Limited* [2011] FCAFC 41 (31 March 2011) [92] (Emmett J).

As noted above, the fair use factors outlined here might have informed one or both of the objective similarity and substantial part tests in the *Larrikin* case. Importantly, an infringement inquiry informed by fair use would have examined whether the use made by Men at Work was an infringing or non-infringing copy of Kookaburra under s. 36(1) of the Act and in line with the constitutional notion of "copyrights".

8.6 Conclusion

The intersection between the Australian Constitution and copyright law is seldom considered in Australian legal analysis. Yet the *Copyright Act 1968*, like all Commonwealth legislation, exists because the federal Parliament has been given the power to enact laws with respect to copyrights in s. 51(xviii) of the Constitution. In this article we have argued, quite simply, that the Copyright Act must be read in a way that fits with this constitutional head of power.

The word "copyrights" in the Australian Constitution is infused with a particular meaning that incorporates the notion of copyright balance—that copyright law is an exercise in balancing the interests of authors in exclusive exploitation of their works with the interests of the public in gaining access to new works. Thus, the constitutional notion of copyright is not that of an unlimited power to prevent all copying. Rather, in order to promote balance, copyright distinguishes between infringing copying and non-infringing copying and grants to the copyright owner only the power to control the former.

Non-infringing copying includes copying of ideas, copying of public domain works (such as where copyright protection in a work has expired) and copying of insubstantial parts of copyrighted works. These are all well accepted limitations on the copyright owner's ability to prevent copying. In this chapter we have argued that non-infringing copying also includes copying to make a fair use of a work.

The principle that copyright infringement does not occur where a person makes a fair use of a work was developed in English case law in the eighteenth and nineteenth centuries. Fair use was generally established where the defendant had made a productive use that did more than colourably shorten or alter the original work for the purpose of evading liability and where the defendant had made an original contribution to the resulting work. Additionally, fairness was shown by a use that did not supersede or prejudice the market for the original work. At the time of including the copyright power in the Constitution, the UK Parliament's understanding of "copyrights" included the notion of fair use as it had been developed in U.K. precedent. The word "copyrights" in the Constitution took its definition from copyright law in 1900 and as it has evolved since, including the principle that a fair use is not an infringement of copyright.

In the *Copyright Act 1968*, infringement is defined is sections 36(1) and 101 (1) as the doing, without licence, of an "act comprised in the copyright". These are the sections that distinguish infringing copies from non-infringing copies in the Act, and which promote copyright's constitutional purpose of maintaining balance between authors and users. An infringing copy is an act comprised the copyright, whereas a non-infringing copy is not. We have argued that space for fair uses of copyrighted works is built into the *Copyright Act 1968* through these sections, because a fair use will not produce an infringing copy and so is not an act comprised in the copyright. We have also argued that this interpretation adheres to the ordinary meaning of the words used in sections 36(1) and 101(1) and that the Australian Constitution, including the constitutional notion of "copyrights", is part of the relevant extrinsic material that may be consulted to confirm this ordinary meaning under s. 15AB(1)(a) of the *Acts Interpretation Act 1901*.

Furthermore, the tests designed to help courts to interpret sections 36 and 101 must also be applied to conform to the constitutional head of power. They must not operate to broaden copyright protection beyond its constitutional scope. For this reason, the tests for objective similarity and substantial part should be applied contextually and in a way that facilitates fair use. The objective similarity test, especially, can be applied to take into account the context of the taking, including whether the defendant has engaged in a productive or transformative use to produce a substantially new work.

In order to promote copyright's purpose, fair use can and should be understood as one of the fundamental principles underpinning each step of the infringement inquiry. "Fair use should be perceived not as a disorderly basket of exceptions to the rules of copyright, nor as a departure from the principles governing that body of law, but rather as a rational, integral part of copyright, whose observance is necessary to achieve the objectives of that law."[201]

References

Journal Articles

Greenleaf G, Bond C (2013) 'Public Rights' in copyright: what makes up Australia's public domain? AIPJ 23(2):111–138

Leval PN (1989–1990) Toward a fair use standard. Harv Law Rev 103:1105–1136

Litman J (2007) Lawful personal use. Tex Law Rev 85:1871–1920

Patterson LR (1998) *Folsom v Marsh* and its legacy. J Int Prop Law 5:431–452

Sims A (2011) Appellations of piracy: fair dealing's prehistory. IPQ 1:3–27

Tehranian J (2004–2005) Et Tu, fair use? The triumph of natural-law copyright. UC Davis Law Rev 38:465–508

Yankwich LR (1954–1955) What is fair use? Univ Chic Law Rev 22:203–215

---

[201] Leval (1989–1990), pp. 1105–1136 at 1107.

Books and Chapters

Alexander I (2010) Copyright law and the public interest in the nineteenth century. Hart, Oxford
Atkinson B (2007) The true history of copyright 1905–2005: the Australian experience. Sydney University Press, Sydney
Burrell R, Coleman A (2005) Copyright exceptions: the digital impact. Cambridge University Press, Cambridge
Cohen JE, Loren LP, Okediji RL, O'Rourke MA (2010) Copyright in a global information economy, 3rd edn. Aspen, New York
Copinger WA (1870) The law of copyright, in works of literature and art. Steven and Haynes Law Publishers, London
Fitzgerald B, Atkinson B (2008) Third party copyright and public information infrastructure/registries: how much copyright tax must the public pay? In: Fitzgerald B, Perry M (eds) Knowledge policy for the 21st century. Irwin Law, Canada, pp 225–268
Kaplan B (1967) An unhurried view of copyright. Columbia University Press, New York
Patry W (1985) The fair use privilege in copyright law. The Bureau of National Affairs Inc., Arlington
Reese RA (2006) The story of *Folsom v Marsh*: distinguishing between infringing and legitimate uses. In: Ginsburg J, Cooper Dreyfuss R (eds) Intellectual property stories. Foundation Press, New York, pp 259–297

Online Publications

Bowrey K (2008) On clarifying the role of originality and fair use in 19th century UK jurisprudence: appreciating 'The Humble Grey Which Emerges as the Result of Long Controversy'. UNSW Law Research Paper No. 2008-58.http://ssrn.com/abstract=1402444
Bracha O (2008) Commentary on *Folsom v Marsh* (1841). In: Bentley L, Kretschmer M (eds) Primary Sources on Copyright (1450–1900). http://www.copyrighthistory.org

Chapter 9
Crown Use: The Government as User of Copyright Material Owned by Other Persons

John Gilchrist

9.1 Introduction

An important differentiating feature of government under the law of copyright in Australia are those statutory provisions dealing with the government's use of other copyright material it receives or deals with in the course of its work. No similar rights are given to other institutions or persons under the *Copyright Act 1968* (Cth). These Crown use provisions provide wide entitlements to the Commonwealth and the States to do any acts comprised within the copyright without the express permission of the copyright owner, but subject to compensation. Similar Crown use provisions are also found in other intellectual property enactments of the Commonwealth.[1]

The Crown use provisions in the *Copyright Act 1968* emanate from a recognition of the needs of government to use copyright material in the exercise of its

---

An earlier version of this work was first published in the (2010) 9 Canberra Law Review 36.

[1] Refer s 163 of the *Patents Act 1990* (Cth) and s 96 of the *Designs Act 2003* (Cth). It would appear that the Crown use provision (s 183 of the *Copyright Act 1968*) is consistent with the *Agreement on Trade-Related Aspects of Intellectual Property Rights* (TRIPS). Article 13, Section 1 (Copyright and Related Rights), of this *Agreement*, which is headed *Limitations and Exceptions*, provides that Members shall confine limitations or exceptions to exclusive rights to certain special cases which do not conflict with a normal exploitation of the work and do not unreasonably prejudice the legitimate interests of the right holder, which is consistent with Berne Convention obligations Australia has long adhered to. Article 31(b), Section 5 (Patents) is more limited and stipulates that 'other use' (that is, use without the authorization of the right holder) is only permitted if, prior to such use, the proposed user has made efforts to obtain authorization from the right holder on reasonable terms and such efforts have been unsuccessful within a reasonable period of time (except in cases of national emergency or public non-commercial use).

J. Gilchrist (✉)
Thomas More Academy of Law, Australian Catholic University, 486 Albert Street,
East Melbourne, VIC 3002, Australia
e-mail: John.Gilchrist@acu.edu.au

© Springer International Publishing Switzerland 2015
B. Fitzgerald, J. Gilchrist (eds.), *Copyright Perspectives*,
DOI 10.1007/978-3-319-15913-3_9

fundamental responsibilities to the community it serves, such as defence, policing, essential communications and emergency relief, without the need to seek prior agreement from copyright owners and without the risk of an injunction to restrain it. The Crown use provisions in the *Copyright Act 1968* are couched in broad language which enable any acts done for 'the services of the Commonwealth or State'. This broad language is a reflection of the broad functions of modern government, which has assumed important regulatory, law enforcement and information-gathering roles across a wide spectrum of community activity in pursuit of goals, such as economic efficiency, better planning, budgeting and development. It is impractical, and sometimes inappropriate, to seek prior agreement with copyright owners if these functions are to be performed effectively.

The government's entitlement to use material for its services without infringement of copyright does not solely arise under the Crown use provisions. It may arise in three ways.

One way is through an implied licence to the Commonwealth or a State to reproduce or even publish copyright material, such as letters, sent to it. For example, a licence to reproduce a letter would normally be implied from the sender of a letter to government, to enable proper consideration of the contents of the letter by ministerial or departmental officers and to assist in the preparation of a reply. This entitlement is further discussed in Part 9.3 of this chapter.

There are also a number of statutory provisions in various Australian jurisdictions which enable the Commonwealth or a State to do acts in relation to copyright material which provide immunity from civil and criminal proceedings. One example is s 90 of the *Freedom of Information Act 1984* (Cth) which provides that where access is given to a document under the Act or where access is given in the *bona fide* belief that access was required to be given under the Act, then no action for defamation, breach of confidence or infringement of copyright lies against the Commonwealth by reason of the authorising or giving of access. Access may be given in the form of a copy of the document.[2] These provisions are discussed further in Part 9.4 of this chapter.

Of greatest importance however, is a provision in Part VII, Division 2 of the *Copyright Act 1968* which enables the Commonwealth and the States to do any act comprised in the copyright in a work or other subject matter if the act is done 'for the services of the Commonwealth or State'.[3] This 'Crown use' provision—s 183 of the *Copyright Act 1968*—and its ancillary provision (s 183A) operate as a statutory licence providing an unfettered entitlement to the Commonwealth and the States to do acts comprised in the copyright in works and other subject matter protected by the *Copyright Act 1968*.

The nature, scope and operation of the Crown use provision in the *Copyright Act 1968*, the extent to which licences may be implied to government to reproduce or

---

[2] Refer s 20 of the *Freedom of Information Act 1984* (Cth).

[3] Under the Act, *the Commonwealth* includes the Administration of a Territory: s 10(1), and a reference to a State includes the Northern Territory and Norfolk Island...: s 10(3)(n).

publish copyright material it receives and the breadth of other statutory rights held by government and their relationship to s 183 of the *Copyright Act 1968*, are discussed in more detail in the remainder of this chapter. In particular, the writer examines arguments for construing s 183 to complement, rather than override, the special defences to infringement, such as s 40 (fair dealing for research or study) which users of copyright material may rely on generally under the *Copyright Act 1968*. The writer concludes that there are good reasons in law and policy for construing s 183 to complement these special defences.

Acts comprised in the copyright in material and, most importantly, the reproduction of copyright information within government agencies and across them, are a management demand required for the effective review and consideration of material and for government agency coordination and interoperability, and such acts are also necessary to fulfil the basic right of all citizens in a democratic society to be informed of, and to have access to, government information. Increased engagement with the community online and the internal transfer of agency information will inevitably increase. These practices of government may test the effectiveness of relying on an implicit licence from the provider of information and the present defences to infringement under the *Copyright Act 1968*. The writer concludes that the High Court decision in *Copyright Agency Limited v New South Wales*,[4] and the changing technology in the way we communicate, suggest a need for an express special defence outside the operation of s 183 permitting certain public uses of copyright material deposited or registered in accordance with statutory obligations under State or Commonwealth law.

9.2 Crown Use

9.2.1 The Scheme of Section 183

The scheme of s 183 is, in essence, set out in ss 183(1), (4) and (5).

The scheme may be summarised as follows. Section 183(1) provides that the copyright in a work or other subject matter is not infringed by the Commonwealth or a State, or by a person authorised by the Commonwealth or a State, doing any acts comprised in the copyright if the acts are done for the services of the Commonwealth or a State.

Section 183(4) provides that where an act comprised in a copyright has been done under s 183(1), the Commonwealth or State shall, as soon as possible, unless it appears to the Commonwealth or the State that it would be contrary to the public interest to do so, inform the owner of the copyright of 'the doing of the act'.

---

[4] *Copyright Agency Limited v New South Wales* [2008] HCA 35.

Section 183(5) provides that where an act comprised in a copyright has been done under s 183(1), the terms for the doing of the act are such terms as are, whether before or after the act is done, agreed or as may be fixed by the Copyright Tribunal.

Section 183(1) is thus expressed as a defence to infringement of copyright as are the special defences to infringement provided in Divisions 3, 4, 5 and 7 of Part III of the Act and in Division 6 of Part IV of the Act, but principally ss 40–53 and ss 103A–104A.[5] One example is s 40 (fair dealing for the purposes of research or study).

Unlike the special defences, the requirements in s 183(4) and s 183(5) oblige the government to inform the copyright owner and to seek agreement on the terms for the doing of the act. This provides a mechanism for securing compensation for the copyright owner. Compensation is also a feature of other statutory licences under the Act, such as those dealing with the copying of works in educational establishments and the copying of works in institutions assisting handicapped readers in Divisions 2 and 3 of Part VB of the Act. It is distinguished from those statutory licences under the Act because the defence to infringement provided by s 183 is not expressed to be conditional on the giving of notice or on any other undertaking to the copyright owner.[6]

The *Copyright Amendment Act (No 1) 1998* (Cth) also inserted provisions aimed at facilitating the payment of equitable remuneration for the copying of material under s 183(1). This is effected through the sampling of copying rather than notifying each instance of copying in accordance with the requirements of ss 183 (4) and (5). The principal provision is s 183A, which enables the Commonwealth or a State to enter into arrangements with an approved collecting society acting on behalf of copyright owners to make payments to the collecting society in relation to copying under s 183(1). Where such arrangements have been made, they override the application of ss 183(4) and (5) and are capable of applying to nearly all copyright material covered by s 183(1). A significant exception is the Crown use of computer programs which can only be subject to the requirements of ss 183 (4) and (5).

Neither s 183A nor its related provisions inserted by the *Copyright Amendment Act (No 1) 1998* alter the defence to infringement of copyright provided by s 183(1).

---

[5] The description 'special defences' is used in this chapter to describe those defences which are available in limited and specified circumstances and which, apart from a few exceptions, do not enable large scale or multiple acts in relation to copyright such as reproduction. The special defences do not provide a right of remuneration to copyright owners. I exclude from the description 'special defences' all the statutory licence schemes under the Act such as those for the manufacture of records of musical works (ss 54–64), multiple copying of works for the teaching purposes of an educational institution (Div 2, Part VB) and copying by institutions assisting handicapped readers (Div 3, Part VB), as well as the Crown use provisions.

[6] Refer, for example, to s 135ZJ or s 135 ZL of the Act, where copying is expressed to be conditional on copying being made solely for the educational purposes of the institution (or of another educational institution), a remuneration notice having been given to the relevant collecting society and the body complying with the marking and record-keeping requirements set out in s 135ZX of the Act.

Section 183A simply provides a sampling scheme for calculating and making payments of equitable remuneration to copyright owners for the copying of their copyright materials in lieu of the notice requirements of ss 183(4) and (5). But other related provisions inserted by the *Copyright Amendment Act (No 1) 1998* facilitate the rights of copyright owners by enabling the recovery of equitable remuneration under the sampling scheme as a debt due to the collecting society. The operation of s 183A and its related provisions is further discussed under Part 9.2.2.4 of this chapter.

9.2.2   The Scope of Crown Use Under the Copyright Act 1968

The defences to infringement provided in the *Copyright Act 1968* have historically been a part of copyright law and represent the balance struck between the rights of the copyright owners and the interests of the users of copyright material—the public—in their access to and dissemination of information. This has been a feature of the growth of this quasi-monopolistic right from its inception. That is, the law has, for many years, recognised that there is a strong public interest in the free flow of information in areas covered by these defences. Governments generate large amounts of information from material supplied to them in their regulatory, statistical, research, law enforcement, management, budgetary, fiscal and other governing roles and also receive large amounts of copyright information and material voluntarily. Information is regularly reproduced into databases, evaluated, dissected and manipulated to produce new information of value to the community or to a segment of it. It is manifestly impractical to seek permission from each copyright owner to use this copyright information in each case, nor should government be fettered in carrying out this work in the public interest by a copyright claim. On the other hand, the use by government of copyright information and material may be substantial and have a significant impact on the exploitation of that material. The balance arrived at in the Crown use provision is to subject the Crown use defence to later agreement on the terms for the doing of the act. The terms almost invariably lead to financial compensation to the copyright owner, although this is not expressed as a requirement in the section.

A fundamental question in relation to the scope of Crown use is whether the government is obliged to use s 183(1) in circumstances where an act would otherwise fall within the protection of the special defences to infringement provided in Divisions 3, 4, 5 and 7 of Part III of the Act and in Division 6 of Part IV of the Act but principally ss 40–53 and ss 103A–104A (the fair dealing provisions, library copying and acts done for the purposes of a judicial proceeding). One illustration of this question is where an officer of a Commonwealth department copies on a departmental copier a reasonable part of a copyright work for the purpose of that officer's research or study within the scope of the fair dealing provision s 40, and the research or study concerns that person's official duties. In these circumstances, is the officer entitled to rely on s 40 of the *Copyright Act 1968* as a defence to infringement or must the Commonwealth rely on s 183(1) and thus be required to give notice of the copying to the copyright owner in accordance with the requirements of s 183 or have that copying sampled and subject to equitable remuneration in accordance with s 183A?

This question goes to the heart of the balance between copyright owners and government users.

The answer to this question in law is not absolutely clear. As a matter of statutory interpretation, it is arguable from a reading of the *Copyright Act 1968* that acts involving the use of copyright material which fall within the special defences to infringement but which are done for the services of the Commonwealth are nonetheless 'acts comprised in the copyright' in the material within the scope of s 183(1). Thus, the procedural requirements of s 183 or s 183A must be adhered to in relation to such acts.

The alternative view, and it is suggested the better view, is that s 183(1) complements the special defences to infringement so that the Crown and citizen alike can rely on those special defences; and that s 183(1) confers on the Crown entitlements to the use of copyright material which are additional to the special defences available to all. That is, only if the use of copyright material for the services of the Commonwealth or State goes beyond that permitted by the special defences is the Commonwealth or State obliged to rely on s 183(1) as a defence to infringement.

The Copyright Law Committee on Reprographic Reproduction (the Franki Committee) stated in its report in 1976:

> 7.10 We think that the Crown, or a person authorised by the Crown, should be entitled to copy a work in the circumstances where a private individual would be entitled to copy it without obligation to the copyright owners. If it be accepted that this is the result presently achieved by section 183, no change in the Act would be required.[7]

There have been a small number of minor amendments made to s 183 since the original passage of the 1968 Act, the most significant of which is s 183(11) inserted by the *Copyright Amendment Act 1980* (Cth). This amendment Act implemented much of the Franki Committee recommendations. No amendment to clarify the operation of s 183 was inserted in the *Copyright Amendment Act 1980* in response to the recommendation contained in paragraph 7.10. No subsequent clarification has been made.[8]

The High Court of Australia in *Copyright Agency Limited v New South Wales* appears to have accepted the complementary view of the Crown use provision:

> The State did not suggest that any of the fair dealing provisions (ss 40-42) or other provisions in Pt III, Div 3 (ss 43-44F) which provide that certain acts do not constitute an

---

[7] Australia. Copyright Law Committee on Reprographic Reproduction (Franki Committee) (1976), p. 57 [7.10].

[8] Section 183A and its related provisions which were inserted by the *Copyright Amendment Act 1998* (Cth) are directed at providing a more practical alternative to the notice requirements under s 183(4) and (5) and do not address this question.

infringement, had any application to the uses of the survey plans described . . . . In cases where these provisions do apply, Pt VII, Div 2 respecting Crown use and equitable remuneration is not engaged.[9]

However, the joint judgment of the High Court in this case did not explore the question beyond that statement, as the application of the special defences was not argued by counsel for the State of New South Wales. Technically, the statement is obiter dicta and can be read equivocally.

9.2.2.1   Arguments in Support of the Wide Scope of Crown Use

There are a number of arguments, based on a reading of s 183 in the context of the Act as a whole, which support the interpretation of s 183(1) that it covers all acts comprised in the copyright in a work or other subject matter if done by the Commonwealth or State for the services of the Commonwealth or State.

The test of infringement in works and other subject-matter is described in ss 36 and 101 of the Act. These sections are expressed in similar terms and together provide that the copyright in a work or other subject matter is infringed by a person who, not being the owner of the copyright, and without the licence of the owner of copyright, does in Australia, or authorises the doing in Australia of, any act comprised in the copyright. The special defences to infringement (such as s 40 and its equivalent s 103C of the Act) are not expressed to limit the exclusive rights but in various circumstances enable acts comprised within the copyright, such as reproduction or communication to the public, to be undertaken beyond a substantial part of a work or other subject matter.

Part VII of the *Copyright Act 1968* is headed 'The Crown' and Divisions 1 and 2 of that Part purport to define the position of the Commonwealth and the States in relation to copyright. An act done 'for the services of the Commonwealth or State' is the subject of s 183 and such an act would not arguably cease to be so characterised simply because the Commonwealth or a State could rely on a special defence to infringement. Section 183 appears to contemplate that acts done for the services of the Commonwealth or the State may otherwise not be an infringement by the person doing them. Under s 183(3):

> (3) Authority may be given under subsection (1) . . . to a person notwithstanding that he or she has a licence granted by, or binding on, the owner of the copyright to do the acts.

An act done for the services of the Commonwealth or State therefore falls within, and is governed by, s 183(1) even though it may also be for a purpose specified in one of the special defences to infringement. However, if the act was not done for the services of the Commonwealth or State then the Commonwealth or

---

[9] *Copyright Agency Limited v New South Wales* [2008] HCA 35 [11].

State may be able to rely on the special defences to infringement of copyright if acting in accordance with those defences.

If this was not the proper interpretation of s 183(1), then it may be argued that it would not have been necessary to insert s 183(11) in the *Copyright Act 1968* by the *Copyright Amendment Act 1980*[10]:

> (11) The copying (*now, by later amendment, reproduction, copying or communication*) of the whole or a part of a work or other subject-matter for the educational purposes of an educational institution of, or under the control of, the Commonwealth, a State or the Northern Territory shall, for the purposes of this section, be deemed not to be an act done for the services of the Commonwealth, that State or the Northern Territory.

That is, if s 183(1) did not apply to the doing of acts by the Commonwealth or a State, which would otherwise be excluded from infringement by virtue of the educational copying provisions in the Act, then it would not have been necessary to insert s 183(11). Following the *Copyright Amendment Act 1980* (Cth), a Commonwealth or State educational institution could only rely on those educational copying provisions.

9.2.2.2 Arguments in Support of the Complementary Scope of Crown Use

The alternative view is that s 183(1) complements the special defences to infringement and does not overlap them.

While s 31 and ss 85–88 describe the rights created by those provisions as 'exclusive rights', the operation of each of those provisions is prefaced by the words 'unless the contrary intention appears'. Those special defences in the *Copyright Act 1968* which provide that the doing of certain acts does not constitute an infringement of copyright and do not provide any entitlement to compensation to the copyright owner, such as s 40 (fair dealing with a work for the purpose of research or study), may be construed as constituting a contrary intention for the purposes of s 31 and ss 85–88 and, therefore, limit the exclusive rights otherwise conferred by those sections. On this basis the doing of an act which by virtue of the special defences does not constitute an infringement of copyright is not the doing of an act comprised in a copyright to which s 183(1) applies. It follows that a notice under s 183(4) is not required to be given in respect of the doing of an act which is not, apart from s 183, an infringement of copyright and which is not, therefore, within the exclusive rights of the copyright owner.

Consistently, while s 183(3) provides that authority to do acts may be given to a person notwithstanding the person has a licence granted by, or binding on, the owner of the copyright, the acts in contemplation are acts comprised in the copyright within the meaning of s 183(1) described. That is, what is done pursuant to a licence granted by the copyright owner would, apart from that licence, amount

---

[10] Inserted by s 24 of the *Copyright Amendment Act 1980* (Cth) No 154 of 1980.

to an infringement of copyright. It does not follow that because s 183(3) expressly contemplates acts which would not amount to an infringement of copyright as a result of the grant of a licence, the section has the effect of more broadly encompassing acts which would not be an infringement of copyright under the special defences in the *Copyright Act 1968*. There are other rationales for the express contemplation of licensed acts in s 183(3). For example, s 183(3) could be relied on in relation to defence activity when it is in the public interest not to notify the copyright owner of the doing of the acts for some time or when the terms of the licence may be unreasonable in the circumstances. In *Copyright Agency Limited v New South Wales*[11] both the Full Court of the Federal Court of Australia and the High Court of Australia accepted that the Crown may rely on an implied licence to do acts comprised in the copyright in material submitted to it, without reliance on s 183.

Similarly, the insertion of s 183(11) does not suggest the section more broadly encompasses acts which would not be an infringement of copyright under the special defences in the *Copyright Act 1968*. The insertion of s 183(11) followed a Franki Committee recommendation that the Crown should not be permitted to rely on s 183 for the making of multiple copies of copyright works for use in government schools and that their recommendations in respect of multiple copying in non-profit educational establishments (which first became s 53B and is now embodied in ss 135ZJ and 135ZL of the Act) should apply to government and non-government schools alike.[12] The insertion was directed at multiple copying and not at the limited copying which may be undertaken under the special defences to infringement of copyright. Section 183 has unlimited scope and, apart from s 183(11), a Commonwealth or State school would be unfettered in its capacity to use copyright material and subject only to the notice and terms requirements of s 183. The purpose of the recommendation which led to the insertion of s 183(11) was to ensure similar treatment of government and non-government schools.[13]

The complementary view is also taken by Campbell and Monotti in their examination of immunities of agents of government from liability for infringement of copyright[14]:

> If agents of government are sued for infringement of copyright, but are not able to rely on any of the statutory exceptions mentioned above, they may nevertheless rely on the

---

[11] [2007] FCAFC 80 (5 June 2007) [152–158] and [2008] HCA 35 [45–47]. This case is discussed in Part 9.3 of this chapter.

[12] Australia. Copyright Law Committee on Reprographic Reproduction (Franki Committee) (1976), p. 57 [7.11].

[13] Curiously, s 183(11) does not cover acts by institutions assisting handicapped readers and institutions assisting intellectually handicapped persons which are not educational institutions but which are nevertheless emanations of the Commonwealth or the States.

[14] Campbell and Monotti (2002), pp. 459 and 462–463. The major professional works on Australian copyright law, Lahore and Ricketson, do not address the interrelationship between the special defences and s 183—refer Lindgren et al. (2004), Vol 1 [28, 561] and Ricketson and Creswell (2002), Vol 1 [12, 275].

provisions in the Act that allow for fair dealing with copyright material. The circumstances in which the fair dealing exceptions operate are limited but they include cases in which copyright material is reproduced for research or study. . . . An act of fair dealing may also be one for the services of the Crown. For example, an officer of a government department may have dealt fairly with copyright material by photocopying an article in a periodical publication for the purposes of the research required of him or her in the course of official duties. In such a case, the fair dealing exception will probably apply rather than the exception created by s 183 of the Act, and its attendant obligation to pay compensation.

The complementary view finds some support from an examination of extrinsic materials concerning the history and purpose of s 183.[15]

Section 183 was inserted in the *Copyright Act 1968* following a Spicer Committee recommendation.[16] The Committee considered the Gregory Committee recommendation that the Crown should be empowered to reproduce copyright material in connection with the equipment of the armed forces and possibly also for civil defence and essential communications, subject to compensation.[17] This recommendation had, to a large extent, been given statutory effect in the United Kingdom.[18] A majority of the Spicer Committee agreed with the view expressed by the Solicitor-General of the Commonwealth that the Commonwealth and the States should be empowered to use copyright material for any purposes of the Crown, subject to the payment of just terms to be fixed, in the absence of agreement, by the Court.

> The occasions on which the Crown may need to use copyright material are varied and many. Most of us think that it is not possible to list those matters which might be said to be more vital to the public interest than others. At the same time the rights of the author should be protected by provisions for the payment of just compensation to be fixed in the last resort by the Court....
> We note that the Commonwealth and the States have a right to use inventions, subject to the payment of compensation, under section 125 of the Patents Act 1952-1955. We recommend the enactment of a provision on similar lines in respect of Crown use of copyright material.[19]

The purpose of the equivalent provision in the *Patents Act 1952* (s 125) was described by Barwick CJ in *General Steel Industries v Commissioner for Railways (NSW)* as providing 'a means of securing the untrammelled use of the invention by the Governments and the authorities of the Commonwealth and of the States'.[20]

---

[15] By virtue of s 15AB of the *Acts Interpretation Act 1901* (Cth) extrinsic materials may be referred to in order to determine the meaning of a provision when the provision is ambiguous or obscure.

[16] Refer second reading speech for the Copyright Bill 1968: Australia, *Parliamentary Debates (Hansard)*, House of Representatives, 16 May 1968, 1536 (N Bowen, Attorney-General), and Australia. Copyright Law Review Committee (1959), p. 77 (Spicer Committee) [404–406].

[17] United Kingdom. Board of Trade (1952) [75].

[18] By provisions of the *Defence Contracts Act 1958* (UK).

[19] Australia. Copyright Law Review Committee (Spicer Committee) (1959), [404–405]. Two members of the Committee were of the view that the Crown's right to use copyright material without the consent of the copyright owner should be confined to use for defence purposes only.

[20] (1964) 112 CLR 125, 134.

The object s 183 would appear to be aimed at is the unfettered use of copyright materials, such as in times of national exigency, where permission of the relevant copyright owners would otherwise need to be obtained.

The basis of the arguments in favour of the wide scope of s 183(1) ultimately lies in the view that Part VII represents the Crown's position under the *Copyright Act 1968* and overrides the operation of other provisions in the Act. That is if, say, an officer of a Commonwealth department copies on a departmental copier a reasonable part of a copyright work for the purpose of that officer's research or study within the scope of the fair dealing provision s 40 of the Act, and the research or study concerns that person's official duties undertaken within the department, the copying must be characterised as for the services of the Commonwealth rather than for that person's research or study. In the absence of such a view, the insertion of s 183(11) in the Act begs the question whether the copying of the whole or a part of a work or other subject matter for the educational purposes of an educational institution of the Commonwealth or a State could have been undertaken in reliance on the educational copying provisions, rather than s 183(1), where that copying was for the services of the Commonwealth or a State. The insertion simply prevents reliance on s 183(1).

Part VII of the Act does not represent a complete code of the Crown's position under the *Copyright Act 1968*. Evidence in support of that proposition is that at least some of the special defences expressly contemplate the Crown. For example, ss 49–51A enable acts to be undertaken by an officer in charge of a library, such as the making of a copy of an article in a periodical publication for a user or for another library, and the scope of these provisions expressly contemplates that the libraries may be administered by the Crown.[21] In addition, s 48A (and its equivalent provision s 104A) provides that copyright is not infringed by an officer of a parliamentary library by anything done for the sole purpose of assisting a member of Parliament in the performance of that person's duties as a member. This does not oblige parliamentary libraries to pay any compensation to copyright owners and would apply to both Commonwealth and State parliamentary libraries.

The consequences of the wide construction of s 183(1) are significant. It would mean that an individual or a person other than the Crown would be able to do certain

---

[21] Section 195A(1)(c) defines 'officer in charge' in relation to a library referred to in the sections to mean 'the officer holding, or performing the duties of, the office or position in the service of the body administering the library the duties of which involve that person having direct responsibility for the maintenance of, and the provision of services in relation to, the collection comprising the library'. Section 195A(1)(a) similarly defines 'officer in charge' in relation to archives. By virtue of s 10(3)(b) a reference to a body administering a library or archives shall be read as a reference to the body (whether incorporated or not), or the person (including the Crown), having ultimate responsibility for the administration of the library or archives. Further, s 51AA enables the making of single working, reference and replacement copies of copyright works by the officer in charge of Australian Archives in certain circumstances. The functions, the strong capacity for executive control, budgetary dependency and accountability to Government *inter alia* evidenced under the Australian Archives' constituent legislation, the *Archives Act 1983* (Cth), suggest the Australian Archives is an emanation of the Commonwealth for the purposes of the Part VII of the Act.

acts comprised in the copyright free of compensation to the author while, in similar circumstances, the Crown would be subject to agreeing on terms or having terms determined by the Copyright Tribunal.[22] That is, expressed generally, the acts which others may make lawfully without compensation would attract a right to compensation under s 183 or s 183A of the Act if done for the services of the Crown.

It is more reasonable in the light of the non-exclusive nature of Part VII dealing with the Crown to adopt the complementary construction of the operation of s 183 (1). That is, those entitlements expressed in s 183(1) in broad terms and which comprise acts which extend far beyond the scope of the limited special defences to infringement are additional to the entitlements enjoyed under other sections of the Act. Additionally, if it is accepted that s 183(1) conflicts with the specific provisions that comprise those limited special defences to infringement in respect of acts undertaken for the services of the Commonwealth or a State—that is, the doing of an act which by virtue of the special defences does not constitute an infringement of copyright is the doing of an act comprised in a copyright to which s 183 (1) applies—it would appear that the maxim of statutory interpretation *generalia specialibus non derogant* applies. This Latin maxim expresses the principle that provisions of general application give way to specific provisions when in conflict. The maxim applies more strictly in the interpretation of provisions in a particular Act, such as the *Copyright Act 1968*, than in the case of conflict between separate enactments.[23] In this case, it follows that s 183(1) gives way to the special defences when in conflict and that s 183(1) gives additional benefits to the Commonwealth and the States beyond the scope of the special defences.

If the Commonwealth and the States are unable to rely upon the special defences to infringement, then government would be placed in a disadvantageous position with respect to its use of copyright material when compared with all other copyright users, such as private institutions, corporations and individuals. Despite the breadth of government functions and powers, and the calls and demands upon it in comparison with other legal users of copyright material, governments would be obliged to remunerate copyright owners in circumstances when other users would not. This would amount to inconsistent policy between the private and public users of copyright material.

Notwithstanding these arguments, the Copyright Agency Ltd on behalf of copyright owners in published works has, since the late 1980s, entered into licensing arrangements with the Commonwealth and the States for the reproduction of these works under s 183. The Copyright Agency Ltd's present agreement with the Commonwealth is based on the premise that the Crown is able to rely on the special defence to infringement of copyright under s 43—reproduction for the purposes of a judicial proceeding or for the purposes of the provision of professional legal

---

[22] The United States Government is able to rely on the doctrine of 'fair use' under s 107 of the US Copyright Act of 1976. Refer US Department of Justice, Office of Legal Counsel (1999): Memorandum from Acting Assistant Attorney-General RE: Whether Government Reproduction of Copyrighted Materials Invariably is a "Fair Use" under Section 107 of the Copyright Act of 1976.

[23] Pearce and Geddes (2011), p. 147; *White v Mason* [1958] VR 79; *Purcell v Electricity Commission of New South Wales* (1985) 60 ALR 652.

advice—but the agreement expressly states that reliance is not placed on other exemptions in the *Copyright Act 1968*.[24] The Copyright Agency Ltd's agreements with the States and Territories also do not appear to include the special defences to infringement as 'copying exempt from payment' within the Data Processing Protocols in those agreements.[25] This appears to be largely attributable to practical difficulties in accurately identifying particular defences when surveying copying.[26]

9.2.2.3   The Effect of Section 183(1) on the Special Defences to Infringement

There is a suggestion in other contexts within the *Copyright Act 1968* that the extent to which Crown servants may be able to rely on one of the special defences to infringement (s 40) could be limited simply because of the existence and effect of s 183(1).

---

[24] Copying is recorded on a sampling basis. Clause 12 of Schedule 8 which deals with survey data protocols provides—

> Exempt - this includes all Commonwealth published and unpublished material as well as material for which a licence has been obtained(subject to verification) or is otherwise exempt from payment because of the utilisation of section 43 of the Copyright Act being a reproduction for the purposes of judicial proceedings or for the purposes of the provision of professional legal advice. (Reliance is not placed on other exemptions in the Copyright Act.)

There is also no express allowance presently made for copying of an insubstantial part of a work. Refer: Australian Government. Attorney-General's Department, *Agreement between Copyright Agency Limited and the Commonwealth for copying of literary works by the Commonwealth – June 2003* (signed 10 June 2003) cal 30 may pdf provided by copyright@ag.gov.au. Refer also Attorney-General's Department, *Australian Government Use of Copyright Material* http://www.ag.gov.au/RightsAndProtections/IntellectualProperty/Pages/Governmentuseofcopyrightmaterial.aspx.

[25] Refer, for example, to the *Agreement between the Crown in right of the State of New South Wales and the Copyright Agency Limited* dated 14 March 2005, Clause 1.1 (definition of copy) and Annexure C to that Agreement, Clause 9 'Copying Exempt from Payment' http://www.copyright.com.au/states_territories.htm and the Interim Rate Agreement between Copyright Agency Limited and Crown in Right of the State of New South Wales [2009] http://www.lawlink.nsw.gov.au/lawlink/legislation_policy/. These Agreements are referred to in Clauses 3.5–3.6 of the current Remuneration Agreement between the Crown in Right of the State of New South Wales and Copyright Agency Limited [2010] http://www.lpclrd.lawlink.nsw.gov.au/lpclrd/lpclrd_copyright/lpclrd_agreements.html. 'The experience since 2003 is that disagreements about which uses are remunerable have led to difficult and protracted negotiations over the amounts payable under the statutory licence. The parties (governments agencies and collecting societies) have not reached agreement over whether fair dealing and other exceptions are available to governments, or over how surveys should be conducted and what should be counted': Australia. Australian Law Reform Commission, *Copyright and the Digital Economy: Final Report* (ALRC Report 122), 332 [15.14] http://www.alrc.gov.au/publications/copyright-reportd-122.

[26] Email from Peter Treyde, Commonwealth Attorney-General's Department, to John Gilchrist, 31 January 2008. However, the Copyright Agency Ltd takes the wide view of the operation of s183 (1) (email from Phillip Stabile, Copyright Agency Ltd, to John Gilchrist, 4 April 2008).

In *Haines v Copyright Agency Ltd*,[27] the New South Wales Director-General of Education had sent a memorandum to school principals containing a statement that s 40 of the *Copyright Act 1968* (fair dealing for research or study) allowed for virtually the same amount and type of copying as s 53B or s 53D without imposing any need to keep records or make payments. Sections 53B and 53D[28] then enabled the multiple copying by an educational establishment of copyright works for teaching purposes but imposed record-making and retention requirements and subjected the educational establishment to claims for payment by copyright owners in respect of that copying. Fox J of the Federal Court, in a judgment with which Bowen CJ and Deane J agreed, made it clear that it was wrong to say that s 40 allowed for virtually the same amount and type of copying as s 53B. Fox J stated:

> What is fair dealing is not fixed by reference to the number of copies, but is to be determined by reference to the facts of each case. An answer to the question must take into account the existence and effect of s 53B (and s 53D). Moreover it is important to the proper working of the sections that a distinction be recognized between an institution making copies for teaching purposes and the activities of individuals concerned with research and study. The memorandum was in relevant respects addressing itself to the former situation.[29]

The Court ordered that the memorandum be withdrawn and destroyed and its reproduction or distribution be restrained.

McLelland J, at first instance, also considered that the availability to schools of the right to make copies under s 53B, upon compliance with conditions designed to provide 'equitable remuneration' to the owners of copyright, must necessarily have an influence upon what amount and type of copying done in a school and could properly be regarded as a fair dealing under s 40. He stated:

> By way of example, it might be anticipated that a teacher who, even if he procured himself to be appointed as agent for every member of his class, made multiple copies for the purpose of classroom study, of substantially the whole of some separately published book, or sheet music, the subject of copyright, would not in ordinary circumstances be likely to be regarded as engaged in 'fair dealing" under s 40, whereas if the teacher were satisfied after reasonable investigation that copies (not being secondhand copies) of the work could not be obtained within a reasonable time at an ordinary commercial price, such multiple copying could legitimately be carried out on behalf of the school under s 53B if the records required by that section were kept.[30]

It is important to note that the Court in *Haines v Copyright Agency Ltd* did not express a view on whether ss 40 and 53B overlapped. It simply stated that it was wrong to say that s 40 allowed for virtually the same amount and type of copying as the statutory licence (s 53B). However, it does not follow from the decision that some copying may not be undertaken legitimately under s 40 which might also be undertaken in pursuance of that statutory licence or in pursuance of s 183. The issue

---

[27] (1982) 42 ALR 549.

[28] Section 53B is now embodied in ss 135ZJ and 135ZL of the Act and s 53D is now embodied in ss 135ZP and 135ZQ of the Act.

[29] *Haines v Copyright Agency Ltd* (1982) 42 ALR 549, 556.

[30] *Copyright Agency Ltd v Haines* [1982] 1 NSWLR 182, 191.

is essentially whether, on the facts of the case, the dealing is fair and for the purposes described; and this must take into account the number of persons a copier is acting on behalf of as well as the extent of the copying. Both are relevant to the factors set out in s 40(2) of the Act in determining whether a dealing is fair.

It may be fair to make a copy of a reasonable portion of a book for the purpose of research or study of the copier or to make a copy each for two persons for their research or study in accordance with their request but unfair for the copier to make a copy each for 60 persons for their research or study in accordance with their request, despite the fact that, individually, each person could make such a copy for himself or herself. It is submitted that the nature of the dealing in the last example is not fair because the scale of the copying affects the character of the dealing. It carries it beyond the notion of individual copying contemplated by s 40.

The copying of a journal article or a reasonable portion of another published work by an individual for that individual's research or study is deemed by s 40(3) of the Act to be a fair dealing with that work for the purpose of research or study. If that individual is a Crown servant acting in the course of that servant's work for the Crown and the copying is for either of those purposes of the Crown servant, then the extent to which Crown servants may be able to rely on s 40(3) is not limited simply because of the existence and effect of s 183. Likewise, there is nothing in the *Haines* decision to suggest that a Crown servant could not undertake acts which otherwise clearly fall within s 40 of the Act, even if that research or study assisted the Crown servant directly or indirectly in that servant's work for the Crown. What the *Haines* decision does suggest is that courts may be reluctant to construe broadly the scope of the special defences, such as s 40, in their application to the Crown.

9.2.2.4   The Operation of Section 183 and Section 183A of the Copyright Act 1968

Assuming the dealings in question do not attract any of the special defences to infringement under *Copyright Act 1968*, how does the defence provided by s 183 and its related provision (s 183A) operate?

Section 183(1) applies when the person doing the otherwise infringing act is either the Commonwealth or a State or a person authorised in writing by the Commonwealth or a State, and the act is done for the services of the Commonwealth or a State.[31]

Two rights of a copyright owner whose work or other subject matter is affected by acts under s 183(1) are expressly protected by s 183(8). That subsection provides that any act done under s 183(1) does not constitute publication of a work or other subject matter and is not to be taken into account in relation to the duration of any

---

[31] An agreement or licence fixing the terms upon which a person other than the Commonwealth or State may do an act comprised in a copyright under s 183(1) is inoperative with respect to the doing of that act after the commencement of the 1968 Act unless it has been approved by the Attorney-General of the Commonwealth or a State (s 183(6)).

copyright. As any act done under s 183 is done without the consent of the copyright owner, the effect of subsection (8) is to avoid subsection (1) being unfairly determinative of the subsistence of copyright in works that would have protection only on the basis of first publication in Australia, and unfairly determinative of the duration of copyright, for example, in the case of a cinematograph film or a sound recording that, upon publication, has a limited term of protection to 70 years after the year of publication. Acts done under s 183(1) are simply acts over which the copyright owner has no control.

Successors in title to any articles sold to them under s 183(1) are protected from any possible infringement action from subsequent resale by reason of s 183(7). By virtue of that provision, successors in title are entitled to deal with the article as if the Commonwealth or State were the owner of copyright.[32] These provisions apply regardless of whether the act is notified under s 183(4) or recorded under s 183A.

The Meaning of 'for the Services of the Commonwealth or State'

Section 183 provides some assistance in determining the meaning of the phrase 'for the services of the Commonwealth or State' by specifying acts which fall within and outside of the phrase. Section 183(2) deems

- the doing of any act in connexion with the supply of goods in pursuance of an agreement or arrangement between the Government of Commonwealth and the Government of another country for the supply to that country of goods required for the defence of that country and
- the sale to any person of such of those goods as are not required for the purposes of the agreement or arrangement,

to be 'for the services of the Commonwealth'.

On the other hand, s 183(11) excludes from the phrase the copying of the whole or a part of a work for the teaching purposes of an educational institution of, or under the control of, the 'Commonwealth, a State or the Northern Territory'.

There are very few reported cases dealing directly with s 183(1) of the *Copyright Act 1968* or other similar Crown use provisions.[33] Judicial consideration of the

---

[32] For the purposes of these and all other provisions in s 183, references to the owner of copyright include references to an exclusive licensee where there is an exclusive licence in force in relation to any copyright (s 183(9)).

[33] Refer comments by Cooper J in *Stack v Brisbane City Council* (1995) 131 ALR 333 at 345 on the meaning of 'the services of'. In *Allied Mills Industries Pty Ltd v Trade Practices Commission (No 1)* (1981) 55 FLR 125 Sheppard J of the Federal Court of Australia held that the Trade Practices Commission was an emanation or agency of the Commonwealth and simply concluded that the use by the Commission of documents in which copyright might subsist in favour of Allied Mills would not be a breach of the *Copyright Act 1968* (Cth) by reason of s 183 as such acts would have been done for the services of the Commonwealth. Most of the documents were relevant to proceedings brought by the Commission against Allied Mills for penalties for breaches of s 45 of the *Trade Practices Act 1974* (Cth). As a matter of precaution the Commission obtained an authority from the Commonwealth to use the various documents.

scope of the phrase 'for the services of the Commonwealth or State' has been largely confined to patent cases.

In *General Steel Industries Inc v Commissioner for Railways (NSW)*,[34] a single judge of the High Court considered whether the defendants in that action could rely on the Crown use provision (s 125 of the *Patents Act 1952* (Cth)) as a defence to an action for infringement of a patent over certain railway vehicle bearing structures.[35] This Crown use provision was similar in language and operation to s 183 of the *Copyright Act* and the major provisions are set out below. The *Patents Act 1952* (Cth) has since been repealed, but there is a revised Crown use provision (s 163) in the current *Patents Act 1990* (Cth).[36]

Section 125 of the *Patents Act 1952* in part provided:

(1) At any time after an application for a patent has been lodged at the Patent Office or a patent has been granted, the Commonwealth or a State, or a person authorized in writing by the Commonwealth or a State, may make, use, exercise or vend the invention for the services of the Commonwealth or State.

. . .

(3) Authority may be given under sub-section (1) of this section either before or after a patent for the invention has been granted, and either before or after the acts in respect of which the authority is given have been done, and may be given to a person notwithstanding that he is authorized directly or indirectly by the applicant or patentee to make, use, exercise or vend the invention.

(4) Where an invention has been made, used, exercised or vended under sub-section (1) of this section, the Commonwealth or State shall, unless it appears to the Commonwealth or State that it would be contrary to the public interest to do so, inform the applicant or patentee as soon as possible of the fact and shall furnish him with such information as to the making, use, exercise or vending of the invention as he from time to time reasonably requires.

(5) Subject to sub-section (2) of this section, where a patented invention is made, used, exercised or vended under sub-section (1) of this section, the terms for the making, use, exercise or vending of the invention are such terms as are, whether before or after the making, use, exercise or vending of the invention, agreed upon between the Commonwealth or the State and the patentee or, in default of agreement, as are fixed by the High Court.

---

[34] (1964) 112 CLR 125.

[35] 'THE COMMISSIONER FOR RAILWAYS ... HEREBY pursuant to s 125(1) of the *Patents Act* 1952 of the Commonwealth of Australia AUTHORIZES AE GOODWIN LIMITED a Company duly incorporated and carrying on business in the State of New South Wales ... (hereinafter called the Contractor) and any of its Subcontractors IN RELATION to the supply by the Contractor to the Commissioner of any article to be used by the Commissioner in or in relation to the exercise of his powers and the operation of the said railways TO MAKE USE EXERCISE OR VEND any invention to which the provisions of the said s 125(1) relate AND TO USE any model plan document or information relating to any such invention which may be required for that purpose....' (1964) 112 CLR 125, 128.

[36] The defence provision is s 163 but ss 163–165 set out a broadly similar notification scheme to that contained in s 183. Exploitation rights are dealt with in Ch 17 Part 2 of the Act: Exploitation by the Crown. Wider rights are provided to the Commonwealth to acquire patents under the Act in Part 3 of Ch 17.

. . .

(8) No action for infringement lies in respect of the making, use, exercise or vending of a patented invention under sub-section (1) of the section.

Section 132 of the *Patents Act 1952* expressly provided that 'references to the Commonwealth include references to an authority of the Commonwealth and references to a State include references to an authority of the State'. Barwick CJ in *General Steel* took the view that the Commissioner for Railways was an authority of the State within the meaning of ss 125 and 132 of the *Patents Act 1952*.

Barwick CJ summarily terminated the action by the plaintiff with costs after being satisfied that the plaintiff's claim did not disclose a reasonable cause of action and was 'manifestly groundless'. He considered

Sub-section (8) of s 125, in providing that no action for infringement shall be brought for what would otherwise be an infringement of the letters patent, emphasises the clear intention of sub-s (1) and with sub-s (7) provides a means of securing the untrammelled use of the invention by the Governments and the authorities of the Commonwealth and of the States. On the other hand, sub-ss (5) and (6) ensure that proper compensation shall be paid to the owner of the letters patent for the acts of a Government or an authority of Commonwealth or State which makes use of the invention.

. . .

The railway system of the State is, in my opinion, undoubtedly a service of the State and the use of the invention in the construction of railway carriages to be used by the Commissioner in that railway system is a use for a service of the State or for the services of the State within the meaning of the expression in the *Patents Act* 1952, whichever may be the proper way to read the final words of s125(1). One could scarcely imagine that sections such as ss 125 and 132, with their evident practical purpose, did not extend to include within the expression the use of the services of the Commonwealth or State, the use of an invention for the purposes of one of the Government railway systems in Australia.[37]

The judgment did not consider the phrase 'for the services of the State' beyond this brief conclusion.

Shortly after *General Steel Industries,* the House of Lords in *Pfizer Corp v Ministry of Health*[38] held that the supply of the patented antibiotic drug tetracycline to National Health Service hospitals for administration to out-patients and in-patients was a use 'for the services of the Crown' and accordingly fell within the Crown use provision (s 46 of the *Patents Act 1949* (UK)). The Ministry of Health had selected a tenderer who had obtained supplies of the drug manufactured in Italy. The United Kingdom patentee claimed, first, that the Ministry had no power under that section to authorise this method of supply and, secondly, that the supply was used for the benefit of the patients and not for the benefit of any service of the Crown. It is the second claim which is germane to this discussion.

Lord Reid stated in respect of this claim:

---

[37] (1964) 112 CLR 125, 133, 134.

[38] [1965] AC 512.

In Victorian times they were the armed services—the navy and the army—the Civil Service, the foreign colonial and consular services, the Post Office, and perhaps some others. Now there are many more Government activities which are staffed and operated by servants of the Crown, and are subject to the direction of the appropriate Minister. But it is not suggested that for this purpose any distinction is to be made between the older and the newer services, and it is not argued that the hospital service is not a service of the Crown.

. . .

The real controversy in the present case turns on the meaning of the word "for"—what is meant by "*for* the services of the Crown"? I think that it is a false dichotomy to treat some patented articles as made or used for the benefit of the department or service which uses them, and others as made or used for the benefit of those persons outside the service who may derive benefit from their use by the service. Moreover, I think that such a distinction would be unworkable in practice. Most, if not all, activities of government departments or services are intended to be for the benefit of the public, and few can be regarded as solely, or even mainly, for the benefit of the department or of members of the service.

. . .

It appears to me that the natural meaning of "use . . . for the services of the Crown" is use by members of such services in the course of their duties. Sometimes, as in the case of the armed services, that use will or is intended to benefit the whole community: sometimes such use will benefit a particular section of the community: and sometimes it will benefit particular individuals. I cannot see any good reason for making a distinction between one such case and another.[39]

Lord Evershed concurred stating:

As pointed out by the learned judges in the Court of Appeal, there is not and cannot be in this day and age a true antithesis between services of the Crown in the sense of services related to the functions of Government as such and services of the Crown in the sense of the provision of facilities commanded and defined by Act of Parliament for the general public benefit.[40]

Lord Upjohn was also of a similar view. Two judges, Lords Pearce and Wilberforce, dissented, arguing that accepting that view is to withdraw from the benefit of the patent either a large or a preponderant part of the customers for whom the invention was made (and supposedly protected by a monopoly of the right to vend). They suggested a more limited interpretation—that the invention must be for the use of the Crown (that is, the use must be by the Crown or its servants)—and that the use must be for the benefit of the Crown or its servants.[41] It would not enable the Crown, in competition with the patentee, to enter into the field of supplying the article to the public.[42]

---

[39] Ibid, 533, 534, 535.

[40] Ibid, 543.

[41] Ibid, 549, 568.

[42] Ibid, 569.

In another patent case, *Stack v Brisbane City Council*,[43] the applicants alleged that they were beneficially entitled to a patent for a water meter assemblies invention. One of the respondents agreed to sell and supply water assembly meters incorporating this invention to the first respondent, the Brisbane City Council (BCC). Another respondent manufactured the meters. The BCC installed the water meters in homes in Brisbane for the purposes of measuring householders' use of the water supply. The water meters were not resupplied to the land owner but remained an asset of the BCC. The applicants sought an injunction restraining the respondents from infringing the alleged patent, damages or an account of profits and delivery to them of all water assembly meters in the possession of the respondents.

The respondents relied on ss 162 and 163 of the *Patents Act 1990* (Cth) as a defence to the infringement complaint.

Cooper J of the Federal Court held that the BCC was 'impressed with the stamp of government' and was an authority of the State within the meaning of s 162 of the *Patents Act 1990*. The water meters were not resupplied to the land owner and were not used in the relevant sense by the landowner. They were a component part of the apparatus by which water was supplied by the BCC for consumption in the territorial area, and charged for by the BCC, the supply being a function of local government. He concluded that the use of the water meters by the BCC as part of its supply of water in the Brisbane local authority area was the exploitation by the BCC as an authority of a State of the invention, for the services of it as such an authority. Thus, he held that the use of the water meters by the BCC was for the services of the State.

Cooper J referred to the majority and minority views in Pfizer Corp, to General Steel and to two English decisions—*Pyrene Co Ltd v Webb Lamp Co Ltd* (1920) and *Aktiengesellschaft fur Autogene Aluminium Schweissung v London Aluminium Co Ltd* (1923)—referred to in General Steel:

> In the reasoning of Lord Wilberforce in *Pfizer Corp* it was the re-supply by the government department in competition to the patentee which underpinned the conclusion that the grant of monopoly rights was not by the exception in s 46(1) of the Patents Act 1949 (UK) to derogate from the monopoly to a greater extent than the right of the Crown to exploit the invention for its own immediate purposes: see [1965] AC at 568.
>
> . . .
>
> The law in this country is no narrower than the minority view in that decision. If the facts in the instant case fall within the minority view in *Pfizer Corp* and the first instance cases referred to above, it is unnecessary for present purposes to determine whether the majority view in *Pfizer Corp* is the law of Australia.[44]

In *Re Copyright Act 1968; Re Australasian Performing Right Association Ltd*,[45] a case dealing directly with s 183, there was some judicial consideration of the meaning of 'for the services of the Commonwealth' but no decision on the point.

---

[43] (1995) 131 ALR 333.

[44] (1995) 131 ALR 333, 348.

[45] (1982) 65 FLR 437.

The Australasian Performing Right Association Ltd (APRA) formulated a licence scheme in which it was willing to grant a licence to the Australian Broadcasting Commission of its members' works which was subject to certain conditions, including the payment of a licence fee calculated with reference to the Commission's gross operational expenditure incurred in the provision of radio and television broadcasting services. The scheme was referred to the Copyright Tribunal pursuant to s 154(1) of the *Copyright Act 1968*. The Commission took a preliminary objection to the Tribunal's jurisdiction to consider the scheme and to make orders confirming or varying it under s 154(4) on the ground that the Commission was an agent or instrumentality of the Commonwealth and, as such, was protected by s 183 of the Act from infringing copyright when broadcasting or televising items in which copyright subsists.

The Tribunal referred three questions of law to the Federal Court. One was whether the Commission was an agent or instrumentality of the Commonwealth for the purposes of s 183 of the Act. The second of relevance was whether broadcasts by radio or television which are conducted by the Commission are done for the services of the Commonwealth within the meaning of s 183(1) of the Act.

All judges of the Federal Court—Bowen CJ, Franki J and Sheppard J—were of the view that the Australian Broadcasting Commission did not fall within the word 'Commonwealth' nor was it an agency of instrumentality of the Commonwealth for the purposes of s 183 of the Act.

On the second question, Bowen CJ and Franki J stated at pp. 444–445:

> No doubt the broadcasting of radio and television programmes by the Commission constitutes a "service" in the sense that it falls within the words "postal, telegraphic, telephonic and other like services" used in s 51(v) of the *Constitution* (*Jones v Commonwealth (No 2)* (1965) 112 CLR 206).
>
> It does not follow that because broadcasting by the Commission is a service within s 51(v), any broadcasting undertaken by the Commission is for the services of the Crown. Indeed, if the Commission is not the Crown, it would seem that it could not properly be said that its broadcasting was "for the services of the Crown". If the Commission is the Crown, then it could be said its broadcasting was "for the services of the Crown" if the view of the majority of the House of Lords in *Pfizer Corporation v Ministry of Health* [1965] AC 512 be accepted for Australian conditions. This was that the phrase "for the services of the Crown" is not restricted to the traditional notion that it relates to services used by the Crown or its servants but in modern times extends also to services provided by the Crown or its servants to members of the public. In view of our conclusion that the Commission is not the Crown it is unnecessary to express a concluded view on this point.

Sheppard J stated at p. 457:

> ... [i]t may be possible for an act to be done for the services of the Commonwealth within the meaning of s 183 of the Act, notwithstanding that the Commission is not the Commonwealth nor an agent or instrumentality thereof. Such a situation might arise if there were broadcast or televised something which was plainly broadcast or televised for the services of the Commonwealth, for example, a radio or television programme put on for the purposes of the Commonwealth Government.

While he also referred to the *Pfizer Corp* case, no opinion was expressed on the majority and minority views in that case.

In *Copyright Agency Limited v New South Wales*, the High Court noted the majority view in *Pfizer Corp* that the formula 'for the services of the Crown' was not limited to the internal activities of government departments but included use by government departments in the fulfilment of duties imposed on them by legislation, and that the expression was broad enough to cover provision of products to the public.[46] The High Court in *Copyright Agency Limited v New South Wales* took a wide view of the scope of s 183 and implicitly adopted the majority view in *Pfizer Corp* of what constitutes 'for the services of the Crown'.

As the High Court stated:

> 61. What is important in respect of the submissions made in this case is that no distinctions are made in s 183(1) between government uses obliged by statute and/or government uses which may be "vital to the public interest" on the one hand, and government uses which reflect considerations more closely resembling commercial uses, on the other.
> 62. Whilst it is not difficult to understand a preference for a policy framed with an eye to such distinctions, no such policy is evinced in the clear and express terms of s 183(1).
> ...
> 70. There is nothing in ss 183(1), 183(5) or 183A, or other provisions relating to the statutory licence scheme, which suggests that governments may make, or take the benefit of, arrangements which would have the effect of circumventing those provisions as they apply to the copying, and the communication to the public, of registered survey plans.[47]

That is, the execution of activities by the Commonwealth, or a State, within its lawful powers and authority, constitutes a 'service' of the Commonwealth or State whether that includes a sale or supply to a third party. In other words, an act is done 'for the services of the Commonwealth or State' if it is done for the purpose of performing a duty or exercising a power which is imposed upon or invested in the executive government of the Commonwealth or State by statute or by prerogative. This is consistent with the wide scope of the acts encompassed by s 183(1), the language of ss 183(2) and (7) and with the broad intention behind the provision manifested in extrinsic materials.[48]

The fact that, in times of peace, government chooses to arrange copyright licences in procurements for its armed forces rather than rely on s 183 is a reflection of government policy and practice[49] but s 183(1) is intended to secure the untrammelled use of copyright material by the governments and emanations of the Commonwealth and of the States in all these lawful circumstances. Sections 183 (4) and (5) and ss 183A and 183B ensure that proper compensation shall be paid to the owner of the copyright for the acts of the Commonwealth or State.

---

[46] *Copyright Agency Limited v New South Wales* [2008] HCA 35 [56].

[47] Ibid. [70].

[48] Refer to judgment of the High Court in Ibid, [8, 55–59, 70].

[49] It has for more than two decades generally been the practice of the Commonwealth to rely on the provision as a last resort.

The Notice Requirement in Section 183

Section 183 imposes an obligation on the Commonwealth and the States to inform the relevant owner of copyright of the act undertaken in reliance upon the provision. The prescribed means of doing this are set out in reg 25 of the *Copyright Regulations 1969*.

Regulation 25(5) requires that a notice be given in the name of the Commonwealth or the State and that it state the International Standard Book Number (if any) or the title or description of the work sufficient to enable the work or other subject matter to be identified. It also requires that the notice specify the act to which the notice relates, state whether the act has been done by the Commonwealth or the State or a person authorised by the Commonwealth or the State and, if the latter, state the name of the person, and state that the purpose of the notice is to inform the owner in pursuance of s 183(4) of the doing of the act.

Regulations 25(2)–(4) require the notice to be served on the owner of the copyright or authorised agent or, where the person giving the notice does not know the address, or the name or address, of the owner of copyright or authorised agent, by notice in the *Commonwealth of Australia Gazette* or *Government Gazette* of the State as the case requires. It is a cumbersome and costly procedure for all but large-scale acts comprised within the copyright in material.

Assuming the acts in question fall outside the sampling arrangements contemplated by s 183A, can the defence provided by s 183(1) be relied on if the Commonwealth or a State undertakes acts which, at some time after the acts are undertaken, it considers are for the services of the Commonwealth or State and then fails to inform the relevant copyright owner? That is, if the Commonwealth or the State simply does nothing to notify the owner of the copying.

There is nothing in the language of s 183(1) to suggest that it is necessary to establish an intention to rely on the section at the time of the doing of the act. Indeed, s 183(3) expressly provides that authority may be given under subsection (1) (that is, to a person authorised in writing by the Commonwealth or a State) before or after the acts, in respect of which the authority has been given, have been done. Section 183(1) is not dependent on any subjective intention of the actors involved at the time of the acts but on the objective test of whether the copying is, in fact, done for that purpose. This, therefore, leads to the conclusion that the defence may be relied on at any time after the acts.

The notice requirements in s 183(4) are not, unlike the notice requirements in other statutory licences, such as ss 135ZJ–135ZL, expressed to be a condition of the operation of the defence. Section 183(7) also refers to the sale of an article 'which is not, by virtue of sub-section (1), an infringement of a copyright'. This clearly contemplates that an act done for the services of the Commonwealth or a State is not an infringement of copyright and supports the view that the defence to infringement is not dependent on informing the copyright owner of the act.

However, s 183(4) clearly imposes an obligation to inform the copyright owner of the doing of the act 'as soon as possible' unless it appears to the Commonwealth or the State that it would be contrary to the public interest to do so.

There is an ambiguity in the way the notification requirement is expressed in s 183(4). The exception 'unless it appears to the Commonwealth or State that it would be contrary to the public interest to do so' is capable of being read as either qualifying the immediately preceding words 'as soon as possible' or the mandatory verb 'shall' preceding those words. The use of commas after 'shall' and 'possible' promotes this response.[50] Lindgren, Rothnie and Lahore appear to suggest that no notice need be given to the copyright owner where it appears to be contrary to the public interest to do so.[51] There are, for example, public interest circumstances such as the security or defence of the Commonwealth where the Commonwealth may not wish to inform the copyright owner. So long as those public interest circumstances continue to exist, then it would seem from either reading of the provision that no notification need be made. Section 183A(6) defines 'excluded copies' from the streamlined arrangements in terms 'where it appears to the government that it would be contrary to the public interest to disclose information about the making of the copies' which is consistent with this view.

If the public interest ceases to exist, such as the cessation of war or armed hostilities or the investigation of terrorist activities, is the Commonwealth then obliged to inform the copyright owner?

It is submitted that notification is required on a reading of s 183(4) in the light of the section as a whole and the underlying economic purpose or object of the Act, which is to protect and reward the originators of certain kinds of creative material by giving them the power to exploit that material. This applies to all excluded copies under the streamlined arrangements. This view has an echo of the Commonwealth's obligations under s 51(xxxi) of the *Australian Constitution* to acquire property on just terms, in this case to provide just terms in dealings with that property which would otherwise be an infringement of the rights of the copyright owner. Further, two important extrinsic materials—the Spicer Committee Report and the second reading speech of the then Attorney-General on the Copyright Bill—appear to support this view.[52]

---

[50] Refer Pearce and Geddes (2011), pp. 164–165 [4.56], where the authors point out that punctuation is a relevant consideration in determining the meaning of a provision even though at the Commonwealth level at least there is no statutory clarification of this principle and courts have at times shown a reluctance to pay regard to punctuation. In four jurisdictions amendments to their Interpretation Acts provide that punctuation in an Act is part of the Act: *Legislation Act 2001* (ACT) s 126(6); *Acts Interpretation Act 1954* (Qld) s 14(6); *Acts Interpretation Act 1915* (SA) s 19; *Interpretation of Legislation Act 1984* (Vic) s 36(3B).

[51] Lindgren et al. (2004), Vol 1 [28, 561].

[52] Refer Australia. Copyright Law Review Committee (Spicer Committee) (1959), [404–405]. 'The occasions on which the Crown may need to use copyright material are varied and many. Most of us think that it is not possible to list those matters which might be said to be more vital to the public interest than others. At the same time the rights of the author should be protected by provisions for the payment of just compensation to be fixed in the last resort by the Court....' and second reading speech for the Copyright Bill 1968, Australia. Copyright Law Review Committee (Spicer Committee) (1959): 'The Bill puts beyond doubt that the Crown is bound by the copyright law. Provision is made, however, [in Pt VII] for the use of copyright material for the services of the

The Impact of Section 183A and Its Related Provisions

From 30 July 1998, the *Copyright Amendment Act (No 1) 1998* (Cth) amended the *Copyright Act 1968* to streamline the system for owners of copyright to be paid for the copying of their works by government. The amendments followed the regime of the statutory licence schemes for copying by educational establishments by providing for a collecting society to be declared by the Copyright Tribunal to administer sampling, collecting and distributing payments in a similar way to the educational copying schemes.

The amendments avoided the operation of ss 183(4) and (5) of the Act by requiring payments for the reproduction of copyright materials by a government to be made the basis of sampling, rather than the statutory method of full record keeping embodied in ss 183(4) and (5), where there is a declared copyright collecting society. The statutory provisions reflected changes in practice that had already occurred between copyright owners and government. These provisions contemplate that a relevant collecting society, which may be declared by the Copyright Tribunal in relation to all government copies or a class of government copies, will distribute the equitable remuneration to the owners of copyright in the material that has been copied and will hold in trust the remuneration for non-members who are entitled to receive it.

The method of working out the equitable remuneration payable may provide for different treatment of different kinds or classes of government copies (s 183A(4)).

Section 183A replicates some of the public interest considerations reflected in s 183. In particular, it does not apply to 'excluded copies' which is defined in s 183A (6) to mean 'government copies in respect of which it appears to the government concerned that it would be contrary to the public interest to disclose information about the making of the copies'. This would include copies made for defence or security purposes. A definition section, s 182B, defines 'government copy' to mean a reproduction in a material form of copyright material made under s 183(1) and, in turn, defines 'copyright material' to cover works and subject matter other than works. Computer programs are specifically excluded from the definition of copyright material and thus from the streamlined arrangements.

Thus, copying of computer programs and copying of any material where there is a public interest in non-disclosure of that copying must be governed by the requirements of ss 183(4) and (5). In addition, acts comprised in the copyright other than reproduction of works and subject matter other than works, which are not done in pursuance of a collective agreement and which are done for the services of

---

Commonwealth or the States upon payment of compensation to the owner of the copyright.' There was very little change from the original 1967 Bill: second reading speech for the Copyright Bill 1967: Australia, *Parliamentary Debates (Hansard)*, House of Representatives, 18 May 1967, 2334–2335 (N Bowen, Attorney-General): 'Provision is made … for the use of copyright material for the services of the Commonwealth or the States upon payment of compensation to the owner of the copyright. These provisions are contained in clause 179 of the Bill, which in this respect follows the relevant provisions of the Patents Act.'

the Commonwealth or a State, would also be governed by the notification and determination requirements of ss 183(4) and (5). For example, if a State government department made an adaptation of a work, such as a translation or cartoon of a literary work, for the services of the State, this act would be governed by ss 183 (4) and (5). Since 2007, the Commonwealth has had a collective agreement with Screenrights for the copying for work purposes of transmissions of television and radio programs based on sampling system under s 183A(3).[53] The Commonwealth also has an agreement with the Australasian Performing Rights Association (APRA) for the public performance of musical works by the Commonwealth, based on an annual fee factored to the number of full time staff, in which APRA waives any right to be notified of the performance of music under s 183.

9.3   Implied Licences to the Commonwealth or a State to Reproduce or Publish Material

Under the *Copyright Act 1968* it is a direct infringement of copyright to do or to authorise the doing of any act comprised in the copyright in a work or other subject matter without the licence of the copyright owner.[54] The effect of a licence given by the copyright owner is to permit what would otherwise have been an infringement of copyright. Licences may be implied from the nature of the work and the surrounding circumstances as well as expressly granted by the copyright owner. Licences may be expressly granted either orally or in writing. Other than in respect of an exclusive licence, there is no requirement under the 1968 Act that a licence be in writing.

An early case dealing with implied licences to government is *Folsom v Marsh*. That case involved the alleged piracy by a commercial publisher, in 'The Life of Washington', of the private and official letters of President Washington (as well as his messages and other public acts). The letters of Washington had been previously published under an agreement with the private copyright owners. The originals of the letters had been purchased by Congress. In *Folsom v Marsh*,[55] Story J dismissed a defence that, because they were in their nature and character either public or official letters or private letters of business, the letters were not the proper subjects of copyright. He observed that the author of letters, whether they are literary compositions or familiar letters or letters of business, possesses the sole and

---

[53] Other than 'excluded copies' and copies for personal use. Screenrights is the trading name of the Audio-Visual Copyright Society Limited which is a declared collecting society under s 182C of the *Copyright Act 1968* (Cth).

[54] Sections 36 and 101. A similar position applies to those indirect infringements under the Act, such as importation for sale or hire (s 102). These indirect infringements require proof of knowledge by the person infringing.

[55] (1841) 9 F. Cas. 342, 2 Story (Amer.) 100. Refer also Bentley and Kretschmer (eds), Primary Sources on copyright (1450–1900).

exclusive copyright therein. Story J went on to say that persons to whom the letters are addressed must have, by implication, the right to publish any letter or letters addressed to them upon such occasions as require or justify the publication or public use of them. He cited as examples:

- to establish a right to maintain a suit at law or in equity or to defend the same, and
- if misrepresented by the writer or accused of improper conduct in a public manner, he may publish such parts of such letters as may be necessary to vindicate his character and reputation, or free him from unjust obloquy and reproach.[56]

He went on to state:

> In respect to official letters, addressed to the government, or any of its departments, by public officers, so far as the right of the government extends, from principles of public policy, to withhold them from publication, or to give them publicity, there may be a just ground of distinction. It may be doubtful, whether any public officer is at liberty to publish them, at least, in the same age, when secrecy may be required by the public exigencies, without the sanction of the government. On the other hand, from the nature of the public service, or the character of the documents, embracing historical, military, or diplomatic information, it may be the right, or even the duty, of the government, to give them publicity, even against the will of the writers. But this is an exception in favor of the government, and stands upon principles allied to, or nearly similar to, the rights of private individuals, to whom letters are addressed by their agents, to use them, and publish them, upon fit and justifiable occasions. But assuming the right of the government to publish such official letters and papers, under its own sanction, and for public purposes, I am not prepared to admit, that any private persons have a right to publish the same letters and papers, without the sanction of the government, for their own private profit and advantage. Recently the Duke of Wellington's despatches have, (I believe) been published by an able editor, with the consent of the noble Duke, and under the sanction of the government. It would be a strange thing to say, that a compilation involving so much expense, and so much labor to the editor, in collecting and arranging the materials, might be pirated and republished by another bookseller, perhaps to the ruin of the original publisher, and editor. Before my mind arrives at such a conclusion, I must have clear and positive lights to guide my judgment, or to bind me in point of authority.[57]

In *Copyright Agency Limited v New South Wales*,[58] the Full Court of the Federal Court of Australia held that the State of New South Wales did not infringe copyright in survey plans registered with the Land and Property Information Division of the New South Wales Department of Lands by making the plans available to the public and to local government and authorities.

Emmett J held on the facts that the survey plans had previously been published and that, by the lodgement of the plans, a surveyor must have been taken to have licensed and authorised the Crown to make available to the public, to copy and to do any other acts required by the Crown's statutory and regulatory planning regime.

---

[56] *Folsom v Marsh* 9 F.Cas.342, 2 Story (Amer) 100, 111.

[57] *Folsom v Marsh* 9 F.Cas.342, 2 Story (Amer) 100, 113, 114.

[58] [2007] FCAFC 80 (5 June 2007).

Copyright in the plans remained with the surveyor. The licence was for the State to do everything that, under the statutory and regulatory framework that governs registered plans, the State was obliged to do with, or in relation to, registered plans.

Emmett J, with whom Lindgren J agreed and with whom Finkelstein J agreed generally, accepted the notion that a surveyor who made the plan must be taken to have licensed and authorised the State to do acts comprised in the copyright in consequence of the lodgement of the plan for registration, regardless of the presence of s 183. To quote from Emmett J's judgement in the case:

> 156 The systems of land holding in New South Wales and the statutory and regulatory framework described above depend in no manner upon the existence of the *Copyright Act*. If s 183 did not exist, it is clear that there would be no utility whatsoever for a surveyor in submitting any of the Relevant Plans for registration unless, by doing so, or assenting to that being done, the surveyor authorised the State to do what it is obliged by the statutory and regulatory regime described above to do, as a consequence of registering the Relevant Plan. Whether or not s 183 has the effect that the doing of the acts, because they are done for the services of the State, are deemed not to be an infringement of copyright, a surveyor must be taken to have licensed and authorised the doing of the very acts that the surveyor was intending should be done as a consequence of the lodgement of the Relevant Plan for registration.[59]

However, on appeal, the High Court took a narrow view of the scope of an implied licence in these circumstances.

> 46. ... On the one hand, the State uses the plans in direct response to lodgement of the survey plans by an applicant to effect, if appropriate, registration, and to issue title. This includes making a working copy of the plans. These uses are directly connected with private contracts for reward between surveyors and their clients for the preparation of plans for the specific purposes of lodgement, registration and the issue of title. On the other hand, there are uses of survey plans by the State which flow from registration and which involve copying the plans for public purposes or communicating them to the public via a digital system.
> 47. Whilst CAL is seeking remuneration and terms only in respect of those latter uses, the submissions did not always distinguish between the two types of uses. As will be explained in these reasons, the statutory licence scheme applies in the circumstances of this case to authorise the State to make copies of the survey plans after registration, for public purposes and for communication to the public, and provides for terms upon which that can be done. The scheme is compulsory in the sense that an owner cannot complain of the permitted use, but the use is allowed on condition that it be remunerated.[60]

The High Court considered that there was nothing in the express terms of s 183 (1) (or its history) which could justify reading down the expression 'for the services of the State' so as to exclude reproduction and communication to the public pursuant to express statutory obligations. The High Court further held that:

> 92. ... a licence will only be implied when there is a necessity to do so. As stated by McHugh and Gummow JJ in *Byrne v Australian Airlines Ltd*:

---

[59] Ibid [156].

[60] *Copyright Agency Limited v New South Wales* [2008] HCA 35 [46, 47].

"This notion of 'necessity' has been crucial in the modern cases in which the courts have implied for the first time a new term as a matter of law."

93. Such necessity does not arise in the circumstances that the statutory licence scheme excepts the State from infringement, but does so on condition that terms for use are agreed or determined by the Tribunal (ss 183(1) and (5)). The Tribunal is experienced in determining what is fair as between a copyright owner and a user. It is possible, as ventured in the submissions by CAL, that some uses, such as the making of a "backup" copy of the survey plans after registration, will not attract any remuneration.[61]

This narrow view suggests copies made for internal administrative purposes, as well as backup copies, would be covered by an implied licence. It is clear in the circumstances of that case that the use which involved copying of the plans for public purposes and later selling the rights to access and use those documents to information brokers and other members of the public via a digital system is not.[62]

Two of the factors the High Court thought were significant in its decision were that the State imposed charges for copies issued to the public, and that equitable remuneration for government uses, which involved copying and communication of the plans to the public subsequent to registration, did not undermine or impede the use for which the plans were prepared, namely lodgement for registration and issue of title. It is dangerous to generalise from the circumstances surrounding the lodgement of these survey plans under the system set by State planning laws more broadly to copyright works received by government in other circumstances, although the decision of the High Court has wider implications for the digitalisation of registration systems and the wider needs of government to disseminate such information, whether enhanced with other information or not.

One simple outcome is that government could increase registration fees to take into account any remuneration payable to the authors of the plans for any public uses or communication of such copyright material and consequent administrative costs. Alternatively, it could require any party lodging material for inclusion in any public registry to expressly licence their copyright material to permit use of the document by government users or for the public purposes contemplated by the government or, as Fitzgerald has pointed out, to provide 'an open licence which permits use of the document both by government and non-government users, such as a non-exclusive Creative Commons Attribution (CC-BY) licence'.[63] The wider implications for government in its own management of information are discussed in Part 9.5 of this chapter.

---

[61] Ibid, [92, 93].

[62] 'At its narrowest, the High Court's decision in *Copyright Agency Ltd v New South Wales* can be read as holding that where third party copyright documents (in this case the survey plans) are lodged with a government registry and the State later sells rights to access and use of those documents to commercial vendors at commercial rates, the State's rights to reproduce and communicate those copyright materials are governed by the statutory licensing arrangements and payment of equitable remuneration under ss 183 and 183A of the Copyright Act 1968': Fitzgerald et al. (2011), p. 430.

[63] Fitzgerald et al. (2011), p. 431.

Implied licences to reproduce or publish copyright material may also arise in a wide variety of circumstances unconnected with government. Licences have been implied by the courts from conduct or from custom of the trade or to give a dealing between the parties', ordinary business efficacy. For example, the editor of a newspaper would normally be regarded as having an implied licence to publish, and to edit, a letter sent to him on a public matter.[64]

As the High Court stated in *Concrete Pty Ltd v Parramatta Design & Developments Pty Ltd*:

> A nonexclusive licence to use architectural plans and drawings may be oral or implied by conduct, or may be implied, by law, to a particular class of contracts, reflecting a concern that otherwise rights conferred under such contracts may be undermined, or may be implied, more narrowly, as necessary to give business efficacy to a specific agreement between the parties. A term which might ordinarily be implied, by law, to a particular class of contracts may be excluded by express provision or if it is inconsistent with the terms of the contract. In some instances more than one of the bases for implication may apply.[65]

The existence and extent of any implied licence to government to do acts comprised in the copyright in material forwarded to government depends on the nature of the material and the circumstances of its submittal.

Where letters, submissions or other correspondence are sent to government from individuals, organisations and other governments, a licence or consent to officials in government to copy that correspondence would normally be implied to enable it to be given timely and proper consideration by relevant Crown servants, Ministers and ministerial staff. Frequently, the drafting of responses to correspondence requires input from a number of different areas of administrative responsibility and copies of correspondence are made to enable contemporaneous consideration by those areas.

Such a licence could, of course, be negated by an express prohibition on copying. It is unusual, or even rare, for letters or submissions or other correspondence to government to be marked 'not to be copied'. In some more sensitive areas of government, such as the Commonwealth Department of Defence, the confidentiality of material may be expressly marked, access may be expressed to be restricted to particular recipients and there may be an obligation to number copies made, particularly in the case of tender documents. But it would be unrealistic to suggest that governments, like other large institutions and organisations, should not normally copy a document received by it to enable it to receive timely and proper consideration.

It is just as strongly arguable that a licence would normally be implied to make a copy of a letter, submission or other correspondence sent to governments to ensure the immediate preservation of the document.[66] For example, a letter sent to a

---

[64] *Springfield v Thame* (1903) 89 LT 242; *De Garis v Neville Jeffress Pidler Pty Ltd* (1990) 18 IPR 292, 302–303.

[65] [2006] HCA 55; (2006) 229 CLR 577 at 595–596 [59] per Kirby and Crennan JJ; see also Gummow ACJ at 584 [16].

[66] This gives business efficacy to the relationship established by the submission of the correspondence.

Minister, which is usually forwarded to the Minister's department for the preparation of a reply, may be copied in the Minister's office for that purpose. When the letter ceases to have currency and is placed in archives, governments may rely on ss 51AA and 51A of the *Copyright Act 1968* to undertake such copying.[67]

In some limited circumstances, governments may have an implied licence to publish or to place publicly online. One circumstance where a licence may be implied is in respect of a public submission on a matter of public moment sent to, or given before, a government committee or commission by a Member of Parliament or a peak body representing a community interest. An example is a submission on a law reform issue. The implication of a licence could only arise in the case of a public submission, that is, a submission made in response to the calling of public submissions by the committee or body concerned and which is submitted on that basis. This is akin to the implication of a licence to an editor of a newspaper to publish a letter on a public matter sent to the editor.[68]

There are other circumstances where correspondence received from Members of Parliament or constituents on matters of public moment may carry an implied licence to publish or place online. An implied licence would almost certainly not extend to cover correspondence sent on private constituent affairs or private commercial matters. A claim of confidentiality on a letter or a submission would negate any such licence simply because it is inconsistent with publication. A licence to publish or to place publicly online would clearly not be implied where there was an express restriction placed on the publication of a document, or more broadly, on its use within government.

Similarly, it may still be open to government to publish official letters addressed to government, or any of its departments, by public officers embracing historical, military, or diplomatic information, as Story J in *Folsom v Marsh* suggests,[69] on the basis of an implied licence, but many of these documents in the present Australian context are likely to be Crown copyright material, having been made by, or under the direction or control of, the Commonwealth or a State. In the case of documents emanating from its own public officers of government, no question of an implied licence to government could possibly arise.

Inevitably, from the very nature of something which is implied, there are likely to be uncertainties about the existence of such a licence. In practice, this deters

---

[67] The former permits a single working copy and a single reference copy of a published or an unpublished work kept in the collection of the National Archives of Australia to be made by the Archives where the work is open to public inspection. The latter, which has application to all non-profit archival institutions (as well as libraries), *inter alia* permits a copy of a work in manuscript form or an original artistic work that forms part of the collection of the archives to be made by the archives for the purpose of preserving the manuscript or original artistic work against loss or deterioration.

[68] Refer *Springfield v Thame* (1903) 89 LT 242 and *DeGaris v Neville Jeffress Pidler Pty Ltd* (1990) 18 IPR 292, 303–303. An implied licence to publish public submissions sent to parliamentary and other public inquiries would normally subsist in the convenor of such inquiries.

[69] *Folsom v Marsh* 9 F.Cas.342, 2 Story (Amer) 100, 113, 114.

reliance upon such a licence. Section 183(1) offers protection from infringement to the Commonwealth and the States where the position is not clear. Section 183 (3) goes even further in that it extends the protection of the provision to a private licencee where written authority is given by the Commonwealth or a State to that person to do acts comprised in the copyright.[70]

9.4   Other Statutory Entitlements to Do Acts Comprised in Copyright

There are a number of statutory provisions in various Australian jurisdictions which enable the Commonwealth or a State to do acts in relation to copyright material which provide immunity from civil and criminal proceedings.[71]

Commonwealth enactments, other than the *Copyright Act 1968*, include laws dealing with freedom of information, archives and parliamentary proceedings in which there are express legal entitlements of government to copy material in its possession without infringing the copyright in the material.[72]

Access to a document may be given to a person under s 20 of the *Freedom of Information Act 1984* (Cth) in one of a number of forms including the provision by the agency or Minister of a copy of the document. Measures passed under the *Freedom of Information Amendment (Reform) Act 2010* (Cth) also require the publication of documents to which access has been given under the Act (and other specified government information) to enable downloading from a website. Under ss 90, 91 and 92 of the *Freedom of Information Act 1984* where access has been given to a document in good faith in the belief that access was required to be given under the Act, or when publication of a document is undertaken in good faith in the belief publication is required under the Act or otherwise, then no action for defamation, breach of confidence or infringement of copyright nor any criminal

---

[70] The agreement or licence providing the authority must be approved by the relevant Commonwealth or State Attorney-General (s 183(6)).

[71] The *Copyright Act 1968* includes special defence provisions enabling the doing of acts comprised in the copyright in works and other subject matter by the judicial and parliamentary arms of government. Section 48A and s 104A are defences to infringement which enable a parliamentary library to do acts comprised in the copyright for the sole purpose of assisting a member of parliament in the performance of that person's duties as a member. Section 43 and s104 are defences to infringement which enable anything done for the purpose of a judicial proceeding or a report of a judicial proceeding. No compensation is provided to the copyright owner under these provisions.

[72] Other examples are ss 720 and 743 of the *Offshore Petroleum and Greenhouse Gas Storage Act 2006* (Cth) which enable the responsible Commonwealth Minister or Titles Administrator in exercise of their powers under to the Act to do any acts comprised in the copyright in a literary or artistic work that are applicable documents (which include lodged applications, reports and returns under the Act). Refer to the discussion in Fitzgerald et al. (2012), p. 160.

action lies against the Commonwealth by reason of the giving of access or the publication of the document.

The measures which require agencies to publish information under the *Freedom of Information Act 1984* have not yet been matched by reforms to the *Archives Act 1983* (Cth). Consequently, there is at present no equivalent in the *Archives Act 1983* to ss 90–92 of the *Freedom of Information Act 1984*. Section 57 of the *Archives Act 1983* merely provides protection from copyright infringement, for defamation, breach of confidence and criminal actions for the giving of access under the *Archives Act 1983*.[73]

No compensation is contemplated by any of these Commonwealth provisions. They operate independently and irrespective of s 183. Neither does s 183 expressly or implicitly refer to these provisions nor do the provisions expressly or implicitly refer to s 183. They have different objects or purposes and are not so wholly inconsistent or repugnant that they cannot stand together.[74] Effect can be given to each provision at the same time.[75] These Acts should thus be accorded independent operation within their given spheres.

Article 9 of the English Bill of Rights 1688/9, which applies to the Commonwealth and to the Australian States by statute or by the common law, provides absolute protection against liability for reproduction of copyright material in debates or proceedings of Parliament.[76] Another widely-expressed provision is s 4 of the *Parliamentary Papers Act 1908* (Cth), which provides that no civil or criminal action or proceeding shall lie against a person for publishing any document or evidence pursuant to an authorisation given by a House of the Commonwealth Parliament, or a committee thereof, under ss 2 or 3 of that Act. Similar provisions exist in State jurisdictions under various State enactments.[77]

---

[73] State Freedom of Information Acts contain bars on actions for defamation and breach of confidence in respect of the giving of access under their several enactments but not bars on actions for copyright infringement although all contemplate the provision of a copy of a document as a form of access. Section 23(3)(c) of the *Freedom of Information Act 1982* (Vic) provides that if the form of access to a document would involve an infringement of copyright, access in that form may be refused and access given in another form. The Commonwealth Parliament under the *Australian Constitution* has exclusive legislative power over copyright.

[74] As Gaudron J stated in *Saraswati v R* (1991) 100 ALR 193, 204,' It is a basic rule of construction that, in the absence of express words, an earlier statutory provision is not repealed, altered or derogated from by a later provision unless an intention to that effect is necessarily to be implied. There must be very strong grounds to support that implication, for there is a general presumption that the legislature intended that both provisions should operate and that, to the extent that they would otherwise overlap, one should be read as subject to the other'.

[75] Refer *Rose v Hrvic* (1963) 108 CLR 353, 360.

[76] For further discussion see Campbell and Monotti (2002).

[77] See for example *Parliamentary Papers Act 1891* (WA) s 1 and the *Parliamentary Papers (Supplementary Provisions) Act 1975* (NSW) s 6, *Parliamentary Committees Act 1991* (SA) s 31. Refer also s 11(1) of the *Parliamentary Privileges Act 1987* (Cth) which provides that no action, civil or criminal, lies against an officer of a House in respect of a publication to a member of a document that has been laid before a House.

No compensation is contemplated by any of these statutory provisions applying in the Commonwealth and States.

In the case of the State enactments, the operation and proceedings of State Parliaments are not immune from the laws of the Commonwealth but are generally unfettered by them. Section 106 of the *Commonwealth of Australia Constitution Act 1901* specifically deals with the saving of each State constitution and provides for its continuance until altered in accordance with the constitution of the State. However, s 106 is expressed to be subject to the *Australian Constitution* and it has not been treated as invalidating a law which otherwise falls within Commonwealth legislative power.[78] Likewise, s 107 of the *Commonwealth of Australia Constitution Act 1901* provides that every power of the Parliament of a colony which has become or becomes a State shall, unless it is by the *Constitution* exclusively vested in the Parliament of the Commonwealth or withdrawn from the Parliament of the State, continue as at the establishment of the State.

The *Copyright Act 1968* clearly falls within a head of Commonwealth constitutional power. The principal question, therefore, is whether s 183 is intended to apply to the publication by State Parliaments of copyright material, that is, to the proceedings of State Parliament. It is clear law that parliamentary privilege is so valuable and essential to the workings of responsible government that express words in a statute are necessary before it may be taken away.[79] In the case of the Parliament of the Commonwealth, s 49 of the *Constitution* requires an express declaration. No express intention to take away either the power of the Commonwealth Parliament or a State Parliament is evident in the *Copyright Act 1968* as a whole or in s 183 specifically and so the provisions of state and federal enactments, which deal with parliamentary publication, stand unfettered by the Act.

9.5   Information Management and Section 183

If the Crown can rely on special defences to infringement of copyright, which enable use of private copyright material, why should it also have wider entitlements to use private copyright material? How are these rights justified on information management principles and other policy considerations?

The special defence provisions, augmented by s 183, reflect the peculiar status of government, and the demands on it, to fulfil in the public interest a wider variety of governing powers and functions within a modern liberal democratic society. This is reflected in the growth of most western governments, especially in the years after

---

[78] *Attorney-General (Qld) v Attorney-General (Cwth)* (1915) 20 CLR 148, 172; *Almalgamated Society of Engineers v Adelaide Steamship Co (Engineers Case)* (1920) 28 CLR 129, 154; *Melbourne v Commonwealth* (1947) 74 CLR 31, 66, 75, 83, *Stuart-Robertson v Lloyd* (1932) 47 CLR 482: *Queensland Electricity Commission v Commonwealth* (1985) 159 CLR 192, *Victoria v Commonwealth* (1996) 187 CLR 416.

[79] *Duke of Newcastle v Morris* (1870) LR 4HL 661, 671, 677, 680.

the Second World War.[80] No other body or institution has the breadth of activity and regulatory, financial, managerial and accountability requirements as modern government.

The information management principles outlined in *Management of Government Information as a National Strategic Resource: a Report of the Information Management Steering Committee on Information Management in the Commonwealth Government*, published in August 1997 by the Office of Government Information Technology, stated that:

> In developing systems for the organisation, transmission and transaction of information, agencies should start from the premise that, subject to privacy legislation, all information content will at some time be transferred across agency boundaries, and design access systems accordingly.[81]

Acts comprised in the copyright in information and, most importantly, the reproduction of copyright information within government agencies and across them, is a management demand required for the effective review and consideration of material, and is also necessary to fulfil the basic right of all citizens in a democratic society to be informed of, and to have access to, government information.

In 2010, the federal government's *Response to the Report of the Government 2.0 Taskforce*[82] agreed that Australian Government agencies should enable a culture that gives their staff opportunity to experiment and develop new opportunities for online engagement with their customers, citizens and communities of interest in different aspects of the agencies' work and to increase the use of online tools for internal collaboration within and between agencies. Increased engagement with the community online and internal transfer of agency information will increase. These practices may test the effectiveness of relying on an implicit licence from the provider of information and the present defences to infringement under the *Copyright Act 1968*. In particular, the High Court decision in *Copyright Agency Limited v New South Wales* and the changing technology in the way we communicate raise the question whether there is any need for express special defences permitting certain public uses of copyright material deposited or registered in accordance with statutory obligations under state or federal law outside the operation of s 183.[83]

In a 2005 report, the Australian Government's Advisory Council on Intellectual Property recommended that the Crown use provisions in the *Patents Act 1990* (as well as the *Designs Act 2003*) be amended to align with the requirements of the TRIPS Agreement.[84] Article 31(b), Section 5 (Patents) of TRIPS is more limited than the provisions of that agreement dealing with copyright and stipulates that 'other use' (that is, use without the authorisation of the right's holder) is only

---

[80] As in most industrialised capitalist democracies, refer generally Wilenski (1982), p. 37.

[81] Australia. Office of Government Information Technology (1997), xxix, 164.

[82] Australia. Department of Finance and Deregulation (2010) [11].

[83] For example, along the lines of ss 47–50 of the *Copyright, Designs and Patents Act 1988* (UK).

[84] Australia, Advisory Council on Intellectual Property (2005) [3].

permitted if prior to such use the proposed user has made efforts to obtain authorisation from the right's holder on reasonable terms and such efforts have been
unsuccessful over a reasonable period of time (except in cases of national emergency or public non-commercial use).[85]

The Advisory Council's recommendation has not yet been legislatively adopted.
It is inappropriate for copyright usage. For reasons earlier advanced, the requirement of prior consent of the copyright owner for the myriad and complex holdings
of rights comprised in most copyright media is impractical and potentially improper
for government to exercise. And to restrict exceptions to cases of national emergency, extreme urgency or public non-commercial use is likely to invite disputes
over the boundaries of these terms. What the majority of the Spicer Committee
foresaw in 1959 were that the needs of government to use copyright material 'are
varied and many'; '[m]ost of us think that it is not possible to list those matters
which might be said to be more vital to the public interest than others'.[86]

To suggest that the government pay remuneration to copyright owners every
time government reproduces their work for another person or communicates a work
online enabling public access to the work, where it is a matter of public record, is
counter to recent reforms requiring and enabling publication of documents accessed
under the *Freedom of Information Act 1982* (Cth).[87] It also places further administrative burdens on government. The balance between copyright ownership and
copyright usage in the information age must take account of the importance of
modern access to, and the wide and free dissemination of, information. This
involves practical as well as in-principle considerations. There is a public interest
in the electronic capture and in dissemination to the public—to councils, public
authorities (such as water and telephone) and other interested institutions and
persons—of survey plans and of their incorporation into digital cadastral databases
with layered and enhanced information from different governmental sources. In the
CAL case, plans could be accessed through Webgov by registered government
users only and a licence fee was charged for delivery of particular plans. There is a
clear public interest in accessing that information and little public interest in
remunerating all authors of all components to the digitalised information which
supports the purposes of the deposited works.

What is fair in terms of the usage of copyright material—the proper balance of
interests between copyright owners and users—must take into account the character

---

[85] World Trade Organization (1994) and the position under Article 13, Section 1 of TRIPS
(Copyright and Related Rights) at n 1.

[86] Australia. Copyright Law Review Committee (Spicer Committee Report) (1959) [404]. In
New Zealand, where the Crown use provision in its *Copyright Act 1994* has a restricted scope
relating to the needs of national security, period of emergency, and the safety and health of the
public or any member of the public and which is subject to equitable remuneration, the law also
provides a number of express non-remunerated provisions enabling copying and other acts by the
Crown for administrative and other purposes in addition to acts done under statutory authority:
refer Copyright Act 1994 (NZ) ss 61–63, s 66.

[87] Refer to the *Freedom of Information Act 1982* (Cth) s 11C.

of what is done and the extent to which it is done. It should not simply be a question of seeking payment for any use of the material in question. This argument was put, and rejected, in the campaign for remuneration for all photocopying of copyright works.[88] In these circumstances, reliance upon s 183 smacks of rent-seeking and, given the nature of the Crown use provision, which compulsorily enables unfettered use of copyright material, it is in the interests of copyright owners and of government that s 183 be used as a last resort.

Section 48 of the *Copyright, Designs and Patents Act 1988* (UK) provides:

> *48 Material communicated to the Crown in the course of public business*
> (1) This section applies where a literary, dramatic, musical or artistic work has in the course of public business been communicated to the Crown for any purpose, by or with the licence of the copyright owner and a document or other material thing recording or embodying the work is owned by or in the custody or control of the Crown.
> (2) The Crown may, without infringing copyright in the work, do an act specified in subsection (3) provided that –
> (a) the act is done for the purpose for which the work was communicated to the Crown, or any related purpose which could reasonably have been anticipated by the copyright owner, and
> (b) the work has not been previously published otherwise than by virtue of this section.
> (3) The acts referred to in subsection (2) are –
> (a) copying the work,
> (b) issuing copies of the work to the public, and
> (c) making the work (or a copy of it) available to the public by electronic transmission in such a way that members of the public may access it from a place and at a time individually chosen by them.
> (4) In subsection (1) "public business" includes any activity carried on by the Crown.
> (5) This section has effect subject to any agreement to the contrary between the Crown and the copyright owner.
> . . .

A special defence of this kind was recommended by one member of the Copyright Law Review Committee in its *Crown Copyright* report.[89] A similar defence also exists under New Zealand law.[90] Such a provision, if adopted in Australian law, should be expressed in a media neutral way so that it encompasses both electronic and hard copy reproduction and communication of the work.[91] It

---

[88] Gilchrist (2011), pp. 65 and 67. The Australian Copyright Council Ltd had made submissions to the Franki Committee that all copying should be remunerated upon the basis that authors should receive a royalty for each copy page made of any work within copyright. In Britain, the Whitford Committee also reached a similar view by concluding that all reprography be remunerated and that fair dealing be confined to hand or typewritten copies.

[89] The author of this chapter. Australia, Copyright Law Review Committee (2005), p. 187.

[90] *Copyright Act 1994* (NZ) s 62. Section 61 of that Act also provides another public administration defence—namely the specific defence to infringement in relation to copying of material open to public inspection or on an official (statutory) register. This provision is similar to s 47 of the *Copyright, Designs and Patents Act 1988* (UK).

[91] Section 48 of the *Copyright, Designs and Patents Act 1988* (UK) was amended by the the the Copyright (Public Administration) Regulations 2014 (UK) to encompass making the work available to the public by electronic transmission, which remedies a limitation of the earlier provision to

would facilitate the fulfilment of a public duty on government. It should, nonetheless, be incumbent on government, which requires the deposit of plans or other material, to make clear in regulatory, statutory or documentary form the uses of the copyright material contemplated by government. No use beyond the purposes expressed should be authorised. It would also change the character of the dealing if the Government was exercising the licence to make a profit from the use of other copyright works rather than simply recouping costs. A proviso could be inserted into this special defence to exclude profit-making activities from the operation of the provision. In this way, the special defence would not unfairly prejudice the legitimate interests of the copyright owner.

On 13 February 2014, the Australian Law Reform Commission Report on its *Copyright and the Digital Economy* reference was tabled in the Australian Parliament with a recommendation that the fair use exception proposed in Chapter 4 of its Report may be relied upon when determining whether a government use infringes copyright. It also proposed expansion of specific Government unremunerated defences to infringement of copyright by recommending:

- a new exception for use of correspondence and other material sent to government similar to the United Kingdom and New Zealand exceptions.
- a separate new exception for uses where statutes require local, state or Commonwealth governments to provide public access to copyright material.[92]

9.6 Conclusion

The broad scope of the Crown use provision should be retained.[93] There are compelling arguments in law and policy for clarifying the interrelationship between the special defences to infringement and the Crown use provision so that copyright

---

enable copies to be shared on the internet. United Kingdom. Intellectual Property Office (2011), p. 108. '7.198 The Copyright Act allows a variety of acts to be performed by public bodies to enable them to discharge their duties effectively…. 7.201 However, although some of these exceptions permit the issuing of copies to the public, this relates only to the issuing of individual copies, for example paper copies. It does not permit copies to be shared on the internet.'

[92] Australia. Australian Law Reform Commission, *Copyright and the Digital Economy* (ALRC Report 122), 349, 350, 347, 344 http://www.alrc.gov.au/inquiries/copyright-and-digital-economy.

[93] The Australian Law Reform Commission released a discussion paper on its *Copyright and the Digital Economy* reference with a draft recommendation that proposed repeal of the statutory licence in Part VII Div 2 of the *Copyright Act 1968* (Cth) in favour of voluntary licensing arrangements. Australia. Australian Law Reform Commission, pp. 283–297. However in its final Report, it recommended the retention of the statutory licence in an amended form so that it was more flexible and less prescriptive. It recommended detailed provisions such as the setting of equitable remuneration, sampling notices and record keeping be removed 'so that more commercial and efficient agreements can be made between the parties'. It did warn however that 'the criticism will be that this reduced prescription comes at a cost – namely, uncertainty and litigation'. Australia. Australian Law Reform Commission, *Copyright and the Digital Economy*

policy is consistent and clear. In particular, it should be made clear that s 183 should complement, rather than override, the special defences to infringement such as s 40 (fair dealing for research or study) which users of copyright material may rely on generally under the *Copyright Act 1968*.

Further, the increased engagement with the community by Australian governments online and the interoperability of information between government agencies, which modern information and communication technologies facilitate, will test the effectiveness of relying on an implicit licence from the provider of copyright material to government and the present defences to infringement under the *Copyright Act 1968*. Reliance by government on s 183 in these circumstances is generally not appropriate. The High Court decision in *Copyright Agency Limited v New South Wales* and the changing technology in the way we communicate suggest a need for an express special defence permitting certain public uses of copyright material deposited or registered in accordance with statutory obligations under state or federal law outside the operation of s 183. Such a provision would recognise the peculiar duties and responsibilities of government and has been recently recommended by the Australian Law Reform Commission.

References

Government Reports

Australia. Advisory Council on Intellectual Property (2005) Review of crown use provisions for patents and designs, November 2005. http://www.acip.gov.au/library/review_of_crown_use_provisions.pdf

Australia. Copyright Law Committee on Reprographic Reproduction (Franki Committee) (1976) Report of the Copyright Law Committee on Reprographic Reproduction. AGPS, Canberra

Australia. Copyright Law Review Committee (2005) Crown Copyright, Canberra

Australia. Copyright Law Review Committee (Spicer Committee) (1959) Report to consider what alterations are desirable in the copyright law of the commonwealth. Canberra

Australia. Department of Finance and Deregulation (2010) Government response to the report of the government 2.0 Taskforce, May 2010. http://www.finance.gov.au/publications/govresponse20report/doc/Government-Response-to-Gov-2-0-Report.pdf

Australia. Office of Government Information Technology (1997) management of government information as a national strategic resource: report of the Information Management Steering Committee on information management in the Commonwealth Government, August 1997

Australia. Australian Law Reform Commission, copyright and the digital economy: discussion paper (DP79). http://www.alrc.gov.au/inquiries/copyright-and-digital-economy

United Kingdom. Board of Trade (1952) Report of the copyright committee (Gregory Committee), Cmd 8662

United Kingdom. Intellectual Property Office (2011) Consultation on Copyright. http://www.ipo.gov.uk/consult-ia-bis0309.pdf

---

(ALRC Report 122), 95, 201–202, 206–208 http://www.alrc.gov.au/inquiries/copyright-and-digital-economy.

US Department of Justice, Office of Legal Counsel (1999) Memorandum from Acting Assistant Attorney-General RE: Whether Government Reproduction of Copyrighted Materials Invariably is a "Fair Use" under Section 107 of the Copyright Act of 1976 (30 April 1999). http://www.loc.gov/flicc/gc/fairuse.html

World Trade Organization (1994) Agreement on trade-related aspects of intellectual property rights. http://www.wto.org/english/tratop_e/trips_e/t_agm0_e.htm

Articles/Monographs

Bentley L, Kretschmer M (eds) Primary sources on copyright (1450–1900). http://www.copyrighthistory.org

Campbell E, Monotti A (2002) Immunities of agents of government from liability for infringement of copyright. Federal Law Rev 30(3):459–473

Fitzgerald B, Fitzgerald A et al (2011) Internet and e-commerce law, business and policy. Lawbook Co, Sydney

Fitzgerald B, Foong C, Fitzgerald A (2012) Copyright exceptions beyond the Copyright Act 1968 (Cth). Canb Law Rev 11(2):160–166

Gilchrist J (2011) The Franki Committee (1976) Report and Statutory Licensing. In: Fitzgerald B, Atkinson B (eds) Copyright future: copyright freedom. Sydney University Press, Sydney, pp 65–71

Lindgren K, Rothnie WA, Lahore JC (2004) Copyright and designs. LexisNexis Butterworths, Sydney

Pearce DC, Geddes RS (2011) Statutory interpretation in Australia, 7th edn. LexisNexis Butterworths, Sydney

Ricketson S, Creswell C (2002) The law of intellectual property: copyright, designs and confidential information, 2nd edn. LBC Thomson Reuters, Sydney

Wilenski PS (1982) Small government and social equity. In: Withers G (ed) Bigger or smaller government? Papers from the sixth symposium of the academy of social sciences in Australia, Academy of Social Sciences in Australia, Canberra, pp 37-70

Chapter 10
Open Content Licensing of Public Sector Information and the Risk of Tortious Liability for Australian Governments

Cheryl Foong

10.1 Introduction

There has been an increasing interest by governments worldwide in the potential uses of public sector information (PSI).[1] An example of advancement in this area is the US government's launch of the data.gov portal in May 2009 as part of the Obama administration's Open Government Initiative.[2] The aim of providing the portal was to increase the ability of the public to find, download, and use datasets generated and held by the US Federal Government.[3] Similarly, the UK government launched the beta version of its data.gov.uk portal in January 2010, providing a single access point to over 2,500 central government datasets available for free re-use.[4] The Australian government is moving in a similar direction by initiating the Government 2.0 Taskforce, with the intent of increasing the openness of government by making public sector information more widely available to promote transparency, innovation and value adding to government information.[5] The Federal Government in its response to the Government 2.0 Taskforce final report supported the use of the Creative Commons Attribution licence as the default

---

[1] See Fitzgerald and Hooper (2009).

[2] See http://www.data.gov.

[3] See About Data.gov at http://www.data.gov/about.

[4] UK Office of Public Sector Information (OSPI) (2010).

[5] See About Government 2.0 Taskforce at http://gov2.net.au/about/. The Government 2.0 Taskforce final report.

C. Foong (✉)
Curtin Law School, Curtin University, Building 407, Level 3, Kent Street, Bentley, Perth, WA 6102, Australia
e-mail: cheryl.foong@curtin.edu.au

© Springer International Publishing Switzerland 2015
B. Fitzgerald, J. Gilchrist (eds.), *Copyright Perspectives*,
DOI 10.1007/978-3-319-15913-3_10

licence for PSI,[6] and formally endorsed this approach in its *Statement of IP Principles for Australian Government Agencies* update of 1 October 2010.[7]

While the issue of access to and reuse of PSI in Australia has been considered by various government agencies and in reports commissioned by governments, there has been no comprehensive statement of policy, principle or practice relating to the publication of PSI under open access regimes by any tier of Australian government.[8] An important legal aspect that has neither been fully canvassed in these reports nor tested in the courts is: can governments[9] incur tortious liability for incorrect or inaccurate information released online under an open content licence?[10] It is imperative that we address this question, because a heightened risk of tortious liability for information released could put a drag on innovation in this area.[11]

In order to fully understand the potential pitfalls and risks in releasing PSI online, this chapter will attempt to apply conventional negligence principles and defences to this yet to be adjudicated situation. In doing so, it will consider the relevance of certain factors including that the information has come from government, is for the benefit of the public, is being provided for free, and the presence of a disclaimer and appropriate information management policies.[12] This chapter concludes that the release of public sector information online under an open content licence is within the bounds of an acceptable level of risk to government, especially where appropriate information management policies and principles are in place to ensure accountability for its quality and accuracy.

---

[6] Australian Government (2010a), pp. 8–10.

[7] Australian Government (2010b).

[8] Fitzgerald (2008), p. 10. See also Victorian Government (2010).

[9] For the purposes of this paper, the terms "government" or "governments" include state, territory and federal governments, and public authorities and agencies.

[10] See for example, Victorian Parliament, Economic Development and Infrastructure Committee (2009), p. 40, where the Committee stated that:

> Wider provision of PSI by the Victorian Government will likely result in instances where errors in information or data, or unintended disclosure, leads to non-government users of PSI or third parties considering legal action against the Government. ...
> For most, if not all, of the PSI released by the Victorian Government . . ., liability will most likely arise through accusations of negligence in the provision of information.

The Committee anticipated that:

> provided sufficient disclaimers accompany the release of PSI, opportunities for Government to incur legal liability will be limited. ...
> However, it is critical that the Victorian Government seek clarity on this issue. . .

See also Victorian Government (2010), p. 20.

[11] See Parchomovsky and Stein (2008), pp. 285 and 288; U of Penn, Inst for Law & Econ Research Paper No. 07-31, available at http://ssrn.com/abstract=1028346. See also Samuelson (2009).

[12] This paper will be limiting its discussion to this specific context of free and open access. For a discussion of potential liability for information released through other means (e.g. formal requests for information at a fee), see Christensen et al. (2008).

10.2   Copyright in Public Sector Information

Public Sector Information (PSI) means a vast range of documents, databases and other information compiled or produced by governments.[13] For example, it includes geographical information (such as meteorological information, spatial and mapping information, mining exploration data and road safety information), public health information, economic and trade statistics, and parliamentary reports.[14] In Australia, it was held in *Desktop Marketing v Telstra*[15] that an "industrial collection" *may* satisfy the originality requirement to sustain copyright, despite minimal intellectual input.[16] Although raw facts and information as such is not capable of being protected by copyright, once it is selected and arranged, the resulting work could be protected as a compilation within the literary works category in Part III of the *Copyright Act 1968* (Cth).[17]

As copyright owners, governments have the exclusive right to copy and to communicate the work to the public.[18] "Communicate" is defined as to "make available online or electronically transmit (whether over a path, or a combination of paths, provided by a material substance of otherwise) a work or other subject matter".[19] Thus, governments hold the right to control the electronic transmission of PSI as well as making it available to the public online via an intranet, the internet or other computer networks.[20]

Unfortunately, governments have often sought to control the right to access and use information under restrictive licensing arrangements.[21] Whilst governments sit

---

[13] Note that this refers to information owned/created by government, and not third party information.

[14] Fitzgerald et al. (2007), pp. 260–261.

[15] (2002) 119 FCR 491.

[16] See further dicta by the High Court in *IceTV Pty Limited v Nine Network Australia Pty Limited* [2009] HCA 14 (Gummow, Hayne and Heydon JJ at [187]–[188]) which casts some doubt on the low originality requirement in *Desktop Marketing v Telstra*. See also *Telstra Corporation Ltd v Phone Directories Company Pty Ltd* [2010] FCA 44, in which Gordon J held at [5] that copyright did not subsist in Telstra's Yellow Pages and White Pages directories because the computer generated compilation had failed the authorship requirement. This case is currently on appeal.

[17] The definition of "literary work" includes "a table, or compilation, expressed in words, figures or symbols": *Copyright Act 1968* (Cth), s 10(1); see Fitzgerald et al. (2007), p. 172.

[18] *Copyright Act 1968* (Cth), s 31(1)(a)(i) and (1)(a)(iv).

[19] *Copyright Act 1968* (Cth), s 10(1).

[20] Fitzgerald et al. (2007), p. 164.

[21] Bushell-Embling (2007).

on the acres of information generated and gathered yearly by governmental bodies, there has been increasing demand for open access[22] to this useful resource.[23] Only recently has the consideration of implementing an open access regime emerged in light of the perceived societal and economic gains.[24] These benefits include:

1. evidence based policy and decision making which contributes to an informed citizen base, whilst facilitating transparency and accountability within government;
2. improving returns on investments by governments, especially when access to publicly funded research is improved;
3. broadening opportunities for commercial exploitation of research data (specifically, leading to the emergence of successful commercial enterprises that create innovative products from repackaged, processed or amalgamated PSI); and
4. in general, enhancing the potential for innovation and creativity throughout society.[25]

10.3 Open Content Licences

The onset of the digital age and the corresponding improvements in the way in which information is disseminated has led to the development of new licence models that allow others to obtain access to and to reuse copyright protected material with minimal unmediated transactions.[26] These licences, referred to as 'open content' licences, are considered a viable alternative to the existing licensing regimes adopted by governments.[27] Whilst a wide range of open content licensing models has developed in recent years,[28] the most recognised open licensing model

---

[22] Open Access is a term generally understood as the making available of material with no or little legal restrictions imposed on the access and use of that material. The term is most commonly used in relation to publicly funded research material such as journal articles (see, for e.g., OAK Law Project: Open Access to Knowledge at http://www.oaklaw.qut.edu.au/ and 'Open Access' on Wikipedia at http://en.wikipedia.org/wiki/Open_access_(publishing)) but is increasingly applied to research data and other forms of information including PSI.

[23] See Victoria, Economic Development and Infrastructure Committee (2008), p. 2; Bushell-Embling (2007); Chillingworth (2006).

[24] Australian Government, Department of Broadband, Communications and the Digital Economy (2008); Note that the Australian Bureau of Statistics (ABS) currently provides access to a majority of its statistical data on the ABS website free of charge under the Creative Commons Attribution 2.5 Licence, see http://www.abs.gov.au/websitedbs/D3310114.nsf/Home/%C2%A9+Copyright?opendocument?utm_id=GB.

[25] Victoria, Economic Development and Infrastructure Committee (2008), pp. 7–14; see also Weiss (2002).

[26] Fitzgerald et al. (2006), p. 10.

[27] Victorian Government (2010), pp. 21–22 (Recommendation 11 and Recommendation 14).

[28] For example AEShareNet Limited, Click-Use Licences, Creative Archive and BBC Commons: Barker et al. (2005), p. 11.

is Creative Commons (CC). The standard permissions under the CC licences are the right to copy the work, to distribute it and to communicate it to the public.[29] The CC licences are a more flexible tool by virtue of their "some rights reserved" terms, allowing copyright holders to grant more extensive rights to the public than under the more traditional "all rights reserved" model.[30] The CC licences make copyright-protected content more "active" by enabling it to be reutilised with a minimum of transactional effort.[31] Using these simple legal tools, combined with the vast digital landscape that we increasingly inhabit,[32] the free-flow of information is greatly enhanced.

The significant proliferation of open content licence usage "in a manner and at a pace that few could have imagined just a few years ago" in modern society has recently been recognised by the most senior specialist intellectual property court in the United States in *Jacobsen v Katzer & Kamind Associates Inc.*[33] Importantly, the Court of Appeals for the Federal Circuit acknowledged the economic and social value of an open access model, stating:

> There are substantial benefits, including economic benefits, to the creation and distribution of copyrighted works under public licenses that range far beyond traditional license royalties.[34]

Although the use of open content licences brings significant benefits to the community and the economy, there still remains a practical reality which may arise if a government chooses to release its information under open content licences: what if the information is incorrect and, as a result, causes loss or damage to citizens or businesses? Will the government be liable for such loss?

10.4 Liability for Incorrect Public Sector Information

In Australia, a person may be liable in negligence to another for the provision of incorrect information or advice (i.e. a negligent misstatement) where there exists a "special relationship" between the parties.[35] However, despite speculation on

---

[29] See for example, the Creative Commons Attribution 3.0 Australia licence, available at http://creativecommons.org/licenses/by/3.0/au/.

[30] van Eechoud and van der Wal (2008), p. 34. See also generally, Fitzgerald and Fitzgerald (2004), p. 455.

[31] Fitzgerald et al. (2007), p. 259.

[32] Fitzgerald and Oi (2004), p. 137.

[33] *Jacobsen v Katzer & Kamind Associates Inc.* 2008 U.S. App. LEXIS 17161 (Fed. Cir. 2008) at pp. 6–7.

[34] *Jacobsen v Katzer & Kamind Associates Inc.* 2008 U.S. App. LEXIS 17161 (Fed. Cir. 2008) at p. 8.

[35] *Esanda Finance Corporation Ltd v Peat Marwick Hungerfords* (1995) 188 CLR 241 at 260 per Toohey and Gaudron JJ.

liability for incorrect data,[36] there do not appear to have been any authoritative decisions on whether a government which releases its public sector information online to the public under an open content licence is in a "special relationship" with the user of the information, and accordingly, whether the government may be held tortiously liable. As Lord Macmillan stated in *Donoghue v Stevenson*:

> The grounds of action may be as various and manifold as human errancy, and the conception of legal responsibility may develop in adaptation to altering social conditions and standards. The criterion of judgment must adjust and adapt itself to the changing circumstances of life. **The categories of negligence are never closed** . . .[37] [emphasis added]

Hence, this paper will proceed in its attempt to apply the elements of negligence and the additional requirements peculiar to negligent misstatements to this novel situation.

10.5   Tortious Liability

For the tort of negligence to be established, the user of the information must prove that:

- the government owed a duty of care to the user;
- the government breached the standard of care appropriate to that duty of care; and
- damage to the user was caused by the government's breach of the duty (where that damage is not regarded as too remote in law).[38]

The main areas of contention arising from these three elements, which will be discussed in turn, are:

1. whether a duty of care exists;
2. the standard of care applicable to the government if a duty is found to exist;
3. whether reliance on the information was reasonable to establish a causative link between the release of the information and the loss suffered; and

Following these in Sect. 10.5.4 of this chapter, the impact of disclaimers on the duty of care is assessed.

---

[36] See Rowland and Macdonald (2005), p. 213.

[37] [1932] AC 562 at 619; cited in *Hedley Byrne v Heller* [1963] 2 All ER 575 at 595.

[38] *Wyong Shire Council v Shirt* (1979) 146 CLR 40 at 44 per Mason J. See further McGlone and Stickley (2005), p. 103. See also Cho (1998), p. 97.

10.5.1   A Duty of Care

In general, a person is under a duty to take reasonable care to avoid causing harm to others, in circumstances where Lord Atkin's neighbour principle, as expounded in *Donoghue v Stevenson,* applies:

> You must take reasonable care to avoid acts or omissions which you can reasonably foresee would be likely to injure your neighbour. Who, then, in law, is my neighbour? The answer seems to be - persons who are so closely and directly affected by my act that I ought reasonably to have them in contemplation as being so affected when I am directing my mind to the acts or omissions that are called in question . . .[39]

However, where a defendant provides advice or makes information available, a "special relationship", in addition to the requirement of reasonable foreseeability from the general principle expressed in *Donoghue v Stevenson,*[40] is essential to ensure that the imposition of liability on the defendant is justifiable. This is because damage flows, not immediately from the defendant's act in disclosing the information or advice, but from the plaintiff's reliance on the information or advice and his action or inaction which produces consequential loss.[41] In other words, it is the actions of the plaintiff, not within the control of the defendant, which links the information or advice to the loss.

The features of this special relationship as expounded by the House of Lords in *Hedley Byrne & Co Ltd v Heller & Partners Ltd*[42] and reiterated by the Australian High Court in *MLC v Evatt*[43] are:

1. The circumstances caused the speaker or a reasonable person in the speaker's position to realize that:

   a. he/she is being trusted by the recipient to give information which the recipient believes the speaker to possess or to which the recipient believes the speaker to have access to, or
   b. to give advice, about a matter upon or in respect of which the recipient believes the speaker to possess a capacity or opportunity for judgment,
   c. in either case the subject matter of the information or advice being of a serious or business nature.

2. The speaker realized or the circumstances are such that the speaker ought to have realized that:

   a. the recipient intends to act upon the information or advice in respect of his/her property or of himself/herself

---

[39] [1932] AC 562.

[40] [1932] AC 562.

[41] *San Sebastian v Minister* [1986] HCA 68; (1986) 162 CLR 340 per Gibbs CJ, Mason, Wilson and Dawson JJ at [15].

[42] [1964] AC 465 at p. 516 per Lord Devlin.

[43] (1968) 122 CLR 556 at 571 per Barwick CJ.

   b. in connection with some matter of business or serious consequence (i.e. an "assumption of responsibility" implied by the law).

3. It is reasonable in all the circumstances for the recipient to seek, or to accept, and to rely upon the utterance of the speaker (i.e. a "reasonable reliance").

   a. Factors for judging reasonable reliance are:

      i. The nature of the subject matter;
      ii. the occasion of the interchange; and
      iii. the identity and relative position of the parties as regards knowledge actual or potential and relevant capacity to form or exercise judgment.

The element of trust between the parties has been described as being the heart of the special relationship.[44] It tends to arise out of an unequal position of the parties which the recipient reasonably believes to exist, especially where the recipient believes the speaker to have superior information or greater capacity than the recipient.[45] Further, the special relationship does not arise unless it is reasonable for the recipient to act on that information or advice, without further inquiry, for the purpose for which it is used.[46]

10.5.1.1 Liability in the Government Context: Open Content Licensing

The "incremental approach" to the law of torts (i.e. the development of the law of torts incrementally through novel cases by reference to analogous cases) has been favoured by the majority of the High Court.[47] Accordingly, we may draw on the principles as discussed in relation to negligent misstatements (which apply equally to advice and information)[48] and attempt to apply them to the dissemination by government of PSI online under open content licences.

The argument that physical injury and damage is direct and obvious, whereas with information or advice no loss results unless the hearer relies and acts upon the

---

[44] *MLC v Evatt* (1968) 122 CLR 556 at 571 per Barwick CJ.

[45] *MLC v Evatt* (1968) 122 CLR 556 at 571 per Barwick CJ (nonetheless His Honour admitted that inequality was not essential for the special relationship to exist).

[46] *Shaddock v Parramatta* (1980) 150 CLR 225 at 231; *Esanda Finance Corporation Ltd v Peat Marwick Hungerfords* (1997) 142 ALR 750 at 768.

[47] *Sullivan* v *Moody*; *Thompson* v *Connon* (2001) Aust Torts Reports ¶81–622; [2001] HCA 59 at [49] and [53] per Gleeson CJ, Gaudron, McHugh, Hayne and Callinan JJ; *Pyrenees Shire Council, Crimmins* v *Stevedoring Industry Finance Committee* (1999) Aust Torts Report ¶81–532; 74 ALJR 1 at [73] per McHugh J.

[48] *MLC v Evatt* (1968) 122 CLR 556 at 571 per Barwick CJ.

information or advice (the loss and damage in a real sense directly arising out of the hearer's actions) was rejected by Barwick CJ in *MLC v Evatt*.[49] As Lord Devlin reasoned in *Hedley Byrne v Heller*[50]:

> A grave defect there would be in the common law if recovery permitted in the case of physical acts or omissions were denied in the case of information and advice given with a lack of due care.[51]

The same argument applies to public sector information (PSI) disseminated online under open content licences. The fact that incorrect information can cause loss or damage cannot be denied.[52] However, it is important to recognise that the context in which the information is shared may be quite different from previous cases involving negligent misstatement. The early cases of *Hedley Byrne & Co Ltd v Heller & Partners Ltd*,[53] *MLC v Evatt*[54] and *Shaddock v Parramatta*[55] were concerned with ascertaining conditions which would attract a duty of care in responding to an inquiry for *specific information*. In addition, the provision of information or assurances by the public authority in *Shaddock v Parramatta*[56] incurred a prescribed fee.

Previous decisions are but illustrations of the general duty of care in its application to particular circumstances of negligent misstatement, because 'the special complications which arise in connection with the imposition of a duty of care on the author of a statement can only be unraveled in a variety of factual situations'.[57] Until there is a clear judicial pronouncement on the issue, the question remains— are the features of a special relationship as identified in these cases still applicable to this situation of government making PSI available online under an open content licence? Indeed, the release of information in the online medium creates another set of factors which may impact on the existence of a duty of care.

---

[49] *MLC v Evatt* (1968) 122 CLR 556 at 567.

[50] [1964] A.C. 465.

[51] *Hedley Byrne & Co. Ltd. v Heller & Partners Ltd* [1964] A.C. 465 at p. 516 per Lord Devlin.

[52] *MLC v Evatt* (1968) 122 CLR 556 at 569.

[53] [1964] A.C. 465.

[54] (1968) 122 CLR 556.

[55] (1980) 150 CLR 225.

[56] (1980) 150 CLR 225.

[57] *San Sebastian v Minister* [1986] HCA 68; (1986) 162 CLR 340 per Gibbs CJ, Mason, Wilson and Dawson JJ.

10.5.1.2   The Online Medium

Where information is made available online (whether by a government agency or otherwise), liability may be greatly expanded.[58] It is difficult to assess how wide the neighbourhood principle extends.[59] Unlike the ginger beer in *Donoghue v Stevenson*[60] which can only be drunk once and in all likelihood by one person only, information may be used by many, perpetuating the damage or causing multiple damages.[61] The features of the relationship become more akin to communications via mass media, rather than a special relationship between the parties. Consequently, there may be good grounds to fear imposition of liability "in an indeterminate amount for an indeterminate time to an indeterminate class".[62]

Thus, it is all the more essential to identify the "relationship of proximity" in order to limit liability for information published to the world at large in this context.[63] However, this concept of proximity does not define legal rules which prescribe an issue of fact on which legal consequence depends.[64] As a result, it has been described as a "label of choice", concealing underlying policy considerations motivating that decision[65] Further, the High Court has criticized it as "a convenient short-hand method of formulating the ultimate question in the case," but one which "provides no assistance in deciding how to answer the question".[66] Instead, by drawing analogies with previously decided cases, combined with a process of induction and deduction, we may systematically identify factors relevant in those cases to finding a duty of care and perhaps identify previously unidentified factors.[67]

---

[58] Fisher.

[59] Stewart et al. (1997), pp. 84 and 97.

[60] [1932] AC 562.

[61] Charlton (1990), p. 16.

[62] *Ultramares Corporation v Touche* 255 NY 170; 174 NE 441 at 444 (1931) per Cardozo CJ. Under Australian choice of law rules, the general principle in tort cases is that the law of the place where the tort arose will apply: *Distillers Co (Biochemicals) Ltd v Thompson* [1971] AC 458 per Lord Pearson at 468. Where PSI is available on the internet, the tort (e.g. publication or dissemination) could potentially be seen to arise at the place where the PSI was downloaded: see for example, *Dow Jones & Company v Gutnick* [2002] HCA 56. Whether an Australian State or Federal government is liable in an overseas jurisdiction for the release of incorrect PSI will depend on that foreign jurisdiction's choice of law rules which are beyond the scope of this paper.

[63] *Sutherland Shire Council v Heyman* (1985) 157 CLR 424, 595 per Deane J.

[64] *San Sebastian v Minister* [1986] HCA 68; (1986) 162 CLR 340 per Brennan J.

[65] Ivankovich (1991), p. 505.

[66] *Sullivan v Moody* [2001] HCA 59 at [48] per Gleeson CJ, Gaudron, McHugh, Hayne and Callinan JJ.

[67] McGlone and Stickley (2005), p. 124 (referring to the 'multi-factorial' approach of Kirby J in *Graham Barclay Oysters Pty Ltd v Ryan* (2002) 211 CLR 540 at [220] and [243], and Spigelman CJ in *New South Wales v Godfrey* (2004) Aust Torts Reports ¶81–741).

In the present context, it would appear that there are several factors (carrying with them corresponding policy reasons) which *may* influence whether a duty of care may be found to exist:

1. the PSI is provided without fee for the benefit of the public;
2. the PSI is proactively provided to the public in general;
3. the PSI is provided by government

Fee Free Provision of PSI for the Benefit of the Public

Although tortious liability is entirely separate from contractual liability and the concept of consideration is not relevant to tort, the provision of PSI by government on a no-fee or non-commercial basis may well present an additional layer of complexity relevant to the application of negligence principles. In commercial transactions where the information or advice is paid for, the acceptance of responsibility by the provider is implicit.[68] Conversely, where the government provider supplies PSI on a no-fee, non-commercial basis, it is arguably reasonable to hold it to a lower standard of legal liability.

In the case of *San Sebastian v Minister*,[69] the plaintiffs argued that the publication of redevelopment feasibility study documents (a plan which was later abandoned) gave rise to a duty of care on the part of the Authority and the Council due to the intention or purpose of inducing developers to develop the land in accordance with the plan. Whilst the intention or purpose of inducing another to act on a representation may be critical to the existence of a duty of care in certain cases,[70] it is not an absolute requirement. It is but one of the various means by which it may be shown that the plaintiff's reliance on the information was reasonable.[71] As Kitto J stated in *MLC v Evatt*[72]:

> Just as words which otherwise would create a contract (because the speaker or writer receives a quid pro quo) are held not to do so if the parties are dealing with one another on a plane where there is really no intention of altering legal relations – as in the case of purely domestic arrangements – so **words giving information or advice without any quid pro quo will be held to entail no legal responsibility for carelessness** if the correct conclusion from the circumstances be that the person who acted upon them could not reasonably have understood them as uttered, as one might say, in the way of business, or (to express it more generally) as uttered on a plane to which legal liability naturally belongs.[73] [emphasis added]

---

[68] *MLC v Evatt* (1968) 122 CLR 556, 586.

[69] (1986) 162 CLR 340.

[70] See for example *Candler v Crane, Christmas & Co.* (1951) 2 KB 164; *Glanzer v Shepard* (1922) 135 NE 275; 23 ALR 1425; also see *Esanda Finance Corp Ltd v Peat Marwick Hungerford (Reg)* (1997) 188 CLR 241, 275 per McHugh J.

[71] *Esanda Finance Corp Ltd v Peat Marwick Hungerford (Reg)* (1997) 188 CLR 241.

[72] (1968) 122 CLR 556.

[73] *MLC v Evatt* (1968) 122 CLR 556 per Kitto J at 585.

The general interest which governments have in promoting or encouraging the digital economy is not a "pecuniary interest" which supports the existence of a duty of care.[74] Conversely, by releasing PSI for free under unrestrictive licensing regimes, the government is putting into practice the overriding principle that 'the community has a right to information held by the [g]overnment'[75]; it is not seeking a private commercial benefit. In *San Sebastian v Minister*,[76] it was ultimately held that reliance on the publication was unreasonable due to the general nature of the documents which contained no representation or assurance about the ultimate level of development or continuing application by the Council.

A duty of care will not be lightly imposed where a government provider does not charge a fee for the information. The courts must consider whether the imposition of such a duty would deter socially desirable activity. In the words of Brennan J in *San Sebastian v Minister*[77]:

> Helpful information and friendly advice, even on matters of the gravest import, will often be proffered without any thought of the informant or adviser being responsible for its truth or soundness. **To impose a legal duty of care on the unsolicited and voluntary giving of any information and advice on serious or business matters would chill communications which are a valuable source of wisdom and experience for a person contemplating a course of conduct.**[78] [emphasis added]

In short, the wide range of PSI which could be released by government to benefit the public presents a strong public policy reason against imposing tortious liability on government in such circumstances.[79]

A General Proactive Publication of PSI

Should there be a duty where general PSI (non-specific to the particular plaintiff) is made available online? Whilst the existence of an antecedent request for information certainly assists in demonstrating reliance, it is by no means essential.[80]

---

[74] See for example *Council of the City of Lismore v Stewart* (1990) 18 NSWLR 718, where the provision of land use information in exchange for a fee was held not to give rise for a contract. Relevant to this finding was the inherently governmental nature of the activity and the fact that the arrangement involved no negotiations. By analogy, the proactive provision of information online is a governmental activity which does not carry with it a commercial intention to induce use of the information by the public.

[75] Queensland Government's comments on the Australian Government's Digital Economy Discussion Paper, available at http://www.archive.dbcde.gov.au/__data/assets/pdf_file/0017/112364/Queensland_State_Government__Chief_Information_Office.pdf.

[76] (1986) 162 CLR 340.

[77] (1986) 162 CLR 340.

[78] *San Sebastian v Minister* (1986) 162 CLR 340, 372.

[79] See generally *The Laws of Australia* Electronic, Torts - Public Policy [33.2.390] (last updated 1 August 2007).

[80] *San Sebastian v Minister* (1986) 162 CLR 340; *MLC v Evatt* (1968) 122 CLR 556, 571–572.

The fact that information is proactively made available to the world by a government does not preclude a duty of care from arising.

All the same, it is undoubtedly of importance to consider the specificity and relevance of that information in relation to the person or class of persons to whom it is directed when determining whether reliance by that particular person or member of that particular class is reasonable. For example, in *Perre v Apand Pty Ltd*,[81] the damage caused was not too remote as it was possible for the respondent to identify precisely who would be affected by an outbreak of bacterial wilt caused by its negligence. Depending on the nature and purpose of the information, it may be possible for the government to identify the class of possible plaintiffs. Arguably, whilst the government may not be able to identify the particular individual users, it may be within contemplation that the information is likely to be downloaded and used by certain categories of people for serious purposes.[82]

Nevertheless, where PSI is released by the government to the general public without a specific request, it may be difficult for the government to foresee how and by whom the information will be used. There is a lesser extent of proximity between the government provider and the user of the information, upon which the government provider may be seen to have assumed legal responsibility. In *Crimmins v Stevedoring Industry Finance Committee*,[83] McHugh J was of the opinion that the imputation of constructive knowledge should be treated with caution, because "it would be a far-reaching step to impose affirmative obligations on a statutory authority merely because it could have or even ought to have known that the plaintiff was, or was a member of a class which was, likely to suffer harm of the relevant kind."[84]

Provision by Government

Where government provides the information, it is more likely to be seen as being in a special relationship with users of the information and it may be seen to have assumed responsibility to the public by making information available. This is largely because a government is often in a better position than the general public

---

[81] (1999) Aust Torts Reports ¶81–516.

[82] See *Mutual Life & Citizens' Assurance Co Ltd v Evatt* (1968) 122 CLR 556 per Barwick CJ at 571:

> the speaker must realize or the circumstances be such that he ought to have realized that the recipient intends to act upon the information or advice in respect of his property or of himself in connexion with some matter of business or serious consequence.

Accepted in *L Shaddock & Associates Pty Ltd v Parramatta City Council* (1981) 150 CLR 225 at 248–249 per Mason J (as he then was); *Tepko Pty Ltd v Water Board* (2001) 206 CLR 1; 178 ALR 634 at [74] per Gaudron J.

[83] (1999) 200 CLR 1.

[84] *Crimmins v Stevedoring Industry Finance Committee* (1999) 200 CLR 1, 42.

to ensure the accuracy of the information released. While this may not always be so where PSI is utilised by people with special skills or knowledge or by large corporations, the argument is especially compelling where the government has a monopoly on important information, and formally sets itself up as the distributor.[85] In this scenario, the public may be seen as being in a position of relative vulnerability.[86]

It has been said that the "risk of indeterminate liability must give way to the more important role attributed to the law of negligence in the form of its deterrent effect".[87] However, the law of negligence does not operate in a vacuum. Finding liability not only affects the defendant government but also society as a whole. If faced with extensive liability, the provision of information may represent such a financial risk that it is prohibitory.[88] Where it is a discretionary undertaking by a government agency, the risk of liability is highly likely to deter the release of information, because there is neither a specific public obligation[89] nor a financial incentive to do so. In determining whether a duty of care should be recognised, the possibility that its recognition might lead to a flood of claims, although not decisive, weighs the balance against the recognition of that duty.[90]

In Queensland, recognition of the constraints applicable to public or governmental authorities is contained s 35 of the *Civil Liability Act 2003* (Qld).[91] Section 35 states that, in deciding whether a public or other authority has a duty or has breached a duty, the following principles apply—

(a) the functions required to be exercised by the authority are limited by the financial and other resources that are reasonably available to the authority for the purpose of exercising the functions;

(b) the general allocation of financial or other resources by the authority is not open to challenge;

---

[85] *L Shaddock & Associates Pty Ltd* v *Parramatta City Council* (1981) 150 CLR 225, 243 per Stephen J. In other words as provider of the information or advice, it has some special expertise or knowledge, or some special means of acquiring information which is not available to the recipient: *Esanda Finance Corporation Ltd v Peat Marwick Hungerfords* (1997) 142 ALR 750, 768.

[86] See *Perre & Ors v Apand Pty Ltd* (1999) Aust Torts Reports 81–516 per Kirby J; *Crimmins v Stevedoring Industry Finance Committee* (1999) 200 CLR 1, [93]–[94] per McHugh J.

[87] Promoted, for example, in *Rosenblum v Adler* 93 NJ 324; 461 A 2d 138 (1983); see Phegan (1997), p. 123.

[88] See Butler (2000), pp. 159 and 163–164.

[89] Note that there will often be a general public obligation in the sense that the government is responsible and accountable to the public. However, in this situation, the risk of liability for release of information is likely to outweigh the risk of liability for *failing* to release information.

[90] *Graham Barclay Oysters Pty Ltd v Ryan* (2002) 211 CLR 540, 665 per Callinan J.

[91] Note the comparable legislation in other Australian jurisdictions except the Northern Territory and South Australia: *Civil Law (Wrongs) Act 2002* (ACT), s 110; *Civil Liability Act 2002* (NSW), s 42; *Civil Liability Act 2002* (Tas), s 38; *Wrongs Act 1958* (Vic), s 83; *Civil Liability Act 2002* (WA), s 5W.

(c)   the functions required to be exercised by the authority are to be decided by reference to the broad range of its activities (and not merely by reference to the matter to which the proceeding relates); and

(d)   the authority may rely on evidence of its compliance with its general procedures and any applicable standards for the exercise of its functions as evidence of the proper exercise of its functions in the matter to which the proceeding relates.

Section 35 reflects the common law principle as espoused by Gleeson CJ in *Graham Barclay Oysters v Ryan* that "decisions as to raising revenue, and setting priorities in the allocation of public funds between competing claims on scarce resources, are essentially political...[and] are ordinarily decided through the political process."[92]

These additional section 35 conditions when taken into account may, depending on the circumstances, lead to the conclusion that there is no duty of care. Alternatively, where a duty of care is held to exist, these principles will again be relevant in assessing whether the duty of care was breached.

10.5.1.3   Does the CLA Bind the Crown in Right of the Commonwealth?

In Australia, the Crown's historical immunity from suit was removed by the various state Crown Proceedings Acts[93] and at the Commonwealth level, the *Judiciary Act 1903* (Cth).[94] Under these Acts, the Crown (both in right of the Commonwealth and in right of the State) is subject to the same common law tortious principles as its subjects and may be held vicariously liable for torts committed by its employees.[95]

As there is no Commonwealth civil liability legislation, question arises as to whether the States and Territories have the legislative power to bind the Commonwealth government under their civil liability legislation. The Queensland legislation is the only state or territory legislation which specifically purports to bind the Commonwealth, so far as it is able to.[96] New South Wales, South Australia, Western Australia and the Northern Territory legislatures provide that their

---

[92] *Graham Barclay Oysters Pty Ltd v Ryan* (2002) 211 CLR 540, [6].

[93] *Crowns Proceedings Act 1988* (NSW), s 5; *Crowns Proceedings Act 1980* (Qld), s 9; *Crowns Proceedings Act 1992* (SA), s 5; *Crowns Proceedings Act 1993* (Tas), s 5; *Crowns Proceedings Act 1958* (Vic), s 23; *Crowns Proceedings Act 1947* (WA), s 5; *Crowns Proceedings Act 1992* (ACT), s 5; *Crowns Proceedings Act 1993* (NT), s 5.

[94] See ss 56, 64.

[95] *Judiciary Act 1903* (Cth), s 64; *Crowns Proceedings Act 1988* (NSW), s 5; *Crowns Proceedings Act 1980* (Qld), s 9; *Crowns Proceedings Act 1992* (SA), s 5; *Crowns Proceedings Act 1993* (Tas), s 5; *Crowns Proceedings Act 1958* (Vic), s 23; *Crowns Proceedings Act 1947* (WA), s 5; *Crowns Proceedings Act 1992* (ACT), s 5; *Crowns Proceedings Act 1993* (NT), s 5. See *Darling Island Stevedoring Lighterage Co Ltd v Long* (1957) 97 CLR 36 per Kitto J at 63; *Stevens v Brodribb Sawmilling Co Pty Ltd* (1986) 160 CLR 16.

[96] *Civil Liability Act 2003* (Qld), s 6.

respective pieces of legislation bind not only the Crown of the respective jurisdiction, but also, so far as able, the "Crown" in all its capacities.[97]

As yet, the courts have not been called upon to decide whether State or Territory civil liability legislation will bind the Crown in right of the Commonwealth. Generally, State laws of general application can bind the Commonwealth. In *Pirrie v McFarlane*,[98] the High Court held that a member of the Air Force was required to hold a Victorian driver's licence when carrying out Commonwealth duties involving the operation of a motor vehicle within Victoria. Therefore, Commonwealth officers, employees and agents must comply with State laws of general application even when undertaking Commonwealth Government activities. However, in *Commonwealth v Cigamatic Pty Ltd (in liq)*,[99] the Court held that States cannot bind the Commonwealth with laws which define or regulate Commonwealth rights or duties towards its subjects or which regulate or control its prerogative rights.[100] These principles were affirmed by the majority of the High Court in *Re Residential Tenancies Tribunal of NSW and Henderson*.[101]

Civil liability legislation are laws of general application which apply to the Crown in regards to actions in which it may choose to engage in exercise of its capacities and functions (i.e. activities which it carries on in common with other citizens).[102] The acts do not purport to govern the capacities and functions of the Crown in right of the Commonwealth.[103] In other words, the legislation covers the civil liability of the Crown should it be negligent in releasing PSI which causes loss, but it does not affect the Crown's ability to release PSI. In short, it is likely that, as far as negligent acts or omissions are concerned, the Commonwealth is bound by State and Territory civil liability legislation, so long as there is no inconsistency with Commonwealth legislation that would attract the operation of s 109 of the Commonwealth Constitution.[104] Even if the State civil liability legislation is held

---

[97] See s 4(1) of the *Civil Liability Act 2002* (NSW); s. 14C of the *Wrongs Act 1958* (Vic); s. 2 of the Civil Liability Act 1936 (SA); s. 5 of the Civil Liability Act 2002 (WA); s. 6 of the Personal Injuries (Liabilities and Damages) Act (NT); s. 5 of the Proportionate Liability Act 2005 (NT).

[98] [1925] HCA 30; (1925) 36 CLR 170.

[99] (1962) 108 CLR 372.

[100] (1962) 108 CLR 372 at 378 per Dixon CJ. This principle was expounded earlier in *Federal Commissioner of Taxation v Official Liquidator of EO Farley Ltd* (1940) 63 CLR 278 at 308.

[101] (1997) 190 CLR 410. The 4/7 majority was comprised of Brennan CJ, Dawson, Toohey and Gaudron JJ.

[102] See *Re Residential Tenancies Tribunal of New South Wales and Henderson* (1996) 190 CLR 410 at 439 per Dawson, Toohey and Gaudron JJ; and at 424 per Brennan CJ:

> ...as to the true operation and effect of *The Commonwealth v Cigamatic Pty Ltd (In liq)*...I would draw a distinction between the capacities and functions of the Crown in right of the Commonwealth and the transactions in which that Crown may choose to engage in exercise of its capacities and functions.

[103] Ibid.

[104] When a law of a State is inconsistent with a law of the Commonwealth, the latter shall prevail, and the former shall, to the extent of the inconsistency, be invalid.

not to apply to the Crown in right of the Commonwealth, general negligence principles at common law will still apply.[105]

10.5.1.4   Is the Provision of Information a Matter of Policy?

A duty of care cannot arise in relation to acts and omissions that reflect the policy-making involved in the exercise of statutory discretions.[106] Whilst the grounds of judicial review of administrative action have ebbed and flowed, there has been one constant—it is not the function of the judicial review court to determine the merits of the exercise of an administrative power.[107] The court is limited to deciding whether that exercise was lawful, and it remains lawful even if the court thinks that it would have been better exercised in another way.[108] Nevertheless, unlike budgetary allocations and the constraints which they entail in terms of the allocation of resources, the courts may be called upon to apply a standard of care to action or inaction that is merely the product of administrative direction, expert or professional opinion, technical standards or general standards of reasonableness.[109]

Consequently, a public authority or governmental body which exercises statutory powers may place itself in a relationship to others which imports a common law duty to take care.[110] For example, the decision whether or not to release certain information, in exercise of a statutory power, would be a policy decision, and cannot as such be subject to a duty of care. However, a duty of care may still arise where operational effect is given to the policy decisions by making information available to the public. Here, a duty of care requiring the government agency to take reasonable steps to ensure the reasonable accuracy of the information may be held to arise.

While a discretionary exercise of powers may involve a combination of policy and operational decisions, "when a duty of care is found to exist, a failure to exercise a statutory power said to be relevant to the cause of negligence in the operational sense is not to be excused merely because the ultimate decision to exercise the power may be classed as a policy one."[111] Therefore, the fact that information is released based on an initial policy decision does not preclude a duty

---

[105] See for example, *Austral Pacific Group Limited v Airservices Australia* (2000) 203 CLR 136.

[106] *Sutherland Shire Council v Heyman* (1985) 157 CLR 424, 468–469 per Mason J (citing *Anns v Merton London Borough Council* (1978) AC 728).

[107] Aronson (2008), p. 2.

[108] Ibid.

[109] *Sutherland Shire Council v Heyman* (1985) 157 CLR 424, 468–469 per Mason J (citing *Anns v Merton London Borough Council* (1978) AC 728).

[110] Torts Commentary Electronic. 'Introduction Special Defendants Time Limits', CCH Australia, [¶1–830].

[111] *Parramatta City Council v Lutz* (1988) Aust Torts Reports ¶80–159, p 67,423 per Kirby P.

of care from arising. However, the fact that information is released by government may have an impact on the applicable standard of care.[112]

10.5.1.5 Is There a Duty of Care?

In summary, where information is pro-actively released online to the public, a relationship of sufficient proximity, which warrants reliance on such information without proper consideration, is unlikely to exist between the government and the user. This is especially so where information is provided free of charge, without any implicit inducement or warranty as to the accuracy of the information.[113] Accordingly, where information is made available online by government to the general public, without expectation of economic profit, a duty of care is not likely to exist.

Simply put, governments are releasing PSI for the benefit of the public. An individual who places undue reliance on the general information provided by a government without proper critical consideration or proper exercise of common sense, and consequently suffers a loss, has not acted reasonably. It should be the individual's responsibility to obtain professional advice before relying heavily on such information. Likewise, where a professional or skilled individual, or a corporation experienced in the particular field is involved, a reasonable reliance on PSI will be even harder to prove.

10.5.1.6 Switching from Duty to Standard of Care and Breach

It must be kept in mind that the elements of reliance and assumption of responsibility are merely illustrations of principles as applicable to previous cases, which cannot be strictly adhered to and applied in every instance. In the present context, the courts may be reluctant to simply deny a duty of care, allowing the government free range to disseminate information without considering its accuracy. This is especially so in light the High Court's decision in *Brodie v Singleton Shire Council*,[114] described as signalling 'a major shift in focus from a duty of care to breach'.[115] In that case, factors which were previously relevant to negating the existence of a duty instead became criteria to be considered and evaluated against the court's conception of reasonableness in the context of the standard of care and breach of that standard.[116]

---

[112] See Sect. 10.5.2.2.

[113] Disclaimers and limitation of liability clauses are discussed in Sect. 10.5.4.

[114] (2001) 206 CLR 512, 577–578 per Gaudron, McHugh and Gummow JJ; 601 per Kirby J.

[115] Aronson (2008), p. 2.

[116] Ibid.

Whilst the role of government is to maintain the public good,[117] it may be difficult to determine which "public good" outweighs another, for example here, the dissemination of valuable information, or the avoidance of potential mishaps from the use of or reliance upon incorrect information. An appropriate balance has to be struck between the need to encourage the dissemination and reuse of data, and the protection of public users. An unnecessarily conservative approach which suppresses the innovative use and re-use of PSI is contrary to the characteristics of a modern democratic government which should be committed to stimulating economic growth and productivity.

Accordingly, the courts may seek to retain judicial flexibility by imposing a duty of care, but provide the government with some leeway by applying a suitably lower standard of care in the circumstances. This way, the courts are able to respond to novel situations in a way that accords with public policy concerns as to whether the state should compensate certain classes of loss.[118]

10.5.2   Standard of Care and Breach

Having discussed factors relevant to the existence of a duty of care, this chapter will now move on to consider the standard of care applicable should a duty of care be held to exist. Arguably, shifting the debate away from duty may lead into a highly policy-oriented discussion of the content and standard of care in the particular context.[119] For instance, where information is provided by government without fee for the benefit of the public, the courts may impose a relatively low standard of care. This way, the government's implementation of PSI re-use and open access policy is encouraged, yet the government is not free to release information without consideration of its accuracy. Similarly, where there is no inducement for the user to rely on the information, the standard of care applicable will be relatively low. This lower standard may be compared to the standard of care which may be expected from a commercial information provider. Thus, the fact that information is provided for free, without expectation of profit, is likely to have a very strong impact on the applicable standard of care.

---

[117] Fitzgerald and Suzor (2005), pp. 412 and 426.

[118] Aronson (2008), p. 2.

[119] Ibid.

10.5.2.1 Civil Liability Legislation

Section 9 of the *Civil Liability Act 2003* (Qld)[120] is relevant to establishing whether a person has breached their duty of care. Section 9(1) states that a person does not breach a duty to take precautions against a risk of harm unless:

(a) the risk was foreseeable (that is, it is a risk of which the person knew or ought reasonably to have known); and
(b) the risk was not insignificant; and
(c) in the circumstances, a reasonable person in the position of the person would have taken the precautions.

Further, section 9(2) specifies that in deciding whether a reasonable person would have taken precautions against a risk of harm, the court is to consider the following (among other relevant things):

(a) the probability that the harm would occur if care was not taken;
(b) the likely seriousness of the harm;
(c) the burden of taking precautions to avoid the risk of harm;
(d) the social utility of the activity that creates the risk of harm.

Although users of PSI may expect a government to ensure the information provided is substantially accurate and that reasonable attempts are made to use error-free procedure,[121] it should be emphasized that the obligation is no more than to use reasonable care *in the circumstances*.[122] Certain information, such as geographic information, is inherently inaccurate.[123] Often, they are the end products of a complex accretion of data from a number of different sources.[124] It is possible for loss or damage to be caused by inherent inaccuracy which would have gone undetected even if the task was carried out competently. As such, a government is not required to ensure that their information is free of error, but rather free of errors which a reasonable public or governmental authority exercising reasonable care in the circumstances would have detected and corrected. Therefore, even if damage is caused by a data error attributable to the government, the action may still fail without the element of fault (i.e. the error was not due to a failure by government to exercise reasonable care). The test is not one of strict liability. In other words, a government is not in breach merely because it releases incorrect information which causes loss to others.

---

[120] Note the comparable legislation in other Australian jurisdictions except the Northern Territory: *Civil Liability Act 2002* (NSW), s 5B; *Civil Law (Wrongs) Act 2002* (ACT), s 43; *Civil Liability Act 1936* (SA), s 32; *Civil Liability Act 2002* (Tas), s 11; *Wrongs Act 1958* (Vic), s 48; *Civil Liability Act 2002* (WA), s 5B.

[121] Stewart et al. (1997), pp. 84 and 98.

[122] *MLC v Evatt* (1968) 122 CLR 556, 573.

[123] Stewart et al. (1997), pp. 84 and 87.

[124] Ibid.

In addition, the courts will take into account the social utility of the activity, i.e. of making PSI openly accessible to the public. If the overall benefit to the community outweighs the harm caused to the individual, it is possible that the injured claimant will not be compensated.[125] However, this principle is unlikely to be extended as far as to allow the incompetent handling and dissemination of PSI. Again, it comes down to whether the defendant government information provider has exercised reasonable care in the circumstances.

10.5.2.2   A Standard of Care Particular to Government

Governments are often in a factually different position to private defendants. The reasonable person, placed in the position of a government would be subject to the statutory and financial constraints which might inhibit its conduct.[126] Thus the standard applicable to government is what ought a reasonable public or governmental authority to have done in the circumstances.[127] Courts have accepted that budgetary, political and other constraints are factors to be taken into account in determining the standard of care and whether it has been breached.[128] This is reflected in s 35 of the *Civil Liability Act 2003* (Qld),[129] which requires consideration of financial and political constrains in determining whether a public authority has breached its duty of care. Thus, if the government lacks the resources necessary to avoid an error, the consequences may be that the failure to do so will not constitute a failure to take reasonable care and therefore no breach will arise.[130]

These statutory and budgetary constraints, combined with the considerations already canvassed in relation to a duty of care—i.e. the information is made

---

[125] See *E v Australia Red Cross* (1991) 31 FCR 299 where the court rejected a claim against the Red Cross Blood Bank in negligence for the supply of HIV-infected blood to a plaintiff. The court took into account the public benefit of the service provided by the Red Cross and the significant problems associated with a potential blood shortage if untested blood had to be discarded. Note that the cause pre-dated the availability of blood tests for HIV antibodies in 1985: Mandelson (1997), p. 284.

[126] *Sutherland Shire Council v Heyman* (1985) 157 CLR 424 at 468–469 per Mason J.

[127] *Crimmins* v *Stevedoring Industry Finance Committee* (1999) Aust Torts Report ¶81–532 [90] per McHugh J, [34] per Gaudron J; *Brodie* v *Singleton Shire Council*; *Ghantous* v *Hawkesbury City Council* (2001) Aust Torts Report ¶81–607 [150] per Gaudron, McHugh and Gummow JJ.

[128] Torts Commentary Electronic. 'Introduction Special Defendants Time Limits', CCH Australia, [¶1–830]; see *Romeo* v *Conservation Commission of the Northern Territory* (1998) Aust Torts Reports ¶81–457; 151 ALR 263.

[129] Note the comparable legislation in other Australian jurisdictions except the Northern Territory and South Australia: *Civil Law (Wrongs) Act 2002* (ACT), s 110; *Civil Liability Act 2002* (NSW), s 42; *Civil Liability Act 2002* (Tas), s 38; *Wrongs Act 1958* (Vic), s 83; *Civil Liability Act 2002* (WA), s 5 W.

[130] Torts Commentary Electronic. 'Introduction Special Defendants Time Limits', CCH Australia, [¶1–835].

available online to the general public "as is" in an unpackaged form by government without expectation of economic profit—means that even if a duty of care is held to exist in the circumstances, the government will be held to a relatively low standard of care. Arguably, the relevant act or omission would be a breach of a duty of care only if no reasonable authority in the defendant government's position would have behaved in the same way.[131]

Provided the government and its agencies or departments, without gross negligence or disregard of the PSI's accuracy, take reasonable steps and precautions in creating, collecting, analyzing, and disseminating the various and voluminous PSI that is created or held by government departments and agencies, the government is not likely to be in breach of the applicable standard of care.

In this respect, implementation of standard systematic protocols throughout the information life cycle (from producing or collecting, recording, disseminating, archiving and analyzing information) may be sufficient to show that reasonable steps were taken to minimize the risk of harm, and therefore show that there has been no breach of the duty of care. Such standard protocols would form part of any whole-of-government or agency Information Management Framework.

10.5.2.3 Information Management Frameworks

An Information Management Framework (IMF) comprises policies, procedures and systems to enable the strategic management of information.[132] Currently, federal government agencies such as the Australian Taxation Office[133] and the Bureau of Meteorology[134] already have IMFs in place as a strategic direction. Similarly, the New South Wales Government has a Natural Resources Information Management Strategy (NRIMS),[135] the Queensland Government has the Queensland Government Information Management Strategic Framework, and the Victorian Govern-

---

[131] This standard is known as *Wednesbury* unreasonableness: *Associated Provincial Picture Houses Ltd v Wednesbury Corporation* [1948] 1 KB 223, 229–230 per Lord Greene MR; see also *Avon Downs Pty Ltd v Federal Commissioner of Taxation* (1949) 78 CLR 353, 360 per Dixon J. The *Wednesbury* standard of unreasonableness expressly applies to public or other authorities in proceedings based on breach of statutory duty: see *Civil Liability Act 2003* (Qld), s 36.

[132] See Information and records management framework – template (webpage), National Archives of Australia at http://www.naa.gov.au/records-management/strategic-information/information-governance/key-documents/framework.aspx.

[133] See the ATO's IMF at https://www.ato.gov.au/About-ATO/Access,-accountability-and-reporting/Information-management/.

[134] See Queensland Department of Environment and Resource Management in consultation with the Bureau of Meteorology Water Division (2009) and Creative Commons Australia (2009).

[135] See NSW Natural Resources Information Management Strategyhttp://www.nrims.nsw.gov.au/policies/imf.html.

ment has committed to the Economic Development and Infrastructure Committee's recommendation for the development of a whole-of-government IMF.[136]

The specified protocols under these IMF's should not be taken for granted as mere standard practice for the sake of consistency. These practices, if credible and reasonable, are important as:

- pre-release precautions to ascertain that sufficient rights attach to the information to allow its release, and therefore to avoid the infringement of copyright; and
- evidence that the government information provider has taken reasonable steps to minimise the risk of harm, that may arise from the release of incorrect information.

Whilst the specifics of these standard protocols are beyond the scope of this article, at the very least, standard protocols should be in place for every stage of the information life cycle, for example:

- collecting the information from credible sources;
- checking the information for noticeable errors before releasing it online;
- updating the information once new information is obtained[137]; and
- clearly detailing the scope and currency of the information.[138]

The adherence to protocols or standards procedures under an IMF, whilst no guarantee that information released will be free of inaccuracies, is cogent evidence that the information provider has acted reasonably in the circumstances.[139] Section 35(d) of the *Civil Liability Act 2003* (Qld)[140] specifically provides that, in deciding whether a public or other authority has a duty or has breached a duty, the authority may rely on evidence of its compliance with its general procedures and

---

[136] Victorian Government (2010). The Victorian Government at p. 8 stated:

A commitment to develop an Information Management Framework
The Victorian Government endorses the committee's overarching recommendation that the default position for the management of PSI should be open access. The Victorian Government further commits to the development of a whole-of-government Information Management Framework (IMF) whereby PSI is made available under Creative Commons licensing by default with a tailored suite of licences for restricted materials.

[137] Note that the information provider has a continuing obligation to correct inaccuracies: *Meadow Gem Pty Ltd v ANZ Executors amd Trustee Co Ltd* (1994) ATPR (Digest) 46–130.

[138] This will be discussed in more detail in the Sect. 10.5.4.

[139] See for example, *Dancorp Developers v Auckland City Council* [1991] 3 NZLR 337 at 353, 354 where the Council provided incorrect information because a vital report was missing from its files. However, the Council had an above average filing system in place and it was held not to be negligent.

[140] Note the comparable legislation in other Australian jurisdictions except the Northern Territory and South Australia: *Civil Law (Wrongs) Act 2002* (ACT), s 110; *Civil Liability Act 2002* (NSW), s 42; *Civil Liability Act 2002* (Tas), s 38; *Wrongs Act 1958* (Vic), s 83; *Civil Liability Act 2002* (WA), s 5 W.

any applicable standards for the exercise of its functions as evidence of the proper exercise of its functions in the matter to which the proceeding relates. Such evidence leaves very little scope for a plaintiff to argue that the information provider was negligent.

10.5.3 Causation and Scope of Liability

Whilst damage is usually the result of a complex set of conditions, the user of the PSI must be able to show on the balance of probabilities that the defendant government's act or omission was causally related to the injury or damage suffered by the user.[141]

Section 11(1) of the *Civil Liability Act 2003* (Qld)[142] is essentially a "but for" test of causation, and states that a decision that a breach of duty caused particular harm comprises the following elements:

(a) the breach of duty was a necessary condition of the occurrence of the harm; and
(b) it is appropriate for the scope of the liability of the person in breach to extend to the harm so caused.

In active systems (e.g. navigation systems), where decision-making on matters of real consequence is delegated to a computer system,[143] it may be easier to causally link the error in data in the system to the damage caused. Conversely, where loss is caused by reliance on incorrect information, contention arises because damage is caused not immediately from a government's act in providing the information, but from the user's reliance on the information.[144] In other words, the factors which establish the existence of a duty of care (for instance, a reasonable reliance) are also relevant to establishing a causal link between the defendant's breach of duty and the harm caused. Therefore, although an unreasonable reliance on the information may break the chain of causation, the question of causation will not arise where a duty of care is found not to exist in the circumstances.

---

[141] *Civil Liability Act 2003* (Qld), s 12; McGlone and Stickley (2005), p. 222; see for example *Barnett v Chelsea and Kensington Hospital Management Committee* [1969] 1 QB 428, where the causal link failed to be established because plaintiff's husband would have died even with medical treatment.

[142] Note the comparable legislation in other Australian jurisdictions except the Northern Territory: *Civil Law (Wrongs) Act 2002* (ACT), s 45(1); *Civil Liability Act 1936* (SA), s 34(1); *Civil Liability Act 2002* (Tas), s 13(1); *Wrongs Act 1958* (Vic), s 51(1); *Civil Liability Act 2002* (WA), s 5C(1); *Civil Liability Act 2002* (NSW), s 5D(1).

[143] Clarke (1988).

[144] *San Sebastian v Minister* [1986] HCA 68; (1986) 162 CLR 340 per Gibbs CJ, Mason, Wilson and Dawson JJ at [15].

10.5.4 Disclaiming Negligence

Having considered the three elements of tortious liability in the context of PSI, it is necessary to consider the effect of disclaimers in preventing a duty of care from arising or as a defence where a duty of care exists.

Most open content licences have express disclaimer of warranty and limitation of liability clauses. For example, clause 5(a) of the Creative Commons Attribution 3.0 Australia licence, headed "Representations, Warranties and Disclaimer"[145] states:

> Except as expressly stated in this Licence or otherwise agreed to by the parties in writing, and to the full extent permitted by applicable law, the Licensor **offers the Work "as-is"** and **makes no representations, warranties or conditions** of any kind concerning the Work, express, implied, statutory or otherwise. This includes, without limitation, any representations, warranties or conditions **regarding**:
>
> i. **the contents or accuracy of the Work**;
> ii. title, merchantability, or fitness for a particular purpose;
> iii. non-infringement;
> iv. **the absence of latent or other defects**; or
> v. **the presence or absence of errors**, whether or not discoverable. [emphasis added]

Clause 6(a) "Limit of Liability" in the licence states:

> To the full extent permitted by applicable law, and except for any liability arising from contrary agreement, **in no event will the Licensor be liable to You on any legal basis (including without limitation, negligence) for any loss or damage** whatsoever.... . [emphasis added]

These clauses, or similar disclaimers, may protect a government information provider from liability, where:

1. the user of the information has accepted the risk; or
2. the user's reliance on the information is unreasonable.

10.5.4.1 Acceptance of Risk

If a user of public sector information consents to the negligence of a government, the government may raise the defence of *volenti non fit injuria* (i.e. no injury is done to one who voluntarily consents).[146] In order to prove the defence and deny a recovery of damages, it must be proven that:

- the user of the PSI had full knowledge of the risk; and
- the user voluntarily accepted the risk.[147]

---

[145] Available at http://creativecommons.org/licenses/by/3.0/au/legalcode.

[146] *Rootes v Shelton* (1967) 116 CLR 383.

[147] McGlone and Stickley (2005), p. 250.

Full Knowledge of Risk

A subjective test is applied in establishing whether the user was aware of the facts and circumstances that gave rise to the risk.[148] Compared to the danger of physical risk, the risk of information being incorrect due to errors in internal information management or collection systems of government may not be as obvious to the general public. Consequently, it is important that government, in publishing PSI for public use, clearly delimits the uses of the information.[149]

Acceptance of the Risk

Acceptance of the licence containing the disclaimer may constitute acceptance of the risk by the licensee. An illustration of such acceptance may be drawn from the UK case of *Ashdown v Samuel Williams & Sons Ltd*,[150] where the plaintiff was injured whilst crossing a railway line she had permission to cross. The defendants, who had negligently shunted a train on the line, had posted notices purporting to exempt the defendants from liability for any injury caused by negligence on their land. It was held that the plaintiff, as a licensee on the land and having read the notice, had accepted the risk of injury on the terms specified by the defendants. Similarly, in using PSI, the user accepts the conditions of use contained in the applicable licence, thereby accepting that any loss caused by errors in the data will not be borne by the licensor.

Again, additional considerations apply where the duty of care is created by the granting of a *gratuitous* licence by the defendant to the plaintiff.[151] As Parker LJ stated in *Ashdown v Samuel Williams & Sons Ltd*: "It is, I think, clear that in granting a licence to enter upon the land the occupier can impose conditions whereby he is absolved from all or some liability which he would otherwise be under at common law."[152] In other words, it is reasonable for the licensor, in granting access without payment in return, to limit its liability; otherwise there would be no incentive to grant access in such a case.

10.5.4.2   Unreasonable Reliance

Potentially, an appropriate disclaimer may operate as a warning, which may be sufficient to discharge the relevant duty of care.[153] Alternatively, where a user

---

[148] *Canterbury Municipal Council v Taylor* [2002] NSWCA 24 (5 March 2002).

[149] See further Sect. 10.5.4.3.

[150] (1957) 1 QB 409.

[151] Lowe (1974), p. 218.

[152] [1957] QB 409, 427.

[153] Torts Commentary Electronic. 'Principles of Liability', CCH Australia, [¶50–690].

utilizes the information without regard to a clear warning against such use, it could be seen as an unreasonable reliance in the circumstances (therefore preventing a duty of care from arising).[154]

For example, liability should not be imputed to government when uninformed users use the information incorrectly,[155] outside of its known limits. In *De Bardeleben Marine Corp v United States*,[156] liability was avoided when a mariner did not have an updated "notice to Mariners" on board a barge that sank, even though these notices were routinely and widely available. The court held that the time had passed at which any reasonable mariner would have conceived an updated chart, and this exonerated the government from negligence liability.[157]

10.5.4.3   What Is an Effective Disclaimer?

To be effective, written disclaimers must be clear, detailed and prominent.[158] As Kirby J stated in *Butcher v Lachlan Elder Realty*[159]: "The more harsh the exemption, the stricter has been the approach of the courts to the duty of the party that seeks to rely upon it to draw it to specific notice."[160] The finer the 'fine print', the more readily will a court draw a conclusion that insufficient notice has been given, so as to take the provision outside the operation of an effective exemption.[161]

A disclaimer is not a catch-all solution to excluding liability, and will be construed strictly.[162] As the duty of care arises by operation of law and not purely by virtue of a person's personal and factual assumption of responsibility, courts are likely to take the view that information providers *may not always* exempt themselves from the performance of a duty.[163] Rather, a disclaimer would be another factor to be taken into consideration with all the circumstances.[164]

---

[154] See *MLC v Evatt* (1968) 122 CLR 556, 585.

[155] Philips (1999), pp. 743 and 769.

[156] 451 F 2d 140 at 141 (5th Cir 1971).

[157] *De Bardeleben Marine Corp v United States* 451 F 2d 140, 149 (5th Cir 1971).

[158] *Butcher v Lachlan Elder Realty Pty Ltd* [2004] HCA 60, [216].

[159] [2004] HCA 60.

[160] *Oceanic Sun Line* [1988] HCA 32; (1988) 165 CLR 197, 229.

[161] *Butcher v Lachlan Elder Realty Pty Ltd* [2004] HCA 60, [219]. For instance, very detailed exclusion clauses were held to be effective in *DHL International (NZ) Ltd v Richmond Ltd* [1993] 3 NZLR 10 by the New Zealand Court of Appeal. Conversely, in *Thornton v Shoe Lane Parking Ltd* [1971] 2 QB 163, an extremely wide exemption clause was held not to absolve the defendant parking company of liability for personal injury caused while the plaintiff was picking up his car. See generally Torts Commentary Electronic. 'Principles of Liability', CCH Australia, [¶50–690].

[162] See for example *Butcher v Lachlan Elder Realty Pty Ltd* [2004] HCA 60; *Bright v Sampson and Duncan* (1985) 1 NSWLR 246.

[163] McGlone and Stickley (2005), p. 336.

[164] Ibid.

In terms of the release of PSI by government, an effective disclaimer should cover details such as data quality, source materials and any known limitations of the data, and include a statement eliminating the provider from any liability for misuse of data.[165] In relation to data currency, the disclaimer should declare the data valid to a certain date, or simply provide the date in which the data was last updated.[166]

In addition to a disclaimer notice, advancement in information technology now means that licence information and the relevant disclaimer can be attached as metadata to the information or dataset released online.[167] This metadata may carry with it a verification link, so that downstream users can always link to the source and check for updates or obtain their information directly.[168] A prominent notice should advise users to check both the metadata and verification link.

Further, where the information can be independently verified or specific professional advice can be sought about its use, government should explicitly warn users to do so before relying on the information. The importance of this warning is evidenced by the recent UK case of *Patchett v Swimming Pool & Allied Trades Association Ltd*,[169] where the defendant website proprietor was held not to owe a duty of care for incorrect statements on its website. This result ensued because the court was of the view that the degree of reliance on the accuracy of the statements which the defendant could reasonably have anticipated was limited by advice that potential customers should obtain additional verification in the form of a further information pack.[170] However, where the government is the sole repository of that information, such a warning is likely to be unreasonable, and therefore ineffective in disclaiming liability.

These steps in ensuring users are adequately informed about the data could avoid improper use of the information, and prevent assumptions about the information's accuracy from arising. This delineation of the limits of the data is important:

• to show that users of PSI have full knowledge of any risks of errors it may carry as a result of these limits (where acceptance of risk is used as a defence); or
• to show that reliance on the information was unreasonable.

Preferably, a disclaimer or exemption of liability should strike an appropriate balance between the rights of the individual on the one hand and potential liability confronting governments.[171] A disclaimer, which clearly sets out the limitations of the information and informs the public when the government will be responsible for errors and when it will not be responsible, avoids a situation whereby information is

---

[165] Stewart et al. (1997), pp. 84 and 111.

[166] Ibid.

[167] See 'Embedded Metadata' at http://wiki.creativecommons.org/Embedded_Metadata.

[168] Ibid.

[169] [2009] EWCA Civ 717 available at http://www.bailii.org/ew/cases/EWCA/Civ/2009/717.html.

[170] [2009] EWCA Civ 717 at [34].

[171] See for example *Mid Density Developments Pty Limited v Rockdale Municipal Council* [1993] FCA 408, [19] & [31].

simply released to be used "at your own risk". It is a step in encouraging the use and re-use of PSI by instilling a degree of confidence in governments' efforts to ensure the information's accuracy, yet shielding governments from an overtly heavy burden of potential liability. For example, the US government's Data.gov portal provides in its Data Policy that:

> For all data accessed through Data.gov, each agency has confirmed that the data being provided through this site meets the agency's Information Quality Guidelines.[172]
>
> . . . . . .
>
> Once the data have been downloaded from the agency's site, the government cannot vouch for their quality and timeliness.[173]
>
> . . . . . .
>
> This Data Policy is intended only to improve the internal management of information controlled by the Executive Branch of the Federal Government and it is not intended to, and does not, create any right or benefit, substantive or procedural, enforceable at law or in equity, by a party against the United States, its Departments, Agencies, or other entities, its officers, employees, or agents.[174]

In comparison, a broad exemption of liability (such as clauses 5(a) and 6(a) of the Creative Commons Attribution 3.0 Australia licence) *in itself* is arguably neither adequate to prove the defence of *volenti* (in the unlikely event that a duty of care and a breach of that duty is found) nor sufficient to show unreasonable reliance by the user. However, the clause will be considered in conjunction with all the relevant circumstances of the case (i.e. matters already canvassed in relation to a duty of care and breach of that duty). If information is released under a Creative Commons licence carrying a broad exemption of liability *combined with* a notice and attached metadata informing users of inherent limitations to the data, and the data provider has adhered to reasonable information management practices and is provided free of charge to the public, then the scope for finding the provider of information liable for inaccuracies is severely limited. In short, the cumulative effect of all these factors combined with the exemption clause is sufficient to deny a plaintiff user's recovery of damages.

10.6 What About Public Sector Information Not Subject to Copyright?

Although copyright may subsist in the compilation as a whole, the Australian High Court held in the recent case of *IceTV Pty Limited v Nine Network Australia Pty Limited*[175] that copyright in a compilation of data is not infringed simply where

---

[172] See "Data.gov - Data Policy" (webpage), at https://www.data.gov/data-policy.

[173] Ibid (Secondary Use).

[174] Ibid (Applicability of this Data Policy).

[175] [2009] HCA 14.

unoriginal portions of the data are taken.[176] The High Court did not overrule its previous decision in *Desktop Marketing v Telstra*[177] in regards to the subsistence of copyright in compilations of data. Nevertheless, in light of Gummow, Hayne and Heydon JJ's obiter remarks that the reasoning in *Desktop Marketing v Telstra*[178] was "out of line with the understanding of copyright law over many years" and had to be treated with caution,[179] it is prudent to consider the application of negligence principles to the release of PSI which may not be subject to copyright.

Where copyright does not subsist in the work, a copyright licence such as a Creative Commons licence cannot attach to it.[180] There are several alternatives to a copyright licence in order to disclaim liability. These include click-wrap contracts, or disclaimer notices on the source website or information metadata. The difference between these alternatives and copyright licensing is that these notices or contract clauses fail to bind downstream users; there is no direct licensor–licensee relationship between the government information provider and the user.[181]

But is it necessary for the disclaimer or warning to be contained in an operative licence to have the requisite legal effect of limiting potential liability to the public? It is submitted that this factor does not have a huge implication on its effectiveness, for there is only one point of divergence. The point of divergence is this: where a licensor–licensee relationship with downstream users does not exist, there is no assumption of liability implied because there is no acceptance of any copyright licence for the use of the work. Acceptance of the copyright licence is not required to enable the lawful use of that information.[182]

In any case, this analysis requires an application of the same tortious principles expressed in *MLC v Evatt*[183] to this new factual scenario. Again, we ask if there was a reasonable reliance or an acceptance of risk in light on the disclaimers/warnings present. A disclaimer/warning may still be effective where it is of sufficient prominence (regardless of whether it is in a licence, contract, website notice or metadata) so as to demonstrate that the user has unreasonably relied upon the information.

---

[176] [2009] HCA 14 at [41]–[43].

[177] (2002) 119 FCR 491.

[178] (2002) 119 FCR 491.

[179] *IceTV Pty Limited v Nine Network Australia Pty Limited* [2009] HCA 14 (Unreported, French CJ, Gummow, Hayne, Heydon, Crennan and Kiefel JJ, 22 April 2009) [188]; see similar remarks of French, Crennan and Kiefel JJ at [52]; See also *Telstra Corporation Limited v Phone Directories Company Pty Ltd* [2010] FCA 44, where Gordon J at [5] held that copyright did not subsist in Telstra's Yellow Pages and White Pages directories because the computer generated compilation had failed the authorship requirement. It appears likely that the decision will be taken on appeal on this and other grounds.

[180] That is, none of the 6 Creative Commons licences (see http://www.creativecommons.org.au/licences); cf CC Zero and the Public Domain Mark (http://creativecommons.org/publicdomain/).

[181] See Fitzgerald et al. (2010), p. 16.

[182] See for example, *Ashdown v Samuel Williams & Sons Ltd* (1957) 1 QB 409.

[183] (1968) 122 CLR 556 at 571 per Barwick CJ.

Moreover, where non-copyright works are obtained downstream, there carries a risk that the information is altered, and disclaimers or metadata are no longer attached to the work (and are no longer effective to limit liability). However, it is submitted that it is very difficult to positively establish a relationship of proximity between a government information provider and a downstream user who utilises that information without verifying its provenance from the source. In other words, reliance on information not sourced directly from the government portal is unlikely to be reasonable in the circumstances. This is especially so where a verification link, which allows the users to check the source website for updates, is included with the information.

Nevertheless, in the case of information not subject to copyright, best practice would be to include the appropriate warnings/disclaimers in a prominent position with the information itself (not merely as a notice on the source website) and also to embed this in the information's metadata. Even if there is no guarantee that the disclaimer will remain attached to the information, it is a preventive measure in limiting liability.

10.7   Conclusion

This chapter has argued that where information is made available by government online to the general public without expectation of economic profit, a court is unlikely to uphold a duty of care on the part of the government body or agency providing access to PSI.

Even if a government body or agency is held to be subject to a duty of care, the duty would be of a relatively low standard compared to the standard of care which may be expected from a firm or private individual providing specific information or advice to another for a fee. Section 35 of the *Civil Liability Act 2003* (Qld)[184] further entrenches this lower standard by requiring that financial and political constrains be taken into account in determining the existence of a duty and whether any duty has been breached. Moreover, these factors must be considered in light of the strong public policy argument that PSI as a publicly funded resource should be made available to the public.[185] The standard of care is also less likely to be breached where government employees have adhered to reasonable information

---

[184] Note the comparable legislation in other Australian jurisdictions except the Northern Territory and South Australia: *Civil Law (Wrongs) Act 2002* (ACT), s 110; *Civil Liability Act 2002* (NSW), s 42; *Civil Liability Act 2002* (Tas), s 38; *Wrongs Act 1958* (Vic), s 83; *Civil Liability Act 2002* (WA), s 5 W.

[185] Bushell-Embling (2007).

management practices, and where there are clear disclosures or warnings about the limitations of the information.

In short, the combined effect of:

i. the circumstances (i.e. PSI proactively being made available online for free under an open content licence);
ii. the public policy arguments for open access;
iii. the adherence to credible information management practices; and
iv. the existence of disclosures or warnings about the limitations of the information and a limitation of liability clause,

means that governments are unlikely to be held tortiously liable for information released under an open content licence, provided they are not grossly negligent in collecting, processing and releasing the information to the public. Where these factors are present, the scope for finding that government information provider liable for inaccuracies is severely limited. The cumulative effect of all these factors is likely to be sufficient to deny a plaintiff user's recovery of damages.

Governments, in carrying out their duties to the public, should be subject to a realistic risk of legal liability, and be prepared to accept that level of risk. A government which adopts a completely risk averse approach by not releasing digitised public sector information is squandering the various opportunities for innovation, economic growth and social engagement that are presented by making the PSI available online under an open access regime.[186]

At the same time, users of freely available public sector information should carefully consider any limitations made explicit to them concerning the information and should ensure that they deal with the information responsibly. In the new online open access space, the public has a shared responsibility with governments in making the most of this valuable taxpayer funded informational resource.

References

Books and Book Chapters

Barker Ed et al (2005) The common information environment and creative commons. Common Information Environment, UK
Charlton S (1990) An introduction to the legal liabilities of information producers. In: Edwards C, Savage N, Walden I (eds) Information technology & the law, 2nd edn. Macmillan Publishers Ltd, UK
Cho G (1998) Geographic information systems and the law: mapping the legal frontiers of the law. Wiley, West Sussex

---

[186] See, Victorian Parliament, Economic Development and Infrastructure Committee (2009), pp. 7–17 and Cutler (2008).

Cutler T (2008) Innovation and open access to public sector information. In: Fitzgerald B (ed) Legal framework for e-research: realising the potential. Sydney University Press, Sydney. Available at http://eprints.qut.edu.au/archive/00014439/

Fitzgerald A, Fitzgerald B (2004) Intellectual property: in principle. Lawbook, Sydney

Fitzgerald B et al (2007) Internet and e-commerce law: technology, law and policy. Lawbook, Sydney

Fitzgerald A, Fitzgerald B, Hooper N (2010) Enabling open access to public sector information with creative commons licences: the Australian experience. In: Fitzgerald B (ed) Access to public sector information: law, technology & policy. Sydney University Press, Sydney. Available at http://eprints.qut.edu.au/29773/

Mandelson D (1997) The new law of torts. Oxford University Press, South Melbourne

McGlone F, Stickley A (2005) Australian torts law. LexisNexis Butterworths, Chatswood

Rowland D, Macdonald E (2005) Information technology law, 3rd edn. Cavendish Publishing, London

Samuelson P (2009) What effects do legal rules have on service innovation? In: Kieliszewski CA, Spohrer J (eds) Handbook of service science. UC Berkeley Public Law Research Paper No. 1421946. Springer, Heidelberg. Available at http://ssrn.com/abstract=1421946

Journal Articles

Aronson M (2008) Government liability in negligence. MULR 2. Available at http://www.austlii.edu.au/au/journals/MULR/2008/2

Butler D (2000) Media negligence in the information age. Torts Law J 8(2):159

Christensen S, Duncan B, Stickley A (2008) Shifting paradigms of government liability for inaccurate information. eLaw Murdoch Univ Electron J Law 15(2). Available at https://elaw.murdoch.edu.au/archives/index.html

Fitzgerald B, Oi I (2004) Free culture: cultivating the creative commons. Media Arts Law Rev 9 (2):137. Available at http://eprints.qut.edu.au/archive/00000122/

Fitzgerald B, Suzor N (2005) Legal issues for the use of free and open source software for government. MULR 29(2):412

Ivankovich IF (1991) Accountants and third party liability — back to the future. Ottawa Law Rev 23:505

Lowe JRM (1974) The exclusion of liability for negligence. Modern Law Rev 37:218

Parchomovsky G, Stein A (2008) Torts and innovation. Mich Law Rev 107:285

Phegan C (1997) Reining in foreseeability: liability of auditors to third parties for negligent misstatement. Torts Law J 5:123

Philips JL (1999) Information liability: the possible chilling effect of tort claims against producers of geographic information systems data. Fla State Univ Law Rev 26:743

Stewart K et al (1997) Geographical information systems and legal liability. J Law Inf Sci 8:84

Reports

Australian Government (2010a) Government Response to the Report of the Government 2.0 Taskforce, May 2010. Available at http://www.finance.gov.au/publications/govresponse20report/doc/Government-Response-to-Gov-2-0-Report.pdf

Clarke R (1988) Who is liable for software errors? Proposed new product liability law in Australia. Department of Computer Science, Australian National University. Available at http://www.rogerclarke.com/SOS/PaperLiaby.html

Fitzgerald AM (2008) Policies and principles on access to and reuse of public sector information: a review of the literature in Australia and selected jurisdictions. Available at http://www.aupsi.org/publications/reports.jsp

Fitzgerald AM, Hooper N (2009) A review of the literature on the legal aspects of open access policy, practices and licensing in Australia and selected jurisdictions. Available at http://www.aupsi.org/publications/reports.jsp

Fitzgerald B et al (2006) Creating a legal framework for copyright management of open access within the Australian academic and research sector. OAK Law Project, Brisbane. Available at http://eprints.qut.edu.au/6099/

Government 2.0 Taskforce final report, Engage: getting on with Government 2.0. Available at http://www.finance.gov.au/publications/gov20taskforcereport/index.html

Queensland Department of Environment and Resource Management in consultation with the Bureau of Meteorology Water Division (2009) Government Information Licensing Framework (GILF) for water: recommended practice. Available at http://www.unidapwaterq.com.au/_resource/downloads/GILF%20for%20H20.pdf

van Eechoud M, van der Wal B (2008) Creative commons licensing for public sector information: opportunities and pitfalls. Institute of Information Law, University of Amsterdam, January 2008. Available at http://www.ivir.nl/publicaties/download/599

Victoria, Economic Development and Infrastructure Committee (2008) Inquiry into improving access to Victorian Public Sector Information and Data: discussion paper July 2008 (Hon. Christine Campbell, MP, Chairperson) Victoria, Victorian Government Printer. Available at http://www.parliament.vic.gov.au/edic/inquiries/access_to_PSI/call_for_submissions.html

Victorian Government (2010) Whole of Victorian Government Response to the Final Report of the Economic Development and Infrastructure Committee's inquiry into improving access to Victorian Public Sector Information and Data. Victorian Department of Innovation, Industry and Regional Development (DIIRD), 4 February 2010. Available at http://www.parliament.vic.gov.au/images/stories/committees/edic/access_to_PSI/Response-to-the-EDIC-Inquiry-into-Improving-Access-to-Victorian-PSI-and-Data.pdf

Victorian Parliament, Economic Development and Infrastructure Committee (2009) Inquiry into improving access to Victorian Public Sector Information and Data (Final report), June 2009. Available at http://www.parliament.vic.gov.au/edic/inquiries/access_to_PSI/final_report.html

Weiss P (2002) Borders in cyberspace: conflicting public sector information policies and their economic impacts, February 2002. Available at http://www.weather.gov/sp/Borders_report.pdf

Online Documents

Bushell-Embling D (2007) Private eyes on public data. The Sydney Morning Herald 25 September 2007. http://www.smh.com.au/news/technology/private-eyes-on-public-data/2007/09/24/1190486224755.html

Chillingworth M (2006) Guardian newspaper campaigns for free public sector information. Information World Review, 17 March 2006. http://www.iwr.co.uk/information-world-review/news/2152217/guardian-newspaper-campaigns

Creative Commons Australia (2009) Bureau of Meteorology to release water data under CC. Creative Commons Australia, 17 November 2009. Available at http://creativecommons.org.au/blog/2009/11/bureau-of-meteorology-to-release-water-data-under-cc/

Fisher FJ, Legal exposures facing the software industry. Lectric Law Library. http://www.lectlaw.com/files/bul17.htm

The Laws of Australia Electronic, Torts - Public Policy [33.2.390] (last updated 1 August 2007)

Torts Commentary Electronic, CCH Australia

UK Office of Public Sector Information (OSPI), Licensing and data.gov.uk launch, PerSpectIves blog, 21 January 2010

Webpages

ATO, Information Management, at https://www.ato.gov.au/About-ATO/Access,-accountability-and-reporting/Information-management/

Australian Government (2010) Statement of IP Principles for Australian Government Agencies. Available at http://www.ag.gov.au/RightsAndProtections/IntellectualProperty/Pages/AustralianGovernmentIPrules.aspx. Last updated 1 October 2010

CC Zero and the Public Domain Mark, http://creativecommons.org/publicdomain/

Creative Commons licences, Creative Commons Australia http://creativecommons.org.au/learn/licences/

Data.gov, http://www.data.gov

Embedded Metadata, Creative Commons, at http://wiki.creativecommons.org/Embedded_Metadata

Government 2.0 Taskforce at http://gov2.net.au/about/

National Archives of Australia, Information and records management framework – template (webpage), at http://www.naa.gov.au/records-management/strategic-information/information-governance/key-documents/framework.aspx

NSW Natural Resources Information Management Strategy, at http://www.nrims.nsw.gov.au/policies/imf.html

OAK Law Project: Open Access to Knowledge at http://www.oaklaw.qut.edu.au/

Open Access on Wikipedia at http://en.wikipedia.org/wiki/Open_access_(publishing)

Chapter 11
Duty and Control in Intermediary Copyright Liability: An Australian Perspective

Kylie Pappalardo

11.1 Introduction

The question of whether technology intermediaries such as internet service providers (ISPs) and website hosts should be liable for acts of copyright infringement by their users has been at the forefront of copyright law for the last three decades. Yet despite a number of high-profile cases grappling with this question,[1] and repeated legislative and policy debates,[2] the law concerning intermediary copyright liability has not developed in a clear and predictable way. In Australia, we still do not have a reliable framework for determining *if* particular intermediaries should be liable for the infringement of third-party users, let alone *to what extent* they should be liable. This chapter considers the liability of so-called "passive" intermediaries, which are those intermediaries—like ISPs—that have not actively helped users to infringe copyright but which face liability because they have not acted to *stop* the infringement. It argues that principles of negligence under tort law, which consider whether the intermediary has a duty to act and whether that duty has been breached,

---

[1] See *Metro-Goldwyn-Mayer Studios Inc., v. Grokster Ltd.* 545 U.S. 913 (2005); *In Re Aimster Copyright Litigation*, 334 F.3d 643, 645 (7th Cir. 2003); *A&M Records, Inc. v. Napster Inc.* 239 F.3d 1004 (9th Cir. 2001); *Roadshow Films Pty Ltd v iiNet Ltd* [2012] HCA 16; *Cooper v Universal Music Australia Pty Ltd* (2006) 156 FCR 380; *Universal Music Australia v Sharman License Holdings Ltd* (2005) 220 ALR 1.

[2] See, for example, the discussions surrounding amendments to the *Copyright Act 1968* following the Australia–United States Free Trade Agreement (AUSFTA), which included the addition of safe harbours for network providers: Rimmer (2006); Burrell and Weatherall (2008), pp. 259–319. See also the debates surrounding the proposed Stop Online Piracy Act (SOPA), detailed in Bridy (2010), pp. 153–164.

K. Pappalardo (✉)
Thomas More Academy of Law, Australian Catholic University, 486 Albert Street, East Melbourne, VIC 3002, Australia
e-mail: kylie.pappalardo@gmail.com

© Springer International Publishing Switzerland 2015   241
B. Fitzgerald, J. Gilchrist (eds.), *Copyright Perspectives*,
DOI 10.1007/978-3-319-15913-3_11

may provide a more coherent framework for assessing the copyright liability of passive intermediaries in Australia. In particular, the concept of control in tort law is far more robust than that currently found in Australian copyright law. This chapter uses the Australian High Court decision in *Roadshow Films Pty Ltd v iiNet Limited* [2012] as a case study to examine the creep of tort principles into copyright analysis and to demonstrate how the High Court used those principles to inform their understanding of an intermediary's control over the infringing actions of its users.

In Australia, intermediary liability is said to arise from the word "authorise" in sections 36(1) and 101(1) of the *Copyright Act 1968*, which provide that copyright is infringed by a person who does or authorises the doing of one of the exclusive acts reserved to the copyright owner. "Authorise" has been held to mean: "sanction, approve, countenance,"[3] and it is on that definition that Australian intermediary liability doctrine is based. The High Court of Australia has recently criticised the fact that authorise has been defined by reference to its dictionary synonyms, especially since the words "sanction", "approve" and "countenance" have no fixed legal meaning within copyright law.[4] "Countenance", for example, has a number of meanings that are not co-extensive with the common understanding of "authorise".[5] Intermediary copyright liability (or authorisation liability, as it is known in Australia) therefore sits on rocky foundations. The doctrine has not developed in a principled manner, resulting in significant ambiguity about the scope of liability for intermediaries in Australia.[6]

A recent decision of the High Court of Australia has subtly shifted the discourse away from these vague definitions in copyright law towards better-established principles in tort. In *Roadshow Films Pty Ltd v iiNet Limited* [2012] the High Court unanimously held that iiNet, Australia's second largest ISP, was not liable for the acts of its subscribers who had communicated copyrighted films to other users over BitTorrent. The Court found that iiNet lacked the power to prevent the infringing uploads except by terminating its contractual relationships with its subscribers (in effect, terminating the subscribers' internet access). Members of the High Court used a notion of control influenced by tort law to hold that a power to prevent infringement at an abstract level (by terminating internet access) did not amount to effective control over infringing users and so did not give rise to a duty to act to prevent the infringements. This was an unusual development, because principles of tort law have never featured prominently in Australian copyright discourse.[7]

---

[3] *University of N.S.W. v Moorhouse* (1975) 6 ALR 193.

[4] *Roadshow Films Pty Ltd v iiNet Ltd* [2012] HCA 16 at [68], [117].

[5] The Oxford English Dictionary includes the following definitions of 'countenance': (noun) support or approval; (verb) admit as acceptable or possible. It defines 'authorize' as "(verb) give official permission for or approval to (an undertaking or agent)". See also *Roadshow Films Pty Ltd v iiNet Ltd* [2012] HCA 16 at [68] (French CJ, Crennan and Kiefel JJ), [125] (Gummow and Hayne JJ).

[6] See, for example, Giblin (2009), pp. 148–177; Ginsburg and Ricketson (2006), pp. 1–25.

[7] See discussion associated with footnote 11.

This chapter will critically evaluate the tort law principles relied upon by members of the High Court in the *iiNet* case. The chapter addresses, primarily, the issue of liability for omissions to act, and argues that in tort law there is a strong onus on the plaintiff to show that the defendant had a duty to act. Whether a duty exists will often depend on whether the defendant was able to exercise effective control over the actions of the wrongdoing third-party. The ability to hinder the third party in some way is not enough to establish a duty to act in the absence of effective control. This chapter argues that an inquiry grounded in control as defined in tort law would provide a more principled framework for assessing the liability of passive intermediaries in copyright. In particular, it would set a higher, more stable benchmark for determining the copyright liability of passive intermediaries, based on the degree of real and actual control that the intermediary can exercise over the infringing actions of its users. This approach would provide greater clarity and consistency than has existed to date in this area of copyright law.

11.2 The Law (in Brief)

In the United States, intermediary copyright liability developed from common law principles originating in tort. Intermediary liability for copyright infringement has traditionally been grounded in legal concepts of vicarious liability, which has its origin in agency,[8] and contributory infringement, which is based upon principles of joint tortfeasorship.[9] By contrast, authorisation liability in Australia derives from statute, as interpreted by the courts. In fact, courts have traditionally denied the relevance of common law tort principles, stating that authorisation liability in Australia is distinct from liability for the acts of agents or employees and liability as a joint tortfeasor.[10]

In Australia, intermediary liability is said to arise from the word "authorise" in sections 36(1) and 101(1) of the *Copyright Act 1968*, which provide that copyright "is infringed by a person who, not being the owner of copyright, and without the licence of the owner of the copyright, does in Australia, or authorizes the doing in Australia of, any act comprised in the copyright."[11] "Authorise" was defined in the

---

[8] The *respondeat superior* doctrine in agency law holds that a principal may, in certain circumstances, be liable for the acts of his or her agent.

[9] Cohen et al. (2010), p. 476.

[10] *WEA International Inc. v Hanimex Corporation Ltd.* (1985) 77 ALR 456; see further *Ash v Hutchinson & Co (Publishers)* [1936] Ch. 489.

[11] The US *Copyright Act 1976* also gives a copyright owner exclusive rights "to do and to authorize" certain acts: 17 USC § 106. Most debates in the US have focused on whether the words "to authorize" provide an independent right that can be directly infringed, or whether they merely refer to liability for contributory infringement. The prevailing position seems to be that the language "to authorize" provides "a statutory foundation for secondary liability": *Capitol Records, Inc. v. Thomas*, 579 F. Supp. 2d 1210, 1221 (D. Minn. 2008). See also *Venegas-Hernandez*

leading case of *University of New South Wales v Moorhouse* (1975) to mean: "sanction, approve, countenance."[12] The *Moorhouse* case was brought as a test case to ascertain whether the University of New South Wales would be liable for making photocopy machines available in its library (where people could take books off the shelves and photocopy them from a small fee) without supervision or display of proper copyright notices. A majority of the High Court found the University liable. The most influential judgment was that of Justice Gibbs, who stated:

> It seems to me... that a person who has under his control the means by which an infringement of copyright may be committed – such as a photocopying machine – and who makes it available to other persons, knowing, or having reason to suspect, that it is likely to be used for the purpose of committing an infringement, and omitting to take reasonable steps to limit its use to legitimate purposes, would authorize any infringement that resulted from its use.[13]

This statement is widely considered to be the model for sections 36(1A) and 101 (1A), which were inserted into the *Copyright Act 1968* in 2000.[14] They provide that in determining whether a person has authorised infringement, the court must take into account:

(a) the extent (if any) of the person's power to prevent the doing of the act concerned;
(b) the nature of any relationship existing between the person and the person who did the act concerned;
(c) whether the person took any other reasonable steps to prevent or avoid the doing of the act, including whether the person complied with any relevant industry codes of practice.

The power to prevent infringement, which loosely correlates to control, is the first factor to which judges must turn their minds. It is therefore an important feature of the authorisation doctrine in Australia. In *Roadshow Films Pty Ltd v iiNet Limited* [2012], the High Court departed from established authority to examine this factor with reference to tort law. Two judges expressly referenced principles derived from tort cases in ascertaining the meaning of control where passive intermediaries have failed to act to stop infringement. The remaining three judges, while not referring to tort principles directly, read down the power to prevent factor in a way that accords with a tort-influenced approach. Section 11.3 describes, in brief, the facts of this case and the tort law references made by the court.

---

v. ACEMLA, 424 F. 3d 50, 58 (1st Cir. 2005); *Subafilms, Ltd. v. MGM-Pathe Commc'ns Co.*, 24 F.3d 1088, 1093 (9th Cir. 1994) (en banc); H.R. Rep. 94-1476 at 61 (1976) ("Use of the phrase 'to authorize' is intended to avoid any questions as to the liability of contributory infringers"); Melville B. Nimmer & David Nimmer, NIMMER ON COPYRIGHT § 12.04 [A][3][a] at 12-85-88; *cf.* Koneru (1996), pp. 87–131.

[12] *University of N.S.W. v Moorhouse* (1975) 6 ALR 193.

[13] *University of N.S.W. v Moorhouse* (1975) 6 ALR 193, 200–201.

[14] *See* Explanatory Memorandum, Copyright Amendment (Digital Agenda) Bill 1999 (Cth), [54]–[56], [122]–[124]; *Roadshow Films Pty Ltd v iiNet Ltd* [2012] HCA 16 at [22], [52] (French CJ, Crennan and Kiefel JJ), [133] (Gummow and Hayne JJ).

11.3   *Roadshow Films v iiNet*

iiNet, Australia's second largest ISP, provides general internet access to subscribers under the terms of its Customer Relationship Agreement. The agreement states, in clause 4, that the subscriber must comply with all laws in using the internet service, and must not use or attempt to use the service to infringe another person's rights. It further provides, in clause 14, that iiNet may, without liability, immediately cancel, suspend or restrict the supply of the service if the subscriber breaches clause 4 or otherwise misuses the service.

In August 2007, the Australian Federation Against Copyright Theft (AFACT),[15] a body which represents the interests of copyright owners and exclusive licensees in films and TV programs in Australia, hired DtecNet Software, a software company, to gather evidence of apparent copyright infringement by Australian internet users. From July 2008 to August 2009, AFACT sent notices ("the AFACT notices") to iiNet on a weekly basis, alleging that iiNet subscribers (identified by IP addresses) were downloading and sharing movies via BitTorrent. In response, iiNet raised two issues: it could not understand AFACT's data, and that an IP address was insufficient to identify a particular internet user. iiNet stated that AFACT should refer its allegations to the appropriate authorities. iiNet did not suspend or terminate any subscriber account under the terms of its Customer Relationship Agreement in response to the AFACT notices, nor did it send warning notices to its subscribers.[16]

The case against iiNet was brought by an alliance of movie studios and media companies, including Village Roadshow, Universal Pictures, Paramount Pictures, Warner Brothers Entertainment, Sony Pictures Entertainment, Twentieth Century Fox and Disney. The movie companies argued that by doing nothing in response to the AFACT notices, particularly by failing to enforce the terms of its Customer Relationship Agreement, iiNet had at least 'countenanced' the infringements. Therefore, by failing to take reasonable steps to prevent subscribers from downloading and sharing infringing copies of films, iiNet had authorised the infringing acts of its subscribers.

The case came to the High Court on appeal from the Full Court of the Federal Court of Australia. The High Court was unanimous in finding that iiNet had not authorised the infringements. The High Court delivered two separate judgments. The first, a joint judgment by Chief Justice French and Justices Crennan and Kiefel, focused on the statutory language in s 101(1A) of the *Copyright Act 1968* to find that iiNet's power to prevent was limited: "It had no direct power to prevent the primary infringements and could only ensure that result indirectly by terminating the contractual relationship it had with its customers."[17] Additionally, the judges noted the inadequacy of the information in the AFACT notices, holding that the

---

[15] Now called the Australian Screen Association: http://www.screenassociation.com.au/.

[16] Description of facts derived from *Roadshow Films Pty Ltd v iiNet Ltd* [2012] HCA 16 at [28]–[35].

[17] *Roadshow Films Pty Ltd v iiNet Ltd* [2012] HCA 16 at [69]–[70] (French CJ, Crennan and Kiefel JJ).

notices did not provide enough evidence to compel iiNet to act.[18] However, it is the second joint judgment by Justices Gummow and Hayne that is of greater interest for the purposes of this chapter. Their Honours drew principles from tort law in finding that iiNet did not have a duty to act to stop subscribers from infringing copyright owners' rights. This is an interesting development, given that Australian courts have seldom relied on tort law in framing authorisation liability.

In their reasons, Justices Gummow and Hayne described the appellants' case by reference to the elements of negligence in tort:

> [C]ounsel for the appellants appeared to accept that their case posited a duty upon iiNet to take steps so as not to facilitate the primary infringements and that this duty was broken because, in particular, iiNet did nothing in that regard.
>
> So expressed, the appellants' case resembles one cast as a duty of care owed to them by iiNet, which has been broken by inactivity, causing damage to the appellants.[19]

Indeed, the appellants had placed significant weight on s. 101(1A)(c) of the *Copyright Act 1968* in arguing that because iiNet had not taken any reasonable steps to "prevent the continuation of the [infringing] acts" it had exhibited indifference about the infringements.[20] They asserted that indifference in the face of knowledge or suspicion of copyright infringement amounted to countenancing infringement. The appellants therefore argued that even though iiNet had not taken any steps to facilitate infringement, it should nonetheless be held liable because it had not acted to stop the infringement. They stated:

> At the least, such conduct amounted to countenancing the infringements of copyright for the purposes of authorization. Despite its denials of authorization, iiNet permitted the users of its internet service to infringe without interruption or consequence. It did so because it did not believe that it was required to act, because 'it had no legal obligation to act'.[21]

The question of whether or not iiNet did have an obligation or duty to act was at the core of Justices Gummow and Hayne's legal analysis. Their Honours referenced several tort law principles in examining the circumstances in which a duty to act to protect another will arise. First, they quoted the following passage from a 1914 article on the tort liability of public authorities:

> The cases in which men are liable in tort for pure omissions are in truth rare. . .The common law of tort deals with causes which look backwards to some act of a defendant more or less proximate to the actual damage, and looks askance at the suggestion of a liability based not upon such a causing of injury but merely upon the omission to do something which would have prevented the mischief.[22]

---

[18] *Roadshow Films Pty Ltd v iiNet Ltd* [2012] HCA 16 at [74]–[75], [78].

[19] *Roadshow Films Pty Ltd v iiNet Ltd* [2012] HCA 16 at [114]–[115] (Gummow and Hayne JJ).

[20] Appellants' Submission in *Roadshow Films Pty Ltd v iiNet Ltd*, No S 288 of 2011, 9 September 2011, 3 [13].

[21] Appellants' Submission in *Roadshow Films Pty Ltd v iiNet Ltd*, No S 288 of 2011, 9 September 2011, 19 [72].

[22] Moore (1914a), pp. 276–291 at 278, quoted by Gummow and Hayne JJ in *Roadshow Films Pty Ltd v iiNet Ltd* [2012] HCA 16 at [108]. This passage had also been cited by the High Court previously, in *Brodie v Singleton Shire Council* (2001) 206 CLR 512 at 551.

Next, their Honours looked to the separate judgments of Chief Justice Gleeson, Justice Gaudron, Justice Hayne and Justice Callinan in *Modbury Triangle Shopping Centre Pty Ltd v Anzil* (2000), a personal injury case.[23] They stated that these judgments were "recent affirmations of the general rule of the common law that in the absence of a special relationship one person has no duty to control another person to prevent the doing of damage to a third."[24]

Justices Gummow and Hayne dismissed the appeal, finding for iiNet. They held that only in a very attenuated sense did iiNet have the ability to "control" the primary infringements, and that for this reason, iiNet could not be liable for failing to act to stop the infringements.[25] Their Honours concluded: "The progression urged by the appellants from the evidence, to 'indifference', to 'countenancing', and so to 'authorisation', is too long a march."[26]

11.4   Tort Liability for Omissions to Act

The principle relied upon by Justices Gummow and Hayne that it is rare, in tort, to find liability for pure omissions, has existing High Court authority. In *Modbury Triangle Shopping Centre Pty Ltd v Anzil* (2000), Chief Justice Gleeson said, "[T]he general rule that there is no duty to prevent a third party from harming another is based in part upon a more fundamental principle, which is that the common law does not ordinarily impose liability for omissions."[27]

For the law to impose liability for an omission to act, there must first be a duty to act.[28] The alleged duty should be specific and clearly articulated.[29] In *Roadshow Films v iiNet*, the appellants claimed that iiNet had a duty to do *something* to prevent the infringements, but they did not state to the satisfaction of the High Court what this something was or ought to be. This created a problem in determining the scope of the apparent duty that iiNet owed to the appellants. A similar problem arose in the *Modbury Triangle* case. There, the respondent worked in a video store in a shopping centre owned by the appellant. The shopping centre had a large

---

[23] *Modbury Triangle Shopping Centre Pty Ltd v Anzil* (2000) 205 CLR 254, 264 (Gleeson CJ), 270 (Gaudron J), 292 (Hayne J), 299–300 (Callinan J).

[24] *Roadshow Films Pty Ltd v iiNet Ltd* [2012] HCA 16 at [109] (Gummow and Hayne JJ).

[25] *Roadshow Films Pty Ltd v iiNet Ltd* [2012] HCA 16 at [146] (Gummow and Hayne JJ).

[26] *Roadshow Films Pty Ltd v iiNet Ltd* [2012] HCA 16 at [143].

[27] *Modbury Triangle Shopping Centre Pty. Ltd. v Anzil* (2000) 205 CLR 254, 265 (Gleeson CJ).

[28] "[I]t is not negligent to abstain from doing a thing unless there is some duty to do it." *Sheppard v Glossop Corp* [1921] 3 KB 132, 145 (Scrutton LJ), quoted in *Brodie v Singleton Shire Council* (2001) 206 CLR 512, 621 (Hayne J).

[29] Moore (1914a), pp. 276–291 at 280.

outdoor car park, in which the respondent had parked his car. The car park was lit until 10 pm. On the night in question, the respondent had closed and exited the video store around 10:15 pm. He walked to his car in the dark, and was assaulted and badly injured by three unknown men. The respondent sued the appellant in tort for damages for personal injury, arguing that the appellant should have acted to protect employees by keeping the car park lights on at least until the last employee had left for the evening. A majority of the High Court found that this did not properly define the scope of the purported duty. It was relevant that the shopping centre had ATMs which were accessible by members of the public all night. Chief Justice Gleeson stated, "If the appellant had a duty to prevent criminal harm to people in the position of the first respondent, at the least it would have had to leave the lights on all night; and its responsibilities would have extended beyond that."[30] Justice Callinan said:

> The respondents initially put their submission on the first issue in very broad terms indeed. They said that the scope of the duty of care owed by a landlord in control of commercial premises to employees of its tenants is to minimize the risk of injury to them by criminal acts of third parties, wherever it is reasonably foreseeable that criminal conduct may take place, and the cost of minimizing or eliminating that risk is reasonable.
> The submission goes beyond any formulation of the duty to be found in any of the decided cases of this country.[31]

Justice Hayne, similarly, thought that the duty alleged by the respondent was not a duty to light the car park. "The failure to light the car park was no more than the particular step which the respondents alleged that reasonable care required the appellant to take."[32] Justice Hayne emphasised the difference between a duty and reasonable steps taken in furtherance of a duty. This is a distinction that also applies in the context of authorisation liability—It is the difference between "power to prevent" under s. 101(1A)(a) of the *Copyright Act 1968* and "reasonable steps [taken] to prevent or avoid [infringement]" under s. 101(1A)(c).

In the *iiNet* case, while the appellants declined to specify what exactly iiNet would be required to do to avoid authorising infringement, they indicated that, at the very least, iiNet should have sent warning notices to the subscribers identified by AFACT as infringing copyright. This is akin to the *Modbury Triangle* respondents arguing that the appellant should have prevented the criminal assault at least by leaving the lights on. Like leaving the lights on, sending a warning notice might constitute a step taken in furtherance of a duty, but it is not the duty itself.

---

[30] *Modbury Triangle Shopping Centre Pty. Ltd. v Anzil* (2000) 205 CLR 254, 266–267 (Gleeson CJ).

[31] *Modbury Triangle Shopping Centre Pty. Ltd. v Anzil* (2000) 205 CLR 254, 296–297 (Callinan J.)

[32] *Modbury Triangle Shopping Centre Pty. Ltd. v Anzil* (2000) 205 CLR 254, 291–292 (Hayne J.)

11.5 The Essential Element: Control

In the *iiNet* case, the primary acts of infringement were committed by third parties whose only relationship to iiNet was a contractual one to acquire internet access. It was not alleged that iiNet helped these third parties to infringe copyright by providing them with the software used to share the digital files or by telling them how to copy and share digital files.[33] iiNet had no connection with or control over the BitTorrent protocol used by the infringing subscribers. Rather, the claim was that iiNet had the power to prevent the infringements under s. 101(1A)(a) but did nothing to stop them. A traditional copyright assessment would look to iiNet's contractual power to terminate or suspend infringing subscribers' accounts under the terms of the Customer Relationship Agreement. This, arguably, constitutes a power to prevent the infringements under s. 101(1A)(a). The copyright-based approach is not particularly nuanced, and provides no means of distinguishing between a technical power to prevent infringement of the kind arguable in the iiNet case and the existence of real and actual control over the infringing acts. The concept of actual control has been more thoroughly explored in tort authorities.

Control was a central feature of the tort law cases referred to by Justices Gummow and Hayne in their reasons. In *Brodie v Singleton Shire Council*, a case dealing with the liability of highway authorities, the court focused on whether the highway authority had control "over the source of the risk of harm to those who suffer injury."[34] In that case, the source of the risk was a faulty bridge that had not been repaired. The court ultimately found that the highway authority did have sufficient physical control over the bridge in question, and so was liable for the plaintiff's injuries that had occurred when the bridge collapsed. Justices Gaudron, McHugh and Gummow stated, "[T]he factor of control is of fundamental importance."[35]

In *Modbury*, the court emphasised that the defendant must have some (real) control over the actions of the third party who caused the harm before liability will follow. Chief Justice Gleeson stated that the appellant in that case "had no control over the behaviour of the men who attacked the first respondent, and no knowledge or forewarning of what they planned to do."[36] Justice Hayne noted that the appellant's ability to control the lighting of the car park was central to the respondent's case. However, this misconstrued the issue of control, which was really about whether the appellant could control the men who assaulted the respondent. Justice Hayne found that the duty asserted by the respondent was a duty "to take reasonable

---

[33] *Cf. Metro-Goldwyn-Mayer Studios Inc. v. Grokster Ltd.*, 545 U.S. 913 (2005); *Universal Music Australia Pty Ltd v Sharman License Holdings Ltd.* (2005) 220 ALR 1.

[34] *Brodie v Singleton Shire Council* (2001) 206 CLR 512, 558–559 (Gaudron, McHugh and Gummow JJ).

[35] *Brodie v Singleton Shire Council* (2001) 206 CLR 512, 558–559 (Gaudron, McHugh and Gummow JJ).

[36] *Modbury Triangle Shopping Centre Pty Ltd v Anzil* (2000) 205 CLR 254, 263 (Gleeson CJ).

steps to hinder or prevent criminal conduct of third persons which would injure persons lawfully on the appellant's premises."[37] He held that this amounted to a duty to take steps to affect the conduct of persons over whom the appellant had no control. He concluded, "No such duty has been or should be recognized."[38]

Justice Hayne in *Modbury* highlighted that the ability to control and the ability to hinder are two different things and should not be confused. To hold the appellant liable for failing to take small steps which might have reasonably hindered the offending behaviour would cast the net of tort liability too wide, by holding the appellant responsible for conduct it could not control and where its contribution to the harm was negligible.[39] Justice Hayne emphasised that the coherence of tort law depends upon "the notions of deterrence and individual responsibility."[40] To hold the appellant liable in circumstances where it had not contributed to the wrong would do nothing to further the goal of promoting individual responsibility for one's actions.

Chief Justice Gleeson made a similar point in his reasons. He said, "The respondents submitted that the appellant assumed responsibility for the illumination of the car park. That submission confuses two different meanings of responsibility: capacity and obligation."[41] In other words, while the appellant owned the car park and decided when to turn the car park lights on and off (capacity), that did not mean that the appellant assumed an obligation to care for the security of people in the car park by keeping the lights on to protect them from attack by third parties.

The principle relied upon in both *Modbury* and *iiNet*, that there is no general duty to control a person to prevent them doing harm to another, is derived from a statement made by Justice Dixon in the 1945 case of *Smith v Leurs*. There, Justice Dixon said:

> It is, however, exceptional to find in the law a duty to control another's actions to prevent harm to strangers. The general rule is that one man is under no duty of controlling another man to prevent his doing of damage to a third.[42]

Smith v Leurs was a personal injury case in which a 13-year-old boy (Leurs) had used his toy slingshot to fire a stone at another boy (Smith), hitting him in the eye and seriously damaging his sight. Smith sued Leurs's parents in negligence, for allowing Leurs to play with the slingshot and for failing to control him in his use of

---

[37] *Modbury Triangle Shopping Centre Pty Ltd v Anzil* (2000) 205 CLR 254, 291–292 (Hayne J).

[38] *Modbury Triangle Shopping Centre Pty Ltd v Anzil* (2000) 205 CLR 254, 291–292 (Hayne J). Justice Gaudron, in her reasons, agreed particularly with Justice Hayne's emphasis on "the significance of control over third parties before the law imposes a duty of care to prevent foreseeable damage from their actions": 270.

[39] *Modbury Triangle Shopping Centre Pty Ltd v Anzil* (2000) 205 CLR 254, 293 (Hayne J).

[40] *Modbury Triangle Shopping Centre Pty Ltd v Anzil* (2000) 205 CLR 254, 293 (Hayne J). On this point, Justice Hayne cites Stapleton (1995), pp. 301–345 at 317. See also, Cane (1997), pp. 3 and 25.

[41] *Modbury Triangle Shopping Centre Pty Ltd v Anzil* (2000) 205 CLR 254, 264 (Gleeson CJ).

[42] *Smith v Leurs* (1945) 70 CLR 256, 261–262 (Dixon J).

the slingshot. There was evidence that Leurs's parents had warned their son of the dangers of playing with a slingshot and had forbidden him to use it outside the limits of their home. The court found that this order was a genuine one and reasonable in the circumstances. There was no evidence that the parents could have expected Leurs to disobey them by taking the slingshot outside his home to play with other boys.[43] As in *Modbury Triangle*, the court distinguished between capacity and obligation. Although the parents certainly had the capacity to deny Leurs the possession of a slingshot, the court held that this was not a reasonable expectation. Chief Justice Latham noted that a slingshot "is a common object in boyhood life. Annoyance rather an actual physical harm is the worst that is normally to be expected from its use."[44]

Both *Smith v Leurs* and *Modbury Triangle* raise interesting points for consideration in the *iiNet* case. Did iiNet have real control over the actions of its infringing subscribers? iiNet had contracts with its subscribers that gave it the capacity to terminate subscriber accounts for breaches of the law. Additionally, the iiNet contracts warned subscribers against infringing copyright.[45] There was some debate as to whether this warning was a genuine one—the appellants argued that unless iiNet was willing to impose measures to deter or prevent infringement, then the warning was a toothless tiger; iiNet countered that it would be willing to take steps if directed by a court order, but it would not act as judge, jury and police on the matter.[46] Ultimately, the court held that in this case, capacity to terminate did not amount to obligation to terminate. The relevant factors were that iiNet's control over its subscribers was indirect at best and its control over use of the BitTorrent protocol was non-existent,[47] and that there was a risk of liability for wrongful termination of subscriber contracts.[48]

A lingering issue is the distinction between control and the ability to hinder, and the point at which failure to act to hinder can attract liability. In *iiNet*, the appellants argued strongly that iiNet should have acted within its capacity to impede infringement, at the very least by sending warning notices to subscribers. As a finding of fact, Chief Justice French and Justices Crennan and Kiefel held, "The information contained in the AFACT notices, as and when they were served, did not provide iiNet with a reasonable basis for sending warning notices to individual customers containing threats to suspend or terminate those customers' accounts."[49] The

---

[43] *Smith v Leurs* (1945) 70 CLR 256, 259 (Latham CJ), 265 (McTiernan J).

[44] *Smith v Leurs* (1945) 70 CLR 256, 259 (Latham CJ).

[45] See *Roadshow Films Pty Ltd v iiNet Ltd* [2012] HCA 16 at [27] (French CJ, Crennan and Kiefel JJ (quoting from iiNet's Customer Relationship Agreement, clauses 4.1, 4.2, 14.2, 14.3)); see also at [37], [66]–[67].

[46] *Roadshow Films Pty Ltd v iiNet Ltd* [2012] HCA 16 at [36] (French CJ, Crennan and Kiefel JJ), [96] (Gummow and Hayne JJ).

[47] *Roadshow Films Pty Ltd v iiNet Ltd* [2012] HCA 16 at [69]–[70], [73], [77]–[78] (French CJ, Crennan and Kiefel JJ), [112], [146] (Gummow and Hayne JJ).

[48] *Roadshow Films Pty Ltd v iiNet Ltd* [2012] HCA 16 at [75]–[76] (French CJ, Crennan and Kiefel JJ).

[49] *Roadshow Films Pty Ltd v iiNet Ltd* [2012] HCA 16 at [78].

AFACT notices had failed to specify how the information contained in them had been gathered, and so the court found it reasonable that iiNet had considered the notices to be unreliable.[50] This leaves open the possibility that had the AFACT notices been more detailed or more transparently evidence-based, iiNet may have been compelled to act on them. It remains, unclear, however, what exactly iiNet would be expected to do. It is arguable that even if the AFACT notices had been more substantial, iiNet would not have been authorising infringement by failing to pass them on. All judges of the High Court were extremely critical of the appellant's reliance on the "countenance" aspect of the *Moorhouse* definition of authorisation ("sanction, approve, countenance").[51] It seems likely that the action (or inaction) of an ISP would need to rise to the level of at least "sanctioning" or "approving" infringement before liability would follow, though what exactly that involves is unsettled.

In determining whether iiNet had taken reasonable steps to prevent the infringements, Chief Justice French and Justices Crennan and Kiefel also placed some emphasis on the wording of s. 101(1A)(c), which includes consideration of "whether the person complied with any relevant industry codes of practice." Their Honours noted "the absence of any industry code of practice adhered to by all ISPs."[52] This suggests that had iiNet been a party to an industry code, their Honours may have read s. 101(1A)(c) to create a duty to adhere to that industry code. Failure to do so might therefore constitute a breach of that duty and provide strong evidence that iiNet failed to take reasonable steps to prevent the infringements, thereby giving rise to legal liability for authorisation.[53]

Justices Gummow and Hayne were more definitive in their conclusion on warning notices. They held that the failure to pass on warning notices did not go to the heart of the matter; warning might or might not have had the effect of forestalling further infringements.[54] iiNet did not have control over how users behaved and there was no evidence as to how users were likely to behave in response to warning notices. "In truth, the only indisputably practical course of action would be an exercise of contractual power to switch off and terminate further activity on suspect accounts. But this would not merely avoid further infringement; it would deny to the iiNet customers non-infringing uses of the iiNet facilities."[55] Their Honours' exercise in distinguishing the small act of passing on warning notices from the broader apparent duty of (contractually) controlling users to

---

[50] *Roadshow Films Pty Ltd v iiNet Ltd* [2012] HCA 16 at [34].

[51] *Roadshow Films Pty Ltd v iiNet Ltd* [2012] HCA 16 at [67]–[68] (French CJ, Crennan and Kiefel JJ), [125] (Gummow and Hayne JJ).

[52] *Roadshow Films Pty Ltd v iiNet Ltd* [2012] HCA 16 at [71] (French CJ, Crennan and Kiefel JJ), see also [139] (Gummow and Hayne JJ).

[53] Although it should be noted that commentators have argued that industry codes requiring ISPs to pass on warning notices and take other measures (including terminating user accounts) are unlikely to be formed post-*iiNet*, given the strong position that ISPs now find themselves in: *see, e.g.,* Lindsay (2012), pp. 53.1–53.24 at 53.18.

[54] *Roadshow Films Pty Ltd v iiNet Ltd* [2012] HCA 16 at [138] (Gummow and Hayne JJ).

[55] *Roadshow Films Pty Ltd v iiNet Ltd* [2012] HCA 16 at [139] (Gummow and Hayne JJ).

prevent infringement is similar to the distinction that Justice Hayne drew in *Modbury Triangle* between the act of leaving the car park light on and the broader purported duty of preventing harm caused by third parties outside the occupant's control. Ultimately, the core consideration is not what small acts iiNet could have done to hinder infringement, but whether iiNet had a specific duty to act in this way.[56]

11.6   Control in Tort and Control in Copyright: Same or Different?

Control has long been a central feature of authorisation liability in Australia. It was central to the findings in *University of New South Wales v Moorhouse*, and the accepted understanding of s. 101(1A)(a) of the *Copyright Act 1968*, which directs a court to consider a person's "power to prevent" the infringement, is that it deals primarily with control. It is reasonable to inquire, then, as to why Justices Gummow and Hayne saw fit to consider the principle of control in tort law when applying the authorisation doctrine in *Roadshow Films v iiNet*, particularly when Australian courts have traditionally rejected the relevance of tort law to intermediary copyright liability. If copyright has its own conception of control, separate to that in tort, is it really helpful to resort to tort law principles?

Tort law principles help in this area because tort's notion of control is more rigorous than that currently found in copyright law. Power to prevent in the *Copyright Act 1968*, for example, speaks to capacity, not obligation. It says nothing about what an intermediary *ought* to do. Tort law's concept of control, on the other hand, is influenced by notions of deterrence and individual responsibility, which ask firstly whether a person has acted wrongfully in his or her exercise of control and secondly what the wider ramifications of imposing liability will be. Is it proper that the person be held liable? How will that person (and persons in similar situations) alter their behavior in response to liability, and is that desirable for the fluid functioning of society? These are public policy question that copyright law provides little scope to ask.[57]

---

[56] This is a point that Justice Hayne made clear in oral arguments (addressing counsel for the appellants): "You cannot take these matters to account in determining whether there is authorisation without first having your concept of what constitutes authorisation. Now, the arguments you have been presently advancing seek to begin with questions of reasonable steps, fasten upon the fact that there is no response to your notice, but then seem, if I may say so, Mr. Bannon, to slide imperceptibly by the word "therefore" to the conclusion that there is authorization." *Roadshow Films Pty Ltd v iiNet Ltd* [2011] HCATrans 323 (30 November 2011).

[57] These questions are sometimes raised in intermediary copyright liability cases, but analysis tends to fall into what Julie Cohen calls the liberty/efficiency binary—either arguments favor finding intermediaries liable to the full extent that they are able to prevent infringement in some way, because this would be economically efficient, or they disfavor finding liability on the grounds

Further, copyright law tends to confuse power to prevent under s. 101(1A)(a) with reasonable steps under s. 101(1A)(c). If causation is not properly addressed,[58] then some reasonable steps may mistakenly be held to affect power to prevent. For example, sending warning notices to internet users might be perceived to have some impact on levels of infringement, so an intermediary might be held liable for authorisation for failing to warn, notwithstanding that this is not a real power to prevent. On one view, iiNet came close to being held liable for this very thing—had there been an industry protocol in place or had the AFACT notices been more comprehensive, it is possible that some judges may have been willing to hold iiNet liable for failing to take any action at all to impede infringement. But this would ignore the fact that no duty to act had been established. In this scenario, iiNet has no greater level of control than it did before. The reasonable steps consideration should not operate to preempt control.

If we view s. 101(1A) through the lens of tort law, however, it becomes clear the way in which paragraphs (a) and (c) relate to each other for omissions to act.[59] Paragraph (a) sets up whether there is a duty to act to prevent infringement (a duty which depends heavily on control) and paragraph (c) considers whether that duty has been fulfilled (or breached) by examining the steps taken by the intermediary. Without a *duty* to act, there can be no breach for failing to act and thus no authorisation.

Where it is claimed that one person should be legally responsible for the acts of another, the duty of care of that person is intimately linked to the level of control he or she is able to exercise over the third party. Duty is dependent on control. Control, therefore, must be clearly defined—control *over what or whom*; control *how*. Power to prevent in copyright is not so specific. Power to prevent can be as straightforward as an on/off switch—technically, iiNet had a power to prevent infringement by terminating user accounts. The power to prevent inquiry is an exercise in ticking a box; it does not call for the same level of careful scrutiny as does the question of control. The *iiNet* High Court—even those judges who did not explicitly refer to tort principles—appeared to be more influenced by a tort conception of control than the copyright concept of power to prevent,[60] and in this sense they diverged from existing approaches to authorisation liability. Under copyright, iiNet had a power to

---

that technology intermediaries need extensive freedom to operate and innovate. See Cohen (2012), pp. 129–153. A tort law analysis may provide a more careful way to interrogate these concerns without automatically favoring copyright holders or intermediaries. Importantly, it may provide scope to consider the interests of internet users within the authorization doctrine.

[58] See further Sect. 11.7.1 below.

[59] For consideration of paragraph (b), see Sect. 11.7.2 below.

[60] See, for example, the exchange between Justice Kiefel and the counsel for the appellants during oral arguments: "Kiefel J: But you have to say control over what. Control over their ability to --- Mr. Bannon: Infringe, yes. Kiefel J: Well, their ability to access the internet. Mr. Bannon: Yes, to access the internet. Kiefel J: That is rather a step removed from their ability to infringe which requires more.": *Roadshow Films Pty. Ltd. v iiNet Limited* [2011] HCATrans 323 (30 November 2011).

prevent infringement by terminating the accounts of infringing subscribers. Under a notion of control influenced by tort law, iiNet did not have a sufficient degree of control over the actions of subscribers for a duty to act to arise.[61] iiNet had no control over the BitTorrent software or the copyrighted content shared by users over BitTorrent. It could not supervise the many subscribers' uses of the BitTorrent software. It could warn, but that is not control. Or it could use its contractual power to terminate the subscribers' accounts, which is a step ill-adapted to the problem. The *iiNet* case is a cogent example of the differences between control under tort and control under copyright, and the poorly defined scope of the latter. This is interesting because a theory of control influenced by tort law could help to bring cohesion and clarity to the doctrine of authorisation liability in Australia.

11.7 Other Points to Note

11.7.1 Causation

It is useful to include a brief note on causation. In negligence cases, the plaintiff must establish that the defendant's breach of his or her duty caused the harm suffered by the plaintiff. Harrison Moore has argued that where the breach is an omission to act, it will be particularly difficult to show that the omission caused the harm.[62] This was illustrated in the *Modbury Triangle* case, where both Chief Justice Gleeson and Justice Hayne expressed doubt as to whether illuminating the car park would have deterred the assailants.[63] Chief Justice Gleeson noted that "facilitate" and "cause" are not the same thing—"[T]he appellant's omission to leave the lights on might have facilitated the crime, as did its decision to provide a car park, and the first respondent's decision to park there. But it was not a cause of the first respondent's injuries."[64] The same point can be made with respect to ISPs like iiNet: while the provision of internet access might have facilitated the infringements, it cannot be said to have caused the infringements. Further, it is not certain that sending warning notices would have deterred infringers or potential infringers.[65] Something more would be required before liability would attach to an ISP in iiNet's position.

---

[61] This is not to say that an ISP will never be liable under a tort-influenced doctrine of authorization. Each case depends on its facts.

[62] Moore (1914b), pp. 415–432 at 416.

[63] *Modbury Triangle Shopping Centre Pty. Ltd. v Anzil* (2000) 205 CLR 254, 263 (Gleeson CJ), 90–291 (Hayne J) ("The conduct of criminal assailants is not necessarily dictated by reason or prudential considerations.").

[64] *Modbury Triangle Shopping Centre Pty. Ltd. v Anzil* (2000) 205 CLR 254, 269 (Gleeson CJ).

[65] See *Roadshow Films Pty Ltd v iiNet Ltd* [2012] HCA 16 at [138] (Gummow and Hayne JJ).

11.7.2   Special Relationship

For omissions to act, the general rule is that in the absence of a special relationship there is no duty to control one person to prevent the doing of damage to another.[66] Tort law recognizes certain categories of special relationships where one person may be held responsible for the conduct of another—these include parents and children,[67] school authorities and pupils,[68] and prison wardens and prisoners.[69] However, while courts may recognise a duty of care arising in particular fact circumstances, it is rare for new categories of "special relationships" to be established in tort.

It is unlikely that a special relationship would ever be shown to exist between copyright intermediaries (especially "passive" intermediaries) and their users, in the sense of a discrete category of relationship under tort. In copyright, the notion of special relationship, particularly in the context of s. 101(1A)(b) which directs courts to consider "the nature of any relationship existing between the person and the person who did the act concerned," is best understood as a reference to the closeness of the relationship between the intermediary and the copyright infringer in so far as that helps to establish or deny a relationship of control.

11.7.3   Unresolved Issues: The Importance of Foreseeability

The dissenting judge in *Modbury Triangle*, Justice Kirby, discussed at length the relevance of the appellant's knowledge or foresight of the harmful actions of the third parties.[70] His Honor stated that the more notice that is provided, the greater the foresight and the more likely it is that the defendant will be liable for failing to

---

[66] *Roadshow Films Pty Ltd v iiNet Ltd* [2012] HCA 16 at [109]; *Modbury Triangle Shopping Centre Pty Ltd v Anzil* (2000) 205 CLR 254, 264 (Gleeson CJ), 270 (Gaudron J), 292 (Hayne J), 299–300 (Callinan J); *Smith v Leurs* (1945) 70 CLR 256, 261–262 (Dixon J).

[67] *Smith v Leurs* (1945) 70 CLR 256, 259 (Latham CJ), 260 (Starke J), 262 (Dixon J); *McHale v Watson* (1964) 11 CLR 384; *Cameron v Comm'r for Rys.* [1964] Qd R 480.

[68] *Commonwealth v Introvigne* (1982) 150 CLR 258; *Geyer v Downs* (1978) 138 CLR 91; *Carmarthenshire County Council v Lewis* [1955] AC 549.

[69] *Home Office v Dorset Yacht Co. Ltd.* [1970] AC 1004; *Ralph v Strutton* [1969] Qd R 348; *New South Wales v Godfrey* (2004) Aust. Torts Reports ¶81–741. See also *Modbury Triangle Shopping Centre Pty. Ltd. v Anzil* (2000) 205 CLR 254, 292 (Hayne J); *cf. Howard v Jarvis* (1958) 98 CLR 177; *Hall v Whatmore* [1961] VR 225.

[70] Justice Kirby referred to evidence that the appellant was aware of the opening hours of the video store and that the respondent worked alone and was required to handle significant amounts of cash; that repeated complaints had been made to the appellant about the lights being turned off too early, accompanied by requests that the lights be kept on until employees had left work; and that in the months preceding the attack, a car window had been smashed, two attempts had been made to break into the ATMs, and a nearby restaurant had been broken into. *Modbury Triangle Shopping Centre Pty. Ltd. v Anzil* (2000) 205 CLR 254, 271–273, 286 (Kirby J).

respond.[71] Justice Kirby also noted that knowledge, or reasonable foreseeability, was a dominant factor in similar US tort cases.[72] This chapter has focused on control, because control has always been the more important element in authorisation liability in Australia.[73] However, knowledge was also a relevant element in the *Moorhouse* case, and featured in the *iiNet* case in relation to the adequacy of the AFACT notices. An interesting question is the extent to which an emphasis on knowledge or foresight might impact upon findings of liability in some cases. This is part of a larger project on intermediary copyright liability and the subject of another paper.

Additionally, it should be noted that the analysis in this chapter is relevant to ISPs and similar "passive" intermediaries. It does not consider those intermediaries that deliberately avoid control, like the defendants in *Metro-Goldwyn-Mayer Studios Inc. v. Grokster*.[74] Different considerations may (and probably should) apply for "bad actors". This, too, is the subject of another paper.

11.8 Conclusion

In the internet age, copyright owners are increasingly looking to online intermediaries to take steps to prevent copyright infringement. Sometimes these intermediaries are closely tied to the acts of infringement; sometimes—as in the case of ISPs—they are not. In 2012, the Australian High Court decided the *Roadshow Films v iiNet* case, in which it held that an Australian ISP was not liable under copyright's authorisation doctrine which asks whether the intermediary has sanctioned, approved or countenanced the infringement. The Australian *Copyright Act 1968* directs a court to consider, in these situations, whether the intermediary had the power to prevent the infringement and whether it took any reasonable steps to prevent or avoid the infringement. It is generally not difficult for a court to find the power to prevent infringement—power to prevent can include an unrefined technical ability to disconnect users from the copyright source, such as an ISP terminating users' internet accounts. In the *iiNet* case, the High Court eschewed this broad approach in favor of focusing on a notion of control which, I have argued, was strongly influenced by principles of tort law. This is an important shift in the

---

[71] *Modbury Triangle Shopping Centre Pty. Ltd. v Anzil* (2000) 205 CLR 254, 283–284 (Kirby J).

[72] *Modbury Triangle Shopping Centre Pty. Ltd. v Anzil* (2000) 205 CLR 254, 277–278 (Kirby J), referring to *Lillie v. Thompson*, 332 US 459 (1947); *Kline v. 1500 Massachusetts Avenue Apartment Corp*, 439 F. 2d 477 (1970); *McClung v Delta Square Ltd. P'ship*, 937 SW 2d 891 (1996); *Ann M v. Pac. Plaza Shopping Center*, 863 P. 2d 207 (1993); *Butler v Acme Markets, Inc.* 445 A. 2d 1141 (1982); *Nivens v 7-11 Hoagy's Corner*, 943 P. 2d 286 (1997); *Piggly Wiggly Southern, Inc. v. Snowden*, 464 SE 2d 220 (1995); *Holley v. Mt Zion Terrace Apartments, Inc.*, 382 So. 2d 98 (1980).

[73] *See University of N.S.W v Moorhouse* (1975) 6 ALR 193.

[74] 545 U.S. 913 (2005).

Australian analysis of intermediary copyright liability, which has never given much emphasis to potential overlap with tort law.

In tort, when a plaintiff asserts that a defendant should be liable for failing to act to prevent harm caused to the plaintiff by a third party, there is a heavy burden on the plaintiff to show that the defendant had a duty to act. The duty must be clear and specific, and will often hinge on the degree of control that the defendant was able to exercise over the third party. Control in these circumstances relates directly to control over the third party's actions in inflicting the harm. Thus, in iiNet's case, the control would need to be directed to the third party's infringing use of BitTorrent; control over a person's ability to access the internet is too imprecise.

Further, when considering omissions to act, tort law differentiates between the ability to control and the ability to hinder. The ability to control may establish a duty to act, and the court will then look to small measures taken to prevent the harm to determine whether these satisfy the duty. But the ability to hinder will not suffice to establish liability in the absence of control.

Just as a tort plaintiff must show a breach of a duty in order to succeed in a negligence action, a copyright plaintiff should be able to point to a duty and breach before succeeding in an authorisation claim against a "passive" intermediary like an ISP. This is appropriate because intermediary liability suits are not like other copyright infringement claims. Intermediary liability cases can have far-reaching ramifications for users who are not parties to the case but on whose allegedly infringing behavior the action is based. Where a court holds that an intermediary must take measures to terminate user accounts or to alter its products or services to impede infringement, then users who have not infringed copyright or who would otherwise have a viable defense to infringement may find their ability to access online services for communication, work and other facets of an internet-enabled life severely constrained. Plaintiffs should therefore be held to an appropriately high standard of proof, to counter the risks of harm to society that an uncertain and easy-to-establish intermediary liability doctrine can pose. In Australia, there needs to be a more coherent framework for determining the copyright liability of intermediaries, especially so-called "passive" intermediaries. Copyright's current approaches are unclear and unpredictable, resulting in an ill-defined scope of liability. Concepts of duty and control informed by tort law may provide the additional benchmarks that copyright law currently lacks.

References

Journal Articles

Bridy A (2010) Copyright policymaking as procedural democratic process: a discourse-theoretic perspective on ACTA, SOPA and PIPA. Cardozo Arts Entertain Law J 30:153–164

Burrell R, Weatherall K (2008) Exporting controversy? Reactions to the copyright provisions of the U.S.–Australia Free Trade Agreement: lessons for U.S. trade policy. Univ Ill J Law Tech Policy 2:259–319

Giblin R (2009) The uncertainties, baby: hidden perils of Australia's authorization law. Aust Intellect Prop J 20:148–177

Ginsburg J, Ricketson S (2006) Inducers and authorisers: a comparison of the US Supreme Court's Grokster decision and the Australian Federal Court's KaZaa Ruling. Media Arts Law Rev 11:1–25

Koneru P (1996) The right "To Authorize" in U.S. copyright law: questions of contributory infringement and extraterritoriality. IDEA 37(1):87–131

Lindsay D (2012) ISP liability for end-user copyright infringements: the High Court Decision in Roadshow Films v iiNet. Telecomm J Aust 62(4):53.1–53.24

Moore H (1914a) Misfeasance and non-feasance in the liability of public authorities. Law Q Rev 30:276–291

Moore H (1914b) Misfeasance and non-feasance in the liability of public authorities (part 2). Law Q Rev 30:415–432

Rimmer M (2006) Robbery under arms: copyright law and the Australia–United States Free Trade Agreement. First Monday 11(3) http://firstmonday.org/ojs/index.php/fm/article/view/1316/1236

Stapleton J (1995) Duty of care: peripheral parties and alternative opportunities for deterrence. Law Q Rev 111:301–345

Books and Chapters

Cane P (1997) The anatomy of tort law. Oxford Press, Oxford

Cohen JE, Loren LP, Okediji RL, O'Rourke MA (2010) Copyright in a global information economy, 3rd edn. Aspen Publishers, New York, p 476

Cohen JE (2012) Configuring the networked citizen. In: Sarat A, Douglas L, Umphey M (eds) Imagining new legalities: privacy and its possibilities in the 21st century. Stanford University Press, Stanford, pp 129–153

Chapter 12
Time Shifting in a Networked Digital World: Optus TV Now and Copyright in the Cloud

Sampsung Xiaoxiang Shi

12.1 Introduction

Technological change has a habit of challenging the law. In times of agitation or upheaval, the law in many instances retreats to what is known or stated from the past; sometimes with a damaging effect on the use of new technologies. A technology that has posed challenges for the law in recent years is known as "cloud computing". In particular, its widespread adoption by consumers, along with relevant business models built around it, has raised new issues for the law of copyright.[1]

A current example of one of these issues involves the recording of TV broadcasts. The established practice for recording television broadcasts is through the use of VCRs or DVRs in the comfort of our own lounge rooms. In July 2011 however, SingTel Optus Pty Limited ("Optus"), one of Australia's largest telecommunication companies, launched a free-to-air TV recording service.[2] This service allowed its subscribers to record their favourite TV shows "in the cloud" on Optus' remote servers. The convenience of this service for subscribers was obvious—by storing the recorded show in the cloud (i.e. in a remote location accessible via the Internet) subscribers had the ability to watch the show "anytime, anywhere" on a wide range of Internet-enabled devices. Given the series of litigation targeting similar services

---

[1] For example, see *RTL Deutschland v. Save.TV Ltd*, (OLG Dresden 14 U 801/07 Urteil vom 12.07.2011—RTL gegen Save.tv); *Cartoon Network, LP, et al. v. CSC Holdings, Inc. et al.*, 536 F.3d 121 (2d Cir. 2008), rev'g *Twentieth Century Fox Film Corp. v. Cablevision Sys. Corp.*, 478 F. Supp. 2d 607, 624 (S.D.N.Y. 2007); *RecordTV Pte Ltd v MediaCorp TV Singapore Pte Ltd*, [2010] 2 SLR 15; [2010] SGCA 43. See also, Chessell (2011).

[2] See Optus' official website http://www.optus.com.au.

S.X. Shi (✉)
East China University of Political Science and Law, Room 416, Chongfa Building,
555 Longyuan Rd., Songjiang District, 201620 Shanghai, China
e-mail: sampsung@outlook.com

© Springer International Publishing Switzerland 2015   261
B. Fitzgerald, J. Gilchrist (eds.), *Copyright Perspectives*,
DOI 10.1007/978-3-319-15913-3_12

in the United States, Singapore and Germany in the past few years,[3] it is not surprising that the controversy of the TV Now service had been brought to Australian courts. On 1 February 2012, Justice Rares of the Federal Court of Australia handed down his decision.[4] However, this decision was overturned by the Full Court of the Federal Court on 27 April 2012.[5] It has been reported that Optus is likely to appeal to the High Court of Australia.[6] This is the first time that the legality of cloud storage and services is being tested in an Australian court, and for this reason the court's decision is likely to have set a precedent in Australian copyright law.[7]

What Optus offered is what copyright scholars commonly refer to as "time shifting". Time shifting—the making of a recording of a broadcast for the purpose of watching the broadcast at a more convenient time—is a common practice amongst individuals. It is exempted from copyright infringement claims by section 111 of the *Copyright Act 1968* (Cth) of Australia provided that the recording is made for private and domestic use only. However, Optus' service moved time shifting from the home to the "cloud" and built a business model around it. This raises questions about whether the s 111 exemption extends to this activity, occasions uncertainty about the application of other copyright law doctrines and challenges some established commercial arrangements between copyright owners and content distributors.

This chapter will undertake a comparative analysis of the legal principles that underpin this case under Australian copyright law and similar cases in the United States and Singapore. It aims to explore how copyright law has been struggling to adapt to solve problems raised by the advent of cloud recording technologies.

12.2 Optus TV Now: The Technology

In essence, the "TV Now" service enabled users to pre-select and record free-to-air television programs, so that the programs could be watched at a more convenient time. The recorded programs could be watched on all kinds of Internet-enabled devices, ranging from smartphones to laptops and iPads.[8] The service involved a complex recording system created and maintained by Optus. A user who subscribed

---

[3] For example, see *supra* note 1.

[4] *Singtel Optus Pty Ltd v National Rugby League Investments Pty Ltd* ("Optus v. NRL") [2012] FCA 34.

[5] *National Rugby League Investments Pty Limited v Singtel Optus Pty Ltd* [2012] FCAFC 59.

[6] Christensenr (2012). See also, Adhikari (2012).

[7] Australian Copyright Council, *Optus dispute with AFL, NRL and Telstra scheduled for December* (28 September, 2011) http://www.copyright.org.au/news-and-policy/details/id/2007/ (16 January, 2012).

[8] The general function of the TV Now system is that it "allows you the freedom to record TV shows anytime, anywhere to play back later at your convenience wherever and whenever you

to this service could log into the service through the Optus myZoo portal using a computer or through an appropriate application installed in a suitable mobile device. After logging in, they would be directed to an electronic program guide or schedule, featuring future television programs on free-to-air channels. Subscribers could then navigate the guide to look for and select the television program to be recorded by clicking on the "Record" button. When the selected program was on air, the recording system would automatically make the recording in four different formats to suit the various devices. Once a user requested to view the recorded program, the TV Now system would transmit a stream of data in the suitable format from Optus' datacentre to the subscriber's device. If no user had instructed that a program to be recorded, no recording would occur.[9]

Optus explained that the availability of channels available to a subscriber on Optus TV Now depended on where the subscriber lived and which TV shows they were already able to view in this region.[10] Subscribers were warned that once a TV show had commenced, they would not be able to start recording that show.[11] They were also unable to access TV listings or record shows from other regions.[12] Once subscribed however, they could watch their recordings anywhere in Australia, so long as they were within an Optus coverage area. The recorded programs would expire and be automatically deleted from the subscriber's list thirty (30) days after recording.[13]

In effect, Optus TV Now had offered its subscribers a time shifting service which in many ways is "similar" to the existing technology including digital video recorder (DVR) or video cassette recorder (VCR). On the other hand, the differences between the new and the old technology are obvious. Unlike the old devices which have largely been superceded by the current market, this new service is empowered by the so-called "mobile cloud computing" technology.[14] It is a complex system combining "cloud computing"[15] with mobile devices. The TV

---

want". See further, What is Optus TV Now http://www.optus.com.au/home/digital-life/tv-now/?sid=HAFeat1:tvnow:OSC:MPOST:OCA:MPOST:19072011 (16 January, 2012).

[9] However, temporary recording may occur for no more than 60 sec in the case of the Apple QuickTime Streaming server. See, [2012] FCA 34, 34.

[10] Ibid.

[11] Ibid.

[12] Ibid.

[13] Ibid.

[14] For further discussion about mobile cloud computing, please see Chang and Park (2011), p. 24; Huang (2011), p. 27, and Kumar and Lu (2011), p. 31.

[15] Cloud computing, as the Australian Academy of Technological Sciences and Engineering (ATSE) explains, "provides a means of accessing a shared pool of configurable computing resources (including networks, servers, storage applications and services) that can be rapidly provided, used and released with minimal effort on the part of users or service providers". See further, Australian Academy of Technological Sciences and Engineering (ATSE), *Cloud Computing: Opportunities and Challenges for Australia* (September 2010) http://www.atse.org.au/resource-centre/func-startdown/263/. See also, Velte et al. (2009), pp. 69–77. See also, Mell and Grace (2011).

Now service offered by Optus is substantially similar to the "Remote Storage" Digital Video Recorder system ("RS-DVR") developed by Cablevision Systems Corporation in the United Sates ("Cablevision")[16] and the Internet-based Digital Video Recorder system ("iDVR") provided by RecordTV Pte Ltd in Singapore ("RecordTV").[17]

Although it carried a "diverse and exciting potential for consumer cloud services",[18] its disruptive power to the established business was apparent to many other stakeholders. For example, this service worried content owners and distributors who asserted that Optus was infringing their rights.[19] In pre-empting a copyright infringement suit against it, Optus, in August 2011, brought an action in the Federal Court of Australia seeking a declaration[20] that its TV Now service was lawful. In response, the Australian Football League (AFL), the National Rugby League (NRL) and Telstra filed cross claims in September.[21] They feared that the service would devalue their exclusive rights in streaming sporting events on the

---

[16] The RS-DVR, developed by Cablevision around March 2006, was a system that used a technology akin to both traditional, set-top digital video recorders like TiVo ("DVRs") and the video on demand ("VOD") services provided by many cable companies. The RS-DVR system allowed Cablevision customers who did not have a stand-alone DVR to record cable programming on central hard drives housed and maintained by Cablevision at a remote location. RS-DVR customers could then receive playback of those programs through their home television sets, using only a remote control and a standard cable box equipped with the RS-DVR software. A group of companies in the television and film industries brought suit against Cablevision, seeking declarative and injunctive relief on the grounds of direct copyright infringement. The plaintiffs claimed that Cablevision, through the operation of its RS-DVR system, would directly infringe their copyrights by making unauthorized reproductions and public performances of their copyrighted works. See, *Cartoon Network, LP, et al. v. CSC Holdings, Inc. et al.*, 536 F.3d 121 (2d Cir. 2008), rev'g *Twentieth Century Fox Film Corp. v. Cablevision Sys. Corp.*, 478 F. Supp. 2d 607, 624 (S.D.N.Y. 2007).

[17] In Singapore, RecordTV Pte Ltd marketed a similar service called iDVR. The iDVR system allowed its registered users to request the recording of MediaCorp TV Singapore's free-to-air broadcasts in Singapore. The broadcasts were recorded on RecordTV's iDVR, which functioned like a traditional digital video recorder ("DVR"), namely, a registered user could select a programme to record, play back and/or delete. The main difference between RecordTV's iDVR and a traditional DVR was that the former was a remote-storage DVR. This meant that the recording was made at RecordTV's premises, with the registered users operating the iDVR system remotely from home or elsewhere via a web browser. In July and September 2007, MediaCorp sent RecordTV cease and desist letters, alleging copyright infringement. In response, RecordTV launched a court action for groundless threats of infringement. See, *RecordTV Pte Ltd v MediaCorp TV Singapore Pte Ltd*, [2010] 2 SLR 15; [2010] SGCA 43.

[18] See also, Currie (2011).

[19] Chessell (2011).

[20] For further information on groundless threats of legal proceedings in relation to copyright infringement, see *Copyright Act of 1968* (Cth) s 202.

[21] The claims and documents filed with Federal Court of Australia, New South Wales Registry can be found here https://www.comcourts.gov.au/file/Federal/P/NSD1430/2011/actions (16 January, 2012). See also, *Optus moves to protect TV Now* (30 August, 2011) The Sydney Morning Herald http://www.smh.com.au/business/optus-moves-to-protect-tv-now-20110829-1jii3.html.

Internet, a lucrative investment for content distributors.[22] Telstra Corporation even threatened to tear up its new $153 million deal with AFL and refuse to consider the potential deal with the NRL for exclusive rights to stream matches live over the Internet, if the TV Now service were to continue in its present form.[23]

12.3   The Legal Issues: Potential Infringement

The central copyright issue in this case, as pointed out by Justice Rares, was whether Optus, through the operation of its TV Now service, infringed the copyright interests of the rightholders. The court was then asked to adjudicate upon seven sub-issues[24]:

1. Who did the acts involved in recording the NRL broadcasts, AFL broadcasts and AFL films for the operation of the TV Now service?
2. Does s 111 mean that the recording was not an infringement of copyright? If s 111(2) [of *Copyright Act 1968* (Cth)] does not apply, is Optus liable for copyright infringement by way of authorisation?
3. When the recording was viewed, who did the acts of electronically transmitting the Copyright Works?
4. When recordings were streamed to a user, was this a communication "to the public"?
5. Did Optus make the Copyright Works available online?
6. If the answer to 5 is "yes", was this to the public?
7. Is the digital file comprising the NRL footage streamed to users an "article" within the meaning of s 103 or an "article or thing" within the meaning of s 111 (3)(d) and, if so, was it distributed for the purpose of trade?

In terms of sub-issues 1, 3, 4, 5 and 6, Justice Rares found that (a) it was the user of the TV Now service, not Optus, who made each recording of a broadcast by clicking on the "Record" button on their device; (b) it was the user, rather than Optus, who transmitted the recording they had recorded; (c) the electronic transmission was not "to the public" and thus not infringing. With regard to sub-issues 2 and 7, his Honour decided that the user did not infringe copyright by making recordings of the broadcasts because it is allowed under s 111, and the subsequent dealing of the recording did not breach s 111(3)(d). In conclusion, his Honour held that Optus' TV Now service did not infringe copyright interests owned by the AFL, NRL and Telstra.[25]

---

[22] See, Edwards (2011a). See also, Edwards (2011b), and Chessell (2011), The Australian.

[23] Battersby (2011).

[24] [2012] FCA 34, 45.

[25] However, this holding did not cover the issue of the temporary copies made in the format suitable for certain Apple devices and stored temporarily for up to 10 sec duration every minute.

Nonetheless, the first instance decision was overturned by the Full Court of the
Federal Court. The full bench of the Federal Court (Justices Emmett, Finn and
Bennett) delivered a unanimous joint judgment that the TV Now service infringed
copyright and Optus could not rely on the specific copyright exception in s 111. The
Full Court reached this conclusion by means of merely focusing on the question of
whether it was Optus or the subscriber that made the copy of each TV broadcast
through the TV Now service. The Full Court determined that "[t]he maker was
Optus or, in the alternative, it was Optus and the subscriber" and "[i]t is unnecessary
for present purposes to express a definitive view as between the two".[26] The
Australian courts' rulings and reasoning share extensive similarities with the
opinion of the judges in the United States and Singapore, yet, substantial variations
are also noticeable. In the following section of this article, these similarities and
variations will be closely examined. The ultimate purpose of doing so is not only to
see how the law operates in different jurisdictions, but to explore how the law can
accommodate technological change and innovation.

12.3.1 Potential Infringement by Copying: Who Did the Acts of Recording?

One of the first and foremost acts covered by copyright is the act of reproduction or
copying.[27] Under the *Copyright Act 1986* (*Cth*) of Australia, reproduction and
copying are governed by the exclusive right to "reproduce the work in material
form" for Pt III works (s 31), and the right to "make a copy" for sound recordings
and cinematograph films (ss 85–86), or the right to "make a cinematograph film of
the broadcast, or a copy of such a film" for sound and television broadcasts) (s 87).
It is apparent that, via the TV Now system, cinematograph films of TV broadcasts
and copyright works included in the broadcasts are being made. This leads us to the
question as to whether the exclusive right of making copies (which subsists in the
broadcasts) and the right of reproduction (which subsists in the copyright materials
on which the broadcasts are based) are infringed. This question can be answered
through the determination of two issues: (1) who did the acts of recording (the
making of the cinematograph films of the broadcasts)? and (2) is the making of the
recordings allowable under copyright law? Issue 1 will be dealt with here, while
issue 2 will be discussed in the next section of this chapter.

This issue was separated from the issued considered in this decision. See, [2012] FCA 34, 34 and
114.

[26] [2012] FCAFC 59, 4.

[27] Although people may say the term "reproduction" and the term "copying" share the same
meaning in common sense, as discussed below, they are used in different contexts in Australian
copyright law.

While determining who did the acts of recording, Justice Rares referred to relevant foreign cases.[28] In *Cartoon Network, LP, et al. v. CSC Holdings, Inc. et al.*,[29] a similar case decided by the courts in the United States, the plaintiffs claimed that by copying programs onto hard disks of the RS-DVR system upon the request of its customer, Cablevision directly infringed their reproduction right. Cablevision defended itself by saying that the creation of hard drive copies was done by consumers with remote controls in their own homes. This argument was not accepted by the U.S. District Court for the Southern District of New York ("District Court"), and a summary judgment was awarded to the plaintiffs and Cablevision was enjoined from operating the RS-DVR system.[30] Cablevision appealed to the Court of Appeals for the Second Circuit ("Circuit Court"). On appeal, the decision of the District Court was reversed by the Circuit Court (for the reasons discussed below). In order to assess infringement of the reproduction right, first of all, the Circuit Court's attention was drawn to the question: who made the copies?

12.3.1.1 Determining the Volitional Conduct That Causes a Copy to Be Made: The United States & Singapore Precedents

The Circuit Court noted that "[a]fter an RS-DVR subscriber selects a program to record, and that program airs, a copy of the program – a copyrighted work – resides on the hard disks of Cablevision's Arroyo Server, its creation unauthorized by the copyright holder".[31] However, "[t]he question is who made this copy".[32] At trial, the District Court was of the opinion that due to Cablevision's unfettered discretion over the choosing of the content for recording, its volitional design, operation and maintenance of the RS-DVR system, and its "continuing relationship" with its RS-DVR customers, the copying of programming to the RS-DVR system was done not by the customer but by Cablevision, albeit at the customer's request.[33]

---

[28] These include *Network Ten Pty Ltd v TCN Channel Nine Pty Ltd* (2004) 218 CLR 273 at 287 [29] per McHugh A-CJ, Gummow and Hayne JJ; *Cartoon Network LP, LLLP v CSC Holdings Inc* 536 F 3d 121 at 138 (2008: CA 2), *Record TV Pte Ltd v MediaCorp TV Singapore Pte Ltd* [2011] 1 SLR 830 at 859–860 [69] per VK Rajah JA with, on the other hand, the view of the district judges in *Twentieth Century Fox Film Corporation v Cablevision Systems Corporation* 478 F Supp 2d 607 (2007 SD NY) at 617–620 (who was reversed by the Second Circuit Court of Appeals in *Cartoon Network* 536 F 3d 121), and *Arista Records LLC v Myxer Inc* (C.D. Ca unreported 1 April 2011; 2011 US Dist LEXIS 109668) at p. 19. See further, [2012] FCA 34, 62.

[29] See, 536 F.3d 121 (2d Cir. 2008), rev'g *Twentieth Century Fox Film Corp. v. Cablevision Sys. Corp.*, 478 F. Supp. 2d 607, 624 (S.D.N.Y. 2007).

[30] *Twentieth Century Fox Film Corp. v. Cablevision System Corp.*, 478 F. Supp. 2d 607 (S.D.N.Y. 2007).

[31] Ibid.

[32] Ibid.

[33] 478 F. Supp. 2d 607 (S.D.N.Y. 2007).

However, the Circuit Court disagreed with that reasoning. The Circuit Court held that those facts found to be dispositive by the District Court were more relevant to the question of contributory liability, which was not at issue in this case. Thus, "on the facts of this case", the Circuit Court concluded that "copies produced by the RS-DVR system are 'made' by the RS-DVR customer, and Cablevision's contribution to this reproduction by providing the system does not warrant the imposition of direct liability".[34] In reaching this conclusion, the Second Circuit explained:

> When there is a dispute as to the author of an allegedly infringing instance of reproduction, *Netcom* and its progeny direct **our attention to the volitional conduct that causes the copy to be made.** There are only two instances of volitional conduct in this case: Cablevision's conduct in designing, housing, and maintaining a system that exists only to produce a copy, and a customer's conduct in ordering that system to produce a copy of a specific program.[35] [emphasis added]

The U.S. Circuit Court ruled that "volitional conduct is an important element of direct liability" and "[in this case] the set of relevant volitional conduct lay with the users rather than Cablevision".[36] The Court's interpretation of the "volitional conduct" that constituted the infringing act was rooted in earlier cases,[37] including *Religious Technology Center v. Netcom On-Line Communications Services, Inc.* ("Netcom")[38] and *CoStar Group, Inc. v. LoopNet, Inc.* ("CoStar").[39] In *Netcom*, the Court refused to hold Netcom directly liable for making copies of copyright works because the Court found that Netcom had not itself taken any affirmative action that would result in the copying of the works. "Although copyright is a strict liability statute", the Court stated, "there should still be some element of volition or causation which is lacking where a defendant's system is merely used to create a copy by a third party".[40] In *CoStar*, the *Netcom* decision was endorsed by both the District Court and the Court of Appeals for the Fourth Circuit. The Circuit Court confirmed that the defendant, as an Internet service provider, was not directly liable for copyright infringement because the defendant was "simply the owner and manager of a system used by others who are violating the plaintiff's copyrights and [was] not an actual duplicator itself".[41]

The Second Circuit's decision in *Cartoon Network* has been followed in several recent cases. In *United States v. ASCAP (In re Cellco P'ship)*,[42] the Court highlighted that "[t]o be held liable for direct infringement ... a defendant must have engaged in conduct that is volitional or causally related to that purported

---

[34] 536 F.3d 121 (2d Cir. 2008).

[35] 536 F.3d 121 (2d Cir. 2008), 131.

[36] Ibid, 131–133.

[37] Ibid, 130–133.

[38] 907 F. Supp. 1361 (N.D. Cal. 1995).

[39] 373 F.3d 544 (4th Cir. 2004).

[40] 907 F. Supp. 1361 (N.D. Cal. 1995), 1370.

[41] 373 F. 3d 544 (4th Cir. 2004), 546.

[42] 663 F. Supp. 2d 363; 2009 U.S. Dist. LEXIS 95630 (S.D.N.Y., 2009).

infringement".[43] In *Disney Enters. v. Hotfile Corp.*,[44] the District Court for the Southern District of Florida held that the law "is clear that the defendants were not liable for direct copyright infringement because they owned and managed Internet facilities that allowed others to upload and download copyrighted material". Nonetheless, *Netcom* and its subsequent decisions have not always been approved and followed in other cases. For example, as noted by the *Hotfile* court,[45] divergent opinions and rulings can be found in *Capitol Records, Inc. v. MP3Tunes*,[46] *Arista Records LLC v. Usenet.com, Inc.*,[47] and most recently in *Perfect 10, Inc. v. Megaupload Ltd., et al.*[48]

In *RecordTV Pte Ltd v MediaCorp TV Singapore Pte Ltd*,[49] a similar case decided in Singapore, the copyright owners also claimed two possible violations of the right of reproduction: (1) by operating and maintaining its website which allowed registered users to request the recording of television broadcasts for viewing it at a later time, RecordTV was liable for making copies of the copyrighted content; (2) RecordTV also authorised the infringement of copyright owner's right of reproduction in the broadcasts and films by subscribers. Only the first claim will be discussed here and the second one will be dealt with later in this chapter.

Both the High Court and the Court of Appeal of Singapore[50] held that "RecordTV did not copy the MediaCorp shows within the meaning of the phrase 'make a copy' in the Copyright Act, and that it was the Registered Users instead who copied the shows by their own actions in requesting the recording of those shows using RecordTV's iDVR".[51] In reaching this conclusion, the High Court relied broadly on the approach adopted by the Circuit Court in *Cartoon Network*,

---

[43] 663 F. Supp. 2d 363, 370.

[44] 2011 U.S. Dist. LEXIS 78387 (decided 8 July 2011).

[45] Ibid.

[46] See, 2009 U.S. Dist. LEXIS 96521, 2009 WL 3364036 (S.D.N.Y., 2009). It was held that a company's knowledge of massive infringement plausibly alleged volitional conduct.

[47] See, 633 F. Supp. 2d 124, 148 (S.D.N.Y. 2009). It was held that a company with a policy encouraging infringement plus the ability to stop that infringement was liable for direct copyright infringement. This case held that a policy encouraging infringement coupled with an ability—but refusal—to stop the massive infringement gave rise to a volitional act. This can be contrasted to the Optus Now service discussed in this paper, where Optus has not encouraged infringed nor refused to stop infringement in circumstances where it had that ability.

[48] See, 2011 U.S. Dist. LEXIS 81931 (decide July 27, 2011). The Southern District of California held that allegations that Megaupload rewarded users who uploaded popular content, which Megaupload knew would likely be infringing, sufficiently alleged volitional conduct, and if true showed that Megaupload was more than a mere "passive conduit" for file storage.

[49] [2010] 2 SLR 15; [2010] SGCA 43.

[50] The Supreme Court of the Republic of Singapore comprises two courts, namely the High Court and the Court of Appeal. Civil and criminal cases heard by the Supreme Court commence in the High Court, which is presided over by a single judge. Appeals from the Subordinate Courts are also heard in the High Court. The Court of Appeal hears appeals against the decisions of High Court Judges in both civil and criminal matters. The Court of Appeal is usually made up of three Judges. See further http://app.supremecourt.gov.sg/default.aspx?pgID=1.

[51] [2009] SGHC 287; [2010] SGCA 43.

and the Court of Appeal did not reject this interpretational approach in its decision. It was apparent to both the High Court and the Court of Appeal that the iDVR was simply a digital version of the traditional DVR/VCR in spite of certain operational differences. The Court of Appeal elaborated that:

> ... these differences are immaterial as they are no more than variations of the same basic model of time shifting. The fundamental objective of time shifting is to allow a show to be recorded on a storage medium so that it may be viewed or listened to at the consumer's convenience after it is broadcast. This is a perfectly legitimate activity so long as it does not constitute copying copyright-protected material or communicating such material to the public contrary to copyright laws.[52]

Consequently, the Singapore courts substantially followed the U.S. Circuit Court's reasoning in *Cartoon Network*. The courts concluded that the iDVR and the traditional DVR/VCR were similar in the following ways:

(a) it is the user who chooses which show to record;
(b) the request to record a show is made to a recording device (the traditional DVR/VCR) or recording system (the iDVR); and
(c) it is the recording device/system which records the selected show.[53]

12.3.1.2   Deployment of the "Volitional Conduct" Concept in Australian Courts

Although Australian courts have not specifically considered the element of volitional conduct in relation to an allegedly infringing act, it appears that the causal connection between a specific act and the infringing outcomes forms part of the court's general analysis. For example, as Justice Gibbs decided in *University of New South Wales v Moorhouse*,[54] the mere provision of a photocopier could not establish a direct act of copying; instead, it amounted to an authorisation of infringing copying in the circumstances at issue.[55] In that case, the University made a photocopier available for use by students and others in a campus library. The University was sued by book publishers for copyright infringement for reproducing or authorising the reproduction of copyright materials. Gibbs J stated:

> In the circumstances of the present case **it is impossible to hold that the University itself did the act of photocopying which was alleged to have infringed the copyright.** Mr. Brennan was not the servant or agent of the University for the purpose of making the copies. Similarly it is impossible to hold that Mr. Brennan made the copies on behalf of the librarian of the University, and for that reason s. 49, which provides that copyright is not

---

[52] [2010] SGCA 43, at 21.

[53] [2010] SGCA 43, 20.

[54] [1975] HCA 26; (1975) 133 CLR 1.

[55] Instead of the doctrines of direct or contributory infringement in the U.S., Australian copyright law, situated in the U.K. tradition, has developed a distinct concept of "authorisation of infringement" with accompanying liability rules. For statutory provisions, see Australia *Copyright Act 1968* (Cth) s 36. For a comparative study of the U.S. law and Australian law, see Ginsburg and Ricketson (2006), p. 1.

infringed by the making of a copy by or on behalf of a librarian under the conditions stated in that section, has no application to the facts of the present case. The University can only be liable if it authorized the doing of the act of photocopying by Mr. Brennan and if that act amounted to an infringement of copyright.[56] [emphasis added]

In regard to the TV Now system at issue, Justice Rares' reasoning was notably in line with Justice Gibbs' in *Moorhouse*.[57] His Honour decided that:

> ... the user of the TV Now service makes each of the films in the four formats **when he or she clicks on the "record" button** on the TV Now electronic program guide. **This is because the user is solely responsible for the creation of those films. He or she decides whether or not to make the films and only he or she has the means of being able to view them. If the user does not click "record", no films will be brought into existence that he or she can play back later.** The service that TV Now offers the user is substantively no different from a VCR or DVR. Of course, TV Now may offer the user a greater range of playback environments than the means provided by a VCR or DVR, although this can depend on the technologies available to the user.[58] [emphasis added]

The essence of Justice Rares' reasoning was that the maker of a recording was the one who initiated a process utilizing technology or equipment that recorded the broadcast, and that the concept of "making a film or recording" was concerned with the acts of creating a copy of a work and the result of bringing a copy of the work into existence by this action.[59] Given the fact that Optus made available to a subscriber a facility (a service) which enabled the subscriber to use that facility to record TV broadcasts and later to view them, Justice Rares held that the recordings could not be said to be created by Optus; instead, it was the result of the subscriber's use of the facility.

On appeal, Justice Rares' proposition was rejected by Justices Emmett, Finn and Bennett jointly for several reasons:

> *First*, the meaning given "make" is, in our view, a contrived one. ... [When the Act refers to "make a copy", it is referring to] so acting as to embody images and sound in an "article or thing" ... or a "record" ... and the essence of it is the idea of making ... a physical thing. ... The issue is not simply how something is made. It is by whom is it made.[60]
>
> The *second* reason ... relates to how the [TV Now] system works. ... We merely note here that a subscriber's clicking on a button labelled "record" may trigger a sequence of actions which result in copies of a selected programme being made, but it does not necessarily follow that the subscriber alone makes that copy.[61]

---

[56] Ibid, 8. Likewise, in both *Universal Music Australia Pty Ltd v Cooper* [2005] FCA 972 *and Universal Music Australia Pty Ltd v Sharman License Holdings Ltd* [2005] FCA 1242 two landmark cases respectively dealing with the liabilities of hyperlink providers and P2P software vendors in the Internet age, the line between the primary acts that directly caused a legal right comprised in copyright to be infringed and the secondary acts that were merely attached to the direct infringement was the key factor investigated by the courts.

[57] In fact, Moorhouse was cited in Justice Rares' decision. See [2012] FCA 34, 67.

[58] [2012] FCA 34, 63.

[59] [2012] FCA 34, 64.

[60] [2012] FCAFC 59, 58.

[61] [2012] FCAFC 59, 59.

Thirdly ... we consider that the system itself has been designed in a way that makes Optus the "main performer of the act of [copying]".[62]

Fourthly, there is some division between federal courts in the United States as how properly to differentiate between "direct" and "contributory" liability for copyright infringement where automated technologies are employed to make copies of copyright material.[63]

The Full Court expressly refused to approach the copyright infringement issues in this case through distinguishing "direct infringement" from "contributory infringement" and also rejected the deployment of the "volitional conduct" concept. The reason for doing so, in the view of the Full Court, is:

> ... because we have our own legislative and common law devices for imposing liability on third persons who are implicated or join in the infringing acts of another as, for example, by authorising the doing of such acts ... or by acting in concert with another to infringe copyright in pursuit of a common design.[64]

In addition, the Full Court was also questioning why a person who designed and operated a wholly automated copying system ought as of course not be treated as a "maker" of an infringing copy where the system itself was configured designedly so as to respond to a third party command to make that copy.[65]

Therefore, the Full Court held that Optus was not merely making available its system to another who used it to copy a broadcast, but captured, copied, stored and made available for reward, a programme for later viewing by another.[66] Put another way, Optus not only had "solicited subscriber utilisation of its Service", it had also "designed and maintained a sophisticated system which can effectuate the making of recordings wanted for viewing by subscribers". Thus, the Court concluded that Optus manifestly was "involved directly in doing the act of copying' and therefore it counted "as a maker of copies for the subscriber".[67]

Following this conclusion, the Full Court considered further: the real issue in consequence is whether Optus alone does the act of copying or whether Optus and the subscriber are jointly and severally responsible for that act.[68] The Court contended that:

> The subscriber, by selecting the programme to be copied and by confirming that it is to be copied, can properly be said to be the person who instigates the copying. Yet it is Optus which effects it. Without the concerted actions of both there would be no copy made of a football match for the subscriber. ...The common design – the production of the selected programme for transmission to the subscriber – informed the solicitation and the taking of a subscription by the subscriber; it was immanent in the service to be provided.[69]

---

[62] [2012] FCAFC 59, 60.

[63] [2012] FCAFC 59, 61.

[64] [2012] FCAFC 59, 63.

[65] [2012] FCAFC 59, 64.

[66] [2012] FCAFC 59, 68.

[67] [2012] FCAFC 59, 75.

[68] [2012] FCAFC 59, 69.

[69] [2012] FCAFC 59, 76.

The Full Court ultimately decided that each cinematograph film and sound recording of the broadcasts and copies of the films was made "either by Optus alone or by Optus and the subscriber"[70]; meanwhile, the Court was of the view that it was not strictly necessary for the Court to determine whether Optus alone was, or Optus and the subscriber were, the maker(s).[71]

12.3.2 Potential Infringement by Communicating to the Public

In the view of the Full Court on, the conclusion that Optus was infringing copyright by making cinematograph film and sound recording of the broadcasts and copies of the films was already sufficient to resolve the legality issue of the TV Now service (system). In consequence, the Full Court decided that it was unnecessary to consider any other alternative grounds raised by each party. However, as Justice Rares' initial conclusion on this issue was different from that of the Full Court, his Honour's attention was drawn to the potential infringement by transmitting the recordings of the TV broadcasts to a subscriber's personal computer, mobile phone or other digital device through the Internet. The transmission occurs when the subscribers want to watch the recorded programs by logging into the service and clicking on a "Play" button.[72] This session considers the legal principles underlying the trial Court's decision concerning whether this transmission could amount to an infringement of the copyright owners' exclusive right to communicate the copyright materials to the public.

12.3.2.1 Who Is the Maker of a Communication?

The right to communicate to the public is composed of two elements, i.e. (1) the act of "communicating", and (2) the communication is made "to the public".[73] Claims of violation of this exclusive right will fail if either one of the two elements are not proven. For example, in *Cartoon Network*, the U.S. Circuit Court rejected the copyright owners' claim simply by holding that the transmission of the recordings was not made "to the public" and leaving the first factor untouched. In comparison, the copyright owners in *RecordTV* also claimed that RecordTV infringed on their

---

[70] [2012] FCAFC 59, 79.

[71] [2012] FCAFC 59, 78.

[72] See further, [2012] FCA 34, 23–26.

[73] See further, *Copyright Act 1968* (Cth), s 10(1)—defining "communicate", s 22(6) and (6A)—provisions related to the communication of a work or other subject matter to the public, s 31(1) (iv) and (b)(iii), s86(c) and s 87(c)—provisions related to the communication of a work or other subject matter to the public.

communication right by transmitting the recordings to consumers at their request for play back. In the first instance, the High Court ruled in copyright owner's favour[74]; however the ruling was rejected by the Court of Appeal. The Court of Appeal concluded that "[i]n our view, RecordTV did not communicate the MediaCorp shows to the public within the meaning of ss 83(c) and 84(1)(d) of the Copyright Act for two reasons: first, we are of the view that there have not been any communications to 'the public' (This will be discussed in detail later in this article); and, second, we do not think that RecordTV was the party which made the communications in question in the present case."[75]

In the case of the TV Now service, once a TV program was recorded Optus allowed the recordings to be played back within 30 days after the recordings were made. In order to enable playing back and watching later, the TV shows recorded by and stored in the TV Now system must be transmitted (communicated) to individual users' local devices which could be personal computers or mobile phones. In other words, upon the completion of a recording, an electronic copy of the TV show would be "communicated", through making the recording available online to those who had subscribed to the service. Similar to the issue with regard to the reproduction right, the first question to be asked here is: who was the maker of the communication?

In his decision, Justice Rares was of the opinion that "the user was responsible for any communication within the meaning of s 22(6) made to his or her device by seeking to play the program that he or she had earlier selected for recording".[76] Under the *Copyright Act 1968* (Cth) of Australia, the maker of a communication is defined, under s 22(6), as "the person responsible for determining the content of the communication".[77] Through the TV Now system, a user can only access and play back the recordings appearing on their playlists which have been created upon their own requests. A communication is initiated by a user when they wish to watch a recording at the time and with the chosen device. In this regard, it is sensible to say that the subscriber, rather than Optus, is the person responsible for determining the content of a specific communication. Therefore, as Justice Rares decided, "by clicking the 'play' button on his or her compatible device, the user communicated the film to his or her device by determining that the film would be made available online or electronically transmitted to that device".[78] His Honour explained that:

It may appear odd that Optus, which has stored the films in its NAS computer, does not "communicate" (make available online or electronically transmit) the film in the

---

[74] [2009] SGHC 287, at 85.

[75] [2010] SGCA 43, at 24.

[76] [2012] FCA 34, 90.

[77] To avoid doubt, it is clarified under 22(6A) that "a person is not responsible for determining the content of a communication merely because the person takes one or more steps for the purpose of: (a) gaining access to what is made available online by someone else in the communication; or (b) receiving the electronic transmission of which the communication consists."

[78] [2012] FCA 34, 94.

compatible format, **but that is because it did nothing to determine the content of that communication**. The user initially chose to record the program so that later he or she could choose to play the film so recorded using the TV Now service. ... Hence, the user, not Optus, is the person responsible for determining the content of the communication within the meaning of s 22(6) when he or she plays a film recorded for him or her on the TV Now service. Thus, the user did the act of electronically transmitting the film within the meaning of ss 86(c) and 87(c).[79] [emphasis added]

Interestingly, Justice Rares was aware that the Singapore Court of Appeal had arrived at a similar conclusion in *RecordTV*, however His Honour was of the opinion that "because their Honours construed somewhat differently worded provisions, their reasoning on this issue is not of assistance".[80]

In *RecordTV*, the Court of Appeal of Singapore disagreed with the first trial judge's finding that RecordTV was the communicator who made the TV shows available to the public. The Court was of the view that the Judge's finding was based on "an overly technical reading of s 16(6) of the *Copyright Act* [of Singapore], which provides as follows: For the purposes of this Act, a communication other than a broadcast is taken to have been made by the person responsible for determining the content of the communication at the time the communication is made."[81] The Court explained:

In order to identify the communicator, s 16(6) of the Copyright Act requires a determination of: (a) the time of the communication ("limb (a) of s 16(6)"); (b) the content of the communication at the time of communication ("limb (b) of s 16(6)"); and (c) the identity of the person responsible for determining that content ("limb (c) of s 16(6)").[82]

The Court was of the view that the recorded TV shows were communicated once they were made available for viewing by the Registered Users who had requested the recording of those shows,[83] and that the relevant content in the present case consisted of specific shows that had been recorded pursuant to the specific requests of a particular Registered User.[84] Consequently, the Court concluded:

[S]ince the only MediaCorp shows that were "communicated" were those shows that appeared on each Registered User's playlist, and since the exact make-up of each playlist depended on the specific shows which the Registered User in question had requested to be recorded, "the person responsible for determining the content of the communication at the time the communication [was] made" would be that Registered User himself. RecordTV would not have been the communicator of the MediaCorp shows for the purposes of s 16 (6) of the Copyright Act.

---

[79] [2012] FCA 34, 95.

[80] [2012] FCA 34, 96.

[81] [2010] SGCA 43, 31.

[82] Ibid, 32.

[83] Ibid, 34.

[84] Ibid, 35.

12.3.2.2 Was the Communication Made "to the Public"?

In determining what was a communication "to the public", Justice Rares looked at the High Court of Australia's decision in *Telstra v. APRA*.[85] The High Court in *Telstra* asked two questions: (a) were the particular audience or intended audience receiving the communication as members of the public outside the communicator's domestic circle; and (b) was the audience of a type that could be described as the copyright owner's public? As His Honour highlighted:

> In essence, the concept is that if a work is communicated in circumstances where the copyright owner can expect a fee, the communication is made "to the public" regardless of whether it is made to only one person or a private audience: *Telstra* 191 CLR at 156-157, 197-200. **Thus, if a work is communicated in a commercial setting it is unlikely to be a private or domestic occasion**.[86] [emphasis added]

The TV Now service was apparently available to the public and anyone in the public in a particular region could subscribe to the service. But would the person who had requested the TV show to be recorded and to whom the specific recording would be communicated qualified as the "copyright owner's public"? Although Justice Rares acknowledged that "the rightholders' public included the users of the TV Now service",[87] his Honour ruled that the communication did not fall within the meaning of "commercial setting" found in *Telstra* because of the operation of the s 111 exemption:

> Here, I am of opinion that no communication "to the public" can occur if the user made the recording he or she communicates by clicking the "play" button, "solely for private and domestic use by watching or listening to the material broadcast at a time more convenient then the time when the broadcast is made" within the meaning of s 111. ...[It is because] **the impact of a user communicating the recording or film to his or her compatible device lacks the element of commercial detriment to the rightholders that Telstra's customers caused by contracting for the music on hold to be played**: cp: *Telstra* 191 CLR 140.[88] [emphasis added]

Obviously, although the Circuit Court in *Cartoon Network* reached a similar conclusion, Justice Rares' reasoning differs from that of the judges in the United States. In *Cartoon Network*, one of the complaints made by the plaintiffs was that

---

[85] [1997] HCA 41; (1997) 191 CLR 140.

[86] [2012] FCA 34, 101.

[87] His Honour held: A user could have watched the broadcasts as they were made and, had he or she done so, would have been part of the viewing public. See, [2012] FCA 34, 102. In addition, His Honour was also of the view that the communication to a user of a film is "part of an overall commercial transaction between Optus and, at least, a subscriber who may also be the user who is bearing the cost of that service". See further, [2012] FCA 34, 103.

[88] Thus, His Honour ruled: Accordingly, a communication made by the user to himself or herself of the film that he or she recorded is not made "to the public". It is a communication that can only be made by the person who made the recording. The fact that the user may be with one or more other persons, such as family members or friends, when the communication is received will not, ordinarily, convert its private and domestic nature to being that of a communication "to the public". See, [2012] FCA 34, 105–106.

Cablevision infringed on their right by engaging in unauthorised "public performances" of the recorded content through the playback of the RS-DVR copies.[89] Cablevision argued that: (1) the RS-DVR customer, rather than Cablevision, did the transmitting and thus the performing; and (2) the transmission was not "to the public" under the transmit clause. Nonetheless, the District Court was of the view that the transmission of the playback copies amounted to a public performance. This view was later rejected by the Circuit Court which decided that "[a]s to Cablevision's first argument, we note that our conclusion ... [that the customer] not Cablevision, 'does' the copying does not indicate a parallel conclusion that the customer, and not Cablevision, 'performs' the copyrighted work".[90] However, the Circuit Court declined to delve into Cablevision's first argument further because "even if we assume that Cablevision makes the transmission when an RS-DVR playback occurs, we find that the RS-DVR playback, as described here, does not involve the transmission of a performance 'to the public'."[91]

The Circuit Court was of the view that it was important, in determining whether a transmission is made to the public, to examine who was "capable of receiving" the performance being transmitted.[92] The Court thus held:

> Because each RS-DVR playback transmission is made to a single subscriber using a single unique copy produced by that subscriber, we conclude that such transmissions are not performances "to the public," and therefore do not infringe any exclusive right of public performance.[93]

In *ASCAP v. U.S.*,[94] the Second Circuit revisited the question of whether an online transmission of a copy of a work was "to the public" if the work had already

---

[89] In the U.S. law, 17 U.S.C.§106(4) grants a copyright owner the exclusive right "to perform the copyrighted work publicly". To perform or display a work "publicly", as 17 U.S.C. §101 provides for, is:

(1) to perform or display it at a place open to the public or at any place where a substantial number of persons outside of a normal circle of a family and its social acquaintances is gathered; or

(2) to transmit or otherwise communicate a performance or display of the work to a place specified by clause (1) or to the public, by means of any device or process, whether the members of the public capable of receiving the performance or display receive it in the same place or in separate places and at the same time or at different times.

[90] 536 F.3d 121, 134.

[91] Ibid, 134.

[92] Ibid, 134–135.

[93] Ibid, 139. Likewise, in *RecordTV*, since every one of the recordings was made privately and individually, the Court of Appeal of Singapore held that "[w]e see no reason why the aggregate of the private and individual communications made to each of the aforesaid Registered users should transform the nature of such communication into 'public' communication". See, [2010] SGCA 43, 26.

[94] *American Society of Composers, Authors and Publishers (ASCAP) v. United States*, 627 F.3d 64 (2d Cir. 2010), cert. denied, 565 U.S. __, (U.S. Oct. 3, 2011)(No. 10-1337). In this case, the Internet companies, including Yahoo! and RealNetworks, sought blanket licenses from ASCAP in

been sold to the receiver.[95] The Court decided: "Just as in *Cartoon Network*, the Internet Companies transmit a copy of the work to the user, who then plays his unique copy of the song whenever he wants to hear it; because the performance is made by a unique reproduction of the song that was sold to the user, the ultimate performance of the song is not 'to the public'".[96] Thus, the Court affirmed the District Court's decision that downloads did not constitute public performances of the downloaded musical works.

The High Court's "commercial setting" scenario in *Telstra* (on which Justice Rares's approach was based) are, in essence, comparable with the Second Circuit's method in *Cartoon Network*, viz the potential audience of a given transmission is dispositive to the question of whether this transmission is "to the public". Consequently, in the view of the trial court, the act of transmitting the recorded TV programs to individual subscriber's digital devices through the Internet does not reasonably fall within the ambit of the communication right because the communication is not made "to the public".

Given the fact that the trial court's conclusions differed substantially from those of the appellate court, each court had to give answer(s) to a different set of subsequent questions; however, each court confronted the application of s 111 of *Copyright Act 1968* (Cth) of Australia which provides for a time shifting exception. To the trial court, since the conclusion was that the subscriber rather than Optus was the maker and communicator of the recordings, the remaining question was whether the subscriber's time shifting of the TV broadcasts through the TV Now system was allowable under the s 111 exception. In alternative, the appellate court had to answer whether Optus's direct involvement in the act of copying could be exempted under the s 111 exception.

12.4 Potential Defences: Time Shifting Exemption

The act of making recordings of the broadcasts may amount to the exercise of a copyright owner's reproduction right or the right of copying as discussed above. This section considers whether any copyright exception may apply to the "use" and "provision" of the TV Now system.

---

order to facilitate their online music services. During the proceedings to establish a reasonable royalty rate, ASCAP claimed that individual downloads counted as public performances, which would cause a copyright holder's exclusive performance rights to be factored into the assessment of fees in addition to the exclusive rights of reproduction and distribution. If downloads were to count as public performances, then each individual download would serve to increase the rate of royalties owed to copyright holders that licensed through ASCAP. Yahoo! and RealNetworks consequently disagreed, citing that downloads involved only reproduction and distribution rights, not performance rights.

[95] 627 F.3d 64, 75.

[96] Ibid.

In copyright regimes, the principle of allowing a consumer to record a television or radio broadcast for private use by watching or listening to the broadcast at a later time has been acknowledged in many countries.[97] In Australia, this "time shifting" exemption makes it legal for a person to make a cinematograph film or sound recording of a broadcast for the private and domestic use of watching the broadcast at a later time, and to reproduce the copyright materials included in the broadcast for this purpose. For this reason, it is lawful for a company to manufacture or sell equipment (such as VCRs and DVRs) that is capable of making and storing the recordings. However, the question is whether the s 111 exception can apply to the TV Now service which takes time shifting from individual consumer's home to the "cloud".

12.4.1 Time Shifting Exception Under s 111

In 2006, several additional categories of copyright exceptions were added to the *Copyright Act 1968* (Cth) of Australia, permitting time-shifting (s 111), device- or space-shifting (s 109A) and format-shifting (ss 43C, 47J and 110AA).[98] These provisions were introduced into the law after an unsuccessful legislative attempt to launch a blank tape royalty scheme which purported to legitimise the home-taping of broadcasts.[99] In response to increasing concerns over the legality of private uses of copyright materials including the common consumer practices of "time shifting" broadcasts, the new exceptions were successfully enacted in the *Copyright Amendment Act 2006* (Cth). This Amendment, for the first time in Australia, "allow [ed] consumers to record most television and radio programs to view or listen to once at a later time (known as 'time shifting')".[100] The Optus TV Now has become the first case to assess the operation of the recently established time shifting exception in Australia.

---

[97] For example, see *Sony Corp. of America v. Universal City Studios, Inc.*, 464 U.S. 417 (1984); *C.B.S. Songs Ltd v Amstrad Consumer Electronics Plc.*, [1987] 2 WLR 1191; [1988] AC 1013.

[98] The new exceptions were introduced into Australian copyright law under the *Copyright Amendment Act 2006* (Cth). The full text of the Act is available at http://www.austlii.edu.au/au/legis/cth/num_act/caa2006213/. However, it is essential to note that these provisions are very technical and specific in application.

[99] The blank tape royalty scheme was introduced into the law in 1989 by Copyright Amendment Act 1989 (Cth). But it was then successfully challenged by the Australian Blank Tape Manufactures Association in the High Court of Australia (See, *Australian Tape Manufactures Associate Ltd v Commonwealth* (1993) 176 CLR 480). As a result, the scheme was removed although the remainder of the 1989 Act was re-enacted by Copyright Amendment (Re-enactment) Act 1993 (Cth).

[100] Ruddock (2006).

As explained above, for the purpose of legitimating the time shifting of copyright materials in Australia, the new copyright exception has been enacted as follows:

COPYRIGHT ACT 1968 - SECT 111
Recording broadcasts for replaying at more convenient time
(1) This section applies if a person makes a cinematograph film or sound recording of a broadcast solely for private and domestic use by watching or listening to the material broadcast at a time more convenient than the time when the broadcast is made.
Note: Subsection 10(1) defines broadcast as a communication to the public delivered by a broadcasting service within the meaning of the Broadcasting Services Act 1992.
Making the film or recording does not infringe copyright
(2) The making of the film or recording does not infringe copyright in the broadcast or in any work or other subject-matter included in the broadcast.
Note: Even though the making of the film or recording does not infringe that copyright, that copyright may be infringed if a copy of the film or recording is made.
Dealing with embodiment of film or recording
(3) Subsection (2) is taken never to have applied if an article or thing embodying the film or recording is:

    (a)   sold; or
    (b)   let for hire; or
    (c)   by way of trade offered or exposed for sale or hire; or
    (d)   distributed for the purpose of trade or otherwise; or
    (e)   used for causing the film or recording to be seen or heard in public; or
    (f)   used for broadcasting the film or recording.

Note: If the article or thing embodying the film or recording is dealt with as described in subsection (3), then copyright may be infringed not only by the making of the article or thing but also by the dealing with the article or thing.
(4) To avoid doubt, paragraph (3)(d) does not apply to a loan of the article or thing by the lender to a member of the lender's family or household for the member's private and domestic use

12.4.1.1 A "Technology Neutral" Provision

This new provision allows a person to make a cinematograph film or sound recording of a broadcast for the purpose of time shifting by providing that the making of the film or recording does not infringe copyright in the broadcast or in any work or other subject-matter included in the broadcast. It is important to note that this time shifting exception is a "technology neutral" provision. As Justice Rares highlighted, "[t]he Parliament must have contemplated that a variety of techniques and technical equipment could be used by a person to make a film of a broadcast".[101]

It means that a person can make a "time shifting" use of copyright materials by means of any device or technology that has the capacity to record and store broadcastings for later watching, listening or reading. Such devices that have

---

[101] [2012] FCA 34, 58.

already been offered in the market-place include the traditional video tape recorder (VTR), the Video Cassette Recorder (VCR), the Digital Video Recorder (DVR), and even digital devices such as personal computers. Therefore, at first glance, there is no reason why an Internet-based recording system such as Cablevision's RS-DVR, RecordTV's iDVR or Optus' TV Now cannot fall within the ambit of this copyright exception. As Justice Rares highlighted, the s 111 exemption "was intended to accommodate the development of technologies and the ordinary ways in which individuals can avail themselves of them".[102]

The concept of "time shifting" was first addressed in *Sony Corp. of America v. Universal City Studios, Inc.*,[103] a landmark case decided by the Supreme Court of the United States (also known as the "Betamax case"). In that case, the Court ruled that the making of individual copies of TV programs by means of the Betamax player, a type of video tape recorder (VTR) developed by Sony, for purposes of time shifting did not constitute copyright infringement because it was a fair use.[104] As Professor Nimmer has highlighted, the U.S. legislators did not intend to create a special exemption from copyright liability for home recording; at most, home recording should be merely defensible under the exiting judicial doctrine of fair use.[105]

---

[102] [2012] FCA 34, 84.

[103] 464 U.S. 417 (1984).

[104] However, the legal foundation underpinning the decisions of the U.S. district court, the Court of Appeals for the Ninth Circuit, and the Supreme Court varied significantly in the Betamax case. Professor Nimmer explained in his monumental work, *Nimmer on Copyright*:

> The United States Supreme Court reversed the Court of Appeals, and held that off-the-air video recording for private use is fair use. In doing so, however, the Supreme Court majority expressly refused to express any opinion on the supposed statutory exemption -- i.e., the issue apart from fair use -- relied upon by the district court n63. The four dissenting justices, by contrast, went to some length to deny that such an exemption exists. In view of the fact that the fair use defense to video home recording is not necessarily applicable to all television broadcasting, and in further view of the possible inapplicability of the Sony fair use decision to audio home taping, it is important to consider explicitly that which the Supreme Court majority declined to address, viz. whether there is a special statutory exemption, apart from fair use, for home audio recording. [references omitted]

See further, Nimmer and Nimmer (2002), §8B.01[D][1][a].

It was also noted by Professor Jessica Litman that although the Supreme Court granted certiorari in the case to decide whether the copyright law permitted consumers to engage in private home copying of television programs the majority ended up crafting its analysis to avoid answering that question definitively. See Litman (2006).

[105] Ibid, §8B.01[D][1][b]. Furthermore, as Professor Nimmer argued, the Supreme Court's decision in the Betamax case that home videotaping constituted air use under the circumstances there presented, this holding did not extend to home audio taping. Ibid, §8B.01[D][2]. After their failure of the Betamax case in the Supreme Court, the U.S. music and entertainment industries lobbied the Congress to make a law that would protect them from the effects of home copying, and later a stator royalty on the sale of blank videotapes. But both attempts failed. See further, Cunard (1996), pp. 245–247.

The fair dealing provisions and other copyright exceptions in Australian law, however, differ substantially from the fair use regime in the U.S. The core difference is that the fair dealing provisions and other copyright limitations in Australia law are very specific, whereas the fair use regime codified in 17 U.S.C. § 107[106] is more general.[107] The U.S. approach to copyright exceptions and limitations "allows for greater debate about the nature, character, purposed and commercial merits of the defendant's use".[108] The Australian approach is much more limited and offers much less flexibility.[109] The provisions for fair dealing and other copyright exceptions enumerated in the *Copyright Act 1968* (Cth) are self-contained exemptions.[110]

---

[106] It provides as follows:

Notwithstanding the provisions of sections 106 and 106A, the fair use of a copyrighted work, including such use by reproduction in copies or phonorecords or by any other means specified by that section, for purposes such as criticism, comment, news reporting, teaching (including multiple copies for classroom use), scholarship, or research, is not an infringement of copyright. In determining whether the use made of a work in any particular case is a fair use the factors to be considered shall include—

(1) the purpose and character of the use, including whether such use is of a commercial nature or is for nonprofit educational purposes;
(2) the nature of the copyrighted work;
(3) the amount and substantiality of the portion used in relation to the copyrighted work as a whole; and
(4) the effect of the use upon the potential market for or value of the copyrighted work.

The fact that a work is unpublished shall not itself bar a finding of fair use if such finding is made upon consideration of all the above factors.

[107] However, a narrow approach to copyright exceptions and limitations is encouraged by international treaties such as the Berne Convention and the TRIPS agreement. The international treaties provide for a "three-step test" requiring that domestic law's limitations on and exceptions to copyright owner's exclusive rights to be limited to (a) certain special cases which (b) do not conflict with a normal exploitation of the work and (c) do not unreasonably prejudice the legitimate interests of the rights holder. See Berne Convention, article 9(2) and TRIPS agreement article 13.

[108] Bowrey et al. (2010), p. 283.

[109] The introduction of a broader United State-style fair dealing was recommended in the report of the Copyright Law Review Committee, *Simplification of the Copyright Act 1968: Exceptions to the Exclusive Rights of Copyright Owners* (1998). However, it has not been accepted by legislators yet. See generally, Fitzgerald and Fitzgerald (2004), p. 171. A similar recommendation can also be seen the report of the *Joint Standing Committee on Treaties of the Australian Parliament on the Australia–United States Free Trade Agreement* (AUSFTA) in 2004. Please see further, Commonwealth of Australia, Joint Standing Committee on Treaties, Report 61, The Australia–United States Free Trade Agreement (June 2004), p. 240, Recommendation 17. See also, Stewart et al. pp. 254–255 and 265–266.

[110] For a use to qualify as "fair dealing", it has to be "fair" and also must fall within one of the categories of exception. Apart from the fair dealing regime in Australian law, there are many "miscellaneous exceptions" to the exclusive rights comprising copyright. These additional exceptions are "specific – each of them allows for a particular act to be done in relation to a copyright

It should also be noted that these enumerations are prescriptive and exhaustive. Therefore, any specific use of copyright materials that involves an exercise of a copyright owner's exclusive rights cannot be held as "fair" or "permitted" unless that use is explicitly covered by an exception enacted in the *Act*.[111] As such, until the specific recording exception was introduced into the *Copyright Act 1968* (Cth) in 2006, it is likely that time shifting constituted copyright infringement.

As a result, the legitimacy of an individual's acts in recording and transmitting a TV program with the Optus TV Now system can only be scrutinized in light of the conditions contained in s 111 of *Copyright Act 1968* (Cth).[112] In order to be protected under the time shifting exception, the subscribers of the TV Now system must satisfy the following conditions set forth in s 111: (a) private and domestic use only; and (b) the application of s 111(3) is not triggered.

12.4.1.2   Private and Domestic Use Only

It is noteworthy that the s 111 exception does not refer to a defence for private copying or time shifting in general.[113] As explained above, the exception is highly specific in light of conditions implicitly or explicitly set forth in the law.

One implied requirement under the s 111 time shifting provision is that the end users should have already paid for their rights to view or listen to the broadcasts or have had other legitimate access granted to them by someone else. As the Attorney-General explained when introducing the 2006 bill, this new exception was to make the law more sensible and defensible by making sure that "ordinary consumers are not infringing the law through everyday use of copyright products **they have legitimately purchased**".[114] [emphasis added] This implicit requirement should not prevent subscribers using the Optus TV Now service from qualifying for protection under s

---

work or other subject matter – but they lack any common underlying rationale". See generally, Fitzgerald and Fitzgerald (2004), pp. 172–182.

[111] But in the U.S., although a specific use is not enumerated as a separate exemption in any provision under the Copyright Act, the use can still be "fair" if it can pass the four-fair-use-factor test set forth in 17 U.S.C. §107.

[112] That is to say, it would not be tested further in Australia under the requirements such as the four fair use factors in the U.S. law under 17 U.S.C. § 107. For further discussion about the four fair use factors in the U.S. law, see Cohen et al. (2010), pp. 529–603.

[113] In contrast, together with a blank media levy system, private copying has been generally allowed in Canadian copyright law since 1997. The levy applies to "blank audio recording media". See further, Part VIII of *Copyright Act* of Canada (R.S.C., 1985, c. C-42).

[114] Commonwealth Attorney-General, *Hansard*, House of Representatives, Thursday, 19 October 2006, 1.

111, as the service merely allows subscribers to record programs from TV channels that they already have the legitimate right to view via their home TV sets.[115]

More importantly, the s 111 time shifting provision explicitly states that this exception may come into operation only if the recording of a broadcast is made "solely for private and domestic use by watching or listening to the material broadcast at a time more convenient than the time when the broadcast is made".[116] That is to say, the exception only applies to individuals, not corporations or institutional copying. In addition, "private and domestic use" is defined as "private and domestic use on or off domestic premises".[117]

12.4.1.3 Practices Excluded Under s 111(3)

Notwithstanding the private copying permitted under s 111(2), a variety of practices are excluded from protection in s 111(3). Subsection (3) provides that s 111(2) is "taken never to have applied if an article or thing embodying the film or recording is: (a) sold; or (b) let for hire; or (c) by way of trade offered or exposed for sale or hire; or (d) distributed for the purpose of trade or otherwise; or (e) used for causing the film or recording to be seen or heard in public; or (f) used for broadcasting the film or recording."[118] In summary, the time shifting exemption allows the making of a cinematograph film of a TV broadcast to be replayed at more convenient time; but it does not permit any commercial dealing or other distribution of the article embodying the film.

---

[115] It is explained as follows:

What channels are available on Optus TV Now?
This depends on where you live will depend on what TV shows are available to you. Your home address determines what TV shows are available in your ACMA TV Broadcast region that you're able to view.

. . .

See, Optus, "Optus TV Now frequently asked questions", http://www.optustvnow.optus.com. au/play/home.do?faq&isPassive=true.

[116] *Copyright Act 1968* (Cth), s 111(1).

[117] *Copyright Act 1968* (Cth), s 10(1).

[118] In addition, the term "article" is defined as "a reproduction or copy of a work or other subject-matter, being a reproduction or copy in electronic form". See, *Copyright Act 1968* (Cth) s 132AA. And, the term "copy" in relation to a cinematograph film, means "any article or thing in which the visual images or sounds comprising the film are embodied". *Copyright Act 1968* (Cth) s 10. No doubt, the "recordings" generated by and stored in the TV Now system can quite easily fall within the ambit of the term "article" or "copy [in electronic form]" governed by s 111(2).

12.4.1.4 Communication Not Covered in s 111

The s 111 exception permits the customers to "make copies" or "reproduce" copyright material for the purpose of time shifting, which, in effect, has created a new limitation on copyright owners' exclusive right of reproduction (for Pt III works) or copying (for Pt IV subject matter other than works). **But it is unclear whether this limitation can apply to the exercise of the exclusive right to communicate copyright materials to the public.**

A plain reading of the text in s 111 suggests that the exemption does not apply to acts that lead to the communication of a work to the public. This answer can be supported by the legislative background of s 111. As mentioned above, the new copyright exception was introduced into the law to legitimize individual consumers' acts in relation to the use of blank tapes for home taping of broadcasts or private copying of copyright works included in the broadcasts. Such traditional practices of time shifting have never related to the doing of acts other than copying. Accordingly, it is unlikely that the doing of other acts including online communication was meant to be covered by this new fair dealing provision, which was so carefully tailored. However, as long as no communication "to the public" could be established as Justice Rares decided in relation to the operation of the TV Now system, no specific permission would be required to transmit the recorded TV programs to the subscribers through the Internet or other data transmission networks.

12.4.2 Applying s 111 to the Use and Provision of the TV Now Service

As mentioned above, both the trial and the appellate court had to resolve the applicability issue of the s 111 in this case. Following the conclusion about who was doing the act of copying, the trial court had to consider whether the individual subscriber, as a user of the TV Now system and a maker of the recordings, could be immune from copyright infringement under s 111.[119] In contrast, the Full Court on appeal confronted the question whether Optus whose acts in making recordings of the TV broadcasts constituted an infringement could invoke this s 111 defence.[120]

In front of the trial court, the rightholders argued that the digital file of the recording of the broadcasts made by the Optus TV Now system was an "article or thing" within the meaning of s 111(3)(d) and that it had been distributed by Optus for the purpose of trade when it was being streamed to a user.[121] These arguments, among others, were rejected by Justice Rares for the following reason:

---

[119] [2012] FCA 34, 45.

[120] [2012] FCAFC 59, 5.

[121] [2012] FCA 34, 107–108.

The purpose of s 111 is to enable individuals to make time-shift recordings. The consequence of the deeming created by s 24 is that the article or thing embodying a recording is Optus' NAS computer. That article or thing is never distributed; it remains at all times part and parcel of Optus' datacentre. The purpose proscribed in s 111(3)(d) must be the user's; i.e. the person for whom s 111(1) and (2) create an exception from liability for infringement. That construction is reinforced by s 111(4) which excludes the operation of s 111(3)(d) where a person in the position of the user (i.e. "the lender") lends "the article or thing" to a member of his or her family or household for the latter's private and domestic use. First, the NAS computer is never in the possession or control of the user and could not be lent. Secondly, the NAS computer is not itself distributed to the user under s 111(3)(d). Rather, that article or thing is used to communicate a copy of the film (i.e. the recording) to the user. **The act of a user causing the recording he or she made to be streamed to his or her compatible device is not a form of distribution. That act is simply the means by which the user can watch the recording he or she wants to see after time shifting the broadcast**. There is no dissipation, division, dispersal or allocation of the recording in its communication by Optus to the user for viewing on his or her compatible device.[122] [emphasis added]

Accordingly, Justice Rares held that, by force of s 111(2), the users (subscribers to the TV Now service) did not infringe copyright in any of the rightholders' broadcasts or films.[123] This contention was, to some extent, accepted by the Full Court. The Court explained as follows:

... For present purposes we will assume that the subscriber in making his or her copies did so for the purposes prescribed by s 111 (there is an evidentiary dispute about this). If the subscriber was sued as a maker of the copies made to provide the programme he or she selected, that person could rely on s 111. No claim has been made against a subscriber, so there is no need to resolve whether any subscriber has been proved to have made a copy for the purpose prescribed in the section.[124]

Nonetheless, the Full Court decided that s 111 offered "no solace to Optus".[125] As discussed above, the Court was of the opinion that the recordings of the TV broadcasts were made either by Optus alone or by Optus and the subscriber jointly.[126] In either of the foresaid contingencies, Optus could not bring itself within the scope of the s 111 exception.[127] It is because, in the view of the Court, there was "nothing in the language, or the provenance, of s 111 to suggest that it was intended to cover commercial copying on behalf of individuals."[128] And the Court continued:

Moreover, the natural meaning of the section is that the person who makes the copy is the person whose purpose is to use it as prescribed by s 111(1). Optus may well be said to have copied programmes so that others can use the recorded programme for the purpose

---

[122] [2012] FCA 34, 111.

[123] [2012] FCA 34, 85.

[124] [2012] FCAFC 59, 92.

[125] [2012] FCAFC 59, 93.

[126] [2012] FCAFC 59, 79, 90–91.

[127] [2012] FCAFC 59, 6, 90–91.

[128] [2012] FCAFC 59, 89.

envisaged by s 111. Optus, though, makes no use itself of the copies as it frankly concedes. It merely stores them for 30 days. And its purpose in providing its service – and, hence in making copies of programmes for subscribers – is to derive such market advantage in the digital TV industry as its commercial exploitation can provide. Optus cannot invoke the s 111 exception.[129]

To sum up, the trial court affirmed that s 111 could apply to the users (subscribers to the TV Now system) and their acts in making the recordings of the TV broadcasts, while the appellate court clarified that the s 111 exception was not applicable to commercial copying, even if such copying was done on behalf of individuals. Put them under closer scrutiny, there is no visible conflict between each court's interpretations of the s 111 exception and its applicability. In essence, the courts' decisions on the legality of the TV Now service had hinged on: who was or were copying?

12.5   Conclusion

It appears that the analytical approach adopted on appeal is convenient to the Full Court but problematic to pave a way to certain and predictable copyright principles in a world of cloud computing. In my view, the Full Court's explanation about the rejection of the deployment of the "volitional conduct" concept for the purpose of identifying who is the conductor of an infringing act is not sufficiently convincing. As discussed earlier, the High Court of Australia did explicitly considered in *Moorhouse* the factors that could give rise to a primary act of infringing or a secondary act of authorizing an infringing act.

In addition, with comparison to Optus' acts of providing the TV Now system, the recording process is more directly related to subscribers' volitional acts of selecting and scheduling a specific TV show to be recorded. In *Cartoon Network*, the Second Circuit Court of the United States pointed out that: "[i]n determining who actually 'makes' a copy, a significant difference exists between making a request to a human employee, who then volitionally operates the copying system to make the copy, and issuing a command directly to a system, which automatically obeys commands and engages in no volitional conduct."[130] To a very large extent, this difference between a request to an independent agent or agency and a command to a system pointed out by the Second Circuit is sensible even in the context of Australian law. For example, in *Brian Kelvin de Garis and Mr Matthew Moore v Neville Jefress Pidler Ltd*[131] ("*De Garis*"), the defendant had acted as an independent agent whose acts were separate from those of its clients. As a result, it was held to be the conductor of

---

[129] [2012] FCAFC 59, 89.

[130] 536 F.3d 121,131.

[131] [1990] FCA 218; (1990) 37. FCR 99; 95 ALR 625. This case will be discussed in details later in this article.

the infringing acts. In contrast, Optus is not acting as an agent of its customers; instead it only provides them the tool which is a centralised system maintained by it.[132]

In conclusion, the time shifting exemption and other copyright exceptions for private uses of copyright materials derived from the conciliation of interests between the copyright owners, the equipment industries, and the consumers.[133] The legislative purpose of these exceptions, stated by (then) Attorney-General (the Hon Philip Ruddock) in the second reading speech for Australia's *Copyright Amendment Act 2006* (Cth) was to be "[to] ensure that we properly reward people but do not unreasonably disadvantage consumers".[134] The same concern about balancing the interests of rightsholders and consumers should inform our analysis of the law as challenged by the advance of technologies and networks.

To echo the sentiments of Justice Rares, given the complex nature of the intangible form of property in our copyright legislation, courts must "discern where the Parliament drew an enforceable line between the exclusive rights to exploit the proprietary interest it created and conferred on the owner of copyright in a work and the ability of others to use and copy that work".[135] Not every use of copyright material requires the permission of or compensation to the copyright holders. The "ability of others to use and copy" a copyright work has always been recognized by the law because maintaining an appropriate balance between property right and public interest is the core of copyright law's construction since its birth and it seems sensible to maintain this principle in the "cloud".

Acknowledgements The author wishes to thank Professor Brian Fitzgerald, Professor Anne Fitzgerald, Kylie Pappalardo, Dr Nicolas Suzor and Cheryl Foong for their help and comments on various drafts of this chapter. This chapter was first published as an article in (2012) 34(8) E.I.P. R. 519 and is reproduced by kind permission of Sweet & Maxwell.

References

Adhikari S (2012) Optus' TV Now High Court appeal no certainty: report. Business Spectator, 1 May 2012. http://technologyspectator.com.au/industry/media/optus-tv-now-high-court-appeal-no-certainty-report. Last visited 6 May 2012
Battersby L (2011) Threat to AFL millions. The Age, 15 September 2011. http://www.theage.com.au/business/threat-to-afl-millions-20110914-1k9qm.html

---

[132] As Justice Rares said, the user initially chose to record the program and Optus' services merely enabled the user to make those choices and to give effect to them. See, [2012] FCA 34, 95.

[133] As Justice Rares pointed out, the conflicts of interests between the electronic equipment industry and the entertainment industry were once remarkably highlighted by Lord Templeman two decades ago in *C.B.S. Songs Ltd v Amstrad Consumer Electronics Plc*, [1987] 2 WLR 1191; [1988] AC 1013.

[134] See further, Ricketson et al. (2009), pp. 408–409.

[135] [2012] FCA 34, 59.

Bowrey K et al (2010) Australian intellectual property. Oxford University Press

Chang K-A, Park I-P (2011) Challenges and enabling technologies in mobile cloud computing. IEEE COMSOC Multimedia Commun Technical Committee (MMTC) E-Lett 6(10):24

Chessell J (2011) Optus TV ignites row over copyright, 27 July 2011. http://www.theaustralian.com. au/business/companies/optus-tv-app-raises-boundary-quarrel/story-fn91v9q3-1226102337757

Christensenr N (2012) Optus mulls TV Now appeal. The Australian, 1 May 2012

Cohen J et al (2010) Copyright in a global information economy, 3rd edn. Wolters Kluwer

Cunard JP (1996) Past as precedent: some thoughts on novel approaches to the Nexus of digital technologies and the arts. Leonardo 29(3)

Currie B (2011) Optus offers free-to-air TV recording for those on the go. iTech Report, 19 July 2011. http://itechreport.com.au/2011/07/19/optus-offers-free-to-air-tv-recording-for-those-on-the-go/

Edwards M (2011a) Cloud hangs over smart device broadcast rights. ABC News, 15 September 2011.   http://www.abc.net.au/news/2011-09-15/mobile-tv-copyright-dispute-goes-to-court/2901084

Edwards M (2011b) Telstra and Optus in dispute over AFL broadcasts. ABC News, 15 September 2011. http://www.abc.net.au/pm/content/2011/s3318709.htm

Fitzgerald A, Fitzgerald B (2004) Intellectual property in Principle. Lawbook Co.

Ginsburg JC, Ricketson S (2006) Inducers and authorisers: a comparison of the US Supreme Court's *Grokster* decision and the Australian Federal Court's *KaZaa* Ruling. Media Arts Law Rev 11(1):1

Huang D (2011) Mobile cloud computing. IEEE COMSOC Multimedia Commun Technical Committee (MMTC) E-Lett 6(10):27

Kumar K, Lu Y-H (2011) Mobile cloud computing: opportunities and challenges. IEEE COMSOC Multimedia Commun Technical Committee (MMTC) E-Lett 6(10):31

Litman J (2006) The story of Sony v. Universal Studios: Mary Poppins meets the Boston stranger. In: Ginsburg JC, Dreyfuss RC (eds) Intellectual property stories, Chap 5. Foundation Press

Mell P, Grace T (2011) The NIST definition of cloud computing (Draft), January 2011. http://csrc. nist.gov/publications/drafts/800-145/Draft-SP-800-145_cloud-definition.pdf

Nimmer M, Nimmer D (2002) Nimmer on copyright. Matthew Bender & Company, Inc.

Ricketson S et al (2009) Intellectual property: cases, materials and commentary, 4th edn. LexisNexis Butterworths

Ruddock P (Attorney-General of Australia) (2006) Major copyright reforms strike balance. Press Release, 14 May 2006

Stewart A et al (2013) Intellectual property in Australia, 4th edn. LexisNexis Butterworths

Velte T et al (2009) Cloud computing: a practical approach. McGraw Hill

Chapter 13
The Development of Copyright Offences in Australia

Steven Gething

13.1 Introduction

A critical driving force behind the development of copyright law has been facilitating the requirements of the various entertainment publishing industries. The orthodox view of copyright law suggests that without the exclusive rights granted by copyright law, the trade in copyright works would simply not be possible,[1] although it has been posited that this is an article of faith rather than an empirical reality.[2]

The offence provisions are no different in this respect. Their rationale is to deter activities that threaten to disrupt the copyright system. Legislators have been heavily lobbied by representatives of the publishing industries, in some jurisdictions even allowing the industry to draft the statutes themselves.[3]

It comes as a surprise to some observers of copyright issues that offences for copyright infringement exist at all. Even more people are surprised that they are far from a modern development. While there may be nothing new per se about the existence of copyright offences in Australia, it is evident that in the past 35 years there has been a substantial increase in the amount of offences and the severity of the potential penalties.

This increase is closely correlated to technological advancements in the domestic reproduction of entertainment media. This has led to a subsequent loss of exclusive control by industry over the ability to reproduce copyright works. The

---

[1] Fitzgerald and Fitzgerald (2004), p. 10; Landes and Posner (1989), pp. 325 and 326.

[2] Atkinson (2007), p. 6.

[3] See Samuelson (2005), p. 1; Litman (2001); Patry (1996), p. 139.

S. Gething (✉)
Thomas More Academy of Law, Australian Catholic University, 486 Albert Street,
East Melbourne, VIC 3002, Australia
e-mail: steven.gething@gmail.com

© Springer International Publishing Switzerland 2015   291
B. Fitzgerald, J. Gilchrist (eds.), *Copyright Perspectives*,
DOI 10.1007/978-3-319-15913-3_13

domestic availability of the Internet has meant the distribution of entertainment media has also been placed out of the exclusive control of copyright owners.

Another factor which has contributed to the development of more offences is the increase in global trade. Australia has entered into a number of treaties that require the signatories to implement offences in their copyright law.

Such technological advancement can be seen as something of a double-edged sword for the publishing industries. It has the potential to create new opportunities for people to produce, copy and disseminate knowledge and entertainment in new forms and by using new methods. However, the same technology can also be used to infringe the property rights granted to copyright owners, particularly where it is made widely available and at low cost.

Innovations in entertainment delivery have been made by both from inside and outside the publishing industries. Innovations originating from outside have been typically treated as a threat to the publishing businesses rather than an opportunity. The ultimate outcome of the application of technological innovation is highly unpredictable.

Inventions that were initially treated as apocalyptic threats by the publishing industries have in retrospect been of great benefit to the industry when they are harnessed for the creation of new markets and products.[4] Conversely, some inventions produced with the support of the publishing industries have failed in the marketplace.

This chapter charts the expansion of the copyright offences in Australia. By chronologically tracking the changes to the law, a more comprehensive understanding can be gained of the factors that have driven the expansion of copyright offences during the last century and beyond. This allows a clearer picture to emerge of the merits of using the criminal law to sustain copyright policy.

13.2 Overview of the Legal Developments

The law of copyright in England and Wales has always contained criminal provisions of some form. Even the original *Statute of Anne* imposed monetary fines payable to the Crown and the copyright holder in moiety.[5] The same offences were of course brought to Australia with the original colonists, and they have remained a part of the Australian legal landscape.

As each colony developed, their respective colonial Parliaments passed new copyright laws. Shortly after the Federation of the Commonwealth of Australia in 1901, a new national copyright Act was enacted in 1905. Since 1905 the Australian Parliament has passed two more copyright Acts. The last of these Acts, the

---

[4] See for example, the reaction of the Motion Picture Association of America to the video cassette recorder, discussed below at Sect. 13.7.

[5] *Copyright Act 1790*, 8 Anne c.19.

Copyright Act 1968 (Cth), is the current Act governing copyright in Australia. All of these Acts, from pre-Federation until the present Act, have contained offence provisions for the infringement of copyright or other related rights, and for dealing in illicit copies of works.

There were three amendments to the offence provisions between Federation and 1980. Since 1980 there have been nine amendments that have substantially increased the scope of copyright offences. Five of these amendments have occurred since 1998, culminating in the current offence provisions brought about by the *Copyright Amendment Act* 2006 (Cth). The rapidity with which these amendments have occurred mirrors the pace with which technological advances in reproductive and distribution of copyright material have occurred, and agreements that Australia has made with its trading partners to harmonise and reciprocate copyright protection. The absence of an organised opposition to the demands of the publishing industries has meant that the scope of the Australian offences has almost never contracted.

This expansion in scope has occurred in four dimensions: (1) the subject matter of copyright has been expanded; (2) the length of copyright protection has increased; (3) new types of offences have been drafted for conduct peripheral to the infringement of copyright and for new related rights; and (4) the culpability required for offences has been lowered. In addition to expanding the scope, the penalties for the offences have also been raised, purportedly to increase their deterrent value.

13.3   Pre-federation

Before Australian Commonwealth was formed in 1901, several Australian states had enacted their own copyright laws, some of which contained criminal sanctions for infringement.

Representing a unique approach in targeting criminals, the *Copyright Registration Act 1887* (Qld) contained an offence of wilfully tendering a false entry in the copyright register, punishable by up to 3 years imprisonment.[6]

The *Copyright Act 1895* (WA) contained two offences, both of which were punishable upon summary conviction by a penalty of up to 10 pounds.[7]

The *Copyright Act 1890* (Vic) was fairly comprehensive. In addition to books,[8] designs[9] and works of fine art[10] were both capable of copyright protection. Each of these categories had its own criminal offence with infringement of a design being

---

[6] *The Copyright Registration Act 1887* (Qld), 51 Vic. No. 2 s 11.

[7] *Copyright Act 1895* (WA), 59 Vic No. 24 ss 15 and 16.

[8] *Copyright Act 1890* (Vic), 54 Vic No. 1076 s 15.

[9] *Copyright Act 1890* (Vic), 54 Vic No. 1076 s 4.

[10] *Copyright Act 1890* (Vic), 54 Vic No. 1076 s 37.

the most severely punished by a fine of up to 50 pounds.[11] The *Copyright Act 1878* (SA)[12] was very similar to the Victorian statute and contained identical offences and penalties.

Even before Federation, it is clear that the colonies of Australia had accepted a need for copyright legislation and the need for criminal sanctions to encourage compliance.

13.4   The *Copyright Act 1905* (Cth)

The first Federal copyright law, the *Copyright Act 1905* (Cth), contained a single summary offence for dealings in "pirated books" or "pirated artistic works", punishable on conviction by a fine of not more than 5 pounds. Pirated books and artistic works were defined as reproductions made in any manner without the authority of the owner of the copyright.[13]

The various types of offending dealings with these books or artistic works were not dissimilar to the contemporary offences: selling; letting for hire; exposing, offering or keeping (possessing) for sale or hire; distributing; or exhibiting in public were all forbidden if the article was a pirated book or artistic work.[14]

The term of the copyright under the *Copyright Act 1905* (Cth) was far shorter than under subsequent Acts. The Australian Parliament adopted the copyright term of the *Copyright Act 1842* (Imp)[15]: the life of the author and 7 years, or 42 years, whichever was the longer.[16]

---

[11] *Copyright Act 1890* (Vic), 54 Vic No. 1076 s 11.

[12] *Copyright Act 1878* (SA), 41 & 42 Vic No. 96.

[13] *Copyright Act 1905* (Cth), 5 Edw.VII c25 s 4.

[14] *Copyright Act 1905* (Cth), 5 Edw.VII c25 s 50 ("If any person – sells, or lets for hire, or exposes offers or keeps for sale or hire, any pirated book or any pirated artistic work; or distributes, or exhibits in public, any pirated book or any pirated artistic work; or imports into Australia any pirated book or any pirated artistic work, he shall be guilty of an offence against this Act and shall be liable to a penalty not exceeding Five pounds for each copy of such pirated book or pirated artistic work dealt with in contravention of this section, and also forfeit to the owner of the copyright every such copy so dealt with, and also to forfeit the plates, blocks, stone, matrix, negative, or thing, if any, from which the pirated book or pirated artistic work was printed or made").

[15] *Copyright Act 1842* (Imp), 5 & 6 Vict. c45.

[16] See Atkinson (2007), pp. 37–41 for a detailed discussion of the events and debate about the length of the copyright term.

13.5   The *Copyright Act 1912* (Cth)

After the passing of the *Copyright Act 1911* (Imp)[17] in the United Kingdom parliament, the Australian Parliament adopted the imperial law by enacting the *Copyright Act 1912*.[18] Section 11(1) of the *Copyright Act 1911* (Imp) contained several summary offences,[19] most of which were already part the *Copyright Act 1905* (Cth).

Curiously, actually making an infringing copy of a work for sale or hire did not constitute an offence until it was included the *Copyright Act 1912* (Cth).[20] The various types of prohibited conduct under these offence provisions have remained virtually unchanged in the copyright law of several former members of the British Empire. A new offence was added under s 11(2) for making or possessing of a plate for the purposes of making infringing copies, or for causing a public performance of a work knowingly and for personal profit.[21]

The *Copyright Act 1912* (Cth) incorporated section 11 verbatim, except for subsection (4), which was of no application in Australia since neither the *Musical* (*Summary Proceedings*) *Copyright Act 1902* (England and Wales)[22] nor the *Musical Copyright Act 1906* (England and Wales)[23] were adopted into Australian law.

---

[17] *Copyright Act 1911* (Imp), 1 & 2 Geo.V c46.

[18] *Copyright Act 1912* (Cth), 3 Geo.V c20 s 8.

[19] *Copyright Act 1911* (Imp), 1 & 2 Geo.V c46 s 11 ("(1) If any person knowingly – (a) makes for sale or hire any infringing copy of a work in which copyright subsists; or (b) sells or lets for hire, or by way of trade exposes or offers for sale or hire any infringing copy of any such work; or (c) distributes infringing copies of any such work either for the purposes of trade or to such an extent as to affect prejudicially the owner of the copyright; or (d) by way of trade exhibits in public any infringing copy of any such work; or (e) imports for sale or hire into the United Kingdom any infringing copy of any such work, he shall be guilty of an offence under this Act, and be liable on summary conviction to a fine not exceeding forty shillings for every copy dealt with in contravention of this section, but not exceeding fifty pounds in respect of the same transaction; or in the case of a second or subsequent offence, either to such a fine or to imprisonment with or without hard labour for a term not exceeding two months. (2) If any person knowingly makes or has in his possession any plate for the purpose of making infringing copies of any work in which copyright subsists, or knowingly, and for his private profit causes any such work to be performed in public without the consent of the owner of the copyright, he shall be guilty of an offence under this Act, and be liable on summary conviction to a fine not exceeding fifty pounds, or in the case of a second or subsequent offence, either to such a fine or to imprisonment with or without hard labour for a term not exceeding two months. (3) The court before which any such proceedings are taken may, whether the alleged offender is convicted or not, order that all copies of the work or all plates in the possession of the alleged offender, which appear to it to be infringing copies, be destroyed or delivered up to the owner of the copyright or otherwise dealt with as the court may think fit. (4) Nothing in this section shall, as respects musical works affect the provisions of The Musical (Summary Proceedings) Copyright Act, 1902, or the Musical Copyright Act, 1906."

[20] *Copyright Act 1912* (Cth), 3 Geo.V c20 The Schedule, s 11(1)(a).

[21] *Copyright Act 1912* (Cth), 3 Geo.V c20 The Schedule, s 11(2).

[22] *Musical* (*Summary Proceedings*) *Copyright Act 1902* (England and Wales), 2 Edw.VII c15.

[23] *Musical Copyright Act 1906* (England and Wales), 6 Edw.VII c36.

One of the major changes the *Copyright Act 1912* (Cth) brought about was the extension of the copyright term to the life of the author and 50 years, thus extending the scope of the criminal provisions. Another major change that dramatically altered the scope of the offence provisions was the granting of mechanical rights,[24] which meant that recordings of literary, dramatic or musical works were both protected by copyright and subject to the same offence provisions.

However, a minor change ran against the general rule and slightly contracted the scope of the offences in one aspect. Under the *Copyright Act 1905* (Cth) it was an offence to distribute a pirated work or book. The distribution under that Act was not qualified, but under the *Copyright Act 1912* (Cth) the distribution had to be either for the purposes of trade or to such an extent as to prejudicially affect the owner of the copyright.[25]

A great many of the countries which adopted the *Copyright Act 1911* (Imp) still retain an offence for distributing an infringing copy to such an extent as to affect prejudicially the owner of the copyright,[26] with the notable exception of New Zealand which limits criminal distribution offences to commercial infringement.[27] The non-commercial distribution of infringing copies has really only in recent times come to the fore, due to the ease with which digital material can be disseminated over the internet.[28]

The penalty for summary conviction under either s 11(1) or (2) was a fine of 40 shillings for each copy dealt with, not exceeding 50 pounds for the same transaction. A second or subsequent offence was punishable by the same fine or by imprisonment for a period not exceeding 2 months with or without hard labour. This was the first time that a person was capable of being imprisoned for a copyright offence in Australia and represented a significant enhancement to the penalty provision.

The development of technological innovations such as cinema, radio and television in the years between the enactment of the *Copyright Act 1912* (Cth) and the *Copyright Act 1968* (Cth) also caused great difficulties for copyright law. However the disputes that they caused between broadcasters and copyright owners were settled through licensing and royalty collection rather than through changes to the criminal law.[29]

The cases of radio and television first illustrate the concept of new technology broadening the range of possible conduct that could constitute an offence, since the playing copyrighted work on a radio or television set in public, knowingly and for

---

[24] *Copyright Act 1912* (Cth), 3 Geo.V c20 The Schedule, s 2(d).

[25] *Copyright Act 1912* (Cth), 3 Geo.V c20 The Schedule, s 11(1)(c).

[26] Examples include countries such as Canada (s 42(1)(c) *Copyright Act 1985*) and Saint Lucia (s 52(1)(d) *Copyright Act 1995*).

[27] *Copyright Act* 1994 (New Zealand), s 198(1)(d)(iii).

[28] For example, the case of *Hong Kong v Chan Nai Ming* [2005] HKLRD 142, where the defendant was convicted under the equivalent offence in the *Hong Kong Copyright Ordinance*.

[29] For a full discussion of these events see Atkinson (2007), pp. 112–136.

private profit, would have constituted an offence under the *Copyright Act 1912* (Cth), s 11(2). Rather than the law moving to capture the new conduct, the new conduct strayed into the realm of the offence.

13.6   The *Copyright Act 1968* (Cth)

The criminal provisions of the *Copyright Act 1968* (Cth), as passed, were not substantially different from those of the *Copyright Act 1912* (Cth), except the offences became housed in s 132[30] and the penalty provisions for those offences were contained in s 133.[31] By this time it had been firmly established that sound recordings and cinematographic films were subject matters capable of copyright protection and the new Act dedicated a new Part IV to the rights in these subject matters. The offence section made it expressly clear that they were to apply to Part IV subject matter.[32]

   The scope of the offences was broadened slightly by altering what the purpose for importing an infringing copy had to be before an offence was committed. Under the *Copyright Act 1912* (Cth) it had been an offence to import an infringing copy for the purpose of selling or letting it for hire.[33] Under the new Act, this was extended to importations for the purpose of[34]: (1) by way of trade, offering or exposing the copy for sale or hire; (2) distributing the article for the purpose of trade or any other purpose to an extent that will affect prejudicially the owner of the copyright; or (3) by way of trade, exhibiting the article in public. A person was required to know

---

[30] *Copyright Act 1968* (Cth) s 132 (circa 1968) ("(1) A person shall not, at a time when copyright subsists in a work- (a) make an article for sale or hire; (b) sell or let for hire, or by way of trade offer or expose for sale or hire, an article; (c) by way of trade exhibit an article in public; or (d) import an article into Australia for the purpose of- (i) selling, letting for hire, or by way of trade offering or exposing for sale or hire, the article; (ii) distributing the article for the purpose of trade, or for any other purpose to an extent that will affect prejudicially the owner of the copyright in the work; or (iii) by way of trade exhibiting the article in public, if he knows the article to be an infringing copy of the work. (2) A person shall not, at a time when copyright subsists in a work, distribute - (a) for the purpose of trade; or (b) for any other purpose to an extent that affects prejudicially the owner of the copyright, an article that he knows to be an infringing copy of the work. (3) A person shall not, at a time when copyright subsists in a work, make or have in his possession a plate knowing that it is to be used for making infringing copies of the work. (4) The last three preceding sub-sections apply in relation to copyright subsisting in any subject-matter by virtue of Part IV in like manner as they apply in relation to copyright subsisting in a work by virtue of Part III. (5) A person shall not cause a literary, dramatical or musical work to be performed in public, knowing that copyright subsists in the work and that the performance constitutes an infringement of the copyright. (6) This section applies only in respect of acts done in Australia.")

[31] *Copyright Act 1968* (Cth) s 133 (circa 1968).

[32] *Copyright Act 1968* (Cth) s 132(4) (circa 1968).

[33] *Copyright Act 1912* (Cth), 3 Geo.V c20 The Schedule, s (11)(1)(e).

[34] *Copyright Act 1968* (Cth) s 132(1)(d) (circa 1968).

that the imported article was an infringing copy before criminal liability was attracted.[35]

The penalty for a first conviction was extended to 10 pounds for each infringing article,[36] not exceeding 200 pounds for the same transaction.[37] Second or subsequent offences could alternatively be punished by a term of imprisonment of not exceeding 2 months,[38] as they could under the *Copyright Act 1912* (Cth).

The *Copyright Act 1968* (Cth) is the same Act that we have today in Australia. There have been a substantial number of amendments to the Act, but only some have amended the offence provisions. These amendments have been made in reaction to a perceived problem caused by the introduction of technological innovations, unfavourable court judgments and to fulfil international treaty obligations.

13.7 The *Copyright Amendment Act 1980* (Cth)

The invention and marketing of the video cassette recorder ("VCR")[39] in the late 1970s caused considerable concern to the motion picture industry, which saw it as a serious threat to its business model. VCRs were capable of recording motion pictures from television broadcasts, which could be copied and distributed, or kept privately as an archive. The motion picture industry approved of neither of these activities, but was particularly concerned about the implications on television aftermarkets.

In the United States, the long-time president of the Motion Picture Association of America Jack Valenti gave testimony before the House of Representatives *Home Recording of Copyrighted Works* hearings in 1982. His doom-laden testimony represented the concerns of the industry at the time. He stated:

> ...now we are facing a very new and a very troubling assault on our fiscal security, on our very economic life and we are facing it from a thing called the video cassette recorder and its necessary companion called the blank tape. And it is like a great tidal wave just off the shore. This video cassette recorder and the blank tape threaten profoundly the life-sustaining protection, I guess you would call it, on which copyright owners depend, on which film people depend, on which television people depend and it is called copyright [...] these machines are advertised for one purpose in life. Their only single mission, their primary mission is to copy copyrighted material that belongs to other people. I don't have to go into it. The ads are here. Here is Sony that tells you that you can record one channel while watching another. You can program to record a variety of shows on four different channels for up to 14 days in advance if you like [...]I say to you that the VCR is to the

---

[35] *Copyright Act 1968* (Cth) s 132(1)(d)(iii) (circa 1968).

[36] *Copyright Act 1968* (Cth) s 133(1)(a) (circa 1968).

[37] *Copyright Act 1968* (Cth) s 133(2) (circa 1968).

[38] *Copyright Act 1968* (Cth) s 133(1)(b) (circa 1968).

[39] See http://en.wikipedia.org/wiki/Videocassette_recorder. Accessed 5 February 2014.

American film producer and the American public as the Boston strangler is to the woman home alone.[40]

The impact of Valenti's testimony was somewhat deflated by the following exchange with Congressman Robert Kastenmeier:

Mr. Kastenmeier: Jack, let me ask you. Do you consider yourself and your family infringers when you engage in that practice?

Mr. Valenti: I consider myself and my family believing what the plaintiffs in this lawsuit said and they said publicly, they have said it to the press, they have said it to the lawyers, they have said it to the courts. They do not intend to file any actions against homeowners now or in the future. I mean, that is obvious and they have said that publicly, Mr. Chairman, so I believe them. As far as I am concerned, I am going to continue taping because the plaintiffs have said they aren't going to do anything to me. I am not committing any crime. They know that.

Mr. Kastenmeier: That wasn't my question.

Mr. Valenti: Do I consider myself an infringer?

Mr. Kastenmeier: When you engage in such practice.

Mr. Valenti: Yes, sir, I do. I am taking somebody else's copyrighted material without their consent and I know damn well I am infringing. But as far as court action or anything else, I am safe. First, it is not a criminal act. Again, the opposition would tell you video, police, and criminals. They show an astonishing lack of the copyright law. They know good and well that that is not a criminal infringement unless you do it for profit. But on the other hand the plaintiffs have said they are moving against anybody in the homes. There is no problem, but I know and everybody else knows they are infringing.[41]

While this hearing had no direct effect on the Australian legislature, it provides a vivid illustration of the level of concern that the VCR initially caused the motion picture industry and the lobbying process that occurs when new copying technologies emerge. The VCR did not have the destructive consequence on the motion picture industry that Valenti portended, instead becoming a lucrative aftermarket for motion pictures.

The Australian response in 1980 to the "problem" of the VCR was to increase the penalty for an offence under ss 132(1) or (2) of the *Copyright Act 1968* (Cth) to $150 per infringing article,[42] and to increase the penalty to $1,500 if the article was a cinematograph film.[43] Second or subsequent offences under either subsection could alternatively be punishable by up to 6 months imprisonment,[44] increasing the maximum term of imprisonment threefold.

---

[40] U.S. Congress, House of Representatives, Committee on the Judiciary, Subcommittee on Courts, Civil Liberties, and the Administration of Justice (1983).

[41] U.S. Congress, House of Representatives, Committee on the Judiciary, Subcommittee on Courts, Civil Liberties, and the Administration of Justice (1983).

[42] *Copyright Amendment Act 1980* (Cth) s 18, amending *Copyright Act 1968* (Cth) s 133.

[43] *Copyright Amendment Act 1980* (Cth) s 18, amending *Copyright Act 1968* (Cth) s 133.

[44] *Copyright Amendment Act 1980* (Cth) s 18, amending *Copyright Act 1968* (Cth) s 133.

13.8   The *Copyright Amendment Act 1984* (Cth)

In 1984, further amendments were made to include provisions related to the transmission of computer programs and the advertisement for supply of infringing copies of computer programs. These provisions were a direct response to the judgment of Beaumont J in *Apple Computer Inc v Computer Edge Pty Ltd*.[45] Beaumont J had held in the case that none of the computer programs in the case were literary works under the *Copyright Act 1968* (Cth)[46] and that the omission by Parliament to make any reference to computers or computer equipment meant computer programs were not afforded copyright protection.[47]

Although the decision was overturned in the Full Federal Court,[48] the Australian Parliament was sufficiently concerned about the implications for the Australian software industry that the *Copyright Amendment Act 1984* (Cth) was passed the week after the Full Federal Court handed down its decision. The Australian Parliament had correctly assessed the fragility of the Full Federal Court decision because it was subsequently overturned by the High Court of Australia.[49] In addition to expressly extending the definition of literary work to include computer programs, the amendment added another subsection to the offence provisions contained in s 132:

> (5A) For the purposes of this section, a transmission by a person of a computer program that is received and recorded so as to result in the creation of an infringing copy of the computer program shall be deemed to be a distribution by the person of that infringing copy.[50]

This amendment meant that the distribution offence in s 132(2) could be applied to cases of software transmitted by telephone modems, an activity that would eventually progress to the transmission of other digital works through the Internet. The addition of a new s 133A also made it a criminal offence to advertise for the supply of infringing computer programs, which was penalised by a fine of $1,500 for a first offence and the same fine or imprisonment for 6 months for a second or subsequent offence.[51]

---

[45] *Apple Computer Inc v Computer Edge Pty Ltd* (1983) 1 IPR 353.

[46] *Apple Computer Inc v Computer Edge Pty Ltd* (1983) 1 IPR 353, 354.

[47] *Apple Computer Inc v Computer Edge Pty Ltd* (1983) 1 IPR 353, 354.

[48] *Apple Computer Inc v Computer Edge Pty Ltd* (1984) 2 IPR 1.

[49] *Computer Edge Pty Ltd v Apple Computer Inc* (1986) 6 IPR 1.

[50] *Copyright Amendment Act 1984* (Cth) s 5, amending *Copyright Act 1968* (Cth) s 132.

[51] *Copyright Amendment Act 1984* (Cth) s 6, amending *Copyright Act 1968* (Cth) s 132.

13.9 The *Copyright Amendment Act 1986* (Cth)

A significant change to the scope of all offences under s 132 of the *Copyright Act 1968* (Cth) was made by the passing of the *Copyright Amendment Act 1986* (Cth). Prior to the amendment, part of the *mens rea* of subsections (1) and (2) was the requirement of actual knowledge that the article in question was an infringing copy. The amendment broadened the *mens rea* of the offence by substituting the words "he knows" to "the person knows, or ought reasonably to know".[52] In addition to broadening the *mens rea* of the offences, the *Copyright Amendment Act 1986* (Cth) also broadened the range of conduct that could constitute an offence by criminalising the possession of infringing copies for the purposes of either[53]: (1) selling, letting for hire, or by way of trade offering or exposing for sale or hire (2) distributing the article for the purpose of trade, or for any other purpose to an extent that will affect prejudicially the owner of the copyright in the work; or (3) by way of trade exhibiting the article in public. This offence section was housed in s 132(2A).

The effect of these changes is illustrated by the case of *Pontello v Giannotis*,[54] which was the first reported prosecution under the *Copyright Act 1968* (Cth) subsequent to the passing of the *Copyright Amendment Act 1986* (Cth). The principle issue in the case was the question of the knowledge of the defendant.[55] Giannotis was a partner in a video hire business who was found to be in possession of a number of infringing copies of copyrighted work for the purpose of letting them for hire, contrary to the new s 132(2A).

Giannotis had acquired infringing copies of some films that had been stolen from his shop[56] from a contact called "Mimo".[57] In his police interview, Giannotis reported the conversation during the transaction between himself and Mimo as being:

> [I said] What did you do, he said don't ask me questions you're happy, I say of course I'm happy, how much cost, he said nothing only if you like to swap some of your movies for some of my movies, and after that we started to swap some movies[58]

It was held that the prosecution had established beyond a reasonable doubt that Giannotis ought to have known that each of the articles were infringing copies for a number of reasons: his history in the video industry; his knowledge of copyright and pirate copies; his knowledge that videos could be copied and the unlikelyhood of

---

[52] *Copyright Amendment Act 1986* (Cth) s 15, amending *Copyright Act 1968* (Cth) s 132.

[53] *Copyright Amendment Act 1986* (Cth) s 15, amending *Copyright Act 1968* (Cth) s 132.

[54] *Pontello v Giannotis* (1989) 16 IPR 174.

[55] *Pontello v Giannotis* (1989) 16 IPR 174, 174.

[56] *Pontello v Giannotis* (1989) 16 IPR 174, 181.

[57] *Pontello v Giannotis* (1989) 16 IPR 174, 181.

[58] *Pontello v Giannotis* (1989) 16 IPR 174, 181.

not appreciating the danger of dealing with a vendor of secondhand tapes.[59]
Sheppard J stated:

> I must confess that the case for holding that there is here demonstrated actual knowledge is
> a strong one, but I must bear in mind, as I have indicated, that the tapes which were
> purchased from Mr Mimo, who said to the defendant to ask him no questions, were not
> necessarily all the tapes which are the subject of the charge. The evidence does not enable
> one to tell. In the result I have reached the conclusion that I ought not to find actual
> knowledge but I do, as I say, find that the defendant ought reasonably to have known that
> each of the articles was an infringing copy of the films in question[60]

The prosecution had relied on the authority[61] of *Taylor's Central Garages
(Exeter) Ltd v Roper*,[62] in which Devlin J (later Lord Devlin) had discussed the
various legal classes of "knowledge". Devlin J stated in that case that the words
"ought reasonably to know" encompass constructive knowledge, which is merely
neglecting to make such enquiries as a reasonable and prudent person would make,
and that generally constructive knowledge has no place in the criminal law.[63]
Giannotis was sentenced to be bound over for 3 years and ordered to pay costs of
$6,500.

In the conclusion of his judgment Sheppard J commented upon the evidentiary
difficulties of proving that a defendant possessed the required degree of knowledge
of the status of the infringing copy. He stated that there the lack of familiarity with
copyright was a problem in the video hire industry and it would be desirable for the
Australian Film and Video Security Office to prepare a short explanation document
for video hire shop owners. He suggested the video hire industry would be helped
by this knowledge, and additionally it would be easier to prove a shop owner or
employee had constructive knowledge that an article was an infringing copy in the
event of a prosecution.[64]

The inclusion of a possession offence in the *Copyright Amendment Act 1986*
(Cth) allowed prosecutions to be brought against shop owners such as Giannotis
without the need for trap purchases or witnessing transactions. An investigator
could gather sufficient evidence from an inspection of the premises, and if the
owner or employee of the shop was still in possession of the infringing copies when
the police visited, they could usually be successfully prosecuted without the need to
prove that the copies had been sold, hired, distributed or exhibited.

The *Copyright Amendment Act 1986* (Cth) implemented a number of other
changes to the offence provisions. It was thought that the scope of the offence of
causing a performance in public would be inappropriately wide if the standard *mens*

---

[59] *Pontello v Giannotis* (1989) 16 IPR 174, 174.

[60] *Pontello v Giannotis* (1989) 16 IPR 174, 185.

[61] *Pontello v Giannotis* (1989) 16 IPR 174, 176.

[62] *Taylor's Central Garages (Exeter) Ltd v Roper* [1951] WN 383.

[63] *Taylor's Central Garages (Exeter) Ltd v Roper* [1951] WN 383, 385.

[64] *Pontello v Giannotis* (1989) 16 IPR 174, 188.

rea element of "ought to know" was applied to the offence.[65] To counter-balance the effect of the change to the *mens rea* element, the circumstances in which the conduct had to occur were altered from "in public" to "in public at a place of public entertainment".[66] A place of public entertainment was defined as including any premises that are occupied principally for purposes other than public entertainment but are from time to time made available for hire for purposes of public entertainment.[67] A new subsection 132(5AA) also made it an offence to cause the performance of a sound recording or a film at a place of public entertainment.[68]

The *Copyright Amendment Act 1986* (Cth) also made substantial changes to the penalties for the offences.[69] The penalty for a first offence was raised to a $500 fine per article for an offence committed by a natural person and a $2,500 fine for an offence committed by a body corporate. If the article was a cinematographic film, the penalty for an offence committed by a natural person could also be punished by not more than 2 years imprisonment, in addition to the existing $1,500 fine for each infringing article. The fine for a body corporate was raised to a $7,500 fine per infringing copy of a cinematographic film.

For second or subsequent offences, the penalty for natural persons was raised to $500 per infringing article, or $1,500 per article and/or 5 years imprisonment if the infringing article was a cinematographic film. The fine for second or subsequent offences committed by a body corporate was also enhanced for cinematographic films: $15,000 per infringing article as opposed to $5,000 in any other case.

13.10   The *Copyright Amendment Act 1989* (Cth)

The *Copyright Amendment Act 1989* (Cth) created a number of offences which were designed to strengthen the protection for performers.[70] The penalties for contravening these offences were prescribed in s 248R and varied in severity according to factors such as the status of the defendant, whether the offence was a first or subsequent offence, whether the infringing article was a sound recording or a cinematograph film and in which court the person or corporation was prosecuted.[71]

The amendment as a whole (inclusive of the civil penalties) was ostensibly implemented to allow Australia to ratify[72] the *International Convention for the Protection of Performers, Producers of Phonograms and Broadcasting*

---

[65] Explanatory Memorandum, Copyright Amendment Bill 1986 (Cth) 46.

[66] *Copyright Amendment Act 1986* (Cth) s 15, amending *Copyright Act 1968* (Cth).

[67] *Copyright Amendment Act 1986* (Cth) s 15, amending *Copyright Act 1968* (Cth).

[68] *Copyright Amendment Act 1986* (Cth) s 15, amending *Copyright Act 1968* (Cth).

[69] *Copyright Amendment Act 1986* (Cth) s 16, amending *Copyright Act 1968* (Cth).

[70] *Copyright Amendment Act 1989* (Cth) s 28, amending *Copyright Act 1968* (Cth).

[71] *Copyright Amendment Act 1989* (Cth) s 28, amending *Copyright Act 1968* (Cth).

[72] Explanatory Memorandum, Copyright Amendment Bill 1988 (Cth) General Outline.

Organizations.[73] However under the convention Australia is only obligated to implement civil laws to protect performance; there is no obligation to provide criminal laws.

One of the more interesting aspects to this amendment is that four of the new offences, found in s 248P, were intended to be strict liability offences. Section 277 of the Explanatory Memorandum to the Copyright Amendment Bill stated:

> The offences contained in [ss 248P(1) to (4)] are intended to be of a strict liability nature and not to be subject to proof of the defendant's actual or imputed knowledge. As unauthorised recording, broadcasting and transmission are practices which are not only direct breaches of the rights conferred on performers but are obviously fundamental to enabling the profit-oriented offences to occur, it was considered appropriate to impose strict liability in order to deter potential offenders[74]

However, the legislation as enacted did not explicitly state that the offences were offences of strict liability, and it is unlikely that a court would have held that the construction of the relevant sections required the assistance of extrinsic material.[75] In the absence of an express *mens rea* element, the courts have consistently held that the *mens rea* should be implied, unless it can be shown that Parliament had intended otherwise.

In *Sweet v Parsley*,[76] the defendant had been charged with being concerned in the management of premises which were used for the purpose of smoking cannabis under s 5(b) of the *Dangerous Drugs Act 1965* (England and Wales). Section 5 (b) did not specify a *mens rea* element. Reid LJ said:

> [...] it is firmly established by a host of authorities that *mens rea* is an essential ingredient of every offence unless some reason can be found for holding that that is not necessary. It is also firmly established that the fact that other sections of the Act expressly require *mens rea*, for example because they contain the word "knowingly", is not in itself sufficient to justify a decision that a section which is silent as to *mens rea* creates an absolute offence. In the absence of a clear indication in the Act that an offence is intended to be an absolute offence, it is necessary to go outside the Act and examine all relevant circumstances in order to establish that this must have been the intention of Parliament. I say "must have been", because it is a universal principle that if a penal provision is reasonably capable of two interpretations, that interpretation which is most favourable to the accused must be adopted.[77]

Lord Morris agreed with Reid LJ:

> [...] it has frequently been affirmed and should unhesitatingly be recognised that it is a cardinal principle of our law that *mens rea*, an evil intention or a knowledge of the wrongfulness of the act, is in all ordinary cases an essential ingredient of guilt of a criminal offence. If follows from this that there will not be guilt of an offence created by statute

---

[73] *International Convention for the Protection of Performers, Producers of Phonograms and Broadcasting Organisations*, opened for signature 26 October 1962, 496 UNTS 43.

[74] Explanatory Memorandum, Copyright Amendment Bill 1988 (Cth) 277.

[75] *Acts Interpretation Act 1901* (Cth) s 15AB.

[76] *Sweet v Parsley* [1969] 1 All ER 347.

[77] *Sweet v Parsley* [1969] 1 All ER 347, 350.

unless there is *mens rea* or unless Parliament has by the statute enacted that guilt may be established in cases where there is no *mens rea*.[78]

The Australian case of *He Kaw Teh v R*[79] also held that there is a presumption that *mens rea* is an essential ingredient in every offence, including offences created by statute.[80] As is the case with many of the criminal provisions in the *Copyright Act 1968* (Cth), the matter was never judicially considered and subsequent amendments have made the possibility of strict liability under the provisions a moot point. However, it is clear that the scope of the offences in the *Copyright Act 1968* (Cth) was once again expanded, this time by creating an entirely new scheme of offences.

13.11 The *Copyright Amendment Act 1998* (Cth)

The *Copyright Amendment Act 1998* (Cth) made major alterations to the existing penalties for both the new offence provisions created by *Copyright Amendment Act 1989* (Cth) and the established offence provisions under ss 132 and 133A of the *Copyright Act 1968* (Cth). The Explanatory Memorandum explains that this was done in response to industry concerns about piracy and for a consistent approach to penalties.[81]

The penalties for offences under ss 132, 248P, 248Q and 248QA of the *Copyright Act 1968* (Cth) were raised to a fine of not more than $55,000 which was expressed in penalty units in accordance with Commonwealth criminal law policy.[82] Penalty units were introduced in 1992 by the *Crimes Legislation Amendment Act 1992* (Cth) with a penalty unit valued at $100.[83] This was raised to $110 by the *Crimes and Other Legislation Amendment Act 1997* (Cth).[84] The fines were therefore expressed as 550 penalty units.

The distinction between first and subsequent offences, and between cinematographic films and other subject matter or works, was removed. In addition to the increased fine, individuals could also be imprisoned for up to 5 years for any of the offences except s 133A. In the context of the criminal law this was quite extraordinary, since the offences remained summary offences. Under s 4G of the *Crimes Act 1914*, all offences against the Commonwealth that are punishable by imprisonment for more than 12 months are indictable offences, unless the contrary intention

---

[78] *Sweet v Parsley* [1969] 1 All ER 347, 352.

[79] *He Kaw Teh v R* (1985) 60 ALR 449.

[80] *He Kaw Teh v R* (1985) 60 ALR 449, 449.

[81] Explanatory Memorandum, Copyright Amendment Bill 1997 (No 2) (Cth) 15.

[82] *Copyright Amendment Act 1998* (Cth) ss 1,4,5 and 6 amending *Copyright Act 1968* (Cth), ss 132, 248P, 248Q and 248QA.

[83] *Crimes Legislation Act 1992* (Cth) s 19 amending *Crimes Act 1914* (Cth).

[84] *Crimes and Other Legislation Amendment Act 1997* (Cth), sch 1(9), amending *Crimes Act 1914* (Cth) s 4AA.

appears.[85] The difference between a conviction on indictment and a summary conviction is important, since the *Australian Constitution* on guarantees a jury trial for offences against the Commonwealth tried on indictment.[86] The amended *Copyright Act 1968* (Cth) did indicate that the offences could be tried summarily, so the right to a jury trial was effectively negated despite the severity of the penalty.

Due to the operation s 4B(3) of the *Crimes Act 1914* (Cth), the maximum fine for a corporation could be five times the pecuniary penalty imposed on an individual, but only if a court saw fit.[87] The penalty for an offence under s 133A was also raised to 15 penalty units and/or 6 months imprisonment for an individual and 150 penalty units for a corporation.[88]

After these amendments, the penalties for offences under the *Copyright Act 1968* (Cth) were at their peak in relation to the culpability required by the offences. It was not until the *Copyright Amendment Act 2006* (Cth) created tiered offences that the penalty for summary offences was reduced to 2 years imprisonment.

13.12   The *Copyright Amendment (Digital Agenda) Act 2000* (Cth)

The rapid developments in communications technologies and digital technology prompted the Australian Parliament to pass the *Copyright Amendment (Digital Agenda) Act 2000* (Cth).[89] During the mid to late 1990s the VCR was being superceded by the DVD, vinyl records and magnetic tapes had largely been replaced by CDs, personal computers had greatly improved computing power and as such were capable of playing CDs and DVD, and Internet connections were made available to domestic users.

These technological developments meant that there was little or no cost associated with the transmission of multiple infringing copies of copyright material,[90] and protection systems for digital products such as DVDs could be circumvented by computers. The greatest strength of digital products is also its greatest weakness: digital reproduction enables lossless reproduction.[91] This is advantageous to manufacturers in that the quality of the product can be maintained, since each copy of a digitally processed work is the same as another. However, this also means that illicit copies of digital media are of the same high quality, to the extent that they can substitute for the genuine article.

---

[85] *Crimes Act 1914*, s 4G.

[86] *Australian Constitution* s 80.

[87] *Crimes Act 1914* s 4B(3).

[88] *Copyright Amendment Act 1998* (Cth) s 3, amending *Copyright Act 1968* (Cth) ss 133A.

[89] Explanatory Memorandum, Copyright Amendment (Digital Agenda) Bill 1999 Outline.

[90] Explanatory Memorandum, Copyright Amendment (Digital Agenda) Bill 1999 Outline.

[91] See http://en.wikipedia.org/wiki/Digital_data. Accessed 5 February 2014.

The use of technological protection measures to prevent and deter copying has not been successful. For example, the motion picture industry instituted a technological protection measure called the Content Scramble System which was designed to prevent the playback of DVDs that lacked an encrypted key which could be any one of 1,099,511,627,776 different keys. In October 1999 a computer program called DeCSS[92] was released via an Internet mailing list called LiViD. The program enabled a personal computer to decrypt the Content Scramble System on a commercial DVD. Once the Content Scramble System is decrypted it is possible to make a perfect reproduction of the DVD. One of the programmers responsible for the DeCSS program was a Norwegian teenager called Jon Lech Johansen,[93] who was unsuccessfully prosecuted by the Norwegian authorities for his involvement. The compromise of the CSS system is but one example of what has been characterised as a technological arms race[94] between the publishing industries and computer hackers to prevent the infringement of copyright. One security expert has been quoted as saying a solution to the problem is impossible, akin to "making water not wet".[95]

To address these problems, the *Copyright Amendment (Digital Agenda) Act* created a number of new offences concerning: (1) circumvention services and devices[96]; (2) the removal or alteration of electronic rights management information[97]; (3) dealings in copies after the removal or alteration of electronic rights management information[98]; and (4) dealing in and using broadcast decoding devices.[99] No offence was created by the *Copyright Amendment (Digital Agenda) Act* 2000 for the private use of broadcast decoding devices, but under the new s 135ANA of the *Copyright Act 1968* it was offence to use such a device for commercial purposes.

The penalties for offences committed under ss 132(1), (2) and (2A) were enhanced by s 133(6AA) if the article was an infringing copy because it was made by converting a work or other subject-matter from a hardcopy or an analogue form into a digital or other electronic machine-readable form.[100] The new penalty

---

[92] See http://en.wikipedia.org/wiki/DeCSS. Accessed 5 February 2014.

[93] See http://en.wikipedia.org/wiki/Jon_Lech_Johansen. Accessed 5 February 2014.

[94] Johnson (2007).

[95] Johnson (2007).

[96] *Copyright Amendment (Digital Agenda) Act 2000* (Cth) s 100, amending *Copyright Act 1968* (Cth).

[97] *Copyright Amendment (Digital Agenda) Act 2000* (Cth) s 100, amending *Copyright Act 1968* (Cth).

[98] *Copyright Amendment (Digital Agenda) Act 2000* (Cth) s 100, amending *Copyright Act 1968* (Cth).

[99] *Copyright Amendment (Digital Agenda) Act 2000* (Cth) s 104, amending *Copyright Act 1968* (Cth).

[100] *Copyright Amendment (Digital Agenda) Act* 2000 s 100A, amending *Copyright Act 1968* (Cth).

did not change the maximum term of imprisonment available, but raised the fine
from 550 penalty points to 850 penalty points.[101]

13.13 The *Copyright Amendment (Parallel Importation) Act 2003* (Cth)

In addition to changing evidentiary presumptions to the ownership of copyright in
works or other subject matter,[102] the *Copyright Amendment (Parallel Importation)
Act 2003* (Cth) amended s 133A of the *Copyright Act (1968)* (Cth).[103] Until this
point s 133A only applied to the advertisement of computer software, but after the
Act was passed the section applied to all infringing copies of works and other
subject matter.

13.14 The *US Free Trade Agreement Implementation Act 2004* (Cth) and the *Copyright Legislation Amendment Act 2004* (Cth)

The next amendment to the offences in the *Copyright Act 1968* (Cth) occurred as a
result of the *Australia–US Free Trade Agreement*,[104] which was ratified by the *US
Free Trade Agreement Implementation Act 2004* (Cth). To implement Australia's
treaty obligations, the Act expanded the criminal provisions related to encoded
broadcasts, making it an offence to receive or distribute encoded broadcasts.[105] The
offences in relation to electronic rights management information were also
expanded by making it an offence not only to deal in infringing copies that had
information removed or altered, but by dealing in the information itself.[106]

The offences under s 132 of the *Copyright Act 1968* (Cth) were also amended to
include the words "with the intention of obtaining a commercial advantage or

---

[101] *Copyright Amendment (Digital Agenda) Act* 2000 s 100A, amending *Copyright Act 1968* (Cth).

[102] *Copyright Amendment (Parallel Importation) Act 2003* (Cth) s 8, amending *Copyright Act 1968* (Cth).

[103] *Copyright Amendment (Parallel Importation) Act 2003* (Cth) s 9, amending *Copyright Act 1968* (Cth), s 133A(1)(a).

[104] *Australia–US Free Trade Agreement*, 18 May 2004, [2005] ATS 1.

[105] *US Free Trade Agreement Implementation Act 2004* (Cth) s 169, amending *Copyright Act 1968* (Cth).

[106] *US Free Trade Agreement Implementation Act 2004* (Cth) s 139, amending *Copyright Act 1968* (Cth).

profit" were the offence had an element concerning trade.[107] This particular amendment had the unintended consequence that the scope of the offences was temporarily narrowed, since instead of amending the offences to read "or with the intention of obtaining a commercial advantage or profit", they instead read "and with the intention of obtaining a commercial advantage or profit". This embarrassing oversight was remedied by the passing of the *Copyright Legislation Amendment Act 2004* (Cth) which amended "and" to "or" in all instances where this occurred.[108]

A new offence was created which made it an offence to engage in any conduct that resulted in an infringement of copyright, which had a substantial prejudicial impact on the copyright owner and occurred on a commercial scale.[109] Quite obviously this broadened the scope of the offence provisions massively. The section was drafted to satisfy Article 17.11.26(a) which requires criminal procedures and penalties to be applied for "wilful copyright piracy on a commercial scale"[110] which includes "significant wilful infringements of copyright, that have no direct or indirect motivation of financial gain".[111] Rather than examine the scope of the existing provisions and fill any gaps, this offence was simply overlaid to satisfy the treaty obligation. It is arguable that it went further than was necessary. The copyright legislation of the United States was not amended to mirror the same scope as this new offence.

Perhaps the greatest change in the scope of the criminal offences in this amendment was the extension of the term of copyright to the lifetime of the author and 70 years[112] or 70 years from the date of first publication or performance.[113]

13.15   The *Copyright Amendment Act 2006* (Cth)

The most recent changes to the offences in the *Copyright Act 1968* (Cth) were made by the *Copyright Amendment Act 2006* (Cth). The Act restructured most of the existing offences to a tiered system of culpability consisting of indictable offences, summary offences and strict liability offences. The explanations given for these amendments were: (1) they would provide police and prosecutors with a wider

---

[107] *US Free Trade Agreement Implementation Act 2004* (Cth) ss 146–153, amending *Copyright Act 1968* (Cth), s 132.

[108] *Copyright Legislation Amendment Act 2004* (Cth) ss 18–28, amending *Copyright Act 1968* (Cth) s 132.

[109] *Copyright Legislation Amendment Act 2004* (Cth) s 154, amending *Copyright Act 1968* (Cth) s 132.

[110] *Australia–US Free Trade Agreement*, 18 May 2004, [2005] ATS 1, art 17.11.26(a).

[111] *Australia–US Free Trade Agreement*, 18 May 2004, [2005] ATS 1, art 17.11.26(a)(i).

[112] *US Free Trade Agreement Implementation Act 2004* (Cth) ss 120–122, amending *Copyright Act 1968* (Cth) ss 33(2), 33(3), 33(5) and 34(1).

[113] *US Free Trade Agreement Implementation Act 2004* (Cth) ss 123–126, amending *Copyright Act 1968* (Cth) ss 81(2), 93 and 94.

range of penalty options to pursue against suspected offenders depending on the seriousness of the conduct[114]; (2) they would draw a clear line between indictable and summary offences, as they were previously inconsistent with the standard Commonwealth criminal law policy in s 4G of the *Crimes Act 1914* (Cth)[115]; and (3) the tiering of the offences would ensure that penalties were reflective of the moral culpability of a particular offence.[116]

While the culpability required for the offences carrying the penalty of 5 years imprisonment were slightly stricter after the amendment, therefore narrowing the scope of the higher tier offences, the inclusion of the strict liability offences meant that the overall scope of the offences is exponentially broader. Since the passing of the *Copyright Amendment Act 2006* (Cth), a person who does not even know of the existence of copyright law can be held criminally liable for a variety of dealings in infringing articles.

In addition to the introduction of the strict liability offences, the *Copyright Amendment Act 2006* (Cth) introduced evidential presumptions for criminal prosecutions relating to the subsistence and ownership of copyright in Part V, Division 5, Subdivision G of the *Copyright Act 1968* (Cth). These provisions allow a rebuttable presumption to be made about who owns copyright in a work or other subject matter and the year of first publication based upon the labelling applied by the manufacturer.

The manner in which the strict liability offences and the new evidential presumptions entered the statute book gives cause for concern. In 2002, the Senate Standing Committee for the Scrutiny of Bills produced a report entitled *Application of Absolute and Strict Liability Offences in Commonwealth Legislation.*[117] On the question of culpability in criminal law the report states as a basic principle:

> [...] fault liability is one of the most fundamental protections of criminal law; to exclude this protection is a serious matter [and] strict liability should be introduced only after careful consideration on a case-by-case basis of all available options; *it would not be proper to base strict liability on mere administrative convenience or on a rigid formula.*[118]

Further to this:

> [...] strict liability should, wherever possible, be subject to program specific broad based defences in circumstances where the contravention appears reasonable, in order to ameliorate any harsh effect; these defences should be in addition to mistake of fact and other defences in the *Criminal Code Act 1995* (Cth). *Strict liability offences should, if possible, be applied only where there appears to be general public support and acceptance both for the measure and the penalty*[119]

---

[114] Explanatory Memorandum, Copyright Bill 2006 (Cth) sch1 pt 1 para 1.7.

[115] Explanatory Memorandum, Copyright Bill 2006 (Cth) sch1 pt 1 para 1.8.

[116] Explanatory Memorandum, Copyright Bill 2006 (Cth) sch1 pt 1 para 1.9.

[117] Senate Standing Committee for the Scrutiny of Bills, Commonwealth Parliament (2002).

[118] Senate Standing Committee for the Scrutiny of Bills, Commonwealth Parliament (2002), p. 283.

[119] Senate Standing Committee for the Scrutiny of Bills, Commonwealth Parliament (2002), p. 283.

The report also recommends that a strict liability scheme should avoid creating a large pool of contravening behaviour, which would result in selective and inconsistent enforcement.[120]

Of particular relevance to the evidential presumptions introduced by the *Copyright Amendment Act 2006* (Cth), the report states:

> [...] strict liability should depend as far as possible on the actions or lack of action of those who are actually liable for an offence, *rather than be imposed on parties who must by necessity rely on information from third parties in Australia or overseas*; offences which do not apply this principle have the potential to operate unfairly[121]

Despite these eminently sensible recommendations, the Senate Standing Committee for the Scrutiny of Bills did not adhere to its own advice when it was charged with scrutinising the Copyright Amendment Bill 2006 (Cth). Instead, the Bill passed the committee stage with the following comments:

> In each case [of strict liability provisions], the explanatory memorandum notes the fact that the imposition of strict liability means that no fault element is required to be proved, and that the offence has a maximum penalty of 60 penalty units and that it will be 'underpinned by an infringement notice scheme to be inserted into the Copyright Regulations.' The explanatory memorandum makes no explicit reference to the Committee's *Sixth Report of 2002: Application of Absolute and Strict Liability Offences in Commonwealth Legislation* or to the *Guide to Framing Commonwealth Offences, Civil Penalties and Enforcement Powers* (the Guide), however, the Committee notes that the new offences appear to fall broadly within the principles stated in the Guide. While the Committee would generally prefer to see a more detailed justification for such offences, it makes no further comment in this case. *In the circumstances, the Committee makes no further comment on this bill.*[122]

The scarcity of information about the strict liability offences in the Bill and an absence any detailed justification for their inclusion, does not appear to have concerned the Committee to any significant degree. The *Guide to Framing Commonwealth Offences, Civil Penalties and Enforcement Powers*,[123] the guide to which the Committee refers, gives substantial weight to the findings of the *Application of Absolute and Strict Liability Offences in Commonwealth Legislation* report. The principles contained within both documents are identical. The only characteristics in the Copyright Amendment Bill 2006 (Cth) that could conceivably be described as falling broadly within the guide are that the strict liability offence are:

(1) not punishable by more than 60 penalty points[124];
(2) are underpinned by an infringement notice scheme[125]; and

---

[120] Senate Standing Committee for the Scrutiny of Bills, Commonwealth Parliament (2002), p. 288.

[121] Senate Standing Committee for the Scrutiny of Bills, Commonwealth Parliament (2002), p. 286.

[122] Senate Standing Committee for the Scrutiny of Bills, Commonwealth Parliament (2007), p. 11.

[123] Minister for Justice and Customs (2004), p. 23.

[124] Minister for Justice and Customs (2004), p. 24.

[125] Minister for Justice and Customs (2004), p. 24.

(3) all elements of the strict liability offences subject to the infringement notice
scheme are elements of strict liability.[126]

It is fairly clear that the normal standards of scrutiny were circumvented to allow
the implementation of the strict liability scheme. What caused the Senate Standing
Committee for the Scrutiny of Bills to ignore its own advice is unclear.

13.16   Conclusion

This chapter demonstrated that the relentless increase in the role criminal law has
played in the Australian law of copyright has been largely prompted by technological advancements and trade agreements. The most telling aspect of this widening in
scope is the frequency in changes that have occurred over the past 30 years.

Between 1905 and 1980 there were only three amendments to the law, and the
changes were relatively insignificant. Beginning with the *Copyright Amendment
Act 1980* (Cth) there were nine amendments to the *Copyright Act 1968* (Cth). Each
amendment has broadened the scope of the offences or increased the severity of the
penalties, culminating in the overhaul of the offence provisions in the *Copyright
Amendment Act 2006* (Cth).

The increase in frequency correlates to increases in two other factors: the power
and availability of copying and distributive technology, and the volume of copyright infringement that this has enabled to occur. If increasing the scope of the
offences and the severity of the penalties were genuinely intended to curtail
copyright infringement and the availability of infringing copies, it would be fair
to say this objective has not been achieved.

References

Atkinson B (2007) The true history of copyright: the Australian experience 1905–2005. Sydney
     University Press, Sydney
Fitzgerald A, Fitzgerald B (2004) Intellectual property in principle. Lawbook, Sydney
Johnson B (2007) Hollywood faces up to DRM flop. http://www.guardian.co.uk/technology/2007/
     feb/22/piracy.newmedia. Accessed 22 Feb 2007
Landes WM, Posner RA (1989) An economic analysis of copyright law. J Leg Stud 18:325
Litman J (2001) Digital copyright. Prometheus Books, New York
Minister for Justice and Customs (2004) A guide to framing Commonwealth Offences, civil
     penalties and enforcement powers. Commonwealth of Australia, Canberra
Samuelson P (2005) Should economics play a role in copyright law and policy? In: Takeyama L
     et al (eds) Developments in the economics of copyright. Edward Elgar, Northampton, pp 1–22
Senate Standing Committee for the Scrutiny of Bills, Commonwealth Parliament (2002) Appli-
     cation of absolute and strict liability offences in Commonwealth Legislation

---

[126] Minister for Justice and Customs (2004), p. 24.

Senate Standing Committee for the Scrutiny of Bills, Commonwealth Parliament (2007) First Report of 2007

US Congress, House of Representatives, Committee on the Judiciary, Subcommittee on Courts, Civil Liberties, and the Administration of Justice (1983) Home recording of copyrighted works. 97th Cong., 2nd Sess., 12 April 1982. Available at http://cryptome.org/hrcw-hear.htm. Accessed 5 Feb 2014

Patry WF (1996) Copyright and the legislative process: a personal perspective. Cardozo Arts Entertain Law J 14:139

http://en.wikipedia.org/wiki/DeCSS. Accessed 5 Feb 2014

http://en.wikipedia.org/wiki/Digital_data. Accessed 5 Feb 2014

http://en.wikipedia.org/wiki/Jon_Lech_Johansen. Accessed 5 Feb 2014

http://en.wikipedia.org/wiki/Videocassette_recorder. Accessed 5 Feb 2014

Afterword: Is Copyright Reform Impossible?[1]

Ian Hargreaves

Is Copyright Reform Impossible? The short answer is: No. It can't be impossible, because it's occurring. If you look at the way that the treatment of copyright is framed in Canada today, versus where it was 5 years ago, it's quite a big change. You would certainly say the same about Israel. You would possibly say the same about Singapore and Korea. And who knows—maybe people will soon be able to say the same about the United Kingdom.

But we don't know yet—the UK reforms that I advocated, and which have been accepted in principle by the government, have been attached to three different legislative vehicles, which have still not all completed their political journeys. The reforms already agreed cover the treatment of orphan works, the regulation of collecting societies, and the rights of designers. But the really controversial bit concerns exceptions and limitations to copyright. Here, the UK—like any other member of the European Union—is able to have access to a slate of exceptions—but it has not taken advantage of those exceptions up to now. I recommended that the UK should take the maximum advantage of those exceptions—which cover things like research, copying for personal use, parody and some educational usages, along with copyright-based products and services for the disabled. I recommended that these things should be taken out of copyright.

Copyright reform is made significantly more likely by a lot of what was being talked about in the previous contributions, including the open access movement. The thing about open access and Crown copyright is that it is, by and large, a decision for the public sector; a set of decisions that governments can make,

---

[1] This afterword was first published in the Journal of Cultural Science http://cultural-science.org/ journal Vol. 7, No 1 (2014): *Creative Industries and Innovation: Facing the Future* 125–126 and is reproduced by kind permission of the publisher.

I. Hargreaves (✉)
Cardiff University, Bute Building, King Edward VII Avenue, Cardiff CF10 3NB, Wales, UK
e-mail: HargreavesI@cardiff.ac.uk

© Springer International Publishing Switzerland 2015
B. Fitzgerald, J. Gilchrist (eds.), *Copyright Perspectives*,
DOI 10.1007/978-3-319-15913-3

whether that concerns openness of access to the government's own data or to data over which government has serious leverage. Politicians of the Right tend to like it because they see it as weakening the bloated engines of government, and politicians of the Left—or liberal-minded politicians of the Left—see it as empowering the citizen and enriching democracy.

When it comes to open access to peer-reviewed academic publications, the argument gets more complicated because the private sector is heavily involved; the main scientific and academic publishers in the world are shareholder-owned businesses—they believe that they have the right to be part of any renegotiation of copyright terms. This is now happening and across the UK and Europe, there has been a significant move to more open access. That is a favourable piece of context for the reform of copyright.

Here's how I think copyright reform is going to proceed. Three things are happening: the first is this trend toward open access; the second is a very unsatisfactorily slow improvement in the licensing of material. One of the biggest problems in commercial copyright is that it is very often the case that users can find material illegally much more easily than they can find it legally.There's a lot of research to support the proposition that if material is made available legally and easily through the technology platforms that people are using or want to use, that people are willing to pay, but that's been a point that is not sufficiently regarded by the rights holder community. This is part of a third phenomenon, which is an insufficient regard in general to the interests of users in a digital context.

The longer that the copyright holding community resists obviously needed change, the greater the danger that the system's illogical, incomprehensible and capricious features will bring it further into disrepute and so render it eventually ineffective.

So, the question is not whether copyright reform is possible, but whether it is going to occur to the extent needed to make copyright effective again as the thing that creators need it to be: namely, a way of enabling creative artists to achieve a fair return from the commercial market for their work, and therefore in the language of economics, to incentivize further production. That's what copyright is supposed to do and I think it's much more likely to be able to do that if it is reformed.

The biggest dilemma that the Internet has caused for copyright is that the Internet requires routine, massive copying in order to function. We need to be able to make a distinction in law—at the centre of law, not on the edge of it, by way of exceptions—between what is sometimes called the expressive purpose of a work and the kind of copying which is non-expressive, which is simply the accumulation of caching data or any other kind of non-expressive data—for example, the kind which is needed in the important and rapidly growing area of data analytics.

One of the things that the copyright industries in the media content domain have failed to understand, is that the game in which they consider themselves the dominant players, is now a game that includes all scientific and medical research, and the huge emerging world of data analytics, which is going to underpin the next big wave of digital change—the provision of digitally afforded services. If you take that very large constituency of interests, it sits in tension with the views of traditional copyright owners. Governments cannot therefore avoid asking questions about the trade off between innovation and economic performance and the 'no-change' stance of rights holders with regard to copyright.

I hope that politicians will also be influenced by some of the other arguments made here today, such as the importance of access to knowledge in less developed economies and among the world's poorer people. Taken together, these things amount to an irresistible force of argument for reform of copyright, whatever the Attorney-General of Australia may say. Change should happen and I think it will.